Studies in the History of Medieval Religion

VOLUME XXXV

MONASTERIES AND SOCIETY IN THE BRITISH ISLES IN THE LATER MIDDLE AGES

Studies in the History of Medieval Religion

ISSN 0955–2480

General Editor
Christopher Harper-Bill

Previously published titles in the series
are listed at the back of this volume

MONASTERIES AND SOCIETY IN THE BRITISH ISLES IN THE LATER MIDDLE AGES

Edited by

JANET BURTON

KAREN STÖBER

THE BOYDELL PRESS

First published 2008
The Boydell Press, Woodbridge

ISBN 978–1–84383–386–4

The Boydell Press is an imprint of Boydell & Brewer Ltd
PO Box 9, Woodbridge, Suffolk IP12 3DF, UK
and of Boydell & Brewer Inc.
668 Mt Hope Avenue, Rochester, NY 14620, USA
website: www.boydellandbrewer.com

A catalogue record for this book is available
from the British Library

This publication is printed on acid-free paper

Printed in Great Britain by
CPI Antony Rowe, Chippenham, Wiltshire

Contents

Female Communities: Nuns, Abbesses and Prioresses

Monasteries and Education

Monasteries and Urban Space

Religious Houses in the Regions

Illustrations

Acknowledgements

The editors would like to thank all concerned with the preparation and production of this book: the contributors to the volume for their patience and willingness to answer our editorial queries quickly and efficiently; our colleagues at the University of Wales, Lampeter, and Aberystwyth University, for their help and encouragement; and the staff of Gregynog Hall, Powys, the University of Wales conference centre, which hosted the colloquium in April 2005 out of which this volume has grown. Thanks are also due to Robert Pearce, Vice-Chancellor of the University of Wales, Lampeter, for an award from the Pantyfedwen fund towards the costs of production of the book, and to Caroline Palmer and all the staff at Boydell and Brewer for their efficiency and kindness throughout the process of seeing it through to final publication.

Janet Burton
Karen Stöber
June 2007

Contributors

Andrew Abram is Teaching Fellow in Medieval History at University of Wales, Lampeter

Janet Burton is Professor of Medieval History at University of Wales, Lampeter

James Clark is Senior Lecturer in Late Medieval History at the University of Bristol

Glyn Coppack is a Senior Inspector of Ancient Monuments with English Heritage

Claire Cross is Professor of History (retired) at the University of York

Kimm Curran is currently the History Postgraduate Co-ordinator for the Subject Centre of History, Classics, and Archaeology, at the University of Glasgow

Martin Heale is Lecturer in Medieval History at the University of Liverpool

Michael Hicks is Professor of Medieval History at the University of Winchester

Emilia Jamroziak is Senior Lecturer in Medieval History at the University of Leeds

Julie Kerr is an Honorary Research Fellow of the University of St Andrews

Colmán Ó Clabaigh OSB is a monk of Glenstal Abbey, Co. Limerick, where he is the monastery archivist

Nicholas Orme is Emeritus Professor of History, University of Exeter, and Hon. Canon of Truro Cathedral

Jens Röhrkasten is Lecturer in Medieval History at the University of Birmingham, and Privatdozent at the Université de Fribourg (Switzerland)

Karen Stöber is Lecturer in Medieval History at Aberystwyth University

Sheila Sweetinburgh teaches for the Postgraduate Centre for Medieval and Tudor Studies at the University of Kent, and for the History Department at Canterbury Christ Church University

Abbreviations

Abp Reg.	Archbishop's Register
ASOC	*Analecta Sacri Ordinis Cisterciensis*
BI	Borthwick Institute, University of York
BIHR	*Bulletin of the Institute of Historical Research*
BL	British Library, London
Bodl.	Bodleian Library, Oxford
BRECP	J. Greatrex, *Biographical Register of the English Cathedral Priories of the Province of Canterbury, c.1066–1540* (Oxford, 1997)
CBMLC	Corpus of British Medieval Library Catalogues
CChR	*Calendar of the Charter Rolls preserved in the Public Record Office*, 6 vols (London, 1903–27)
CCR	*Calendar of the Close Rolls preserved in the Public Record Office*
CPL	*Calendar of Entries in Papal Registers Relating to Great Britain and Ireland: Papal Letters*, ed. W. H. Bliss, C. Johnson, J. A. Twemlow, M. J. Haren (London, 1893– in progress)
CPR	*Calendar of the Patent Rolls preserved in the Public Record Office*
EHR	*English Historical Review*
Emden, BRUC	A. Emden, ed., *A Biographical Register of the University of Cambridge to AD 1500* (London, 1963)
Emden, BRUO	A. Emden, ed., *A Biographical Register of the University of Oxford to AD 1500*, 3 vols (Oxford, 1957–9)
Emden, BRUO, 1501–1540	A. Emden (ed.), *A Biographical Register of the University of Oxford AD 1501–1540* (Oxford, 1974)
HMC	Historic Manuscripts Commission
HRH	*The Heads of Religious Houses: England and Wales: I, 940–1216*, ed. D. Knowles, C. N. L. Brooke and V. C. M. London, 2nd edn (Cambridge, 2001); *II, 1216–1377*, ed. D. M. Smith and V. C. M. London (Cambridge, 2001)
JEH	*Journal of Ecclesiastical History*
Knowles, MO	D. Knowles, *The Monastic Order in England. A History of its Development from the Times of St Dunstan to the Fourth Lateran Council 940–1216*, 2nd edn (Cambridge, 1963)
Knowles, RO	D. Knowles, *The Religious Orders in England*, 3 vols (Cambridge, 1948–59)
LP Hen. VIII	*Letters and Papers, Foreign and Domestic, of the Reign of Henry VIII, preserved in the Public Record Office, the British Museum, and elsewhere in England*, 23 vols in 38 (London, 1862–1932)
Monasticon	W. Dugdale, *Monasticon Anglicanum*, ed. J. Caley, H. Ellis and B. Bandinel, 6 vols in 8 (London, 1817–30)

MRH	D. Knowles and R. N. Hadcock, *Medieval Religious Houses: England and Wales*, 2nd edn (London, 1971)
NLT	*Narrative and Legislative Texts from Early Cîteaux*, ed. Chrysogonus Waddell (Cîteaux: Commentaria Cisterciensia, 1999)
ns	new series
ODNB	*Oxford Dictionary of National Biography*, ed. H. Matthew and B. Harrison (Oxford, 2004)
PRO	The Public Record Office
Prob. Reg.	Probate Register
RCAHMS	Royal Commission on the Ancient and Historical Monuments of Scotland
RS	Rolls Series
RSB	*The Rule of St Benedict*, ed. and trans. D. O. Hunter Blair, 5th edn (Fort Augustus, 1948)
Soc.	Society
STC	*A Short-Title Catalogue of books printed in England, Scotland and Ireland and of English books printed abroad, 1475–1640*, first compiled by A. W. Pollard and G. R. Redgrave, 2nd edn., revised and enlarged, begun by W. A. Jackson and F. S. Ferguson, completed by Katherine F. Pantzer, 2 vols (London, 1976, 1986), vol. 3, *Printers and Publishers' Index*, other indexes and appendices, cumulative addenda and corrigenda by K. F. Pantzer, with a chronological index compiled by Philip R. Rider (London, 1991)
Test. Ebor.	*Testamenta Eboracensia*, ed. J. Raine and J. Raine jnr, 6 vols, Surtees Soc. IV, XXX, XLV, LIII, LXXIX, CVI (1836–1902)
TNA	The National Archives
TRHS	*Transactions of the Royal Historical Society*
Twelfth-Century Statutes	*Twelfth-Century Statutes from the Cistercian General Chapter*, ed. Chysogonus Waddell (Cîteaux: Commentaria Cisterciensia, 2002)
VCH	*Victoria County History*
VE	J. Caley and J. Hunter, eds, *Valor Ecclesiasticus temp. Henr. VIII auctoritate regia institutus*, 6 vols (London, 1810–34)
YAJ	*Yorkshire Archaeological Journal*
YASRS	Yorkshire Archaeological Society, Record Series

Introduction

Monasteries and Society in the British Isles in the later Middle Ages

JANET BURTON and KAREN STÖBER

In 2001 Joan Greatrex wrote in her chapter on recent developments in monastic history that 'in the last twenty years there has been an impressive increase of interest in the study of monastic history'.[1] The present volume is reassuring testimony that the developments so welcomed by Greatrex have not ceased since she applauded them some five years ago. On the contrary, monastic history continues to go from strength to strength: scholars continue to explore uncharted territories and they are reassessing the findings of earlier generations of historians such as Dom David Knowles through the use of previously neglected sources, documentary, literary, archaeological and artefactual. More attention has been paid to those 'lesser' religious houses, for which the surviving evidence does not always abound. Different kinds of questions have been asked by historians, whose primary interest is gradually shifting from a predominantly institutional approach to late medieval monasticism to an increasingly socio-cultural-economic one. In this context, the external relations and networks of religious communities, be they with patrons and benefactors or with other secular authorities including the Crown, have received particular consideration.

The fifteen chapters in this collection represent the proceedings of an international conference on 'Monasteries and Society in the later Middle Ages', organised by the History Departments at Aberystwyth and Lampeter and held in April 2005 at Gregynog Hall (Powys). The conference brought together scholars from different institutions working on diverse aspects of monastic history and focused on the wide range of contacts which existed between religious communities and the laity in the later medieval British Isles.

Advances in approaches to medieval monastic history are not solely a matter of investigating new and hitherto unexploited sources, valuable though that is

---

[1]   J. Greatrex, 'After Knowles: Recent Perspectives in Monastic History', in *The Religious Orders in Pre-Reformation England*, ed. J. G. Clark (Woodbridge, 2002), pp. 35–47 (p. 35).

for deepening our understanding of this central medieval phenomenon. It is clear that historians are now questioning some of the older assumptions about monastic life in the later Middle Ages, and setting new approaches and a new agenda. The present volume is in line with these developments in a number of ways. First of all, as the title indicates, the scope is not limited to England. A conscious attempt was made when planning both the conference from which this collection grew and the volume itself to escape the dominant context of 'English' and to look at Ireland (Colmán O' Clabaigh), Wales (Karen Stöber) and Scotland (Kimm Perkins-Curran, Emilia Jamroziak), as well as distinctive regional contexts within England, from Yorkshire in the north to Cornwall in the south west, from Kent in the south-east, to Shropshire and the Welsh borders. Indeed authors have been prepared to look further afield at regions offering meaningful analogies to their own, as Emilia Jamroziak looks to Poland and Brandenburg for political situations akin to those on the Anglo-Scottish borders.

The papers range in time from the thirteenth to the sixteenth centuries. Traditionally – within an English context – the twelfth century has been seen as the century of growth, while the centuries that followed have been perceived as a period of gradual decline leading to the Dissolution of the 1530s, when failing monastic houses, with dwindling numbers of religious who were at best lukewarm in their observance and at worst corrupt, teetered on the brink of self destruction. While the work of eminent scholars has done much to redress the balance, there is still a sense in which the 'late medieval' period is perceived as intrinsically inferior to the great centuries of monastic life. This collection, in line with many recent studies, sees in the later Middle Ages in Britain a rich and vibrant monastic culture which was different from that of earlier centuries, but far from in decline.

The essays that form this collection are for convenience grouped into six sections but there is much overlap between them. The sections serve, however, to highlight those themes with which monastic historians are engaging. The collection opens with four chapters that look at a range of contacts between religious communities and the outside world. In the opening essay of this section, Karen Stöber discusses the social networks of monastic communities in late medieval Wales. She addresses the many ways in which these religious communities were involved with the outside world, considering the ties which formed between the Welsh monasteries and their patrons and benefactors, as well as the relations with the lay community more widely, either through the authority of kings and popes, or through trade or hospitality. This chapter demonstrates that the relationships between the monks and nuns of medieval Wales and the outside world much reflect those to the east of Offa's Dyke while showing a number of unique features, notably the role assumed by some Welsh Cistercian communities as patrons of the Welsh bards.

In her essay on Cistercian hospitality, Julie Kerr investigates further some of the issues raised in the previous chapter. As providers of hospitality, Cistercian houses played a role which was fundamental to monastic life, for St Benedict had enjoined his community to treat guests as they would Christ himself. Such an injunction had to be obeyed, but accommodated within the particular demands of Cistercian observance, with its restrictions on overly close relations with patrons, and on women entering their houses. Her wide ranging discussion looks at how different types of visitors (fellow monks and abbots on visitation or travelling to the General Chapter, lay people, women) were received, accommodated, fed, and entertained, in the Cistercian monasteries of Britain. As the obligation of hospitality demonstrated, no monastery or nunnery, however far from the beaten track, could remain aloof from the outside world – from visitors on the road, from patrons who sought burial for a member of their family, from benefactors who appeared in the chapter house seeking to be accepted into confraternity, from visiting Welsh bards. However, some institutions were more susceptible to outside pressures than others because of the politically unstable conditions of the area in which they were located.

Focusing on the often violent experiences of monastic communities in border regions, Emilia Jamroziak looks at the interconnections between monks, borders and violence: at how monks prevented or, if this failed, minimized threats of violence against them. Within a British context she looks at three monasteries in a border area that saw an increase in military activity in the thirteenth and fourteenth centuries: Melrose, Dundrennan, and Holm Cultram Abbey on the Anglo-Scottish border. Their fortunes and coping strategies are contrasted with three monasteries on another border, between Brandenburg, Denmark and Greater Poland. What emerges is an important study of the impact on Cistercian monasteries of the fragmentation of political power and the damage that ensued – but also the possibilities for patronage.

In his paper on headship of religious houses, Martin Heale looks at the important question of the election of late medieval superiors and in particular the chronology and significance of external intervention in such appointments. This is a detailed and closely argued paper, which for the first time highlights where superiors were taken from, the processes of election, and the significance of outside interference, where it occurred, and what this reveals about relations with lay and ecclesiastical authorities.

The next three chapters, under the general heading, 'Religious Houses and their Patrons and Benefactors', offer a closer assessment of some of the topics raised in the opening section. One such theme is the relationship between monastic houses and their founders, patrons and benefactors. The first of these papers takes us to medieval Ireland. The arrival of the Dominicans in Dublin in 1224 marks the first Irish contact with the mendicant movement. The friars quickly emerged as one of the most influential forces in Irish Church and society, adapting themselves to the challenges and difficulties of life in a colonial and frontier society. Colmán O' Claibaigh explores the symbiotic relationship that the friars enjoyed with both Gaelic and Anglo-Norman patrons, a task made harder by the paucity of surviving sources. Using the case of the Observant Franciscans at Adare in Co. Limerick and the Fitzgerald family, he examines patterns of patronage of mendicant communities in medieval Ireland, and the manner in which the friars established new foundations and secured support for extensive building projects in both the towns and boroughs of the Anglo-Norman colony and in the predominantly rural environment of Gaelic Ireland.

Given the ethnically divided nature of late medieval Irish society, the politics of almsgiving is explored, while particular attention is paid to the Irish friars' development of support networks on both sides of this divide.

Underscoring the point made in the previous chapter, that relationships between religious houses and their patrons and benefactors had many facets, the next essay focuses on the regular canons and their supporters. In his essay Andrew Abram demonstrates that the often-underrated and neglected houses of Augustinian canons were a significant force in medieval society. As he shows, however, significance is not always directly related to the size of a community or its material wealth. Through an intensive study of the cartulary of one such house – Wombridge Priory in Shropshire – Abram argues that the canons attracted, and perhaps more importantly were able to retain, the support of a handful of local knightly families. This was despite the fact that the priory was located in an area where competition for endowments was intense; the canons forged enduring relationships through kinship, property and lordship, and through ritual with their patron saint. This is only one manifestation of a wider phenomenon of the social contacts enjoyed, to a greater or lesser extent, by all monasteries: all interacted with their neighbours and with the local community; all had wider social responsibilities; many were involved in political life.

In one way the perception of the later Middle Ages as a period of decline is sustainable. Only a handful of new monastic foundations occurred after 1300, and new endowments to existing monasteries diminished. Michael Hicks explores the reasons for the way in which benefactors apparently turned their backs on monastic patronage. His paper looks at questions of religious fashion and taste, but especially at the economic factors that multiplied many-fold the costs of endowments and new buildings, sharply curtailed new projects, diminished the pools of potential religious founders and benefactors, and accentuated the emphasis on those accountable and tailored expressions of individual and public piety that were characteristic of the late Middle Ages.

Two papers, with different emphases, turn the focus onto women's communities, which have so often been neglected in traditional accounts of monastic life in Britain, but which have over the last fifteen years or so started to receive the attention they deserve. Janet Burton looks at the evidence for recruitment in the nunneries of late medieval Yorkshire and for the women who became nuns. Like other papers in the collection, hers deals with small and poorly endowed houses. Drawing on a diversity of materials, from charters, archbishops' registers, wills, and court records, she is able to draw some tentative conclusions about the origins of Yorkshire female religious and to point the directions for future research. She does not merely produce a list of names: what emerges is a sense of the vibrancy of communities of female religious – even if ambition to secure the headship of a nunnery and the concentration of family interests might lead to friction and loss of harmony. Clearly the nunneries formed an integral part of the wider communities in which they were located.

In a paper that complements that of Martin Heale on the headship of male monastic communities in England, Kimm Perkins-Curran looks north of the border, and argues for the existence of close connections between the prioresses of the Scottish nunneries and interests outside the house – notably with local families – and that these as much as any religious duties influenced or indeed defined their duties.

An underpinning dynamic of the paper by James Clark is that it is only recently that historians have come to appreciate the continuing role of the religious orders in the education of the laity in the late medieval period in England, through monastic almonry schools, the support offered by individual monks to boys and youths as they pursued their studies, the provision for the education of the laity within the liberty of a monastic house, and the sponsoring of exhibitions and scholarships for religious to support university study. Clark here offers a new appraisal of the role of the monasteries in education. This is one of the themes in Glyn Coppack's study of the importance of the Carthusian order in later medieval England. The Carthusians were an order that went out of their way to avoid society, discouraging guests and making the point that they sought seclusion for the benefit of their own souls. At least that is what the early twelfth-century customs of Prior Guiges de St-Romain demanded. However, documentary evidence suggests that this requirement was not taken literally in the later Middle Ages, with charterhouses accepting large numbers of lay burials, giving grants of confraternity, lending books (which were not always recovered) to laymen, and allowing members of the community to correspond with and advise individuals outside the community. The documentary evidence is complemented by the archaeological and Coppack's assessment of the significance of the contents of the Carthusian cell recovered by excavation gives a very clear impression of what Carthusian life comprised.

In addition to Colmán O' Clabaigh's paper on the friars in Ireland two other papers focus on the role of the mendicants, one of which takes a broad canvas, and the other a more focused treatment of the operation of the friars in one urban context. Jens Röhrkasten investigates the question of Franciscan legislation dealing with relations with lay society. The friars depended to a very large degree on the constant material support given by lay society. This included regular support for their everyday expenses as well as the granting of substantial contributions for the provision of chapels, churches, and convents. It is well known that the forms in which this support was given and the degree to which it was accepted had an impact on the Franciscans' practices and also led to a deep division within the order, which experienced a profound crisis in the phase of its formative development. Röhrkasten analyses legislation that was designed to unite this order and to preserve the founder's ideal while allowing the community a realistic basis for its material existence. These texts provide an important insight into the general problems affecting relations between friars and laypeople. Seen in conjunction with external sources, they allow a reconstruction of Franciscan–lay relations in some localities and regions.

It is with the lesser mendicant order of the Austin friars that Sheila Sweetinburgh is concerned and in particular their presence in Canterbury. Her paper explores the dynamic of the role and place of the Austin friary in the city, using approaches drawn from social anthropology regarding space, gift exchange, and performance. The activities of the friars are set against the backdrop of the social and economic problems of the later Middle Ages.

The collection ends with two papers that consider the impact of monasticism in a regional context. Cornwall was not a great monastic county. Of the twelve monasteries existing there by 1250, only three – Bodmin, St Germans, and Launceston – were independent houses of significant size, all of them reorganisations of earlier minsters. The remaining nine were small cells of English or French mother houses. The Benedictines, Augustinians, and one tiny Cluniac body were alone represented, and six of the little houses did not survive beyond the fifteenth century. Even the larger were scarcely of national importance, and the records of their internal life are dominated by the disciplinary problems so familiar from episcopal visitations all over England. Such a description might encourage us to write off the history of monasticism in Cornwall, but such a judgement would be based on incomplete consideration. Closer study of the Cornish monasteries reveals a different side to them, which has to date been all but overlooked by historians. Local people evidently regarded the houses as having some spiritual value. Most of the monasteries occupied ancient religious sites, had shrines or relics, and were visited by the public to attend services or by way of pilgrimage. One, St Michael's Mount, was the chief centre of pilgrimage in Cornwall. Although the records of their cultural life are few, at least two houses had book collections, three sent members to university, and one possesses other evidence of writing and study. Finally one house, Tywardreath, made a remarkable recovery during the fifteenth century from an endangered alien priory to an independent house, with a full complement of monks recruited locally. Researching the Cornish monasteries confirms how important it is to consider the evidence of merit alongside that of mediocrity, and to compensate for the fact that our knowledge of small monasteries is skewed in the direction of unfavourable visitation reports.

Finally, Claire Cross looks at the mutual involvement of the monastic order and local society at the very end of the monastic centuries. Roche Abbey, founded by two local landowners in a narrow rocky valley near Tickhill in south Yorkshire in 1147, had an annual income of a little over £260 in the reign of Henry VIII. The suppression of this otherwise unexceptional Cistercian monastery is of particular interest because a near contemporary description of the destruction of the house happens to have survived. Even more intriguingly, from the evidence of their wills and a unique letter testimonial for ordination of one of their number, we know that several of its former members remained in close contact with each other after the Dissolution. In collaboration with former monks of the Cistercian abbey of Rufford across the county border in Nottinghamshire, they may just possibly have been in the process of trying to reassemble their community on the restoration of Catholicism under Mary Tudor. With the aid of wills and the voluminous suppression papers, Claire Cross reconstructs the relationship between the abbey and local lay society in the Henrician period, details the mechanism of dismantling the monastery in the summer of 1538, and traces the fortunes of the former Roche monks in the secular church after the abbey's surrender.

Together these papers offer insight into important interactions between two types of society in medieval Britain, the monastic houses and the broader communities of which they were a part.

THE MEETING OF THE WORLDS

1

The Social Networks of Late Medieval Welsh Monasteries

KAREN STÖBER

They were never numerous: little more than forty houses of monks, canons and nuns ever flourished in late medieval Wales. Yet the religious houses of the Principality were so inextricably linked to the society in which they operated that they can scarcely be separated from it at all. Laymen and laywomen, after all, were responsible for the foundation of Wales's abbeys and priories[1] and contributed to their upkeep, as well as maintaining a range of other types of contact with their abbots and priors, as varied as trading connections and religious services.

The last quarter of the eleventh century saw profound changes in Welsh monasticism, when a number of small Benedictine cells were established by Norman settlers on their newly acquired Welsh lands, and the establishment of a religious foothold to some extent mirrored the Norman advancement into Wales.[2] The Benedictines were closely followed by most of the other main religious orders, although not all of them were equally successful. The Cluniacs, present on Welsh soil from the 1120s, established only two marginal cells here, one in Malpas (Monmouthshire), the other in St Clears (Carmarthenshire), and only one single house of Premonstratensian canons ever flourished.[3] The rather moderate achievement of these religious groups stands in sharp contrast to what can justifiably be described as medieval Wales's monastic success story, the Cistercian monks. Although little more than a dozen in number, plus two nunneries, the Cistercian houses came to dominate the Welsh monastic stage

---

[1] The small Augustinian priory of St John the Evangelist in Carmarthen (founded before 1127), and the Cistercian abbey of Whitland (Carmarthenshire, 1140), both established by Bernard, bishop of St David's, were exceptions to this rule.

[2] On the religious expansion of the Norman settlers in Wales, see R. R. Davies, *The Age of Conquest: Wales 1063–1415* (Oxford, 1987), pp. 172–210. Note also M. Heale, *The Dependent Priories of Medieval English Monasteries* (Woodbridge, 2004), pp. 48–9.

[3] Talley Abbey, or *Talyllychau* (Carmarthenshire), was founded between 1184 and 1189 by Rhys ap Gruffudd, the Lord Rhys.

like no other religious order.[4] Unlike in England, they were both more numerous and more influential than the regular canons, who enjoyed such popularity east of Offa's Dyke. Nonetheless, between the first decade of the twelfth century and the middle of the thirteenth, the reforming spirit of the Augustinian canons was instrumental in the transformation of the characteristic Welsh *clas* system into priories of their order, in time taking over the remaining existing native religious communities.[5] Continental monasticism thus gradually but effectively replaced the older Welsh monasteries, and by the mid-twelfth century new monastic foundations were in existence both in *Pura Wallia* and in the Anglo-Norman dominated parts of Wales. By the later Middle Ages, the abbeys and priories of Wales had become established, if frequently small, institutions, which formed part of a society with which they interacted on many levels. The different groups with whom the communities of monks, canons and nuns were involved – their patrons and benefactors, their neighbours, other religious communities, their trading and business partners, their rulers and their bards – all contributed to shaping their identity. While the extent to which we can now reconstruct the various types of contact between the religious and the lay community in late medieval Wales is to a considerable extent dictated by the spread and the nature of the surviving evidence, what can be said with some certainty is that these contacts existed and that they are perhaps more crucial to our understanding of Welsh monasticism during this period than has hitherto been appreciated.

Founders and patrons

In her will of 10 October 1367 Agnes, countess of Pembroke, made a bequest to the small Benedictine priory of St Mary's, Abergavenny (Monmouthshire).[6] The monastery, which had been founded by Hamelinus de Barham at the turn of the eleventh century, had by this time passed into the patronage of the Hast-

---

4   The Cistercian abbeys of Wales have been the focal point of Welsh monastic studies to date. Note D. M. Robinson, *The Cistercians in Wales: Architecture and Archaeology 1130–1540* (London, 2006); D. H. Williams, *The Welsh Cistercians* (Leominster, 2001); J. F. O'Sullivan, *Cistercian Settlements in Wales and Monmouthshire, 1140–1540* (New York, 1947); R. Richards, 'The Cistercians and Cymer Abbey', *Journal of the Merioneth History and Records Soc.* 3 (1957–60), 233–49; E. Roberts, 'The Impact of the Cistercians on Welsh Life and Culture in North and Mid Wales', *Denbighshire Historical Soc. Transactions* 50 (2001), 12–23; J. Burton, '*Homines sanctitatis eximiae, religionis consummatae*: the Cistercians in England and Wales', *Archaeologia Cambrensis* 154 (2005), 27–49; H. Pryce, 'Patrons and Patronage among the Cistercians in Wales', *Archaeologia Cambrensis* 154 (2005), 81–95, and by the same author note also the numerous charters to Welsh Cistercian abbeys reproduced in *The Acts of Welsh Rulers 1120–1282* (Cardiff, 2005).
5   Among them the old monasteries of Bardsey and Beddgelert (both in Caernarfonshire), and the priories at Penmon (Anglesey) and Penmon's dependency on Puffin Island, off the Anglesey coast.
6   N. H. Nicolas, ed., *Testamenta Vetusta* (London, 1826), I, 72.

ings family,[7] then earls of Pembroke; and Agnes's late husband Laurence, lord Hastings, earl of Pembroke, had been interred in the priory church some twenty years previously. With her bequest to the prior and convent of St Mary's, Agnes acknowledged and reinforced the patronal link between herself, via her husband, and the Benedictine community of Abergavenny. Laurence, lord Hastings, had inherited the patronage of St Mary's when he acquired the wealthy earldom of Pembroke in 1339, and by choosing the priory church as his mausoleum he emphasised his role and standing as patron of the house, as well as continuing an existing burial tradition.[8]

As members of the upwardly mobile Anglo-Norman nobility in Wales, Lord Hastings and his wife Agnes represent what formed the majority of monastic patrons in the fourteenth-century Principality. The monasteries and nunneries of Wales almost exclusively owed their existence to the pious initiative of two groups of lay folk, namely the native Welsh nobility on the one hand and the Anglo-Norman settlers on the other, and by the later Middle Ages the majority of Welsh abbeys and priories were under the patronage of a relatively small number of noble families, of whom the de Clares, earls of Gloucester, and the earls of Norfolk were the most prominent. By the time of the Dissolution of the Monasteries two and a half centuries later, the picture of monastic patronage of Welsh abbeys and priories had undergone significant changes, as the nobility was increasingly superseded in their patronal role by the English Crown, while several houses had by then failed altogether.[9]

This basic information is, in many cases, all that we know about the later medieval patrons of Wales's monasteries and nunneries. Unlike many of their English counterparts, the religious houses of medieval Wales have not normally left abundant records of their patronage histories. There is more than one reason for this. First, the Welsh monasteries and nunneries were not normally their patrons' only religious houses or the main focus of their pious generosity. This contributed to the fact that they were, second, often inadequately endowed by their patrons and ultimately remained impecunious institutions, which did not always generate extensive sets of records. And third, their archives were repeatedly raided and dispersed during the recurring Welsh wars and at the Dissolution.[10]

---

[7] For Dugdale's copy of the *Historia fundationis cum fundatoris genealogia* see *Monasticon*, IV, 615–16.

[8] A number of earlier burials of members of the Hastings family are known, and in some cases their tombs can still be seen in the church today. The effigies of John de Hastings (d. c. 1325) and William de Hastings (d. c. 1348) are among them.

[9] For instance the small Benedictine priories at Cardiff (Glamorgan) and Goldcliff (Monmouthshire), and the Cluniac cell at St Clears (Carmarthenshire), all ceased in the fifteenth century.

[10] It is known that their archives had in some cases been substantial. From Margam Abbey, for example, a fourteenth-century list survives which names 242 titles then in its library. None of these is known to have survived. See D. Huws, *Medieval Welsh Manuscripts* (Cardiff, 2000), pp. 3, 11.

Despite being thus in some respects disadvantaged, it would be wrong to say that Welsh monasteries were entirely neglected by their hereditary patrons. The fervour of early monastic founders like the Lord Rhys may have cooled somewhat by the fourteenth century, but bequests continued to be made by patrons to several of their houses, grants were confirmed, and some existing burial traditions continued. The monks of Margam, for instance, enjoyed the generous attention of their patrons, the de Clares and their successors, on a number of occasions and over several generations.[11] The descendants of the founder, Robert, earl of Gloucester, and their families, continued his legacy throughout the thirteenth century.[12] During the fourteenth century, Lady Alionora de Clare and her husband, William la Zouche, displayed particular generosity towards the monks of Margam. As well as giving them the advowson of the church of St Cunit,[13] the pair re-granted certain lands to the abbey in February 1329, from which Alianora's father had 'unlawfully ejected the monks' during his lifetime.[14] When the patronage of the abbey passed to the Despensers at the death of the last de Clare earl of Gloucester in 1314, members of this family maintained the tradition of bequests to the house. In 1338, Hugh le Despenser the younger confirmed his predecessors' gifts and privileges, as well as extending the monks' rights.[15]

Margam may be a particularly well documented example of patronal generosity towards a Welsh monastery, but it was by no means the only one. Among the others, the Augustinian priory of Llanthony Prima (Monmouthshire) also benefited considerably from its patrons' grants, which included significant lands and properties in Ireland.[16] And the descendants of the founders of Strata Marcella Abbey (Montgomeryshire) similarly upheld their support of the small Cistercian community there.[17] That patronal support was not necessarily always financial or restricted to transactions involving land, is illustrated by a charter of 1367 to Strata Marcella Abbey, by which John de Charleton, lord of Powys, 'gives, grants and confirms to William, abbot of Stratamarchell, and the convent of the same place, their right to hold a court of all their tenants'.[18] Half a century later the lord of Powys, Edward de Charleton, confirmed all his predecessors'

---

[11] Of the 'fine Cistercian monastery of Margam', Gerald of Wales said with some admiration that 'of all the houses belonging to the Cistercian order in Wales, this was by far the most renowned for alms and charity' (*Gerald of Wales: The Journey through Wales / The Description of Wales*, trans. L. Thorpe (Harmondsworth, 1978), p. 126).

[12] Particularly noteworthy is the generosity shown by Amicia, wife of Richard de Clare, of whose charters to the abbey numerous survive (W. de Grey Birch, *A History of Margam Abbey* (London, 1897), pp. 235–9).

[13] Ibid., p. 302.

[14] Ibid., pp. 300–1.

[15] Ibid., p. 307.

[16] See E. St John Brooks, ed., *The Irish Cartularies of Llanthony Prima and Secunda* (Dublin, 1953). Note also the recent Ph.D. thesis by Arlene Hogan (Trinity College Dublin, 2006).

[17] See G. C. G. Thomas, ed., *The Charters of the Abbey of Ystrad Marchell* (Aberystwyth, 1997).

[18] Ibid., pp. 228–9.

gifts and privileges to the abbey, 'for the welfare of the souls of his parents', the 'noble lords of Powys'.[19]

As well as granting rights and privileges, a monastic patron might offer his monks his protective support. In the mid-fourteenth century, Margam Abbey came under the protection of Ralph Stafford, who was through his wife descended from the de Clare co-heiress Margaret.[20] And not long before the patronage of the house reverted to the Crown, George, duke of Clarence, patron of Margam, made known his special protection of the monastery to his officers in Glamorgan.[21] The initiative did not always lie with the patrons, however, and in April 1306, for example, the Benedictine monks of Monmouth petitioned their patron about the seisin of certain mills.[22]

Contributions towards the repair or extension of a monastery were another common act of patronal support. At St Dogmael's Abbey (Pembrokeshire), late medieval building work saw the transformation of the distinctive north transept of the abbey church in the early sixteenth century.[23] It is conceivable that the religious community was supported in this project by the descendants of the abbey's founders, the lords of Cemais.[24] Similarly, in about 1300 the small Benedictine priory of Ewenny (Glamorgan) underwent several alterations to its outer buildings at the instigation of its patrons, when a tower was added to the cemetery gate and two of the priory gates were refashioned.[25] A further indication that late medieval building projects involved the patrons of a religious house is given by the retiling of floors in monastic churches. The best surviving evidence for this activity in late medieval Wales comes from the heraldic tiles found in the Cistercian abbeys of Neath and Margam.[26] At Neath Abbey, fragments of these tiles are still *in situ* in the eastern and the northern ambulatory.[27] Among the most famous survivals of this kind in Wales are the floor tiles of Strata Florida, many of which are still in place in the south transept chapels of the former conventual church.[28]

Naturally these bequests and gifts were not entirely selfless acts, nor were they the fruit exclusively of a patronal sense of obligation or even of belonging. Perhaps the most eagerly sought-after return-services were the spiritual benefits enjoyed by sponsors of monasteries, and among these none was as important as

---

[19] Ibid., pp. 230–3.
[20] Birch, *History of Margam*, p. 317.
[21] Ibid., pp. 348–9.
[22] TNA (PRO) SC1/48/82.
[23] Ornamental traces of this elaborate addition are still visible on the north transept walls, which now form the most substantial remains of the abbey.
[24] The remains of burial evidence in the north transept seem to support this.
[25] C. A. Ralegh Radford, *Ewenny Priory / Priordy Ewenni* (London, 1976), p. 8.
[26] Some show the *three chevrons* of the de Clare family, others the arms of the Despensers.
[27] J. M. Lewis, *The Medieval Tiles of Wales* (Cardiff, 1999), p. 31 (ill. 107, p. 122) and A. L. Jones, *The Medieval Heraldic Inlaid Paving Tiles of Neath Abbey*, Heraldry in Glamorgan, vii (Bridgend, 1996), p. 30.
[28] Among these is a tile showing the coat of arms of the Despenser family. See D. M. Robinson and C. Platt, *Strata Florida Abbey, Talley Abbey* (Cardiff, 1998), p. 32.

the care for the donor's soul after his or her death. Interestingly, although the religious houses of later medieval Wales were a popular burial choice for many local notables, they rarely tended to be chosen as family mausolea by their hereditary patrons. The effigies of the lords Hastings at Abergavenny are an impressive exception to this rule, but in most cases, as already mentioned, the patrons of the Welsh abbeys and priories also held the patronage of one or more monasteries in England (and beyond), where they normally chose to be buried. Their Welsh monastic possessions could not normally match those of their English houses, which had moreover often held the family sepulchre for generations, as at Tewkesbury Abbey (Glos.) in the case of the de Clares and their successors, or at Thetford Priory (Norfolk) in the case of the dukes of Norfolk. Apart from the Hastings tombs in the priory church of Abergavenny, the fifteenth-century burials of members of the Herbert family, earls of Pembroke, at Tintern stand practically alone in this category.[29] However, relatives and associates of the patrons of Strata Florida Abbey,[30] and possibly of St Dogmael's, are known to have requested burial in these monasteries.[31] And very likely there were others – relatives and kinsfolk of the patronal families – who remain unrecorded and whose graves have left no traces.

Patrons could be involved in the monastic affairs in other ways as well. They might be instrumental in negotiating corrodies for family members or retainers. Thus the prior of the Benedictine house at Monmouth (Monmouthshire) is known to have made arrangements with his patron, the duke of Lancaster, regarding corrodies.[32] Corrodians, whether or not supplied at the instigation of a monastery's patron, were another point of contact between religious communities and the outside world, and in Wales the custom was practised up until the Dissolution. In 1530 a certain John Howe, in return for the substantial payment of £20, was provided with accommodation, subsistence, and other commodities at the Cistercian abbey of Valle Crucis.[33]

There can be little doubt that the heirs of the founders of the Welsh monasteries and nunneries were involved in a whole range of other activities with the religious houses under their patronage, at least until the fifteenth century, when the majority of them finally lost their patronal rights to the Crown. Little further evidence unfortunately survives about other, especially more mundane types of contact between the Welsh monasteries and their patrons, at least in part for the reasons stated above. One consequence of this situation was that in the absence of engaged and active patrons, religious communities often looked elsewhere for

---

[29] G. E. Cockayne, *The Complete Peerage of England, Scotland, Ireland, Great Britain and the United Kingdom*, ed. H. V. Gibbs et al.,14 vols in 15 (London, 1910–98), X, 387.

[30] Many of these, up to 1275, are recorded in the *Brut y Tywysogion*. See T. Jones, ed., *Brut y Tywysogion or The Chronicle of the Princes* (Cardiff, 1955).

[31] The redecorated north transept of St Dogmael's Abbey, mentioned above, may have housed graves, or possibly memorials, to the patrons or chief benefactors.

[32] TNA (PRO) E315/37/195.

[33] TNA (PRO) E315/91/61.

the support they needed to maintain themselves. They did not always have to look far, for this support often enough came from neighbouring families.

Neighbours

That everybody needs good neighbours was a truism for religious communities in late medieval Wales. There is ample evidence to suggest that many local families chose to become involved with neighbouring or nearby monasteries by supporting them financially and with lands and properties. In return, some of these men and women sought to be associated with the religious communities, benefit from their services, religious and otherwise, and, ultimately, enjoy the privilege of burial within the convent walls.[34] During their lifetimes, these benefactors often enjoyed the hospitality of the monks or canons, and this might include the right to hold court or otherwise assemble in certain parts of the conventual buildings.[35] The impression that monastic hospitality could be lavish in fifteenth-century Wales is also given by the poets who were fortunate enough to enjoy it on many occasions.[36] One of the chief social obligations of religious communities was the regular distribution of alms, an activity which tied the monks firmly into the local society, and the Benedictine monks at Ewenny Priory (Glamorgan) were in no way unusual in providing each year, 'on the anniversary of Maurice de Londres, first founder', certain alms to the poor.[37]

There was undoubtedly a sense of loyalty to their local religious communities, not least due to the social welfare provided by the monks, which encouraged benefactions from the neighbouring lay community, many of whose charters still survive. Again the evidence is unevenly distributed, but this should not be taken to mean that the less well documented houses did not experience the support of local benefactors, merely that the documentation has not survived to prove this. Substantial evidence does, however, survive in the shape of numerous grants from local families to some religious communities, including Margam Abbey.[38] As well as being the beneficiary of bequests from neighbours and other benefactors, the Margam community also did business with their local lay community. In return for lands given to them by John, son of John Nichol of Kenefeg, the monks gave him 'daily one conventual loaf, two loaves called "Liuersouns" and

---

34 See B. J. Golding, 'Burials and Benefactions: an Aspect of Monastic Patronage in Thirteenth-century England', *England in the Thirteenth Century*, ed. W. M. Ormrod (Woodbridge, 1986), pp. 64–75.

35 Up until the 1280s, the abbots of Strata Florida Abbey regularly played host to their patrons and benefactors, as in 1238, when 'all the princes of Wales swore allegiance to Dafydd ap Llywelyn ap Iorwerth at Strata Florida' (*Brut y Tywysogion*, p. 235).

36 On Welsh monasteries as patrons of the bards see below, pp. 22–4.

37 Birch, *History of Margam*, p. 338.

38 Notable among these are grants from members of the family of De Avene (Davene): ibid., pp. 309–13.

a gallon of beer, half a mark silver for wages, four pairs of shoes, price 12d, a quarter of oats, and pasture for two beasts'.[39]

From the small Cistercian abbey of Strata Marcella, a collection of charters survives to illustrate the network of local families involved with the convent, often over several generations. At some point during the 1240s and 1250s, 'Iewaff Wachan son of Iewaff son of Henri' confirmed his father's gifts to the abbey, as well as granting the community 'about an acre of cleared land called Grofft Adam' and certain rights relating to the use of his lands;[40] and around the same time one Llywelyn ap Meredudd sold his land called Pennantigi to the monks of Strata Marcella.[41] Like the monks of Margam the monks of Strata Marcella were actively engaged in a range of business transactions involving lay folk. On 10 March 1532 the monks, under the leadership of their abbot, John Goyddvarche, leased the rectory of the parish church of St Bynoe of Berrew to Nicholas Pursell, a baker from Shrewsbury.[42] To Gutun Goch ap Dafydd they leased 'a tenement called Tyddyn y Purse' for the term of 99 years in December 1529,[43] and Gutun ap Deio ab Iorwerth obtained the lease of 'a parcel of land called Dol'r Ychen Issa, half a meadow called Gweirglodd Gadwgan and two other parcels called Kae Pwll Gwrgene and Y Koetkae Gwernog' at an annual rent of 20s.[44]

Not unlike monastic patrons, powerful neighbours might provide support and protection of a religious house. In 1279 'Roger de Moles and Howel son of Meuric were assigned to hear and determine the complaints and trespasses that Cynan ap Marduc ab Owain and his tenants committed upon the abbot and convent of Strata Florida'.[45] Support and protection were often enough needed by the Welsh monks and nuns, for the relationships of religious communities with both local families and with neighbouring monasteries were not always amicable or peaceful. Thus quarrels over lands between Margam and Neath soured that relationship over a long time. The close proximity of the two abbeys perhaps inevitably occasioned friction, as their dispute over hill pastures in the early thirteenth century demonstrates.[46]

The small Monmouthshire priory of Goldcliff allegedly experienced a particularly difficult time at the hands of its quarrelsome neighbours. In the 1320s the priory was embroiled in the repercussions of rebellion against the king,[47] and in the 1330s a long drawn-out dispute regarding the succession to the position of prior disturbed the peace of the community. During these years Goldcliff's priors repeatedly petitioned Edward III for help following a number of break-ins

---

[39] Ibid., p. 298.
[40] Thomas, *Charters of Ystrad Marchell*, pp. 224–5.
[41] Ibid., p. 225.
[42] Ibid., p. 237.
[43] Ibid., pp. 236–7.
[44] Ibid., p. 238.
[45] *Calendar of Various Chancery Rolls: Supplementary Close Rolls, Welsh Rolls, Scutage Rolls. A.D. 1277–1326* (London, 1912), p. 179.
[46] Birch, *History of Margam*, pp. 181–2.
[47] *Ancient Petitions Relating to Wales*, pp. 102–3.

and robberies by the rebels, who carried off the monastery's valuables.[48] The troubles of Goldcliff Priory culminated in 1332, when Dan William Martel, a monk from Tintern (Monmouthshire), attempted to drive out Goldcliff's prior by falsifying a number of papal bulls. Together the rebels 'fell upon the priory by force and arms', chased away the prior, and 'robbed him of all his goods'.[49] To ensure that such a hostile situation could not arise in the first place, the monks of Strata Marcella received the protection of the bishop of St Asaph, who issued a command to 'all the clergy and laity' during the final quarter of the thirteenth century, to ensure the welfare of the abbey, on pain of excommunication.[50]

The range of relationships between the late medieval Welsh abbeys and priories and their neighbours and local lay community thus had many manifestations, ranging from amicable to hostile. Between the two parties there existed a degree of mutual dependence, which necessitated their contact in a range of situations as varied as the spiritual services offered by the religious, the provision of various services by lay folk as employees of the religious communities, or straightforward business transactions. Where the immediate neighbours of the religious were concerned, the two parties normally knew each other personally and often had long-standing relationships with each other, and this proximity brought with it the inevitable friendships and frictions of neighbourhood relations. Lamentably little is known about the kind of daily or regular contacts between the Welsh religious communities and their neighbours, the beneficiaries of their almsgiving, or the visitors to their houses. All these contacts took place in Wales as they did elsewhere, but unless they turned into memorable events, they were unlikely to leave more than a trace in the records. But the social networks of the Welsh monasteries stretched much further than their local lay communities, beyond their neighbourhoods and as far as the halls of the Welsh nobility, the royal courts in London and the papal curia in Rome.

Wider society

As residents on the geographical margins of medieval Welsh society, the religious communities could not fail to be drawn into the events surrounding this society. That they were considered to be a part of society and as such responsible for the fulfilment of certain duties emerges from the different types of surviving correspondence conducted between Welsh religious communities and the wider world. Among them are a number of royal orders, reminding heads of religious houses of their responsibilities for the local community, including their obligation to ensure the safe passage of travellers through their woods by maintaining,

---

48 According to a statement made by William, prior of Goldcliff, the intruders 'by force and arms, broke the treasury of the priory … and carried off chalices, basins, cruets and censers of silver-gilt and several muniments which were within, and likewise the common seal of the place' (ibid., p. 118).

49 Ibid., pp. 65–6.

50 Thomas, *Charters of Ystrad Marchell*, pp. 226–7.

and in some cases extending or widening, the public roads. Thus on 10 January 1278 the abbot of Strata Florida was advised by the king 'that the passes through the woods in divers places in Wales' including those crossing his land 'shall be enlarged and widened', so that 'the passage for those traversing them may be safe and open.'[51] The response to this order was evidently not entirely satisfactory in the eyes of the authorities, for little more than two years later, on 10 June 1280, a further order was issued to the same abbey, ordering further action in this respect.[52]

Taking responsibility for the upkeep of thoroughfares through the unsafe Welsh woods was not the only way in which religious communities took an active part in the social life of medieval Wales. One important point of contact was through trade with the lay community, both locally and further afield. Even those monasteries that had achieved a high degree of self-sufficiency, notably the Cistercians, were not entirely independent from external trading contacts. This became increasingly manifest as time went by and the dependence on the purchase of goods, especially luxury goods, increased with the gradual less-ening of economic autonomy. If the poets can be believed, the wine that flowed so freely in the Welsh Cistercian abbeys was often imported, from Germany, Burgundy or Gascony, and judging by the sense of wonder they expressed at the sight of the banquets allegedly served by the abbots of Strata Florida, Strata Marcella and Valle Crucis, the dishes put before the poets on these occasions are likely to have contained more than average local fare.[53]

More significant still for the exposure of monks and canons to the wider world were the occasions which took members of the religious community out of the enclosure of their monastic compounds and occasioned contact with fellow travellers, but these tend not to have left much of a trace in the records. Particu-larly noteworthy, and much better documented, was the involvement of Welsh religious communities in the political life of the day. Much has been made of the debate which effectively divides the Welsh Cistercian abbeys into 'Welsh' and 'Anglo-Norman' (or, by our period more appropriately, 'English') communi-ties, and although one must treat this convenient 'division' with a great deal of caution, it must not be discarded.[54] To some degree the association with one or the other part of society was reflected in the political loyalties of the religious house, particularly in times of open conflict, as during the Edwardian campaigns of the late thirteenth century or Owain Glyn Dŵr's revolt in the early fifteenth. That more than one Welsh Cistercian community was embroiled in the political upheavals and unrests of the later Middle Ages is evident from the number of

[51] *Calendar of Welsh Rolls*, p. 171.

[52] Ibid., pp. 184–5.

[53] Note, for instance, the frequent mention of wine consumed at the table of Dafydd ab Iorwerth, abbot of Valle Crucis (J. Ll. Williams and I. Williams, ed., *Gwaith Guto'r Glyn* (Cardiff, 1961), e.g. pp. 287–9, 291, 299–300, 301, 304, 308), or at that of Dafydd ab Owain, sometime abbot of Strata Florida and of Strata Marcella (Gwynn Jones, T., ed., *Gwaith Tudur Aled* (Cardiff, 1926), pp. 15–18).

[54] See also F. R. Lewis, 'Racial Sympathies of Welsh Cistercians', *Transactions of the Honour-able Soc. of Cymmrodorion* (1938), 103–18.

documents of 1281, in which their support of Llywelyn ap Gruffudd is implicit.[55] Their involvement is further confirmed by numerous royal charters obliging religious communities to make payments of fines for their collaboration with the enemies of the king, or granting them compensation for damages suffered during the war of 1282–3.[56]

It has already been indicated that the Welsh abbeys and priories were not exempt from royal orders, as their obligation to clear the roads through the woods shows. Demands made by the Crown, however, went further than this and could include compulsory financial assistance to the English king. This might prove to be a serious burden to the less prosperous Welsh monasteries, as in 1347, when the abbot of Basingwerk informed Edward III of his inability to comply with his request for financial aid.[57] Unwelcome payments imposed on religious houses are known to have caused Welsh abbots and priors to rise to the defence of their communities. Thus Philip, abbot of Strata Florida, wrote to Edward I in November 1278 requesting the authorisation of the abbey's representative 'to negotiate concerning unjustified exactions from their house'.[58] On the other hand, the English king could be a source of support for ailing religious houses, especially where patronal funding or protection was lacking; and the confirmation of gifts and privileges of later medieval Welsh monasteries often fell to the Crown. In the early 1320s, for instance, the prior and convent of the Benedictine priory of Brecon, which originated as a cell of the royal abbey at Battle (Sussex), informed Edward II that they were 'greatly impoverished by the disturbance in [Wales] and they pray the king to have regard to their condition and poverty and to command that their charters be viewed in the Chancery and be confirmed'.[59]

Aside from the Crown and the nobility, both English and Welsh, the religious houses of Wales were naturally involved with the spiritual authorities, from the bishops at local level all the way up to the pope. The monasteries of Wales had regular dealings with their local bishops. However, episcopal involvement in the affairs of the Welsh abbeys and priories was not restricted to local bishops, nor even to national ones, as a fifteenth-century commission by Jordan Orsini, bishop of Albano, to the abbot of Margam demonstrates.[60] As regards contacts with the papal curia in Rome, the religious communities of late medieval Wales, just like monasteries elsewhere in western Europe, did occasionally have reasons to communicate with the pope. In a bull of Pope Alexander IV, dated 3 March

---

[55] J. G. Edwards, ed., *Littere Wallie. Preserved in the Liber A in the Public Record Office* (Cardiff, 1940), e.g. pp. 25, 45.

[56] For some acknowledgements of receipts of 'compensation for ecclesiastical damages in the Welsh war' see ibid., p. 96 (Cymer Abbey); p. 82 (Bardsey Abbey); p. 132 (the Cistercian nunnery of Llanllyr); p. 84 (Basingwerk Abbey), and p. 61 (Beddgelert Priory).

[57] TNA (PRO) SC1/37/183.

[58] TNA (PRO) SC1/20/189.

[59] *Ancient Petitions Relating to Wales*, pp. 30–1.

[60] Birch, *History of Margam*, pp. 341–2. This commission, incidentally, gives evidence for a further way in which heads of religious houses in Wales, as elsewhere, were involved with the lay community, namely in overseeing marriages among lay folk.

1261, the pontiff confirmed various grants and privileges to Margam Abbey by its benefactors, including the site of the house, numerous granges, 'mills, lands, vineyards, fisheries, pastures, woods, and other belongings'.[61] And as late as 1423 Martin V intervened in a dispute between an abbot of Margam, the bishop of Llandaff, and a local farmer.[62]

There were few areas of medieval Welsh society in which religious houses were not in one way or another involved, and this involvement included both spiritual and wholly secular activities. Yet while all the occasions of contact between monasteries and lay society discussed above were to some extent a common experience for late medieval religious communities across the British Isles, there was one area which was unique to the Welsh houses, and indeed to a select number of Welsh houses, almost exclusively Cistercian abbeys, and that was their role as patrons of the Welsh poets.

Welsh monasteries as patrons of the bards

With the end of the era of the Welsh princes in 1282 and Edward I's campaign to 'order and organise [stabiliret et ordinaret] that land',[63] the former Welsh ruling classes experienced considerable structural changes. One notable casualty of these changes was the patronage they had provided to Wales's poetic élite: the Edwardian conquest effectively brought to an end the age of the so-called beirdd y tywysogion, the poets of the princes.[64] With the loss of their traditional patrons, literary patronage had to be sought elsewhere, and this role was adopted chiefly by two main parties, namely the uchelwyr, that is, the Welsh nobility, on the one hand, and the abbots of some Welsh Cistercian monasteries on the other.[65] Consideration of the latter opens up an entirely new perspective on late medieval Welsh Cistercian social life, as well as granting an insight into the pantries, the abbots' lodgings and the social networks of the heads of Welsh Cistercian abbeys.

> The house of wholesome malt, house of the white bread,
> House of the bragget and the bright-topped tower.
> House of the numerous servants at dinner,
> House of the poets, long may it continue![66]

Thus the fifteenth-century poet Guto'r Glyn sang the praises of the Cistercian abbey of Valle Crucis, also known as Glyn Egwestl or Glyn-y-Groes (Denbigh-

---

[61] Ibid., pp. 272–3.

[62] Ibid., p. 341.

[63] H. Rothwell, ed., *The Chronicle of Walter of Guisborough*, Camden Soc. 89 (1957), p. 222.

[64] A. D. Carr, 'The Historical Background, 1282–1550', *A Guide to Welsh Literature, 1282–c.1550*, ed. A. O. H. Jarman and G. R. Hughes (Cardiff, 1997), especially pp. 4–10.

[65] On the Cistercian abbots as patrons of the poets, see also C. T. Beynon Davies, 'Y Cerddi i'r Tai Crefydd fel Ffynhonnell Hanesyddol', *National Library of Wales Journal* 18 (1974), 268–86.

[66] Williams, *Gwaith Guto'r Glyn*, p. 300.

shire). In this and many other poems, Guto emphasised the bond which had been wrought between the abbots of abbeys like Strata Florida and Valle Crucis and the fourteenth- and fifteenth-century Welsh bards. That these bonds were often strong and continued after the poets' deaths is shown by the fact that several of them are known to have received burial in the precincts of the religious houses whose abbots they lavished with such elaborate praise.[67] Religious houses were not alone in playing an instrumental part in the composition, promotion and preservation of the vernacular literary heritage; however, what are unique are the relationships which seem to have developed in some instances between poets like Guto'r Glyn, Gutun Owain, Tudur Aled and others, and Cistercian abbots, and the extraordinary glimpse into the world beyond the precinct walls which their work allows us. Needless to say, in Guto's poems to Cistercian abbots we have to allow for a fair portion of poetic licence, for the bulk of his work is straightforward praise poetry, fashioned in much the same way in which he might praise a competent ruler or a successful soldier.[68] Poetic conventions aside, the surviving poems nonetheless provide us with an intriguing and singular perspective of Welsh monastic life.

Perhaps the most colourful portrayal of Cistercian abbots comes from the verse of Guto'r Glyn, foremost praise-poet of his time and, interestingly, in his subject matter one of the least religious of the later medieval Welsh bards. In his poems he emphasised the hospitality and generosity he experienced at the hands of the Cistercian abbots, in particular those of Strata Florida and Valle Crucis.[69] It was in the latter abbey that Guto ended his life towards the close of the fifteenth century, and at his death he received a lavish funeral feast at the hands of the abbot, which was witnessed by Guto's contemporary, the poet Gutun Owain, who was in turn responsible for compiling the abbot's genealogy, and who was moreover associated with the Cistercian abbey of Basingwerk (Flintshire).[70] The poems bear witness to some of the activities in which the Cistercian abbots were involved, including the practice of gift-giving. Thus the poet Tudur Aled requested a stallion from Dafydd ab Owain, abbot of Conway, on behalf of a certain Lewys ap Madog from Llaneurgain,[71] the Kidwelly-born poet Ieuan Deulwyn asked a certain Huw Lewys from Brysaeddfed for a hawk

---

67 According to tradition Dafydd ap Gwilym lies buried beside Strata Florida Abbey. Less conspicuous are the unmarked burial places of Gutun Owain in the same monastery, and those of Guto'r Glyn and, according to some, Iolo Goch, in Valle Crucis. We know from a poem by Guto'r Glyn that the poet Llywelyn ab y Moel died in the abbey of Strata Marcella (Williams, *Gwaith Guto'r Glyn*, pp. 14–16).

68 While he described men of war as 'brave eagles', or 'fearless hawks', Guto's religious men were invariably generous, learned and holy (Williams, *Gwaith Guto'r Glyn*, e.g. p. 21).

69 Note also K. Stöber, '"Ei fardd wyf"– Guto'r Glyn and Rhys, abbot of Strata Florida' (unpublished M.Phil. thesis, University of Glasgow, 1998).

70 J. E. Caerwyn Williams, 'Gutun Owain', *Guide to Welsh Literature*, ed. Jarman and Hughes, pp. 242–3, 245. For Gutun Owain's elegy to Guto'r Glyn, see Williams, *Gwaith Guto'r Glyn*, pp. 316–17.

71 B. O. Huws, ed., *Detholiad o Gywyddau Gofyn a Diolch* (Caernarfon, 1998), p. 66. On Tudur Aled see also E. Rowlands, 'Tudur Aled', *Guide to Welsh Literature*, ed. Jarman and Hughes, pp. 298–313.

on behalf of the abbot of the Premonstratensian abbey of Talley,[72] and Guto'r Glyn thanked the abbot of Valle Crucis for the gift of a buckler.[73] The poems also provide some rare descriptions of the conventual buildings of some of the praised abbeys, with special emphasis on their stained glass, leaden roofs and tiled floors,[74] while the abbots are frequently eulogised for their wisdom and education, making the monasteries true 'centres of learning'.[75]

What the work of these men accentuates is the important function played by the Cistercian abbots in the literary realm, where 'monastic and bardic institutions merge'.[76] The abbots are treated much in the manner of secular lords in the praise-poetry of the bards, who thereby provide an exceptional insight into their non-monastic activities within the monasteries. As well as providing an indication of the social networks of the abbots, the poems also hint at their leisure pursuits and, not least, their diet. A particularly intriguing aspect of the nature of late medieval Welsh monasteries is the manner in which they effectively took over from the Welsh princes as traditional patrons of the bards and assumed this role in all its secular guise.

However much they strove for a remote, spiritual existence, 'far from the concourse of men', in Wales, as elsewhere in the late medieval British Isles, monastic communities regularly interacted with the lay community, both the local lay community and wider society, including kings and popes. They were embroiled in their conflicts, political, social and economic, and the nature of medieval Welsh society meant that ties, often close ties, between individuals and individual religious houses were not only likely, but inevitable. The monasteries of late medieval Wales thus possessed an international, yet at the same time a strongly local flavour. While they resembled their fellow communities elsewhere in their religious activities, in their dealings with neighbours and secular and religious authorities, they retained some unique characteristics, which mark them out among their counterparts in the rest of the British Isles.

---

[72] Huws, *Cywyddau Gofyn a Diolch*, pp. 54–6.

[73] Williams, *Gwaith Guto'r Glyn*, pp. 296–8.

[74] Guto describes the lead and the glass of Valle Crucis Abbey, its wax candles and its 'web of stone walls' (ibid., pp. 294, 300).

[75] The abbot, Dafydd ab Iorwerth, is variously called a teacher and a scholar ('Athro i bawb … ysgolhaig'): ibid., p. 308).

[76] Caerwyn Williams, 'Gutun Owain', *Guide to Welsh Literature*, ed. Jarman and Hughes, p. 242.

2

Cistercian Hospitality in the Later Middle Ages

JULIE KERR

The monks of Meaux Abbey, Yorkshire, likely welcomed the General Chapter's decision that men and women of honest character might enter their abbey church to view the miracle-working crucifix recently commissioned by Abbot Hugh (1339–49). However, they were soon to regret this, for according to the chronicle of the house hoards of women flocked to the abbey not out of devotion, but rather to have a good look around the church and take advantage of the monks' hospitality. No doubt news that the crucifix had been carved from a nude model had made a visit to Meaux all the more compelling.[1] This lively account of curious Yorkshire women in the fourteenth century provides an appropriate opening for this analysis of Cistercian hospitality in the later Middle Ages. This paper begins by considering how central hospitality was to Cistercian life – and just how compatible, given that the White Monks sought to establish sites 'far from the haunts of men'.[2] It explores how the Order sought to welcome guests warmly without impeding the daily observance of monastic life. It moves on to discuss the recipients of Cistercian hospitality. Who visited these abbeys? Why? How were they provided for during their stay? A final section considers how important the Cistercians' hospitality was to their friends, neighbours and passers-by. The analysis draws on material from England, Scotland and Wales to provide an overview of Cistercian hospitality from the thirteenth century until the Dissolution of the religious houses. It reflects work in progress since more extensive research is required to explore regional differences and also changes over time.

Hospitality and the Cistercians

> Let all guests be received as Christ Himself for He will say, 'I was a stranger and you took me in.' And let fitting honour be shown to all, especially to those who are of the household of the faith and to strangers.[3]

---

[1] E. A. Bond, ed., *Chronica Monasterii de Melsa*, 3 vols, RS (1868–88), III, 35–6.
[2] 'Instituta Generalis Capituli apud Cistercium', clause I, in *NLT*, p. 454.
[3] *RSB*, chapter 53.

In chapter 53 of his *Rule*, Benedict addresses the reception of guests and makes hospitality an integral part of Benedictine life. As faithful devotees of the *Rule*, the Cistercians implemented Benedict's prescriptions to the letter. His instructions on hospitality are echoed – and modified – in the twelfth-century Cistercian customary, the *Ecclesiastica Officia*, which was the backbone of Cistercian observance from the twelfth century onwards.[4] The Cistercians' commitment to unity and uniformity of practice meant that they produced an extremely detailed customary; accordingly, we now have a clear idea of how hospitality ought to have been administered from the moment the guest knocked at the door.[5] Given that every Cistercian abbey was to own a copy of the customary, it is appropriate to summarise its directives for the administration of hospitality.

The *Ecclesiastica Officia* effectively implemented a shuttle system, or a relay, whereby representatives of the community received guests courteously from early morning until Compline, when the door of the monastery was shut and no outsiders were admitted. Hospitality was thus confined to a specific area of the precinct, and the monks were able to continue their daily routine without undue disruption. Whenever a guest knocked at the door, he was greeted courteously by the porter or his assistant and asked the reason for his visit. In a show of humility the porter bowed before the guest and seated him in his cell while he notified the abbot. If the Divine Office was in progress, the visitor was asked to wait in silence for the duration of the Hour since it was not their custom to speak at such times. Indeed, the porter was to remain in silence with his hood drawn while his brethren celebrated the Office. As soon as the abbot learned of the guest's arrival he, or whoever was presiding, appointed two monks to put on their copes and hoods and welcome the visitor formally on behalf of the community. Meanwhile the porter briefed the visitor on how to behave during his stay. Upon their arrival in the porter's cell the monks prostrated themselves before the guest, to adore Christ in him. They then led him to pray, perhaps in the gatehouse chapel or at a side altar in the church, or even in the parlour.[6] Thereafter they gave the blessing, bowed and finally extended the Kiss of Peace for, as Benedict warned in his *Rule*, for 'fear of delusions of the devil' the kiss should not be given until after the guest had prayed. Once the visitor had been rendered safe in this way, he was edified with the Divine Word and shown to the guesthouse. Here, he was introduced to the guestmaster, the monastic obedientiary entrusted with the care of guests and the hospice, whose duties are dealt with in chapter 119 of the customary.[7]

---

4   D. Choisselet and P. Vernet, eds, *Les Ecclesiastica Officia Cisterciens du XIIème siècle* (Reiningue, 1989) [*EO*], chapters 87 and 120 (pp. 246–8, 334–6).

5   This is quite different to the evidence for contemporary Benedictine practice which is discussed in J. Kerr, *Monastic Hospitality: the Benedictines in England c.1070–c.1250* (Woodbridge, 2007).

6   The account of three mysterious strangers received at Melrose suggests they were taken to pray in the oratory: see G. J. McFadden, 'An Edition and Translation of the *Life of Waldef*, Abbot of Melrose, by Jocelin of Furness' (Ph.D. thesis, University of Columbia, 1952), p. 139.

7   *EO*, chapters 87 and 120 (pp. 246–8, 334).

Every Cistercian abbey ought to have had guest provision of sorts, since early legislation stipulated that before any community moved to a new site there ought to be a guesthouse, oratory, refectory and gatehouse.[8] Relatively little is known of the layout and design of guesthouses, although more is being revealed from work on sites such as Tintern, Fountains and Kirkstall.[9] The guesthouse complex might include a hall and chamber or chambers. It was generally situated to the west of the lay-brothers' range and was well out of ear- and eye-shot of the claustral area. The nature of guest accommodation would have varied depending on the needs and resources of each community. The guestmaster, or hosteller as he was also known, was in charge of the complex and was invariably assisted by at least one lay-brother. He was to provide for guests according to their standing, and decided where each visitor should be accommodated and how he should be served at table. The hosteller was also to make sure that, in accordance with chapter 53 of the *Rule*, the Maundy was administered to guests. Each week two monks were assigned to help him. It is interesting to note that the Benedictines seem to have largely dispensed with this practice and were reprimanded for their negligence by the German Cistercian, Idung of Prüfening.[10]

In accordance with the *Rule of St Benedict*, Cistercian abbots were to dine with visitors in the guesthouse and certain concessions were granted so that they could entertain visitors appropriately without compromising their ideals.[11] They were permitted to break their fasts to dine earlier with visitors, but were not then to eat later with the brethren. The abbots might enjoy finer food in the guesthouse than was served in the monks' refectory, but were not to indulge in gluttony or partake in revelry.[12] While guests were served richer and more appetising fare than the monks, they were not sumptuously entertained – at least, not in the early days. Eggs and cheese were forbidden on Fridays and on customary fast days and meat was prohibited at all times.[13] Inevitably, some used hospitality as an excuse to overindulge. Abbot Gervase of Louth Park confessed that he had dined sumptuously in the guesthouse while his monks had famished in the refectory.[14] There are several rather colourful examples of lavish and even riotous tables, notably, Abbot Hugh of Beaulieu's disorderly behaviour in 1215 when he was reprimanded by the General Chapter for drinking 'wassail' in the presence of three earls and forty knights, for having a dog with a silver chain to guard his couch, eating his food from a silver plate, and 'receiving the ministra-

---

8   *Capitula* IX, 'of the building of abbeys', *NLT*, p. 408.
9   For a summary of this work, see D. Robinson, *The Cistercians in Wales: Architecture and Archaeology 1130–1540* (London, 2006), pp. 161–3.
10 *Idungus, Dialogus duorum monachorum*, in *Cistercians and Cluniacs: The Case for Cîteaux*, ed. J. Leahey and trans. J. O'Sullivan (Kalamazoo, 1977), pp. 3–141 (p. 137).
11 *EO*, chapter 110 (p. 312).
12 Ibid.; *RSB*, chapter 53.
13 Statute 1191: 37 in *Twelfth-Century Statutes*, p. 228; 'Instituta Generalis Capituli', clause XXIV (*NLT*, p. 466).
14 C. H. Talbot, ed., *The Testament of Gervase of Louth Park*, ASOC 7 (1951), 32–45 (p. 39).

tions of obsequious secular attendants'.[15] This particular allegation may have given rise to Gerald of Wales's account of Henry II's impromptu visit incognito to a Cistercian house whose abbot allegedly entertained his visitor to a long drinking session 'in the English fashion', with both men pledging each other *Wril* and *Pril* until the early morning.[16]

There are indications that hospitality remained integral to Cistercian life throughout the Middle Ages. Cistercian sources praise abbots and communities on account of their exemplary hospitality, suggesting this was seen as a good thing, and the care of guests is often addressed in visitation reports. The foundation history of Fountains Abbey commended Abbot John (1203–11) for his generosity at table, and for managing to exercise hospitality even during the persecution of King John's reign.[17] When the abbot of Hailes visited Buckfast in 1422, he ordered the abbot to receive guests and strangers well and cheerfully, according to the long-established tradition of the house.[18] The very fact that facilities for guests were built, furnished and maintained, that revenues were earmarked for hospitality and requests to appropriate churches were granted so that communities could continue to receive guests appropriately are further indications of the importance of hospitality. Moreover, a number of statutes were issued by the General Chapter relating to the care of guests. The monks were reminded to welcome guests warmly, in accordance with the words of the Apostle, and to show particular kindness to those of the faith, fellow Cistercians and anyone joined in fraternity with the Order.[19]

A large proportion of the General Chapter's statutes relate to visiting Cistercians. This may seem rather incongruous given that members of the Order were not, strictly speaking, guests and as part of the wider family took their place with the host community in the refectory, dormitory and choir. But the ruling relates in part to the requirement that all abbots attend the yearly chapter meeting at Cîteaux. This meant that a large number of Cistercians were on the road in late summer and early autumn and relied on a warm welcome from their brethren along the way. Communities that refused to admit visiting abbots or extended a rather frosty welcome might be reprimanded by the General Chapter. Ralph Haget, abbot of Fountains (1190–1203), was brought to task on two occasions. He was punished for showing 'unequal hospitality' to abbots travelling to the General Chapter, presumably abbots from the houses in Scotland, and for receiving his Father Immediate, Abbot Guy of Clairvaux, less reverently than was deemed appropriate.[20] The fact that letter templates were prepared for

15 J. M. Canivez, ed., *Statuta Capitulorum Generalium Ordinis Cisterciensis ab Anno 1116 ad Annum 1786*, 8 vols (Louvain, 1933–41), I, 1215: 48.
16 Gerald of Wales, *Speculum Ecclesiae*, in *Giraldi Cambrensis Opera*, 8 vols, ed. J. Brewer, J. F. Dimock and G. F. Warner, RS (1861–91), IV, 3–354 (pp. 213–15).
17 J. S. Walbran, J. Raine and J. T. Fowler, eds, *The Memorials of the Abbey of St. Mary of Fountains*, 3 vols, Surtees Soc., 42, 67, 130 (1863–1918), I, 125–6, 114.
18 C. Harper-Bill, 'Cistercian Visitation in the Late Middle Ages: the Case of Hailes Abbey', *BIHR* 53 (1980), 103–114 (p. 106).
19 For example, Canivez, *Statuta*, III, 1299: 4 (pp. 298–9); 1348: 7 (pp. 510–11).
20 *Twelfth-Century Statutes*, 1199: 45 (p. 436); 1200: 23 (p. 462).

abbots to complain about poor hospitality they had received and for the host community to write and apologise, certainly suggests that Ralph's behaviour was by no means exceptional.[21] Visiting abbots also had responsibilities, for if the system was to work effectively, it was vital that they did not make unreasonable demands but acted with humility. On several occasions abbots were warned to respect their host communities and not to exhaust their supplies or patience. In 1221 the General Chapter stipulated that abbots from England and Ireland needing to stay at Whitland for more than fifteen days should provide hay for their horses and be satisfied with whatever the community set before them.[22] Monks and lay-brothers of the Order might also seek hospitality from their fellow brethren. The London house of Stratford Langthorne was evidently inundated by visiting Cistercians who were in the city to conduct business or to deal with litigation. The General Chapter took action in 1219 and restricted these visits to a maximum of three days in a fortnight; anyone who needed to remain longer was to provide his own beverages and provender for his horses.[23] It was clearly not the presence of these men that was at issue but the cost of sustaining them.

The guests

The wide network of relationships that linked the Cistercian community with its locality, the country and the Order at large, brought a wide range of people to the house. The *Beaulieu Account Book*, compiled c. 1270, contains an impressive and diverse list of would-be visitors that includes royalty, barons, church dignitaries, messengers, mariners and grooms.[24] If, however, we are to believe the rather cynical ranting of the rector of St Keverne (Cornwall), this is not so much a reflection of the extensiveness of the monks' hospitality as the exhaustiveness of their list. When Beaulieu requested to appropriate the rector's church in 1235 to support its hospitality, he replied that the community had already received an annual rent of £1000 and required no more, especially as their monastery was in a desert place and had no need for visitors. He also claimed that the monks hardly ever admitted a guest and used these revenues for debauchery.[25]

An abbey's location, its relationship with benefactors, and also its resources would have obviously had an impact on the volume and diversity of guests received. The coastal locations of Margam, Basingwerk, Whitland and Neath meant they were inundated with visitors travelling to and from Ireland. Travellers heading to the port of Southampton might break their journey at Beaulieu,

---

21 Ibid., p. 147.
22 Canivez, *Statuta*, I, 1220: 22 (p. 521). See also *Twelfth-Century Statutes*, Statute 1189: 4 (p. 150); Canivez, *Statuta*, III, 1287: 12 (p. 239), 1288: 9 (p. 242).
23 Ibid., I, 1218: 41 (p. 493); 1219: 11 (p. 505).
24 S. F. Hockey, ed., *The Account Book of Beaulieu Abbey*, Camden Soc., 4th series, 16 (1975), pp. 271–6. For a summary, see C. Talbot, 'The Account Book of Beaulieu Abbey', *Cîteaux in de Nederlanden* (1958), 189–210.
25 Cited in R. A. R. Hartridge, *A History of Vicarages in the Middle Ages* (Cambridge, 1930), p. 224.

and Netley Abbey complained of the number of mariners that arrived on its doorstep. Melrose Abbey, which was conveniently located along the Roman road connecting England to Tweedale and the Lothians, had more than its fair share of dignitaries, and could boast a guest list that included Edward III, James I, James IV and James V.[26] The level of demand for hospitality was also affected by political developments. Military campaigns in Scotland and Wales meant that a number of Cistercian houses were obliged to entertain royal troops and might even be used as military headquarters. Prince Llywelyn ap Gruffydd stayed with his men at Aberconwy and its properties on several occasions in the 1270s, and Edward I quartered here during the final months of his Welsh campaign in 1283.[27] The monks of Sweetheart were called upon to entertain Edward I during the Scottish Wars of Independence, and the king was a frequent visitor at Holm Cultram at this time; in fact, Edward was here on 5 July 1307, the day before he died at Burgh on Sands.[28] The presence of these men would have been disruptive and financially draining, if not devastating. Strata Florida evidently suffered severely following Henry IV's stay with his troops in the autumn of 1401. According to the chronicler, Adam of Usk (d. 1430), the English used the church as a stable, stripped the abbey of its plate, and left the community on the verge of disbanding. The king clearly felt some responsibility for this damage and the following April ordered that reparations be paid to the monks.[29] The prudent might, however, profit in these times of adversity. The monks of Basingwerk acted shrewdly in August 1277 when they found Edward I and his men encamped on their doorstep and sold him property, probably Sovereign Grange, for the princely sum of 55 marks.[30]

Cistercian abbeys were also used as venues to conduct political or ecclesiastical negotiations. Accordingly the monks might find themselves at the heart of contemporary affairs. This was especially true of Melrose which was well-equipped and situated, and also, as Oram points out, one of the few places large enough to accommodate an extensive gathering, especially by the time of James IV (1473–1513) whose predecessors had pulled down the major Scottish castles in the central and eastern parts of the Borders.[31] In January 1209 the Yorkshire barons did homage to Alexander II in the chapter-house of Melrose. A particularly notable assembly gathered here in April 1424 when James I stopped off at the abbey on his return from captivity in England and, before a large

[26] D. H. Williams, *The Welsh Cistercians* (Leominster, 2001), p. 144; F. G. Cowley, *The Monastic Order in South Wales 1066–1349* (Cardiff, 1977), pp. 204–5; L. Butler and C. Given-Wilson, *Medieval Monasteries of Great Britain* (London, 1979), p. 306; R. Fawcett and R. Oram, *Melrose Abbey* (Stroud, 2004), pp. 50, 54, 58.

[27] Williams, *Welsh Cistercians*, pp. 31, 39.

[28] F. Grainger and W. G. Collingwood, eds, *The Register and Records of Holm Cultram*, Cumberland and Westmorland Antiquarian and Archaeological Soc. Record Series 7 (1929), pp. 133, 139. For Holm Cultram see also the paper by Emilia Jamroziak, below, pp. 40–50.

[29] C. Given-Wilson, ed. and trans., *The Chronicle of Adam of Usk 1377–1421* (Oxford, 1997), pp. 144–5.

[30] Williams, *Welsh Cistercians*, p. 35.

[31] Fawcett and Oram, *Melrose Abbey*, p. 54.

gathering of the Scottish nobility, was formally invested with royal power.[32] The Welsh royal succession was secured at Strata Florida in 1237/8, when all the princes in the land gathered at the abbey to swear fealty to Prince Llywelyn's son, the lord David; Edward I secured the loyalty of the bishop of Glasgow at Holm Cultram in October 1300.[33] Meaux Abbey in Yorkshire was actively involved in effecting peace between Prince Edward and the rebellious men of Holderness in 1260. The sub-prior of the house was a chief negotiator, and a meeting of the sheriff and the knights of the locality, along with the squires, free tenants and a multitude of common people was held in the monks' chapel. Everyone was then entertained in the abbey's guesthouse and according to the chronicler, the community had never before refreshed so many. But this was before the monks were inundated by the women of Yorkshire.[34]

A ceremonial occasion, such as the dedication of the abbey church, would have attracted crowds of visitors requiring hospitality. The cost did not necessarily fall on the monks. The bishop of Winchester provided for everyone who attended the dedication of Waverley Abbey in 1278. This was no mean feat, given that the celebrations and feasting lasted nine days, and over seven thousand dishes were handed out on the first day alone. The guest list was extensive, but does not seem to have included the king and queen who attended the dedications of the royal abbeys of Beaulieu (1246), Hailes (1251), and Vale Royal (1277).[35]

By the later Middle Ages a number of Cistercian abbeys possessed a relic or object of veneration that drew crowds of visitors, such as the cross in the church at Dore and the miracle-working crucifix at Meaux that proved so popular with the local women.[36] An image of the Virgin in the Chapel-at-the-Gate of Merevale Abbey allegedly attracted so many pilgrims that in 1351 they were almost crushed to death.[37] The Holy Blood at Hailes made this one of the most popular pilgrim sites in the country and costly building work was undertaken to construct a suitable shrine in the east end of the abbey church. At a formal ceremony on 14 September 1270 the abbots of Hailes and Winchcombe placed the phial in its new shrine.[38] The building expenses were soon recouped, for the pilgrim trade could be extremely lucrative. Indeed, when the monks of Tintern and Basingwerk required financial aid after the destruction of their buildings in the fifteenth century, they encouraged pilgrimage to the galilee chapel at

32 Ibid., p. 50.

33 Williams, *Welsh Cistercians*, pp. 27, 144; *Register of Holm Cultram*, p. 133.

34 *Chron. Melsa*, III, 35–6.

35 *Annales Monasterii de Waverlei*, in H. R. Luard, ed., *Annales Monastici*, 4 vols, RS (1864–9), II, 390; J. K. Fowler, *A Guide to Beaulieu Abbey* (London, 1928), p. 37; Matthew Paris, *Chronica Majora*, ed. H. R. Luard, 7 vols, RS (1872–84), V, 262; J. Brownbill, ed., *The Ledger Book of Vale Royal Abbey* (London, 1914), pp. 11–12.

36 Harper-Bill, 'Visitation of Hailes', 105. Vale Royal had a portion of the Holy Cross that had been given by the king, *Vale Royal Ledger Book*, no. 8 (pp. 9–10).

37 R. Midmer, *English Medieval Monasteries* (London, 1979), p. 218.

38 J. G. Coad, *Hailes Abbey*, 2nd edn (London, 1993), p. 22. Edmund had bought this phial in 1267 from the Patriarch of Jerusalem.

Tintern and Basingwerk's shrine at Holywell.[39] At the time of the Dissolution, the Holy Cross at Garendon drew about £10 annually from local pilgrims.[40]

Communities retained their links with friends and family. Monks might occasionally return home and members of their family might visit the monastery several times a year. In 1553 the abbot and monks of Coupar Angus agreed to set aside a proportion of the revenues for the entertainment of their friends.[41] While the *Ecclesiastica Officia* makes little if any reference to visiting relatives they are specifically mentioned in a late thirteenth-century account book of Beaulieu Abbey; this assigns them to the first of four categories of visitors, which includes the most respectable guests. Relatives of the monks were permitted to visit Beaulieu once or twice a year, to stay for two nights and leave after they had eaten on the third day unless they had received special permission from the abbot to remain longer.[42] This two-night restriction seems to have been fairly widespread and is echoed in many contemporary Benedictine customaries.[43] In accordance with Cistercian legislation Beaulieu did not, in theory, receive women as guests but to avoid insult refreshments were provided for female relatives and other honourable women.[44] They were perhaps entertained at or outside the abbey gate similar to Dore Abbey where, from 1318, women who had come to venerate the cross in the abbey church might, if courtesy dictated, be lavishly provided for at the gate.[45] Female relatives visiting Hailes were granted more extensive privileges for in 1437 it was conceded that any of the monks' mothers or sisters who had travelled a long distance might stay the night within the precinct.[46] Cistercian hospitality to women and a reluctance to admit females within their precincts requires closer analysis.

The entertainment of women

> Women, hawks and dogs, except those ready barkers used to drive thieves from houses, do not enter the gates of the monastery.[47]

Whilst early Cistercian legislation banned women from entering the monastery, and all guests were therefore male, it was agreed that dignified women should

[39] Williams, *Welsh Cistercians*, p. 55.

[40] W. Humphrey, *The Cistercian Abbey of St Mary, Garendon* (Loughborough, 1982), pp. 22, 64; Midmer, *English Monasteries*, p. 148.

[41] C. Rogers, ed., *Register of the Cistercian Abbey of Cupar Angus*, 2 vols (London, 1880), II, no. 115 (pp. 109–10).

[42] *Account Book of Beaulieu Abbey*, p. 271.

[43] See Kerr, *Monastic Hospitality*, pp. 184–8; see also Canivez, *Statuta*, I, 1210: 12 (p. 371), for attempts to control the duration of relatives' visits.

[44] *Account Book of Beaulieu Abbey*, p. 276.

[45] Harper-Bill, 'Visitation of Hailes', p. 105.

[46] Ibid., p. 111.

[47] Walter Daniel, *The Life of Aelred of Rievaulx*, ed. and trans. F. M. Powicke (London, 1950), p. 12.

be refreshed in the vill.[48] This total exclusion was short-lived and women were soon granted access to the abbey church on certain specified occasions.[49] The rest of the monastery buildings remained out of bounds and even royal women were forbidden to stay overnight.[50] When Queen Eleanor remained at Beaulieu for almost three weeks after the dedication ceremony in 1246, to care for the young Prince Edward who had fallen ill, there were serious repercussions. The prior and cellarer, who had also served meat to guests attending the dedication, were dismissed.[51] The monks of Hailes had served meat to visitors at the dedication of their church in 1251 yet were not seemingly reprimanded by the Order, which suggests that Beaulieu was punished essentially for lodging the queen.[52] The Cistercians' official stance was quite different to the Benedictines at this time. Stephen's queen, Matilda, evidently stayed with the monks of St Augustine's, Canterbury, when the royal foundation at Faversham was under construction. Abbot Geoffrey of St Albans (1119–46) actually built a chamber for the queen, where she might reside when visiting the abbey. The chronicler of St Albans states that she was the only woman at this time permitted to stay within the precinct.[53]

Over the years individual abbeys might negotiate more flexible terms and, as previously noted, some women might even stay the night. Most concessions simply granted access to the church. A papal receipt of 1401 allowed women to enter the abbey church at Kirkstall on those days when access was given to men, but prohibited them from the other offices.[54] Entry to the monastic buildings might on occasion be conceded to certain named females. In 1336 the wife and daughter of the patron of Meaux were granted access to the monastery between Prime and Compline, but were not to stay the night.[55] These concessions were by no means universal, and in 1472 the monks of Holm Cultram were warned that no women should enter the abbey precinct.[56]

---

48 'Instituta Generalis Capituli', clause VII, in *NLT*, pp. 459–60.
49 Canivez, *Statuta*, I, 1157: 10 (p. 61), 1157: 58 (p. 67); *Twelfth-Century Statutes*, Tre-Fontane, c. 1160: 24 (p. 706).
50 In 1205 the General Chapter reprimanded Pontigny, where Queen Ingelburga of France had stayed for two days, and investigated claims that she had stayed for six days at Quarr Abbey, on the Isle of Wight. In 1250 Innocent IV conceded that noble women might enter the monasteries but were forbidden to spend the night or eat meat: Canivez, *Statuta*, I, 1205: 10 (pp. 308–9), 1205: 59 (p. 319); II, 1250: 23 (p. 350).
51 *Waverley Annals*, p. 337.
52 *Chronica Majora*, p. 262.
53 Gervase of Canterbury, *Opera Historica*, ed. W. Stubbs, 2 vols, RS (1879–80), I, 139; H. T. Riley, ed., *Gesta Abbatum Monasterii Sancti Albani*, 3 vols, RS (1867–9), I, 79.
54 *Memorials of Fountains*, I, no. xliii (pp. 205–6).
55 *Chron. Melsa*, I, 35–6.
56 *Register of Holm Cultram*, pp. 149–50.

The guest complex

What facilities were there for guests staying at Cistercian abbeys? It was noted earlier that the hospice was invariably situated to the west of the lay-brothers' range. In most houses this would have formed a complex of buildings, providing different accommodation for guests in accordance with their standing.[57] The precise nature of facilities would have varied depending on the size and resources of the abbey, and the number of guests expected. Basingwerk attracted so many visitors that the community built new guest quarters in the early sixteenth century. Edward I gave stone to Stanley Abbey in 1280 to build a chamber for his own use, and seemingly stayed here in the spring of 1282.[58] Whenever the guesthouse was empty it might be used by the community to hold meetings. Thomas Burton's succession to the abbacy of Meaux in the late fourteenth century was ratified by the abbot of Fountains in the abbey's guest house. The feud that ensued was ultimately resolved in a chamber here.[59]

At Fountains Abbey in Yorkshire, there are significant remains of two guest-houses. Geophysical survey of the site in 1992 revealed the structure and layout of a large aisled hall that lay adjacent. The guest complex stood to the west of the lay-brothers' range and had its own drainage system to flush the latrines.[60] There may have been stables for visitors' horses as there were, for example, at Kirkstall and Kingswood.[61] Fountains may also have had a hospice outside the abbey gates to accommodate women and perhaps those who arrived after Compline when the gates had been shut. There was certainly a hospice of sorts outside the West Gates of the abbey in the sixteenth century, and a hospice is known to have stood outside the gates of Hailes in the fifteenth century.[62]

---

[57] The Empress Matilda (d. 1169) made a grant to Mortemer, Rouen, for the erection of two stone houses so that there would be separate accommodation for merchants, the poor, religious and the rich: *Le Recit de la Fondation de Mortemer*, ed. J. Bouvet, *Collectanea Ordinis Cisterciensium Reformatorum*, 22 (1960), pp. 149–68 (p. 159).

[58] Colin Platt, *The Abbeys and Priories of Medieval England* (London, 1984), pp. 202–3; Walter de Gray Birch, *Collections towards the History of the Cistercian Abbey of Stanley* (1876), pp. 46–7.

[59] *Chron. Melsa*, I, lxii–lxx; III, 239–40, 264. The guesthouse at Bury St Edmunds was similarly used in the early thirteenth century, when Hugh of Northwold's election to the abbacy was disputed: R. M. Thomson, ed. and trans., *The Chronicle of the Election of Hugh, Abbot of Bury St. Edmunds and Later Bishop of Ely* (Oxford, 1974), p. 108.

[60] For this and subsequent details of the hospice buildings, see G. C. Coppack, *Fountains Abbey: the Cistercians in Northern England* (Stroud, 2003), pp. 59–60; G. Coppack and R. Gilyard-Beer, *English Heritage Guide to Fountains Abbey, Yorkshire* (London, 1993), pp. 59–61.

[61] V. R. Perkins, 'Documents Relating to the Cistercian Monastery of Kingswood', *Transactions of the Bristol and Gloucestershire Archaeological Soc.* 22 (1899), 178–256 (p. 220).

[62] Robert and Ellen Dawson, keepers of the West Gates, were to build stables by their house or the hospice for their own horses and those of their guests: D. J. H. Michelmore, ed., *The Fountains Abbey Lease Book*, YASRS, 140 (1981), no. 276 (pp. 291–3). Robert Butler was warden of the hospice outside the gates of Hailes Abbey in 1442, Harper-Bill, 'Visitation of Hailes', 112.

The two guesthouses at Fountains would have afforded comfortable lodgings for distinguished visitors, and were furnished with fireplaces, latrines and even rose windows. Others were less sumptuously provided for in the adjacent hall, which is now marked by a single stone table leg. The allocation of guests to lodgings according to their standing was commonplace. Gerald of Wales was none too pleased when, on the abbot of Whitland's orders to his daughter houses in Wales and especially Strata Florida, he was no longer to be received as the archdeacon or bishop-elect but shown to the public hall, 'with the common folk and the noise of the people'.[63] This was not only a slight to Gerald's dignity but a prospectively rough experience. An 'untoward event' occurred in the guesthall refectory of Margam Abbey in the late twelfth century, when one young man struck another and was the next day found dead on the very spot where he had thrown his punch.[64]

Although there is archaeological evidence for amenities such as fireplaces and latrines, there is little documentary evidence of how these guest complexes were furnished. Surviving accounts and inventories shed some light on this problem. An early sixteenth-century compotus of Sibton Abbey records that the guest-master was assigned certain rents to buy beds and bedlinen for the guesthouse, to cover the floors with rushes and wash the household linen.[65] An inventory compiled at Vale Royal in the early sixteenth century reveals that the hospice here had a suitable couch with coverlet, a featherbed with three mattresses, and six pairs of sheets. The abbot's chamber was more extensively furnished, having a couch with ten coverlets, four mattresses, twelve pairs of linen sheets and two featherbeds.[66] Cleanliness ought to have been a priority and Alexander of Neckam (1157–1217) recommended changing straw regularly lest guests were troubled by fleas and suffered insomnia.[67]

Refreshment and recreation

The provision of food and drinks was integral to hospitality and most visitors would have expected refreshment of sorts and a more appetising fare than the monks. The account book of Beaulieu Abbey, c. 1270, reveals that the quality, quantity and type of food and drink served to guests were dependent on their standing. Most who dined here received herring to supplement the staple fare of

---

63 *De jure et statu menevensis ecclesiae*, trans. in H. E. Butler, *The Autobiography of Gerald of Wales* (Woodbridge, 2005), p. 226.

64 Gerald of Wales, *The Journey through Wales*, trans. L. Thorpe (Harmondsworth, 1978), p. 127. A brawl in the abbot of Furness's stables in 1246 resulted in the death of the baker, who was stabbed by a visiting groom: T. Beck, ed., *Annales Furnesiensis* (London, 1844), p. 207.

65 A. H. Denney, ed., *Sibton Abbey Estates: Select Documents*, Suffolk Record Soc., 2 (1960), pp. 37, 140–41.

66 *Vale Royal Ledger Book*, appendix F, pp. 191–2.

67 'The *Sacerdos ad altare*', in *Teaching and Learning Latin in Thirteenth-Century England*, ed. T. Hunt, 3 vols (Cambridge, 1991), I, 250–73 (p. 265).

bread, ale and pottage, but the more distinguished might enjoy hake or salmon. 'Special friends' and those whom the community held dear were served wine if they dined with the abbot.[68] According to the eulogies of Welsh bards who extolled the generosity of their hosts, guests visiting Basingwerk might sip choice wines and home-brewed cider, and feast on venison, wild game and seafish. It is hardly surprising that so many visitors sought refreshment at Basingwerk and had to be served in two sittings.[69] The account book of Abbot Greenwell of Fountains (1442–71) reveals that he served partridges, oysters, quails, figs, walnuts, pears, venison and fish.[70] Greenwell's successors evidently dined just as finely for excavations in the nineteenth century uncovered a variety of meat bones as well as oyster, mussel and cockle shells.[71] When Edward II visited Robertsbridge he was served an array of delicacies that included swans, oxen, cheese, wine and ale. These were provided by the abbot and also the local gentry, but Edward probably brought with him his accustomed supply of favourite fruits and spices.[72] By the later Middle Ages the abbot's guests would have dined sumptuously and might also have enjoyed minstrels and players.[73]

Lavish entertaining on this scale might seem far removed from early Cistercian practice for, as mentioned above, while guests were to be served finer foods than the monks, their diet was by no means sumptuous. This frugality was remarked upon by contemporaries. The twelfth-century satirist, Walter Map, attributed the Spartan fare in the Cistercian guesthall to the monks' stinginess and a desire to hoard everything. John of Salisbury complained that their refusal to serve guests meat was 'foreign to all civility, not to say humanity'.[74] Needless to say rules were not always observed and meat was, as we have seen, occasionally served to guests before it was officially sanctioned in 1335.

There were changes also to where guests ate. Whereas early legislation stipulated that the abbot should dine with all visitors in the guesthall, there is evidence that by the late twelfth century some abbots dined with favoured guests in private chambers. Ralph of Coggeshall (d. post 1224) described how three Templars who visited his abbey were initially shown to the guesthall. When the lay-brother officiating noted their noble appearance he made arrangements for them to be refreshed in the abbot's private chambers but the Templars refused,

---

[68] *Account Book of Beaulieu*, pp. 271–6.

[69] For a summary of these tributes, see Robinson, *Cistercians in Wales*, pp. 163, 215–20; see also the essay by Karen Stöber, above, pp. 11–24.

[70] *Memorials of Fountains*, III, 14, 19, 25, 49, 50, 51, 56, 61, 89.

[71] Coppack, *Fountains Abbey*, p. 141.

[72] W. H. Blaauw, 'Visit of King Edward the Second to Battle and Other Parts of Sussex in 1324', *Sussex Archaeological Collections* 6 (1853), 41–53 (p. 44); G. M. Cooper, 'Notices of the Abbey of Robertsbridge', *Sussex Archaeological Collections* 8 (1856), 140–76 (pp. 173–4).

[73] In the fifteenth century Fountains made payments to minstrels, to players from Thirsk and Ripon, a fool from Byland and 'a strange fabulist': *Memorials of Fountains*, III, 17, 18, 19, 59, 60, 61.

[74] Walter Map, *De Nugis Curialium*, ed. and trans. M. R. James, rev. C. N. L. Brooke and R. A. B. Mynors (Oxford, 1983), p. 86; John of Salisbury, *Ioannis Saresberiensis Episcopi Carnotensis Policratici*, ed. C. Webb, 2 vols (Oxford, 1909), II, 326.

claiming they were not accustomed to dine in private chambers.[75] There are also signs that the refectory did not remain an exclusively Cistercian zone. Injunctions issued following the visitation of Hailes in 1394 stipulated that no secular should be invited to dine in the convent on a regular basis. An exception was made if some very great advantage would come of this and the secular in question was of good repute, lest something untoward occurred that might detract from the honour of the Order. Unfortunately it is not stated what this might be, but the clause underlines the importance of reputation and public opinion at the time. It is notable that seculars were to be kept out of the monks' dormitory at Hailes in case they laughed at the simplicity of the bedding there.[76]

How did guests pass their time during their visit? Some who stayed at the abbey simply used the monastery as a base and James V (1513–42) lodged at Melrose when hunting in the Borders in November 1539.[77] Other guests visited the abbey specifically to meet and talk with the abbot or another member of the community. In 1252 Isabella of Arundel received papal permission to enter Waverley Abbey to consult with the abbot, seemingly to seek advice about the foundation of Marham Abbey.[78] Spiritual care was integral to any visit and guests were blessed and taken to pray upon their arrival. Visitors might also hear the monks preach a sermon. When Simon de Montfort visited Waverley with his wife and two sons in April 1245, the party attended Mass and heard a sermon in the chapter-house. In December 1344 the bishop of Lincoln granted forty days indulgence to everyone who visited the chapel of St Mary outside the gate at Furness, to hear the monks preach here.[79] Visitors might also expect to satisfy their curiosity and look around the abbey church and other buildings. The antiquary and traveller, William Worcester, had a thorough scrutiny of Tintern Abbey when he stayed there for three nights in September 1478, and has left a detailed description of the church and measurements he took of the infirmary buildings, the chapter-house and cloister.[80] There were also more frivolous ways to pass the time. A stone board for a game similar to Tic Tac Toe or Nine Men's Morris was found at Byland Abbey, and a chess piece was recovered at Kirkstall. Guests might also play cards to while away the hours, and James IV passed Christmas at Melrose in this way, in 1496.[81]

75 Ralph of Coggeshall, *Chronicon Anglicanum*, ed. J. Stevenson (London, 1875), p. 134.
76 Harper-Bill, 'Visitation of Hailes', 109–10.
77 Fawcett and Oram, *Melrose Abbey*, p. 58.
78 *Waverley Annals*, p. 345.
79 Ibid., p. 336; *Coucher Book of Furness*, II:3 (pp. 803–4).
80 William gives these measurements in his own steps: J. H. Harvey, *William Worcester, Itineraries* (Oxford, 1969), pp. 58–62.
81 Fawcett and Oram, *Melrose Abbey*, p. 54.

The Cistercian reputation for hospitality

Hospitality was clearly an important part of Cistercian life, but how valuable were the monks' services to others? The sheer number of guests that the monks provided for and the fact that communities such as Margam were overwhelmed by a continuous flow of strangers for the very reason that they were in remote places and the only source of hospitality, certainly suggests that the Cistercians' contribution was significant and in some cases indispensable. Moreover, Cistercian hospitality was not confined to the monastery precinct. The monks might provide refreshments and lodging at their granges and properties, and offer 'roadside services', that is refreshments for travellers to purchase on their journey. In 1558 Abbot Donald and the monks of Coupar Angus granted land in Galloraw to Robert Alexander and his wife, on the understanding that the couple built 'ample buildings' and ensured that the cellar was stocked with wine, drinks and food, which might be sold to the abbot and monks of Coupar, their servants and also to guests arriving on the seacoast of Angus.[82] James I (1394–1437) clearly appreciated the value of such services, for he granted the monks of Kinloss the right to bake bread in an old brewery that stood on their lands and to cook flesh and fish when required, that they might sell this to travellers and others.[83] In 1558 it was agreed that the feuar[84] of Boghall should maintain a hospice here for guests, complete with stalls and food, so that the abbot, convent and other travellers might purchase supplies on their journeys.[85]

A final and more explicit testimony to the value of the Cistercians' hospitality is the fact that certain abbeys were singled out by contemporaries for their noteworthy work. The Welsh bard, Guto'r Glyn (fl. c.1435–c.1493) remarked that the monks of Strata Florida fed many rich and poor folk. While it was in Guto'r Glyn's interests to pay tribute to his hosts, these were not simply empty words, for one reason put forth by the Crown in 1557 for the restoration of Strata Florida was that the monks might 'devoutly extend hospitality'.[86] Significantly, when Cleeve was omitted from the list of abbeys to be suppressed the royal receiver, Thomas Arundell, assumed that the monastery was perhaps to be spared on account of the good hospitality it provided and the high reputation of its seventeen priests.[87] The northern houses also made an impact. Robert Aske, the Yorkshire barrister who played a prominent role in the Pilgrimage of Grace, declared that hospitality had disappeared with the monasteries, since they alone could afford shelter and refuge to pilgrims, corn dealers and travellers in the

---

[82] *Register of Cupar Angus*, ii, no. 208 (pp. 167–9 at p. 168). These ample buildings included a large hall and chambers, and a stable with straw, hay and oats.

[83] J. Stuart, ed., *Records of the Monastery of Kinloss* (Edinburgh, 1872), p. xxxviii.

[84] Scots' term for lease-holder; long-term fixed rent.

[85] *Register of Cupar Angus*, II, no. 220 (pp. 178–80, p. 179).

[86] Williams, *Welsh Cistercians*, p. 143.

[87] R. W. Dunning, 'The Last Days of Cleeve Abbey', *The Church in Pre-Reformation Society: Essays in Honour of F. R. H. Du Boulay*, ed. C. M. Barron and C. Harper-Bill (Woodbridge, 1985), pp. 58–67 (p. 59).

remote and barren parts of the North.[88] At the time of the Dissolution it was said that of all the religious houses in the North of England the Cistercian abbey of Byland made the greatest contribution to hospitality.[89]

The administration of hospitality was inherent to the Christian and monastic life but clearly it needed to be controlled lest the presence of outsiders and their entertainment within the precinct led the monks astray. Accordingly, hospitality was confined to a specific part of the precinct and entrusted to certain members of the community; no visitors were admitted after Compline and there were restrictions on how long guests might stay. While arrangements were modified over time to suit contemporary needs, hospitality remained pivotal, if altered. Indeed, the Cistercians' generous hospitality was remembered and celebrated some fifty years after the Dissolution by a priest from Rotherham, Michael Sherbrook, whose family had known the monks of Roche and had, in fact, witnessed the spoliation of the house. Reflecting on the loss of the monasteries Sherbrook paid tribute to their liberal hospitality,

> No traveller left without a night's lodging, meat, drink and money; he was not asked from where he came or to where he would go. Thus, they fed the hungry and gave drink to the thirsty, clothed those who needed clothing, and comforted the sick, sore and lame, and helped strangers to lodging within their gates … they were seldom without gentlemen strangers or others, who always sat at the abbot's table; for he for the most part kept a table by himself only for entertaining strangers.[90]

88   A. Savine, *English Monasteries on the Eve of the Dissolution* (London 1909), p. 241.
89   G. W. O. Woodward, *The Dissolution of the Monasteries* (London, 1966), p. 111.
90   Michael Sherbrook, 'The Fall of the Religious Houses', in *Tudor Treatises*, ed. A. G. Dickens, YASRS, 125 (1959), 89–142 (p. 94). On Roche see also Claire Cross, 'Monasteries and Society in Sixteenth-Century Yorkshire: the Last Years of Roche Abbey', below, pp. 229–40.

3

Cistercians and Border Conflicts: Some Comparisons between the Experiences of Scotland and Pomerania

EMILIA JAMROZIAK

The political, social and economic landscape of Europe changed significantly between the twelfth and the fourteenth centuries. This change was also very noticeable in the ways in which religious houses functioned and interacted with the society around them. The traditional view, which now survives only in popular literature, presents a contrast between the image of twelfth-century monastic life – one of strictness and simplicity – with that of the 'corruption' of the fourteenth century and beyond.[1] Although this antithesis is clearly oversimplified, there is no doubt that for Cistercian houses in many ways – the layout of their precincts, the use of their buildings, their economic activities and the very character of their contacts with the lay world – their lives were very different by the late Middle Ages from what they had been in the twelfth century. In many respects these changes reflect what happened in the broader society from which the members of the monastic communities were recruited. For example, the appearance of individual cells for monks instead of communal dormitories reflects the greater attention given to the comforts of life among the nobility and wealthy urban classes in the later Middle Ages.

The Cistercian Order became significantly fragmented by the fourteenth century and based more around national boundaries than the earlier pan-European network. This was to a large extent a result of the papal schism between 1378 and 1417. The support offered to different popes by Cistercian monasteries in different parts of Europe contributed to the formation of the national provinces of the Cistercian Order in the early fifteenth century. The impact of change was not uniform throughout Europe and the two regions that are discussed here show particularly striking and important characteristics.

The northern frontiers of Europe had witnessed rapid and successful expansion of Cistercian monasticism in the twelfth century, but in the fourteenth

---

[1] Kaspar Elm, 'Mythos oder Realität? Fragenstellungen und Ergebnisse der neueren Zisterzienserforschung', in *Zisterzienser: Norm, Kultur, Reform – 900 Jahre Zisterzienser*, ed. Ulrich Knefelkamp (Berlin, 2001), pp. 3–9.

century they became subject to violence and economic pressure on a significant scale. The contrast between the situations in these two centuries is symptomatic of a shift in the character of the frontier regions and changes in the importance of borders. On a generalised level it can be said that borders in the earlier period were permeable and much less linear than in the fourteenth century, and that this had a significant impact on the monasteries in the frontier regions.

The discussion in this paper is based on case studies of six Cistercian abbeys, three located on the English-Scottish border and three in Pomerania and Neumark which formed a frontier between Brandenburg, Denmark and the duchy of Greater Poland. The examples taken from Scotland are Melrose Abbey, a daughter house of Rievaulx Abbey, which was founded in 1136 by King David I of Scotland; Dundrennan Abbey, also a daughter house of Rievaulx, founded in 1142 by Fergus lord of Galloway; and finally Holm Cultram Abbey, a daughter house of Melrose, which was founded in 1150 by Prince Henry, son of David I. The examples I shall be discussing from Pomerania are Kołbacz Abbey, a daughter house of Esrum Abbey founded in 1174 by Warcisław Świętobrzyc; and in Neumark two further Cistercian foundations, both daughters of Kołbacz Abbey – Marienwalde, founded c. 1280 by Margraves Otto IV and Conrad and his son John VI, and Himmelstädt, founded in 1300 by Margrave Albrecht III.

The traditional view of the expansion of Cistercian monasteries in northern Europe and other frontier regions, such as the Iberian Peninsula, has primarily focused on two themes. The first stresses the perceived availability of empty land as a key feature that attracted monasteries; the second characterises these religious houses as an element of 'border control' by lay patrons.[2] The second of these assumptions has been questioned and largely discarded in the last decades, but this does not mean that frontier conditions did not exhibit distinctive features as areas of new monastic foundations. In this paper I will argue that it was above all the fragmentation of power in these regions that provided very favourable conditions for the new religious orders in the twelfth century, and I will explore why by the fourteenth century the change in the character of the borders so profoundly affected those Cistercian houses located in Scotland and in Pomerania.

The fragmentation of political power and the presence of centrifugal forces can be observed in the parallel examples from Scotland and Pomerania. In both regions these conditions were particularly favourable for the emergence of Cistercian monasteries. Fergus, lord of Galloway, was one of the most ambitious semi-independent rulers of the Hiberno-Norse seaboard. His political aspirations were high as he aimed to be independent from the Scottish king, David I. It would be too crude to say that Fergus's religious patronage activities were a copy-cat of David I's, but there is undoubtedly a striking similarity in the support offered by the lord of Galloway for the 'new religious orders' (Cistercian, Augus-

---

2   The most developed concept of monasteries established along a border as a defence line has been proposed by Walter Kuhn, 'Kirchliche Siedlung als Grenzschutz 1200 bis 1250 (am Beispiel des mittleren Oderraumes)', *Ostdeutsche Wissenschaftliche Jahrbuch des Ostdeutschen Kulturrates* 9 (1962), 6–55.

tinian and Premonstratensian) and the activities of the Scottish king. The similarity goes even further, as Melrose and Dundrennan had the same mother house of Rievaulx in Yorkshire. For Fergus, becoming founder and patron of a Cistercian monastery was a way of asserting his status and his political position in relation to King David I. The ideological significance of Fergus's foundations has been emphasised by Andrew McDonald, who has linked the lord of Galloway's connections with England (through his marriage to the illegitimate daughter of King Henry I) and with the Norse dynasty of Man, as well as his personal friendships with Abbot Ailred of Rievaulx and his possible connections with St Malachy of Armagh, as key non-Scottish influences on Fergus's religious activities.[3] The new abbey benefited directly from the fragmentation of power in south-western Scotland and the desires of local leaders to subscribe to a particular model of the pious nobleman and ruler. The contrast between the 'barbarian' culture of Galloway and the new religious foundation coming from the mainstream of western culture was noted by the contemporary clerical sources.

> It is a wild country [Galloway] where the inhabitants are like beasts, and altogether barbarous. ... Rievaulx made a foundation in this savagery, which now, by the help of God, who gives the increase to a new plantation, bears much fruit.[4]

The contrast of the new – both religiously and culturally represented by the founder and the monastery – with the old of the local environment emphasises the importance of the foundation and the 'civilising' qualities represented by the patron.

This pattern is closely reflected in the foundation of another Cistercian monastery in the second of the frontier regions that I am investigating. The oldest and most important of the Cistercian houses in Pomerania was Kołbacz. The abbey was founded in 1174 by Warcisław, a close relative of Duke Bogusław I of Stettin, as a daughter house of Esrum Abbey in Denmark. The foundation occurred at the time of military and political pressure exerted by the Danish king, Valdemar I, who initiated expansion into the southern Baltic coast. He made several military expeditions to Pomerania, one of which resulted, in 1173, in the Danish capture of Stettin.[5] However, there were also local ambitions involved in the foundation of the abbey. Saxo Gramaticus praised Warcisław, the founder, for his particular piety and true Christianity in a semi-pagan land.

---

[3]   Andrew McDonald, 'Scoto-Norse Kings and the Reformed Religious Orders: Patterns of Monastic Patronage in Twelfth-century Galloway and Argyll', *Albion* 27:2 (1995), 187–219 (pp. 192–3, 202–9); J. G. Scott, 'The Origins of Dundrennan and Soulseat Abbeys', *Transactions of the Dumfriesshire and Galloway Natural History and Antiquarian Soc.* 63 (1988), 35–44 (pp. 45–6).

[4]   Walter Daniel, *The Life of Aelred of Rievaulx and the Letter to Maurice*, ed. and trans. F. M. Powicke, introduction by Marsha Dutton, Cistercian Fathers Series, 57 (Kalamazoo, 1994), pp. 124–5.

[5]   Wolfgang Ribbe, 'Politische Voraussetzungen und Motive der Ansiedlung von Zisterzienser in England und Deutschland', in *Zistercienser: Norm, Kultur, Reform – 900 Jahre Zisterzienser*, ed. Knefelkamp, pp. 30–32.

The governor of the city was Warthyszlavus, who was also closely related to Bogis-zlavus and to Kasimirus. He was almost entirely out of sympathy with his fellow countrymen, and so zealous in propagating and endowing the Catholic faith that it was hard to believe that he was a Slav by blood, and had been brought up a barbarian; for in order to win over his superstitious country from its erroneous worship, and set before it an example by which to correct its fond belief, he invited over from Denmark men of monkish persuasion, built a cell on his own estates, and enriched it with numerous and extensive revenues.[6]

This passage accordingly paints a fairly stereotypical picture of a 'good barbarian' and echoes the description of Dundrennan's foundation written by Walter Daniel. However, importantly, this passage comes in the middle of the narrative of the siege of Stettin by the Danish army. This hints at a particular background and political context for Warcisław's Cistercian foundation. He accepted Danish overlordship as a condition of the surrender of Stettin, which appeared to have offered him power-building opportunities. Some German and Polish historians have seen this co-operation as part of Warcisław's attempt to carve out a duchy for himself or even, with Danish help, to eliminate Bogusław I; others have seen the foundation as part of an 'internal mission' aimed at Christianising Pomerania.[7] In fact, these two interpretations do not contradict each other. The founder was at best a second generation Christian, as Pomerania began to be Christianised only in the 1120s. By establishing Kołbacz Abbey Warcisław was also mani-festing his status as a powerful Christian lord and subscribing to a particular model not dissimilar to that followed by Fergus. At the same time Warcisław was trying to assert some kind of independence from the duke of Stettin, which provides another parallel with the situation in south-western Scotland. Most importantly, in both regions Cistercian houses benefited from the fragmenta-tion of power and the opportunities for patronage that were connected to it. By founding Cistercian monasteries people like Fergus and Warcisław were subscribing to a particular model of fashionable piety and expressing religious and political aspirations. In this sense, the instability of these borders was a posi-tive factor for the White Monks.

The next critical point for the importance of frontiers came in the fourteenth century, but the situation by then was markedly different. Since the 1290s the Anglo-Scottish wars created a hostile border environment between the two countries. As much as Melrose, Dundrennan and Holm Cultram benefited from the cross border patronage of families with lands in both northern England and southern Scotland, this became increasingly difficult and eventually impossible

---

6 Saxo Grammaticus, *Gesta Danorum Heroumque Historia*, ed. Eric Christiansen, 3 vols (Oxford: British Archaeological Reports, International Series, 118, 1981), II, 528–9.

7 Stella Maria Szacherska, *Rola klasztorów duńskich w ekspansji Danii na Pomorzu Zachodnim u schyłku XII wieku* (Wrocław, 1968), p. 42; Thomas Hill, *Könige, Fürsten und Klöster: Studien zu den dänischen Klostergründungen des 12. Jahrhunderts* (Frankfurt am Main, 1992), p. 200; Kazmierz Bobowski, *Skryptorium dokumentowe klasztoru cystersów w Dargunie do końca XIII wieku* (Wrocław, 1991), p. 27.

to sustain in the course of the fourteenth century.[8] It would not be an oversimplification to say that the wars 'created' the border in a sense that it became a line that cut off connections between communities on both sides. As Geoffrey Barrow explained, because so much of the political, economic and religious power of the Scottish kingdom was located in the south, the question of the border was much more a concern for the Scottish ruler than the English kings until the sixteenth century. The border was a result of a

> series of compromises between northern rulers, who failed to extend their power as far south as they would have wished, and southern rulers who despite their greater wealth and potentially bigger armies lacked the resources to subjugate and permanently occupy the northern part of the island of Britain.[9]

By the fourteenth century the political autonomy of Galloway was gone and, although the Scottish wars of independence created a group of powerful lords of the Scottish Marches, the establishment of new religious foundations was not one of their key activities. By the second half of the fourteenth century the earls of Douglas became the leading magnates in the region. Their support was a key element of the protection that monastic houses there, particularly Melrose Abbey, desperately needed when faced with frequent English military campaigns.[10] In that period power was also fragmented in southern Scotland, but no longer in such a way as would be favourable to religious houses. The borders became contested lines and monasteries there came to be among the many victims of these circumstances. The deterioration of living conditions in the fourteenth century, in comparison with the twelfth and thirteenth centuries, affected not only religious houses but lay society as well, creating an economic strain that affected all sections of society.[11] This does not mean that religious houses were powerless or passive, but ultimately there was very little they could do to 'fight back'. The direct attacks by enemies' armies were not the only problem: wars on the fourteenth-century borders resulted in a broad spectrum of violence.

The texts produced in the Cistercian houses in that period highlight the impact of violence on monastic communities. The *Annals of Kołbacz*, a key source for the history of that house, show a conventional, but not overly narrow

---

[8] Keith Stringer, 'Identities in Thirteenth-century England: Frontier Society in the Far North', in *Social and Political Identities in Western History*, ed. Claus Bjørn, Alexander Grant, and Keith J. Stringer (Copenhagen, 1994), pp. 28–66.

[9] G. W. S. Barrow, 'The Anglo-Scottish Border: Growth and Structure in the Middle Ages', in *Grenzen und Grenzregionen – Frontières et regions frontalières – Borders and Border Regions*, ed. Wolfgang Haubrichs and Reinhard Schneider (Saarbrücken, 1993), pp. 197–211 (pp. 197, 200–201).

[10] Michael Brown, 'The Development of Scottish Border Lordship, 1332–58', *Historical Research* 70 (1997), 1–22; Michael Brown, *The Black Douglases: War and Lordship in Late Medieval Scotland, 1300–1455* (East Linton, 1998), pp. 184–90.

[11] Barrow, 'The Anglo-Scottish Border', p. 207.

horizon.[12] First of all they include a number of entries which are pertinent to the key events in Europe – appointments and deaths of popes, successions of emperors, French and English kings, and crusades. There are also a small number of lines devoted to events concerning the Cistercian Order. Second, on six occasions there is information about events in Denmark, mainly the deaths of kings, the last being mentioned in 1325. Third, the annals contain a number of entries related to Pomerania and Brandenburg. Among them are frequent records of the deaths of dukes of Stettin, margraves of Brandenburg and bishops of Kammin. Besides that, natural phenomena such as solar eclipses are mentioned in keeping with the style of this type of document. Finally, a large part of the annals is taken up by the events in the abbey itself, for example the deaths of the abbots and building work on the abbey church. Among the local news are records of attacks by lay neighbours of the abbey in the second half of the thirteenth century. In fact, such entries became a dominant theme of the annals in the first half of the fourteenth century. The first of these attacks was carried out in 1321 by Duke Otto I of Stettin and his sons, who took control of the abbey's grange in Horst (Turza), expelling monks and lay brothers from that property. The duke sold this land to the abbey in 1316, but clearly changed his mind concerning the transaction. His tactic was effective, for the monks made him a second payment of 200 pounds of denars in 1342 to be allowed to repossess the grange.[13] It seems that ducal abuse of the abbey was copied by the neighbours of Kołbacz who attacked the house on several occasions in the 1320s. First, on 20 August 1325 the neighbours of the abbey, the Mellentin family, stole horses from the grange in Przylep and Gardzica. The action was initiated by an unnamed apostate lay brother from this family who had some major grievances against the abbey.[14] Then, in March 1326, granges in Glinna, Czarnowie were burned down by sons of Wedel, a vassal of the abbey, who resided in Lyndow. Fifteen days later his other sons from Korytowa burned down the abbey grange in Gardzica.[15]

Finally, in 1329 an apostate lay brother, William, and his brother John Wasenborg mounted a campaign against the abbey. On 10 August William burned down a mill belonging to a monastery in Brody and two granges in Zaborsk and Przylep. The latter grange had a church or chapel and three monks were

---

[12] There are two editions of the Annales of Kołbacz. The older one contains mistakes and omissions: *Monumenta Germaniae Historica: Scriptores*, vol. 19, ed. G. H. Pertz (Hanover, 1866), pp. 710–20. All the references in this paper are to the second edition in Roger Prümers, ed., *Pommersches Urkundenbuch* [hereafter PUB], I (2) (Stettin, 1877), pp. 467–96.

[13] *PUB*, I (2), 487; *PUB*, XI, no. 6017.

[14] Ibid., I (2), 487.

[15] Ibid., I (2), 487–8; on the Wedel family see Helga Cramer, 'Die Herren von Wedel im Lande über der Oder. Besitz und Herrschaftsbildung bis 1402', *Jahrbuch für die Geschichte Mittel- und Ostdeutschlands* 18 (1969), 63–129; Edward Rymer, 'Udział rodu Wedlów w ekspansji margrabiów brandenburskich na Pomorze Środkowe i Wschodnie w latach 1269–1313', in *Pomerania Mediaevalis: Pomorze słowiańske i jego sąsiedzi, X–XV w*, ed. Jerzy Hauziński (Gdańsk, 1995), pp. 45–60.

kidnapped from there and taken to William's castle in Ukiernica.[16] One of them managed to escape and the others – Arnold of Rzepin and John of Stargard – were tortured and hanged the following day. Their names and the circumstances of their deaths are listed in the monastic necrology and a little verse is included in the annals to commemorate the murdered monks.[17] Then, on 19 October, John Wasenborg came to the abbey with an armed band and threatened to destroy the granges. The community offered him 701 marks and 50 pounds of pepper. Finally, the annals note with satisfaction that God did not permit such crime to be left unpunished and that William and John were captured and executed.[18] The fury of the brothers can be explained by a grant of Duke Otto I, dated 1 October, in which he gave the manor of Ukiernica to Kołbacz Abbey. The charter described the property as being held by William a *conversus* of Kołbacz from the duke 'by feudal tenure', but there is no indication that William gave consent to the act and he is not listed as a witness either.[19] The ducal grant might have been a response to the events of 10 August and clearly inflamed the conflict between the brothers and the abbey.

It appears from the annals that these difficult neighbours became a real preoccupation of the abbey as damages became more severe. This type of problem was not isolated to Kołbacz but rather symptomatic of the time and region. The disparity in the economic resources of the abbey and those of its lay neighbours made Kołbacz an obvious target for disgruntled or impoverished tenants and neighbours. The situation was quite unlike that in southern Scotland and northern England, where the economic disparity between the abbeys and their lay neighbours was not so marked. Kołbacz Abbey was by far the wealthiest landholder in the region, and steadily pushing out many of the lay neighbours. In the thirteenth century many Cistercian abbeys found that a common arrangement that benefited the economic expansion of their estates was for lesser knights to sell land to the abbey in return for life-long rents. In addition, many knights of lesser and middling status were vassals of the abbey holding land from the Cistercians by feudal tenure. In the second half of the fourteenth century, after the crises caused by the Black Death when the abbey lost much of its peasant workforce, the process of estate consolidation led to the eradication of most of the knightly vassals of Kotbacz. This process occurred between 1356 and the early fifteenth century, in which period the monastery paid its vassals between 60 and 1200 denars of Stettin in order for the land to be returned to the direct control of the monastery.[20] As the examples above show, although attacks on the actual precinct of the monastery also occurred, the real targets were the granges

---

16 *PUB*, I (2), 488.

17 Ibid., I (2), 495, 489.

18 Ibid., I (2), 488–489.

19 Ibid., VII, no. 4516.

20 Edward Rymar, 'Osadnictwo wiejskie i własność ziemska na obszarze ziemi pyrzyckiej w XII–XV wieku', *Zeszyty Pyrzyckie* 5 (1972–4), 192–3, 230–4; Helena Chłopocka, *Powstanie i rozwój wielkiej własności ziemskiej opactwa cystersów w Kołbaczu w XII–XIV wieku* (Poznań, 1953), pp. 246–8.

which could be singled out for a simple theft of goods (as in the case of horses taken from Prilop), or for repossession of land encroached on and forcibly held (as in the case of Duke Otto's actions in 1321). The repeated cases of burning and deliberate damage to the assets of Kołbacz Abbey by the Wedels and the Wasenborg brothers indicate real or perceived grievances against a dominant and powerful institution.

Unlike Kołbacz Abbey, which had relatively little connection with its mother house of Esrum after the end of Danish influence in the southern Baltic region in the 1220s,[21] Melrose and Dundrennan Abbeys maintained close and frequent connections with Rievaulx, as did Holm Cultram with Melrose. During the peaceful twelfth and thirteenth centuries Holm Cultram received lands in Galloway in Kirkgunzeon, Colvend, Kirconnell and Mabie, as well as salt-works on the northern shore of the Solway. Dundrennan held tenements in Egremont in Cumbria, whilst Melrose Abbey had houses in Carlisle as well as extensive lands in the Cheviot Hills in north-western Northumberland.[22] With the onset of the Anglo-Scottish wars contacts between a mother house and its daughters on the other side of the border were often disturbed or even cut off. In February 1327 King Edward III allowed the abbot of Holm Cultram to go to Scotland to visit the abbot of Melrose and to survey the abbey estates in Galloway, but that was under a condition that 'none of his [the abbot's] retinue take letters with them to the prejudice of the realm, or reveal any of its secrets'.[23] The transborder links and connections which were much valued and profitable for the monastic communities in peacetime could render them suspicious to lay authorities at more uncertain times.[24]

The extent to which Holm Cultram was subject to violence and destruction caused by war shows how the emergence of a hostile border during the wars of independence impacted on the monastic houses of the area. Major destruction was inflicted upon the abbey during the Scottish attack of 1315–16 and for a while the monks had to find shelter in neighbouring religious houses. King Edward II made a request to Tintern Abbey in south Wales and other Cistercian houses to provide for the monks of Holm Cultram until their own monastery was repaired and the estates productive again.[25] Throughout the first half of the fourteenth century the abbey suffered repeated damage due to the Scottish raids, but also impoverishment on account of frequent, unpaid 'purchases' by the English royal army going northwards. The abbey itself and its granges served as

21 Stella Maria Szacherska, *Rola Klasztorów duńskich w ekspansji Danii na Pomorzu Zachodnim u schyłku XII wieku* (Wrocław, 1968), p. 60.

22 Stringer, 'Identities in Thirteenth-century England', pp. 54–5, 66.

23 Joseph Bain et al., eds, *Calendar of Documents Relating to Scotland 1108–1516 preserved in the PRO London* (Edinburgh, 1881), III, no. 906.

24 For further example of difficulties in maintaining contact between Melrose Abbey and its daughter house in Cumbria see *Calendar of Documents Relating to Scotland*, III, no. 605.

25 F. Grainger and W. G. Collingwood, eds, *The Register and Records of Holm Cultram*, Cumberland and Westmorland Antiquarian and Archaeological Soc. Record Series, 7 (1929), p. 141.

storage facilities for the English, which exposed Holm Cultram to further attacks by the Scots.[26]

In the second half of the fourteenth century the situation in Scotland became extremely difficult for religious houses. King David II and King Edward III both considered Melrose to be within their jurisdiction, used it as a residence and as a base and issued contradictory letters of protection. However David II appears to have been aware and concerned about the cross-border difficulties facing his favourite abbey of Melrose and allowed the community to remain on good terms with the English – an essential strategy in this region – whilst protecting its lands and interests in Scotland.[27] With the renewal of open warfare in the 1380s, Melrose was at first spared by the English army of the duke of Lancaster, John of Gaunt, in return for a large payment in 1384. Besides the financial gain, John of Gaunt might have been reluctant to attack Melrose on account of the connection with the earls of Douglas who by that time were the most important benefactors and protectors of Melrose and would not have taken very kindly to an attack on 'their house'.[28]

The trail of destruction can also be observed very sharply through applications for compensation directed to the English and Scottish kings. Holm Cultram applied in 1315 to King Edward II for compensation on account of the abbey having 'been plundered and spoiled in the Scottish wars, and of late burned and wasted, their cattle driven, horses, oxen, and cows to the value of £500'.[29] The community claimed impoverishment and helpfully suggested to the king that he should give them the advowson of the church of Burgh in Westmorland, which he rejected. Similar requests were made throughout the fourteenth century by the abbeys of Melrose and Holm Cultram in connection to the outright destruction of buildings and granges or confiscation of goods.[30]

The most striking example of how the fragmentation of power in the twelfth century favoured the emergence of Cistercian houses on the frontier in contrast with the situation in the fourteenth century when the borders became 'linear' comes from Neumark. The last of the Cistercian houses established in this region was Himmelstädt. It was plagued by violence and encroachment from its lay neighbours from the very beginning of its existence. The founder, Margrave Albrecht III, from the junior line of the Ascanians, was a nephew of Duke Otto I of Stettin. The original endowment of the monastery was substantial and encompassed fifteen villages and a large forest. Some historians have assumed that the charter making the grant must have been a forgery since it was not confirmed by Albrecht's successors.[31] Albrecht died in December 1300, a few months after the

---

[26] *Register of Holm Cultram*, pp. 142–4. Colm McNamee, *The Wars of the Bruces: Scotland, England and Ireland, 1306–1328* (East Linton, 1997), p. 95.

[27] Brown, *The Black Douglases*, p. 187.

[28] Richard Fawcett and Richard Oram, *Melrose Abbey* (Stroud, 2004), p. 43; Brown, *The Black Douglases*, p. 187.

[29] *Calendar of Documents Relating to Scotland*, III, no. 529.

[30] Ibid., III, nos 529, 967, 1157, 1561.

[31] Edward Rymar, 'Cystersi na terytorium Nowej Marchii przed i w trakcie jej tworzenia oraz ich stosunki z margrabiami brandenburskim z dynastii askańskiej', in *Historia i kultura*

foundation, and the next margrave, Herman, who was the last of that dynasty, contested the original grant of his predecessor. In fact, in the following decades the abbey did not enjoy control of much of its original endowment. This does not necessarily indicate that the documentation of the original generosity of the margrave was forged by the monks. The problem lay elsewhere. The strong opposition by Albrecht's successors was not motivated by the illegality of the monks' claims to the property, but rather by a more fundamental difficulty in establishing a Cistercian monastery in the frontier region of the fourteenth century. During the period between 1319 and 1323 Neumark was ruled by the dukes of Stettin, who were generous towards other Cistercian houses, including Marienwalde, which was located further east than Himmelstädt, and which had itself already existed for three decades by the time of the latter's foundation in 1300.[32] Marienwalde Abbey was moderately successful in building economic dominance over the lesser knights and towns in the area following the successful example of this strategy used by its mother house of Kołbacz.

Even so, in 1337 most of the estates of Himmelstädt Abbey were in the hands of Margrave Ludwig and much else was held by various local knights. In the mid-fourteenth century the abbey was still in the process of erecting basic buildings. The first abbot appears in the sources only in 1372. In 1389 Pope Boniface IX finally ordered an inquest, at the request of the mother house in Kołbacz, into encroachments on Himmelstädt's lands, which resulted in an unimpressive grant of compensation from Margrave John of Luxemburg in the form of a strip of marshland north of the abbey.[33] The miserable situation of that house and the pressure from its neighbours were so severe that the monastery could not function for decades. This failure to prosper was partly due to the untimely death of the founder, and to dynastic changes and thus to a lack of noble support, but mostly to the fact that it was too late to establish a Cistercian abbey that could thrive in the unstable frontier region. The socio-economic landscape was crowded with a number of lesser landholders who could not – and did not wish to – become benefactors, and the appearance of the new religious house was perceived by its neighbours as an encroachment on their rights. The volatile political situation did not encourage generosity to monasteries. Moreover, fashions and expectations had also changed, and mendicant houses became more popular than traditional rurally based monastic houses (with two Dominican and five Franciscan houses in the region); in addition, several wealthy houses of the Hospitallers already held substantial amounts of land in Neumark, further dampening the prospects for Himmelstädt's prosperity.[34]

cystersów w dawnej Polsce i ich europejskie związki, ed. Jerzy Strzelczyk (Poznań, 1987), pp. 207–8; *Codex Diplomaticus Brandenburgensis* [hereafter *CDB*], ed. Adolph F. Riedel (Berlin, 1838–63), vol. 18, nos 13, 6, 28.

32   Edward Rymar, 'Opactwo cysterskie w Bierzwniku (rozwój uposażenia i osadnictwa)', *Przegląd Zachodniopomorski* 15 (1971), 37–62 (pp. 47–8).

33   Gahlbeck, *Zisterzienser*, pp. 196–219; *CDB*, vol. 18, pp. 411, 414.

34   Jan Harasimowicz, 'Sekularyzacja klasztorów w Nowej Marchii w XVI wieku', in *Klasztor w społeczeństwiu średniowiecznym i nowożytnym*, ed. Marek Derwich and Anna Pobóg-Lenartowicz (Opole, 1996), p. 401.

The six case studies discussed here exhibit some of the characteristics typical of Cistercian monasteries on the northern frontiers of medieval Europe. The southern coast of the Baltic and southern Scotland in the twelfth century shared significant similarities in terms of the fragmentation of political power as well as a mixture of 'indigenous' and western-European cultural influences. For the noblemen aspiring to varying degrees of independent political power, becoming a founder and patron of a Cistercian house was an aspirational gesture and a sign of subscribing to a particular model of the pious Christian nobleman. The situation in the fourteenth century shows a sharp contrast to the situation two hundred years earlier; it also shows important differences between Scotland and Pomerania and Neumark. The emergence of borders as divisive lines by the fourteenth century largely destroyed the important links of Scottish houses with northern England as well as those of Holm Cultram with southern Scotland. The experience of war and destruction was a common one for the six houses discussed here (although it was already prominent in Pomerania in the thirteenth century, a peaceful time in Scotland). 'Local' violence, largely executed by neighbours and including attacks on monastic granges and theft, was widespread in Pomerania, whilst sources do not reveal similar trends in Scotland. This was largely related to the overwhelming economic domination of the Cistercian monasteries over their neighbours in the former region, which was never the case in Scotland. I am not trying to claim that the fourteenth century was a peaceful period for the Cistercian monasteries in the hinterlands of Europe, but this time was a turning point for the ways in which monastic communities interacted with lay society, in very sharp contrast to the twelfth-century relationship. In short, political fragmentation, and to some degree even instability, created extremely favourable conditions for the Cistercians in the twelfth century, whilst the volatility and wars of the fourteenth century cut across frontiers and made border lines more rigid, thus creating a hostile environment and a very different set of issues.

4

'Not a thing for a stranger to enter upon': The Selection of Monastic Superiors in Late Medieval and Early Tudor England[*]

MARTIN HEALE

Medieval England is not known for democracy. Indeed, it has been remarked that the selection of heads of autonomous religious houses by their communities comprised 'the only consistently "free" and comparatively democratic elections in late medieval England'.[1] To a certain extent, the freedom of late medieval English monasteries to elect their own heads serves as an indication that these institutions were no longer of central importance in the political life of the kingdom. This right had only sporadically been allowed to their Anglo-Norman forbears at a time when the heads of major abbeys occupied a position of much greater public significance; and the nomination of bishops remained tightly controlled by the monarchy throughout the medieval period and beyond. Nevertheless, the ability freely to select their own heads – in accordance with monastic rules and canon law – was a privilege far from universally enjoyed among the monasteries of later medieval Europe. Institutions which controlled so much wealth and patronage were always vulnerable to external interference, both lay and ecclesiastical, and English monasteries were fortunate in their comparative immunity from institutionalised lay involvement in elections, papal provision and commendatory abbots in the later Middle Ages.[2]

---

[*] The reliance of this essay on the researches of Professor David Smith will be evident to all. Not only have I made extensive use of the materials he assembled for his *HRH*, but he has also made available to me, with characteristic generosity, considerable information from his forthcoming *HRH*, III. I am also very grateful to Professor Smith and to Dr Matt Houlbrook for their helpful comments on a draft of this essay, and to all those who responded to my paper at the Gregynog conference.

[1] R. B. Dobson, *Durham Priory 1400–1450* (Cambridge, 1973), p. 83. The heads of a number of late medieval colleges were also freely elected by their membership.

[2] For examples of external interference in monastic elections in a variety of contexts, see: J. Wallace-Hadrill, *The Frankish Church* (Oxford, 1983), pp. 289–91; D. Knowles, 'Essays in Monastic History 1066–1215, I. Abbatial Elections', *Downside Review* 49 (1931), 252–78, and *Christian Monasticism* (London, 1969), pp. 119–21; G. Coulton, *Five Centuries of Religion*, 4 vols (Cambridge, 1923–50), III, 425–47; D. Hay, *The Church in Italy in the*

Studies of monastic elections in later medieval England, focusing in particular on the form and ceremonial of these occasions, have concluded that the majority seem to have been canonical and uninhibited.[3] It is true that little evidence of overt interference can be found in fourteenth- and fifteenth-century England, but the possibility that bishop, patron or some other external authority might exert influence behind the scenes cannot be discounted. Levels of informal interference will always remain mysterious, but one potential index of outside involvement in monastic elections is available to historians: the frequency with which monastic superiors were taken from other religious houses. This is evidently a rough indicator, since communities might willingly elect a head from another institution, whereas external agencies might intervene in favour of an internal candidate (as was relatively common in the late 1520s and the 1530s). However, as Dom David Knowles noted when studying monastic elections in post-Conquest England, when given free rein religious houses tended to be conservative electors:

> The first choice of a community electing freely fell almost invariably upon one of their own number. They obeyed a perfectly natural instinct followed by most religious communities at the present day, and by such secular bodies as the Fellows of a College. By electing one of their number they satisfied *esprit de corps*, avoided the danger of an unknown tyrant and secured the rule of one with whose methods and character they were familiar. There was, besides, the natural if not exalted consideration that the abbatial dignity was the crown of a career, the highest honour in the gift of the house, not a thing for a stranger to enter upon. Only in the direst distress, financial or spiritual, would a great community willingly choose an outsider.[4]

Elections of outsiders could certainly cause considerable friction, as at Glastonbury or Peterborough in the late eleventh century or Keldholme and Burton in the later Middle Ages.[5] The convents of Spalding, Osney and Selby exhibited great concern about the possibility of external appointments in the sixteenth century; whereas the monks of St Albans in the 1330s were apparently willing to resort to murder rather than accept the machinations of Richard of Ildesle, a monk of Abingdon, to attain the headship of their house.[6] Moreover, there is

Fifteenth Century (Cambridge, 1977), pp. 74–6; M. Dilworth, *Scottish Monasteries in the Later Middle Ages* (Edinburgh, 1995), pp. 12–25; R. Storey, 'Papal Provisions to English Monasteries', *Nottingham Medieval Studies* 35 (1991), 77–91.

3   E.g. Knowles, *RO*, II, 248–52; Dobson, *Durham Priory*, pp. 82–8; R. Vaughan, 'The Election of Abbots at St Albans in the Thirteenth and Fourteenth Centuries', *Proceedings of the Cambridge Antiquarian Soc.* 47 (1953), 1–12.

4   Knowles, 'Abbatial Elections', 262.

5   Knowles, *MO*, pp. 114–15; H. Loyn, 'Abbots of English Monasteries in the Period Following the Norman Conquest', in *England and Normandy in the Middle Ages*, ed. D. Bates and A. Curry (London, 1994), pp. 95–103; and see below, pp. 55–6, for the problems at Keldholme and Burton.

6   *LP Hen. VIII*, IV(ii), no. 4708, XII(ii), no. 1120; H. T. Riley, ed., *Gesta Abbatum Monasterii Sancti Albani*, 3 vols, RS (1867–9), II, 284–92. On a visit to St Albans to gauge the convent's reaction to his attempts to gain the abbacy through papal provision, Ildesle was

an obvious *prima facie* correlation between external appointments to religious houses and well-attested external involvement in the selection of monastic superiors. In both post-Conquest England and late medieval Scotland, when explicit outside intervention in monastic elections was common, external appointments were a regular occurrence.[7] Yet examples of this kind of appointment are much harder to find in late medieval England, when elections were to all appearances free.

Incidences of the importation of heads from other religious houses in late medieval England therefore merit closer scrutiny. Their study can potentially shed valuable light on levels of lay and ecclesiastical interference in monastic affairs, an important but obscure element in the relations between monasteries and society. Tracing patterns of external appointments has two further advantages. First, monastic elections to houses of non-exempt orders are well recorded throughout the later Middle Ages, with bishops' registers and government records (for houses in royal patronage) providing relatively full information about the provenance of individual superiors. Thanks to the remarkable and indefatigable researches of Professor David Smith, many of these references are now readily accessible.[8] Second, the records of monastic elections are fairly uniform throughout the later Middle Ages and early Tudor period. This allows the reliable plotting of trends of elections up to 1540, without the common concern that apparent developments in early sixteenth-century England were the product of increased evidence rather than genuine changes in praxis. Historians of the late medieval church have often tended to avoid questions concerning change over time, an approach often dictated by the nature of the surviving evidence. Mapping trends of external appointments to religious houses, however, permits a chronological approach to this subject. The patterns that emerge are unambiguous and suggest a significant shift in relations between monasteries and the lay authorities in early Tudor England. Together with considerable anecdotal evidence, they point to the conclusion that royal intervention in monastic elections (common in twelfth- and thirteenth-century England) was unusual throughout the later Middle Ages, but increased markedly during the second half of Henry VII's reign. Government involvement in elections intensified during the rule of his son and by the 1530s was relatively widespread. This chronology of royal interference provides a novel dimension to our understanding of pre-Reformation English monasticism and the Dissolution, and suggests that current approaches which see the Henrician Reformation as a 'bolt out of the blue' may need to be reassessed.

---

informed that 'having no regard for any sentence whatever, [they intended] to seize him and butcher him cruelly, as a most dreadful example to all such future provisors'. Ildesle fled, and sensibly, since Walsingham opined that there were men in the abbey at that time who would indeed have carried out these threats.

7   Knowles, 'Abbatial Elections', 252–78; *HRH*, I; D. Watt and N. Shead, eds, *The Heads of Religious Houses in Scotland from the Twelfth to Sixteenth Centuries* (Edinburgh, 2001).
8   *HRH*, II. The final volume of the series, detailing monastic heads down to the Dissolution, will soon be ready for publication. The evidence for exempt orders is uneven, and accordingly this study will focus primarily on the Benedictine and Augustinian orders.

*

Before 1215 external appointments to religious houses were common in England. The Anglo-Norman and Angevin kings played an overt and conspicuous part in the selection of heads, either nominating them outright (William I, William II, Henry I) or selecting candidates from a shortlist presented to them by the relevant convent (Henry II, Richard I, John).[9] This practice need not be viewed as an abuse. As Knowles noted, it was the kings' ability to import abbots from the continent that allowed the thoroughgoing reform of English monasticism after the Conquest; and the frequent interchange of superiors in twelfth-century England created an atmosphere of mutual exchange and renewal.[10] However, King John's grant of free election to all collegiate and conventual churches in November 1214, in accordance with developing canon law, brought about a significant change of practice among the great abbeys and priories of medieval England. The impact of this charter was not immediate, and evidence of continued lay involvement in monastic elections can be found during the long reign of Henry III. English bishops complained in 1253 that 'no one can be promoted in cathedral or conventual churches unless intruded by the king', and repeated this charge in 1257; and there is good evidence that Henry III exerted influence on elections to Pershore and Peterborough abbeys in 1250 and 1251 respectively.[11] It should also be noted that major houses continued to receive heads from other communities relatively frequently between 1214 and 1272, although not at the rate of the preceding period.[12]

However, from the third quarter of the thirteenth century – the period when explicit cases of lay interference in monastic elections become exceptional – external appointments of this kind are rare. Between 1272 and 1485, the vast majority of elections to the larger Benedictine male and female houses favoured internal candidates, and only a handful of outside appointments are recorded (see Table 1). Between 1272 and 1350, six superiors were appointed from other houses. However, three of these six appointments were papal provisions, whereas a further two heads (Robert of Langdon, abbot of Burton, and Matilda of Upton, abbess of Godstow) were in fact former inmates of those houses who had transferred to different communities a few years earlier.[13] Between 1350 and

---

9   Knowles, MO, pp. 395–403. It would appear that all lay patrons enjoyed similar rights in twelfth-century England: S. Wood, English Monasteries and their Patrons in the Thirteenth Century (Oxford, 1955), p. 45.

10 Knowles, MO, pp. 300, 401.

11 Wood, English Monasteries, pp. 40–74, esp. pp. 67–9; CPR 1247–58, p. 211; HRH, II, 56.

12 Examples of external appointments to major Benedictine houses can be found from Bardney, Burton, Chester, Crowland, Evesham, Glastonbury, Milton, Pershore, Peterborough, St Benet of Hulme, Selby, Shaftesbury, Shrewsbury, Tavistock, Thorney, Westminster, St Mary's Winchester, Whitby and Worcester over these years: HRH, II, 15–88, 537–626.

13 William of Tanfield (Durham), Bonus (Tavistock) and John de Devenys (St Augustine's Canterbury) were all provided to their offices by the pope: CPL, II, 40, 265, III, 240; for Longdon and Upton see, VCH Staffordshire, III, 335, 213; HRH, II, 562–3.

1399, not a single major Benedictine house is known to have elected a head from outside their convent. Over the first half of the fifteenth century, only two external appointments in monasteries of this kind took place. The promotion of Gilbert Multon, a monk of Crowland, to Bardney Abbey in 1448 was made by the bishop of Lincoln, having ruled that the convent's nominee, the prior, John Bracy, was unsuitable.[14] Robert Ownesby's appointment to the headship of Burton in 1430 was even more controversial. The account of this election in the Burton registers indicates that this choice was made under considerable pressure from William Heyworth, bishop of Coventry and Lichfield, who like Ownesby had been a monk of St Albans. After stout resistance during the election process, the Burton monks took their case to Rome and in 1433 managed to secure Ownesby's resignation.[15]

These were the only two external appointments to major Benedictine houses over the century leading up to 1450, and just three more followed between 1450 and 1485. One of these three, the election of John Dunster, prior of Bath, to St Augustine's Canterbury in 1482, was a rare papal provision;[16] and the other two appointments (William Wroughton to Chertsey Abbey in 1462 and William Walwayn to Evesham Abbey in 1469) were also unusual. Wroughton, a monk of Winchester Cathedral Priory, had headed a commission on behalf of Bishop Waynflete into the dilapidations of Thomas Angewyn, abbot of Chertsey. Angewyn was duly deposed, and Wroughton selected in his place after the convent had given the bishop the right to choose a successor. However, nearly three years later Wroughton was himself deprived, and the monks of Chertsey surprisingly re-elected Angewyn; an act suggesting that Wroughton's replacement of the former head had not won the full support of the convent.[17] William Walwayn, meanwhile, had already transferred from Worcester to Eynsham (after a highly chequered career at the cathedral priory) a few months before his election as abbot of the latter house. Given his record of disruption at Worcester, the reason for his warm reception at Eynsham is far from clear.[18]

It can be seen, therefore, that external appointments to major Benedictine houses in the period 1272 to 1485 were exceedingly rare, and where they occurred the selection of outside candidates could be the cause of some controversy. It is also notable that very few (if any) instances of large houses themselves nominating a head from another house can be found, and that where outside interference is discernible it is ecclesiastical rather than lay agency that can be traced. This is in sharp contrast to the preceding two hundred years, when monks from other houses were regularly promoted to the headship of major Benedictine houses, with the Crown heavily involved in the selec-

---

14 TNA, C84/47/5; *CPR 1446–1452*, pp. 116–18. I am very grateful to Professor David Smith for bringing this example to my attention.

15 HMC, *Report on the Manuscripts of Lord Middleton, preserved at Wollaton Hall, Nottinghamshire* (HMSO, 1911), pp. 248–51; *VCH Staffordshire*, III, 209.

16 *CPR 1476–1485*, pp. 310, 346; *CPL*, XIII(ii), 812–13.

17 *CPR 1461–1467*, pp. 180–1, 380; *VCH Surrey*, II, 60.

18 Emden, *BRUO*, III, 1977; *BRECP*, pp. 887–8.

tion of superiors. This pattern would seem to support the common conclusion that secular interference was unusual in larger monasteries in this period (see note 3). Houses of this size were in a minority, however, and it is necessary to consider the evidence for elections in the smaller (non-exempt) monasteries in late medieval England before more general conclusions can be drawn.

Starting with the nunneries, few of which were exempt from episcopal jurisdiction, there are again remarkably few examples of external appointments in the later Middle Ages. Professor Smith has identified only twelve such cases between 1272 and 1485, from elections to over 130 houses (see Table 2).[19] All of these examples, with the exception of Matilda of Upton's promotion to Godstow (which, as we have seen, was not a genuine external appointment), involved smaller houses of nuns. Where evidence survives, the selection of these heads generally seems to have been made by the diocesan. Denise de Horsulle, a nun of Broomhall, was appointed prioress of Kington St Michael in 1326 after the election was devolved to Archbishop Reynolds of Canterbury by lapse of time; and it is likely that the selection of Margery, a nun of Lambley, to the headship of St Bartholomew's, Newcastle in 1361, when only two nuns remained in the convent, was also made by the diocesan.[20] Rather more acrimonious was Archbishop Greenfield of York's appointment of Joan of Pickering, a nun of Rosedale, to the headship of Keldholme Priory in July 1308. This choice was fiercely opposed by the Keldholme community, four of whom were sent to other houses for resisting their new head, and the priory was placed under interdict. Despite the archbishop's strenuous attempts to restore order, Joan resigned in February 1309 and returned to Rosedale.[21]

The rarity of external appointments among nunneries of all sizes in later medieval England corresponds closely to the pattern found for major Benedictine monasteries. However, the experience of smaller male houses in this period departs quite considerably from this trend. Indeed, external appointments to lesser houses of (autonomous) Benedictine monks and Augustinian canons were relatively common throughout the later Middle Ages. Benedictine houses such as Alcester, Canwell, Sandwell and Walden are each known to have elected three or four external superiors between 1272 and 1485, and about forty such appointments can be traced from smaller, independent Benedictine houses over this period.[22] Even more strikingly, Professor Smith has located nearly two hundred examples of external appointments to houses of Augustinian canons

[19] HRH, II, 537–626; private communication from Professor David Smith.

[20] HRH, II, 576, 590.

[21] W. Brown and A. H. Thompson, eds, The Register of William Greenfield, Lord Archbishop of York 1306–1315, 5 vols, Surtees Soc., 145, 149, 151–3 (1931–40), III, nos 1188, 1192, 1198, 1213, 1216, 1218, 1221 and 1224; HRH, II, 574–5. Interestingly, there was also considerable opposition to this election from the nuns' lay neighbours. See also Janet Burton, 'Cloistered Women and Male Authority: Power and Authority in Yorkshire Nunneries in the Later Middle Ages', Thirteenth Century England X, ed. Michael Prestwich, Richard Britnell and Robin Frame (Woodbridge, 2005), pp. 155–65.

[22] HRH, II, 18–19, 65–6; private information from Professor David Smith. This figure includes naturalised alien priories (see below).

over the same period.[23] The large majority of these instances come from small priories, such as Torksey and Charley, who imported six and eight superiors respectively from other communities between 1272 and 1485. Why male and female experience in this area should be so markedly different must be a matter of speculation. It may be that nunneries were more resistant than houses of monks and canons to superiors from outside their communities; but perhaps the most likely explanation for this trend is the size of female convents, with even the poorest nunneries rarely containing fewer than five inmates.[24] For this reason, smaller nunneries would have been less likely to find themselves dangerously bereft of inmates, and more likely to house an appropriate internal candidate for promotion than was the case for poor male priories.[25]

One or two further observations concerning the large number of external appointments to lesser male houses over the later Middle Ages can be made. It is clear that these appointments were most common among houses of Augustinian canons. In many instances, we do not know who was responsible for the selection of the promoted canon, and whether or not this reflected a considered decision by the convent itself. However, in a large number of cases it would seem that the choice of superior was made by the diocesan. The records of seventy-five elections of this kind explicitly state that the appointment of the external candidate was made by the bishop or his deputy.[26] A canon might be collated by the diocesan for a number of reasons, such as the inadequate number of inmates in the convent (as at Bodmin Priory in 1349, after the devastation caused by the Black Death), internal conflict over the selection of a new head (as at Thurgarton in 1284), or lapse of time (as at Missenden in 1348).[27] It is also noticeable that the majority of imported Augustinian heads came from houses within the same diocese. Five of the eight priors transferred to Charley were canons of neighbouring Ulverscroft; and two of the three external heads of Bilsington in this period (as well as two more in the early sixteenth century) came from nearby Leeds Priory. Imported heads came from priories of all sizes, with 106 different houses providing the nearly two hundred promoted canons. This 'democratic' exchange of heads appears to have been a late medieval development, since more than half of the canons promoted to the headship of other Augustinian houses between 1214 and 1272 came from the communities of Dunstable or Osney (presumably an indication of high levels of observance at these two houses). Other differences between pre-1272 and post-1272 appointments can also be discerned. In the earlier period, appointments were made to both smaller and larger houses of canons, with heads imported into important priories such as Carlisle, Dorchester, St Frideswide's Oxford and Southwark. In

23 *HRH*, II, 327–490; private information from Professor David Smith.
24 R. Gilchrist, *Gender and Material Culture, The Archaeology of Religious Women* (London, 1994), pp. 42–4.
25 For some observations on the office of prioress in an English context see Janet Burton, 'Looking for Medieval Nuns', below, pp. 113–23.
26 *HRH*, II, 327–490; private information from Professor David Smith.
27 *HRH*, II, 339, 471–2, 425.

contrast, very few external appointments to major Augustinian houses can be found after 1272. Similarly, the pre-1272 appointments were a little less local than later medieval examples, with 24% of promoted heads being drawn from a different diocese compared to 18% between 1272 and 1485.

Although external appointments to Augustinian houses continued at a steady rate throughout the period 1216 to 1485, there was therefore a discernible shift in the pattern of promotions after 1272. The profile of pre-1272 appointments – with the advancement of canons taken from a restricted number of important houses, to the headship of great and small monasteries alike throughout the entire realm – corresponds to that of Benedictine elections of this period, when lay intervention in monastic elections remained acceptable. In contrast, the typical post-1272 appointment of a local canon to a small and often demonstrably struggling priory suggests a decision made at the behest or prompting of the diocesan. It may be that several of these selections were made by the canons themselves, and Henry Knighton's account of the exporting of four canons of Leicester to rule other houses during the rule of Abbot Clowne implies that these choices were made by the convents concerned on account of Leicester's high spiritual reputation. However, for the three of these elections where additional evidence about the selection of the Leicester canons survives, it is clear that the appointment was in fact made by the diocesan: by lapse of time (as we have seen) at Missenden in 1348 and at Wellow in 1374, and on the invitation of the convent at Mottisfont in 1352.[28] It seems likely, then, that the diocesan was the driving force behind the majority of these elections in the later Middle Ages. Indeed, the identification of suitable inmates for promotion to struggling religious houses must have been an important (if rarely cited) facet of the bishop's supervision of the monasteries of his diocese.

Although many fewer examples of external appointments to lesser, independent Benedictine houses can be found between 1272 and 1485, these do come from a much smaller sample of houses. It is also notable that a large number (twenty-two out of forty-one) of these appointments involved a particular category of Benedictine monastery: the seventeen alien priories naturalised in the late fourteenth and early fifteenth centuries (see Table 3). Blyth Priory alone received eight superiors from outside its convent over these years, whereas there were four external appointments at Monmouth and three at Eye during the same period.[29] This series of appointments was not only unusual in its frequency, but also appears different in certain respects from the selection of external candidates to the headship of nunneries and houses of Austin canons in late medieval England. First, several heads were selected from monas-

---

[28] G. Martin, ed., *Knighton's Chronicle 1337–1396* (Oxford, 1995), pp. 200–1; HRH, II, 425, 483, 426.

[29] Appointments of this kind might cause friction. On the election of Thomas Cambridge as prior of Eye in 1440, the second monk of Bury to be promoted to that office within ten years, Abbot Curteys of Bury commented archly in his register that Cambridge quickly felt overburdened by this honour, 'if indeed it should be called an honour': BL, Add. MS 7096, fol. 129a.

teries outside their own order, including monks from the Cluniac houses of St Andrew's Northampton, Pontefract and Thetford. And second, half of these new heads came from houses in a different diocese from their new priory. This casts some doubt over whether the diocesan was generally responsible for these appointments, and it is significant that the available records rarely if ever indicate that the presentation was granted to the bishop, unlike those pertaining to elections in houses of Austin canons.

How then can we explain this spate of external appointments to naturalised alien priories, a trend that continued after 1485, with at least fifteen further instances in the fifty years up to 1535 (see Table 3)? It is likely that a number of different factors were operative in these selections. Some appointments may have been made freely by the convent concerned, and others through episcopal influence.[30] In a number of examples (such as the promotion of Robert Eton as prior of Abergavenny), the appointee was the first head of the house since its denization and therefore necessarily drawn from another community. Nevertheless, there are signs that appointments to former alien priories were sometimes the product of external secular interference. Blyth Priory, which so regularly imported heads after its denization, was in the king's patronage and may have been subject to royal intervention in some of its elections. The priory was described as 'donative' at the time of the appointment of Nicholas Hall, a monk of Pontefract, in 1438, whereas the headship of the house was said to have been 'granted' by the king to new priors in 1447 and 1458, terminology which is highly unusual for late medieval monastic elections.[31] Another hint that royal influence might have played a part in some elections involving naturalised alien priories comes from the promotion of four monks of Westminster Abbey to the headships of such houses in fifteenth- and early sixteenth-century England. The significance of the large number of external appointments to former alien priories remains difficult to judge. But it is possible that the king and other lay patrons, who had enjoyed considerable powers over these houses and their endowments during times of Anglo-French hostility, were not wholly prepared to relinquish influence thereafter.

It seems clear, therefore, that the patterns of external appointments to the headship of religious houses reveal something of the changing relations between the monastic order and the lay and ecclesiastical authorities in medieval England. The scarcity of such appointments in the later Middle Ages for all orders other than the Augustinian canons would seem to support the orthodox conclusion that monastic elections in late medieval England were generally 'free and democratic'. Signs of lay interference in elections, moreover, with the

---

[30] The appointment of Thomas Sudbury, prior of Northampton, to Folkestone Priory in 1502 was made by Archbishop Morton after the deposition of Prior Thomas Banes: C. Harper-Bill, 'The Priory and Parish of Folkestone in the Fifteenth Century', *Archaeologia Cantiana* 93 (1977), 195–200 (p. 199). For Sudbury's earlier career, see R. Graham, 'The English Province of the Order of Cluny in the Fifteenth Century', in *English Ecclesiastical Studies*, ed. R. Graham (London, 1929), pp. 81–6.

[31] CPR 1436–1441, p. 226; CPR, 1446–1452, p. 102; CPR, 1452–1461, p. 470.

possible exception of those involving naturalised alien priories, are very hard to find, with the bishop by far the most important outside influence. Indeed, it is even possible to find examples where royal wishes were explicitly disregarded in this period, most notably Westminster Abbey's election of William Colchester as abbot in 1386, despite three messages sent by Richard II recommending John Lakingheath as the most suitable candidate.[32] The contrast with monastic elections held before c. 1250 is stark.

However, the examination of patterns of election reveals one final and suggestive trend: a significant upturn in external appointments to major houses from the 1490s. As we have seen, the great Benedictine monasteries of fourteenth- and fifteenth-century England were led almost exclusively by men and women who had been trained within their own convents. This, however, began slowly to change during the reign of Henry VII (see Table 4). Between 1495 and 1509, seven heads of major Benedictine abbeys were chosen from outside their communities. From 1509 to 1529 a further seven external appointments were made, and ten more during the 1530s. Therefore, following a period of over two hundred years when – aside from papal provisions and elections of former members of the communities concerned – only four heads of major Benedictine houses were selected from outside their own convents, twenty-four such appointments were made in a little over forty years.[33] Some sense of proportion should be retained since only about a quarter of elections to major Benedictine houses in this period were affected, but the change in ratio is nonetheless dramatic: from one election every fifty-five years promoting an external candidate (1272–1495) to more than one such election every two years (1496–1536). This would suggest that a significant change in the relationship between monasteries and external influences was taking place between the late fifteenth century and the 1530s.

Closer examination of these elections reveals that they have considerably more in common with pre-1272 elections than those late medieval examples involving Benedictine houses, nunneries and the Augustinian canons. The majority of these appointments (seventeen out of twenty-four) imported monks from other dioceses, and there is little indication in the bishops' registers that the diocesan played a major part in the choice of heads. Furthermore, in several cases the selection of a superior points strongly to the influence of an important patron. The first of these abbots to be appointed from another house was Thomas Rowland, prior of Luffield (and a former monk of Durham), who was made abbot of Abingdon in April 1496. Since Luffield Priory had been suppressed by Henry VII to endow his chantry in the previous year, it seems very likely that this appointment was the king's compensation for Rowland; and

[32] L. Hector and B. Harvey, ed., *The Westminster Chronicle 1381–1394* (Oxford, 1982), pp. 176–9. I am grateful to Professor David Smith for reminding me of this episode.

[33] Significantly, only two of these elections involved nunneries (Elstow in 1524 and Wilton in 1534). It should also be noted that external appointments were not confined to the Benedictine order in these years, but can also be traced for larger Augustinian, Cluniac, Cistercian and Premonstratensian houses.

it is also significant that he was not the unanimous choice of the Abingdon convent.[34] Similarly, a number of the regulars promoted to the headship of other houses between 1515 and 1529 had close connections with Cardinal Wolsey. Both Thomas Marshall (appointed abbot of Chester in 1527 and abbot of Colchester in 1533) and John Stonywell (made abbot of Pershore in 1526) were monks of St Albans, the abbey held *in commendam* by Wolsey from 1522.[35] John Salcot, a monk of Colchester elected abbot of St Benet Hulme in 1517 (and subsequently abbot of Hyde and bishop of Salisbury), was the brother of William Capon, Wolsey's chaplain.[36] Wolsey also wrote to Bishop Atwater of Lincoln in 1516 recommending Thomas Chaundler, abbot of Wymondham (and formerly a monk of Canterbury Cathedral Priory and prior of Horsham), 'the flower of St Benet's order', for the vacant abbacy of Eynsham, to which Chaundler was duly appointed.[37]

Additional evidence exists for interference in monastic elections by both Henry VII and Cardinal Wolsey. The houses of Great Malvern, Ramsey and St Mary's York, along with the English Cistercians, disbursed large sums to Henry VII for the 'privilege' of free election under the aegis of Edmund Dudley; and, in his *Tree of Commonwealth* (1509/10), Dudley himself advised Henry VIII that 'it were a graciouse and a noble acte that the Churche of England were restorid to hur free election after thold manor, and not to be lettyd therof by meanes of you, oure souuereigne lord, nor by meanes of any of your subiectes as farforth as you may help yt'.[38] Wolsey's involvement in monastic elections is well known, and there is evidence to suggest that the Cardinal made substantial profits from this activity, including from the promotion of Thomas Marshall.[39] From the second half of the 1520s, both Wolsey and Cromwell were monitoring monastic elections closely, although their patronage was generally given to internal candidates.[40] This intensifying interference caused some disquiet, featuring in the charges made against Wolsey on his fall, and in Thomas Starkey's *Dialogue between Pole and Lupset*, which criticised 'electyonys both of byschoppys abbottys and pryorys, wych are made other by the prynce or some

---

[34] *VCH Berkshire*, II, 58; *CPR 1494–1509*, pp. 55, 56.

[35] J. Ward, 'Marshall, Thomas (d. 1539)', *ODNB*, pp. 869–70; Knowles, *RO*, III, 340–2; *LP Hen. VIII*, IV(ii), no. 3227. Marshall had been prior of Wallingford, and may well have been promoted in compensation for the closure of this house by Wolsey in 1528; whereas Stonywell had been prior of Tynemouth, another cell of St Albans.

[36] A. Louisa, 'Capon [Salcot], John (d. 1557)', *ODNB*, IX, 994. Salcot wrote to Wolsey in 1525 having heard from his brother and Dr Lee that the Cardinal was intending to promote him: *LP Hen. VIII*, IV(iii) app. 38, p. 3091.

[37] *LP Hen. VIII*, II(i), no. 2724.

[38] S. Gunn, 'Edmund Dudley and the Church', *JEH* 51 (2000), 509–26 (pp. 510, 517–18); D. Brodie, ed., *The Tree of Commonwealth. A Treatise Written by Edmund Dudley* (Cambridge, 1948), p. 25.

[39] P. Gwyn, *The King's Cardinal. The Rise and Fall of Thomas Wolsey* (London, 1990), pp. 316–30; Knowles, *RO*, III, 161; BL, Stowe MS 141, fol. 10.

[40] *LP Hen. VIII*, passim.

other grete mannys authoryte', which were the cause of 'grete destructyon of the gud ordur in the church'.[41]

The rise in the rate of external appointments to major Benedictine houses after Wolsey's fall suggests an intensification of government interference. The promotions of John Salcot (to Hyde Abbey), William Repps (to St Benet Hulme) and William Boston (to Burton Abbey) followed soon after all three monk-scholars helped to secure the University of Cambridge's support for the King's divorce in March 1530.[42] The selection of Robert Catton as abbot of St Albans in 1531 also seems to have been heavily influenced by the king, who warned the monks against choosing their preferred internal candidate and who received five manors from Catton soon after his appointment in an exchange of property very much to the king's advantage.[43] Money certainly changed hands during the election of Cecily Bodenham, prioress of Kington St Michael to the headship of Wilton Abbey in 1534.[44] And Henry Holbeach (later bishop of Rochester and Lincoln) was appointed prior of Worcester in 1536 following a letter of support by Cranmer and a highly irregular election in which only two of the four *compromissorii* chosen to elect the new prior were monks.[45]

Therefore, the re-emergence of regular external appointments to major houses in the early Tudor period should be seen as symptomatic of greater external involvement in the selection of superiors and in monastic affairs more generally. Indeed these appointments of regulars from other houses may have contributed to this situation in themselves. Where appointments to the headship of houses were confined largely to internal candidates, the patronage of individual monks by external authorities was considerably less worthwhile: in any given house, a patron (and ambitious monk) may have had to wait many years for the next election. But in a climate where the promotion of superiors from other houses was commonplace, the patronage of individual religious became much more viable and profitable: in effect, a job market was created, comparable to that which existed for other ecclesiastical benefices. By the later 1520s, this developing state of affairs is reflected in correspondence between members of the lay and ecclesiastical elites. In October 1527, William Franklin, archdeacon of Durham, and Sir William Bulmer wrote to Wolsey, having heard of the cardinal's intention to make the prior of Tynemouth (another St Albans monk) abbot of Peterborough, to request the headship of Tynemouth for Dr

[41] *LP Hen. VIII*, IV(iii), no. 6075; T. Mayer, ed., *Thomas Starkey, A Dialogue between Pole and Lupset*, Camden 4th series, 37 (1989), p. 87.

[42] *LP Hen. VIII*, IV(iii), nos 6247, 6276, 6331, V, no. 166 (53); D. Leader, *A History of the University of Cambridge, I: The University to 1546* (Cambridge, 1988), p. 327. Boston was also an old friend of Archbishop Cranmer: D. MacCulloch, *Thomas Cranmer. A Life* (New Haven, 1996), pp. 20, 94, 136, 369.

[43] *LP Hen. VIII*, V, nos 78, 405; J. Clark, 'Reformation and Reaction at St Albans Abbey, 1530–58', *EHR* 115 (2000), 297–328 (p. 300); *LP Hen. VIII*, V, no. 78.

[44] Friends of one Cecily Lambert were said to have been willing to pay Cromwell £100 for her election, while Cecily Bodenham is known to have incurred debts in securing the post: *VCH Wiltshire*, III, 239–40.

[45] *LP Hen. VIII*, IX, no. 97; *BRECP*, p. 824.

Peter Lee, a monk of Durham; and in 1535, when Prior More of Worcester was arrested on a treason charge, both Cranmer and Richard Gresham, mayor of London, wrote to Cromwell requesting the position for monks of their acquaintance, the latter even offering £100 for the favour.[46] Connected to this trend was the contemporaneous appearance of a new phenomenon in English monastic history: the serial abbot. The examples of John Salcot and Thomas Marshall, careerist monks who met very different fates, have already been cited, together with that of Thomas Chaundler. Similarly, Matthew Mackerell, a canon of Cockersand, attained the headship of Alnwick and then Barlings, while John Salisbury of Bury St Edmunds became head successively of Horsham and Titchfield; and both men were also appointed suffragan bishops.[47] Career patterns of this kind would have been unthinkable a generation earlier and are indicative of broader changes taking place within the monastic order in early Tudor England.

Many of the recorded examples of interference in monastic elections from the 1530s involved rival internal candidates: a reminder that external appointments can only be a rough index of outside involvement.[48] It is also likely that patterns of superiors chosen from other communities can reveal much more about governmental intervention in monastic affairs than local patronal interference, which would tend to adjudicate between inmates of the same house.[49] Nevertheless, the ebb and flow of external appointments to religious houses over the Middle Ages corresponds very closely to the more anecdotal evidence for government intervention in monastic elections both before 1272 and after 1485. In the absence of any way of knowing what went on behind the scenes in the vast majority of monastic elections in late medieval and early Tudor England, external appointments provide one of the best available guides to changing relations between monasteries and the secular authorities. The avail-

---

[46] *LP Hen. VIII*, IV(ii), no. 3478, IX, nos 97, 184. As we have seen, one of Cranmer's candidates, Henry Holbeach of Crowland, was chosen. Pressure might also come from ecclesiastical sources, and in February 1528 William Marton, abbot of Bardney, wrote to Thomas Heneage of Wolsey's household, asking him to petition the cardinal for the promotion of one of Marton's own monks to the headship of Spalding: ibid., IV(ii), no. 3964.

[47] For Salcot, Marshall and Chaundler, see above p. 61; Mackerell and Salisbury also experienced the vicissitudes of the Henrician court, with the former executed for alleged involvement in the Lincolnshire Rising of 1536 and the latter made dean of Norwich after surrendering Titchfield: M. Bowker, 'Mackerell, Matthew (*d*. 1537)', *ODNB*, XXXV, 494–5; I. Atherton, 'Salisbury, John (1501/2–1573)', *ODNB*, XLVIII, pp. 710–11.

[48] E.g. Knowles, *RO*, III, 339–40.

[49] It may be a product of the increasing survival of evidence that the early sixteenth century affords a greater number of examples of patronal interference in monastic elections (usually in favour of internal candidates) than the preceding period: e.g. R. Hoyle and H. Summerson, 'The Earl of Derby and the Deposition of the Abbot of Furness in 1514', *Northern History* 30 (1994), 184–92; *LP Hen. VIII*, V, no. 1614 (Muchelney); VI, no. 1376 (Buckland); VII, no. 1096 (Hulton), app. 17 (Croxton); XII(i), no. 822 (Tynemouth); G. Baskerville, *English Monks and the Suppression of the Monasteries* (London, 1937), pp. 45–71. Alternatively, this may be interpreted as lay patrons following the interventionist lead of the government.

able data strongly suggests that government interference was rare throughout the later Middle Ages, but that royal intervention intensified considerably in the generation leading up to the Dissolution. Since the suppression of the majority of English monasteries would proceed by government pressure on individual superiors to surrender their houses, this finding is of real interest.

The particular chronology suggested by this study also prompts reflection. It may well be significant that the pattern of government involvement in monastic elections bears more than a passing resemblance to the chronology of lay intervention in monastic property – which, like free election, was protected by canon law in the later Middle Ages. As I have argued elsewhere, there were very few closures of religious houses in the later Middle Ages, with the exception of the significant but atypical opportunities provided by alien priories for the redeployment of monastic resources in fifteenth-century England. A gradual change can then be discerned from the final years of the fifteenth century, with Henry VII's closure of four monasteries in 1495–1507, a trend greatly extended by Wolsey and then taken up more widely by laymen in the 1530s.[50] It is also worth underlining that lay interference in monastic elections (as with monastic property) seems to begin in the reign of Henry VII and not that of his son. Although theories about a 'new monarchy' after 1485 have been widely questioned, it does appear that Henry Tudor adopted a more interventionist policy towards the church than his predecessors. Steven Gunn has shown how ecclesiastical taxation increased during the reign, along with complaints from the clergy about the Crown's undermining of various clerical rights.[51] Gunn concludes his fine study of Edmund Dudley and the church by noting how laymen at the heart of Henry VII's government set out 'to extend royal power over the Church, [and] to exploit the Church's resources for their own benefit … and to accept that the clergy needed improving and that the laity, led by the king, had the right to tell them so'. For Gunn, this development 'does not account for the Henrician Reformation, but it does help us to understand the course it took'.[52] The evidence for the first Tudor king's relations with the monasteries of his realm suggests that this is also true more specifically for our understanding of the Dissolution. The years around 1500 were an important turning point in the relations between monasteries and Crown, and church and Crown more generally, and it is hard to explain satisfactorily the reforms of the 1530s without reference to this backdrop.

Yet it would be wrong to conclude that any kind of lay influence over monastic affairs was necessarily damaging or a precursor of the hostile policies of the late 1530s. Lay patrons (including the Crown) regularly intervened in the business of their houses in order to restore solvency or to prevent an

---

[50] M. Heale, 'Dependent Priories and the Closure of Monasteries in Late Medieval England, 1400–1535', *EHR* 119 (2004), 1–26.

[51] Gunn, 'Edmund Dudley', pp. 513–18.

[52] Ibid., pp. 525–6.

unsuitable head causing damage.[53] It may well also be the case that several of the external appointments taking place after 1495 were in favour of talented and deserving monks. Several of those patronised, including Thomas Barton, Anthony Dunstan, Thomas Chaundler, Henry Holbeach, Thomas Marshall, William Repps, John Salcot and John Stonywell, had enjoyed prominent academic careers before their promotion, and had apparently come to the attention of the government as a result.[54] It is also significant that during these very years there was a sharp upturn in the number of (university-educated) monks and canons made bishops or suffragans. Sixteen appointments of monks and canons to English or Welsh bishoprics were made in as many years from 1494 to 1509, compared to just ten preferments over the previous seventy-five years; and a further seven monks and canons were promoted to the episcopal bench during the reign of Henry VIII (interestingly, all after 1533).[55] It is very likely that these two striking developments were linked, and that what we see from the second half of Henry VII's reign is greater royal interest in monastic affairs and increased interplay between the secular and monastic spheres. In ordinary circumstances, this development might have been beneficial for the monastic order, but in the very different climate of the 1530s it could only strengthen Cromwell's hand. When trying to understand the remarkable ease with which England's greater monasteries went down between 1538 and 1540, the growing dependence of heads of religious houses on the Tudor government in the generation leading up to the Dissolution should be seen as an important factor.

[53] E.g., K. Wood-Legh, *Studies in Church Life in England under Edward III* (Cambridge, 1934), pp. 1–37; Wood, *English Monasteries*, pp. 136–60.

[54] Emden, *BRUO*, I, 399–400, III, 1791; Emden, *BRUO, 1501–1540*, pp. 29, 330, 382; M. Bowker, 'Holbeach, Henry (d. 1551)', *ODNB*, XXVII, 580–1; I. Atherton, 'Rugg, William (d. 1550)', *ODNB*, XLVIII, 101; A. Louisa, 'Capon [Salcot], John', *ODNB*, IX, 994. Barton, Chaundler, Dunstan, Holbeach and Stonywell had all served as wardens/priors of monastic colleges in Oxford or Cambridge prior to their promotions.

[55] R. B. Dobson, 'English and Welsh Monastic Bishops: the Final Century, 1433–1533', *Monasteries and Society in Medieval Britain*, ed. B. Thompson (Stamford, 1999), pp. 348–67; R. Haines, 'Regular Clergy and the Episcopate in the Provinces of Canterbury and York during the Later Middle Ages', *Revue Bénédictine* 113 (2003), 407–47. For the twenty-one known monastic suffragans appointed between 1485 and 1534, see *Handbook of British Chronology*, ed. E. Fryde, D. Greenway, S. Porter and I. Roy, 3rd edn (London, 1986), pp. 284–7. This list is probably not complete, and further appointments were made between 1534 and 1540.

Table 1. External appointments to the headship of major Benedictine monasteries, 1272–1485
(Sources: *HRH*, II, *CPR, CPL, VCH, BRECP*, private communication from Professor David Smith)

Superior	Position	Year
1. Matilda of Upton (Amesbury)	Abbess of Godstow	1304
2. William of Tanfield (Wetheral)	Prior of Durham	1308
3. Richard of Gainsborough (Spalding)	Abbot of Bardney	1318
4. Bonus (Larreule-en-Bigorre)	Abbot of Tavistock	1327
5. Robert of Langdon (Tutbury)	Abbot of Burton	1329
6. John de Deveyns (St Swithun's Winchester)	Abbot of St Augustine's Canterbury	1347
7. Robert Ownesby (St Albans)	Abbot of Burton	1430
8. Gilbert Multon (Crowland)	Abbot of Bardney	1448
9. William Wroughton (St Swithun's Winchester)	Abbot of Chertsey	1462
10. William Walwayn (Worcester)	Abbot of Eynsham	1469
11. John Dunster (pr. Bath)	Abbot of St Augustine's Canterbury	1482

Table 2. External appointments to the headship of nunneries, 1272–1485
(Sources: *HRH*, II, *VCH*, private communication from Professor David Smith)

Superior	Position	Year
1. Christine of Winchester (pr. Farewell?)	Prioress of Langley	?1281/2
2. Matilda of Upton (Amesbury)	Abbess of Godstow	1304
3. Alice of Beverley (Nunkeeling)	Prioress of Nunburnholme	1306
4. Joan of Pickering (Rosedale)	Prioress of Keldholme	1308
5. Isabel Couvel (Arthington)	Prioress of Arden	1324
6. Denise de Horsulle (Broomhall)	Prioress of Kington St Michael	1326
7. Margery (Lambley)	Prioress of Newcastle	1361
8. Joan Holkene (Cook Hill)	Prioress of Pinley	1366
9. Alice Myntyng (Whistones)	Prioress of Pinley	1427
10. Margaret Danby (St Bart. Newcastle)	Prioress of Neasham	1428
11. Katherine Colyngrygge (Little Marlow)	Prioress of Flamstead	1454
12. Margaret Fages (Clerkenwell)	Prioress of Castle Hedingham	1476

Table 3. External appointments to the headship of naturalised alien priories, 1390–1535
(Sources: *HRH, II, CPR, LP Hen. VIII, VCH*, E. Pearce, *The Monks of Westminster* (Cambridge, 1916), private communication from Professor David Smith)

Superior	Position	Year
1. Thomas Fakenham (Bermondsey)	Prior of Eye	1391
2. Robert Eton (Christ Church Canterbury)	Prior of Abergavenny	1417
3. John Gaynesburgh (Selby)	Prior of Blyth	1421
4. John Assheford (St Augustine's Canterbury)	Prior of Folkestone	1427
5. Robert Toppeclif (St Mary's York)	Prior of Blyth	1430
6. John Cotyngham (St Mary's York)	Prior of Blyth	1431
7. Silvester Bolton (Bury)	Prior of Eye	1431
8. Thomas Gedney (Westminster)	Prior of Tutbury	1433
9. Richard Horton (Gloucester)	Prior of Monmouth	1433
10. Robert Blythe (Northampton)	Prior of Tickford	1434
11. Nicholas Hall (Pontefract)	Prior of Blyth	1438
12. Thomas Cambrygge (Bury)	Prior of Eye	1440
13. John Twining (Gloucester)	Prior of Goldcliff	1441
14. Thomas Bolton (Pontefract)	Prior of Blyth	1447
15. William West (Lenton)	Prior of Blyth	1451
16. James Onysbury (Gloucester)	Prior of Monmouth	1455
17. William Buckland (Westminster)	Prior of Deerhurst	1462
18. Thomas de Leghe (Great Malvern)	Prior of Monmouth	1464
19. Reginald Mathon (Great Malvern)	Prior of Monmouth	1465
20. Robert Scotes (St Mary's York)	Prior of Blyth	1465
21. William Kirkby (Holy Trinity York)	Prior of Tickford	1468
22. William Massam (Durham)	Prior of Blyth	1472
23. John Redman (Westminster)	Prior of Totnes	1499
24. Thomas York (Whitby)	Prior of Tickford	1501
25. Thomas Chaundler (Christ Church Canterbury)	Prior of Horsham	1501
26. Thomas Sudbury (pr. Northampton)	Prior of Folkestone	1502
27. Thomas Broke (pr. Snelshall)	Prior of Tickford	1503
28. Robert Hyll (Tavistock)	Prior of Totnes	1503
29. Thomas Gardyner (Westminster)	Prior of Blyth	1507
30. John Baynebrig (Horsley)	Prior of Blyth	1511
31. John Thornton (pr. Dover)	Prior of Folkestone	1513
32. Robert Burton (Winchcombe)	Prior of Monmouth	1520
33. Richard Evesham (Evesham)	Prior of Monmouth	1524
34. Edmund Coker (Glastonbury)	Prior of Totnes	1527
35. William Motlowe (Gloucester)	Prior of Abergavenny	1530
36. Richard Taylbus (Bermondsey)	Prior of Monmouth	1534
37. John Salisbury (Bury)	Prior of Horsham	1534

This table does not include external appointments preceding the naturalisation of the house. It is quite possible that two sixteenth-century heads of Horsham should be added to this list, although no concrete evidence has been found to link Priors William Castleton and Lancelot Wharton to the so-named priors of Norwich and Rumburgh.

Table 4. External appointments to the headship of major Benedictine monasteries, 1485–1540
(Sources: *CPR*, *LP Hen. VIII*, *VCH*, *BRECP*, Emden, *BRUO* and *BRUC*, *ODNB*, private communication from Professor David Smith)

Superior	Position	Year
1. Thomas Rowland (pr. Luffield)	Abbot of Abingdon	1496
2. John Lovell (St Mary's York)	Abbot of Whitby	1499
3. William Eynesham (pr. Tickford)	Abbot of Whitby	1501
4. William Gedding (Ramsey)	Abbot of Crowland	1504
5. Robert Depyng (Crowland)	Abbot of Selby	1504
6. John Benested (St Albans; pr. Tynemouth)	Abbot of Whitby	1504
7. William Compton (Tewkesbury)	Abbot of Pershore	1504
8. John Salcot (Colchester)	Abbot of St Benet Hulme	1517
9. Thomas York (pr. Northampton)	Abbot of Whitby	1517
10. Thomas Chaundler (abb. Wymondham)	Abbot of Eynsham	1517
11. Thomas Barton (Westminster)	Abbot of Colchester	1523
12. Agnes Gascoyne (St Mary Northampton)	Abbess of Elstow	1524
13. John Stonywell (St Albans; pr. Tynemouth)	Abbot of Pershore	1526
14. Thomas Marshall (St Albans; pr. Wallingford)	Abbot of Chester	1527
15. Anthony Dunstane (Westminster)	Abbot of Eynsham	1530
16. John Salcot (abb. St Benet Hulme)	Abbot of Hyde	1530
17. William Repps (pr. Norwich)	Abbot of St Benet Hulme	1530
18. William Boston (Peterborough)	Abbot of Burton	1531
19. Robert Catton (pr. Norwich)	Abbot of St Albans	1531
20. Thomas Marshall (abb. Chester)	Abbot of Colchester	1533
21. William Boston (abb. Burton)	Abbot of Westminster	1533
22. Robert Hamlyn (Tavistock)	Abbot of Athelney	1533
23. Cecily Bodenham (pr. Kington)	Abbess of Wilton	1534
24. Henry Holbeach (Crowland)	Prior of Worcester	1536

RELIGIOUS HOUSES AND
THEIR PATRONS AND BENEFACTORS

5

Patronage, Prestige and Politics:
The Observant Franciscans at Adare

COLMÁN Ó CLABAIGH

The village of Adare in Co. Limerick is one of the principal tourist attractions in the south-west of Ireland. The efforts of the local landlords, the Wyndham-Quin earls of Dunraven, in the late nineteenth century produced a picture postcard streetscape more reminiscent of the Cotswolds than of rural Ireland. At the heart of the village lies a remarkable ensemble of medieval ecclesiastical and secular buildings dating from the village's heyday as the manorial caput of the Fitzgerald earls of Kildare.[1] The Fitzgeralds gained possession of the manor in the early thirteenth century and it remained theirs until it was forfeited to the earls of Desmond, following the Kildare rebellion in 1534. The surviving structures consist of the Fitzgerald or Desmond castle, constructed at various stages between the thirteenth and fifteenth centuries; the thirteenth-century parish church of St Nicholas; a monastery of Trinitarian friars founded by Geoffrey de Marisco in the early thirteenth century and now serving as the Roman Catholic parish church;[2] a house of Augustinian friars founded in 1316 by James Fitz Thomas Fitzgerald, first earl of Kildare, and now the Anglican parish church.[3] In the fifteenth century a chantry chapel was established adjacent to the parish church and in 1464 a friary was established for Observant Franciscans by Thomas Fitzgerald, seventh earl of Kildare, and his countess, Johanna, daughter of James Fitzgerald, the seventh earl of Desmond. This last foundation is unique in Ireland in that documentary, testamentary and architectural evidence disclose a pattern of patronage that demonstrates the close symbiotic relationship between the friars and the leading figures of the Anglo-Irish and Gaelic elites.

---

[1] Caroline, Countess of Dunraven, *Memorials of Adare Manor* (Oxford, 1865).
[2] Aubrey Gwynn and R. N. Hadcock, *Medieval Religious Houses: Ireland* (Dublin, 1970, repr. 1988), p. 217.
[3] Ibid. p. 295. See also R. F. Hewson, 'The Augustinian Priory, Adare', *North Munster Antiquarian Journal* 1 (1938), 108–12.

The Franciscans in Ireland

The establishment of the Irish Franciscan province by the general chapter of the Friars Minor at Assisi in 1230 formally brought Irish church and society into contact with one of the most vibrant and creative movements in the late medieval church. As was the case elsewhere in Europe, the Franciscans in Ireland underwent a period of rapid expansion and, by 1325, when the first wave of foundations ceased, thirty-two friaries had been established.[4] The pioneers of the Irish province were for the most part Englishmen who naturally gravitated to the towns and boroughs of the Anglo-Norman colony. Here they found a ready forum for their ministry and the material support necessary for their mendicant lifestyle. In time the friars also shared in the colony's experience of decline as a result of depopulation, absenteeism and economic recession. Growing insecurity in the face of the Gaelic revival of the late thirteenth and early fourteenth centuries led to increased ethnic tension between Gaelic and Anglo-Irish friars.[5] While recent studies have challenged the veracity of the reports that sixteen friars were killed by their confreres at the provincial chapter in Cork in 1291, it is clear that the province was ethnically polarised by events such as the Bruce invasion of 1316–18.[6] A reform of the province in 1325 effectively gerrymandered the Gaelic friaries into the custody of Nenagh. While this arrangement was rescinded in 1345 Anglo-Irish friars continued to dominate the province and the first Gaelic friar to attain the office of provincial minister was William O'Reilly who was appointed c. 1445.[7]

The second wave of expansion, which began in the early fifteenth century, saw the friars move into Gaelic and Gaelicised territories. Their imposing Gothic friaries, with distinctive tapering bell towers, are as much a symbol of that newly prosperous and confident society as are the tower houses of the lords and chieftains who patronised them.[8] This expansion was closely associated with the austere Observant reform whose constitutional arrangements provided a mechanism for Gaelic friars to escape the hegemony of the Anglo-Irish authorities of the order. This political dimension should not be overstated however as the Observants quickly won the respect of all sections of society and the reform was eventually accepted by the majority of the older founda-

4   Francis Cotter, *The Friars Minor in Ireland from their Arrival to 1400* (St Bonaventure, New York, 1994); Patrick Conlan, *Franciscan Ireland* (Athlone, 1988), pp. 7–32.
5   John Watt, *The Church and the Two Nations in Medieval Ireland* (Cambridge, 1970), pp. 175–83.
6   Cotter, *Friars Minor*, pp. 33–40.
7   Bernadette Williams, ed., *The Annals of Ireland by Friar John Clyn* (Dublin, 2007), pp. 182, 232.
8   Roger Stalley, 'Gaelic Friars and Gothic Design', in *Medieval Architecture and its Intellectual Context: Studies in honour of Peter Kidson*, ed. E. Fernie and P. Crossley (1990), pp. 191–202; idem, 'The End of the Middle Ages: Gothic Survival in Sixteenth Century Connacht', *Journal of the Royal Soc. of Antiquaries of Ireland* 133 (2003), 5–23.

tions.[9] Their pastoral activities led to a quickening of devotion among their lay followers with their promotion of the Third Order or Tertiary rule being particularly effective. From the ranks of these lay tertiaries a new form of religious life emerged, that of the Third Order Regular or Regular Tertiaries. This consisted of members, generally men, living the vowed life in community as professed religious. Between 1426 and 1527 forty-six houses were established for these tertiaries, the majority of which were situated in Gaelic territories.[10] The Observants also garnered lay support by issuing letters of confraternity, granting a share in their spiritual exercises and ascetic practices to their lay benefactors and supporters.[11] Thus, by the 1530s, Ireland was host to over one hundred Franciscan communities, the majority of which were reformed or Observant houses. In comparison England, though a much wealthier and more densely populated country, supported seventy-one Franciscan communities, of which only six were Observant.[12] In addition the friars enjoyed considerable prestige as spiritual and moral authorities, and Gaelic noblemen were reported to hold them in such reverence as to endure corporal punishment at their hands.

The friars and the Fitzgeralds

The paucity of late medieval Irish source material makes it very difficult to provide an analysis of the relationship of the Irish friars with their patrons and benefactors comparable to those available for the English province of the order. Sufficient material survives, however, to provide a reasonably comprehensive account of the relationship between the mendicant friars, particularly the Franciscans, and the various branches of the most prominent of the Anglo-Norman families, the Geraldines or Fitzgeralds. The family emerged from relatively modest origins in Wales, tracing their descent from a union between Henry I's castellan, Gerald of Windsor, and Nesta, daughter of Rhys ap Tewdwr. Though among the first Anglo-Normans to arrive in Ireland in 1169 their rise to prominence was consolidated during the lifetime of Maurice Fitzgerald II, second Baron Offaly and Justiciar of Ireland from 1232 to 1245.[13] The arrival of both the Dominicans and Franciscans in Ireland also corresponded with his career and he was credited with the foundation of the Franciscan house in Youghal in 1224 or, more likely, 1231, which, by the late fifteenth century was believed to be the proto-friary of the order in Ireland. Maurice's involvement in 1235 with Richard de Burgh in the conquest of the western province of Connacht brought him extensive territories in the west and north-west of Ireland and he consolidated his territories by a process of encastellation and the

9   Colmán N. Ó Clabaigh, *The Franciscans in Ireland, 1400–1534* (Dublin, 2002).
10 Ibid., pp. 80–105.
11 Joseph A. Gribbin and Colmán N. Ó Clabaigh, 'Confraternity Letters of the Irish Observant Franciscans and their Benefactors', *Peritia* 16 (2002), 459–71.
12 *MRH*, pp. 189–95.
13 Brendan Smith, 'Fitzgerald, Maurice (c. 1194–1257)', *ODNB*, XIX, 832–33.

foundation of religious houses. In 1245 he built a castle at Sligo and in 1253 established a Dominican priory in the town. He retired to the Franciscan friary in Youghal and died in the habit of a friar on 29 May 1257. The late fifteenth-century martyrology from the Youghal friary lists the details of an indulgence proclaimed by a number of local bishops on the occasion of his death and he enjoyed something of a local cultus as Francis O'Mahony (alias Matthews), a seventeenth-century Franciscan minister provincial and historian, demonstrates.[14] The Franciscan friaries at Ardfert (c. 1253), Askeaton (1420); Clane (1258); Clonmel (1269) and Kildare (c. 1254) and the Dominican houses at Sligo (1252); Tralee (1243) and Youghal (1268 or 1271) acknowledged various members of the different Geraldine families as their principal founders. Other houses, such as the Dominican priories at Limerick and Kilmallock, received Fitzgerald patronage at later stages in their history. Once established these foundations remained sources of dynastic pride as descendants of the founders continued to act as friends, benefactors and protectors of the communities.

In addition to enjoying the spiritual benefits of establishing a religious house founders discovered that the friaries and their inmates also served a number of social roles. They provided a place for members of the family who embraced the religious life: the first to receive the habit in Adare was Theodoric Fitzmaurice, presumably of the lineage of the Fitzmaurice Lords of Kerry, and in 1616 the surviving altar plate from Adare was in the custody of Friar Thomas Fitzgerald.[15] They also provided a secure environment to which members, like Maurice Fitzgerald in Youghal, could honorably retire and prepare for death in the friar's habit. Individual friars fulfilled important roles as confessors, counsellors, intermediaries, negotiators and trustworthy witnesses in the patrons' temporal affairs. Another important dynastic function was that of custodians of the family's traditions and reputation: the 1523 addition to the library catalogue of the Observant house at Youghal, Co. Cork, listed a chronicle of the Fitzgeralds among the collection.[16] The seventeenth-century Dominican friar Dominic O'Daly compiled a history of the family in which he recorded many of the early legends of the family and its association with the Dominican priory in Tralee.[17] He was a member of one of the families of hereditary bardic poets that the Fitzgeralds had patronised: a Cu Uladh O'Daly, described as the 'great poet', is listed alongside the Geraldine benefactors of the Adare foundation and was responsible for building a chapel in the transept.

---

[14] Ó Clabaigh, *Franciscans in Ireland*, p. 115; Pádraig Ó Riain, 'Deascán Lámhscríbhinní: a Manuscript Miscellany', *Journal of the Cork Historical and Archaeological Soc.* 108 (2003), 62–8; Brendan Jennings, ed., 'Brevis Synopsis Provinciae Hiberniae FF Minorum', *Analecta Hibernica* 6 (1934), 139–91 (p. 182).

[15] Brendan Jennings, ed., 'Brussels MS 3947: Donatus Moneyus, De Provincia Hiberniae S. Francisci', *Analecta Hibernica* 6 (1934), 12–138 (pp. 63–4).

[16] Ó Clabaigh, *Franciscans in Ireland*, p. 175. The earliest section of the catalogue dates to 1491.

[17] Dominic de Rosario O'Daly, OP, *Initium, incrementa, et exitus Familiae Geraldinorum Desmoniae Comitum, Palatinorum Kyrriae in Hybernia* (Lisbon, 1655), translated by C. P. Meehan, *The Rise, Increase and Exit of the Geraldines, Earls of Desmond* (Dublin, 1878).

Perhaps the most important dynastic function of the friaries was to serve as worthy places of burial for their principal patrons, a role that Friar Donatus Mooney saw as vital for the preservation of the Franciscan houses in the early seventeenth century.[18] The Franciscan house at Kildare received the remains of a number of members of the principal branch of the family, the Barons Offaly and their descendants, the early earls of Kildare.[19] The Franciscan friary in Askeaton, Co. Limerick was specifically established in 1420 by James Fitzgerald, earl of Desmond, as the place of sepulture for him and his descendants.[20] The Dominican house in Tralee and the Franciscan friary at Ardfert were the burial places of the Fitzmaurice lords of Kerry and a number of the Fitzgibbon White Knights were buried at the Dominican priory in Kilmallock, Co. Limerick.[21]

The Observants in Adare

We are unusually well informed about the foundation and early years of the first Observant community in Adare in the diocese of Limerick. Friar Donatus Mooney, whose 1618 report on the state of the Irish province is the main source of information for the period, gives a list of the principal benefactors of the foundation which he obtained from James Hickey, sometime syndic or lay financial administrator of the community, and which, in accordance with both the provincial and general statutes of the Observants, was read in chapter each Friday so that the friars might pray for their benefactors.[22] He also refers to the existence of the Adare register with other registers of the province in 1618 and it is possible that this was the 'liber de Athdare' known to the antiquarian Sir James Ware.[23] Ware, quoting the lost statutes of the Irish Observants, states that the Adare house was the first to be built for the reformers[24] and this seems plausible, even though other sources record the foundation of Enniscorthy and Sherkin Island in 1460.

The church of the Friars Minor at Adare was dedicated in honour of St Michael the archangel, on the 19th November, 1464, the feast of St Pontianus, Martyr

---

18 Jennings, 'Brussels MS 3947', p. 17.
19 Goddard H. Orpen, 'The Fitzgeralds, Barons of Offaly', *Journal of the Royal Soc. of Antiquaries of Ireland* 64 (1914), 99–113.
20 John O'Donovan, ed., *The Annals of the Kingdom of Ireland by the Four Masters*, IV (Dublin, 1856), pp. 842, 843.
21 Katherine Walsh, 'Franciscan Friaries in pre-Reformation Kerry', *Journal of the Kerry Historical Soc.* 9 (1976), 16–31; Arlene Hogan, *Kilmallock Dominican Priory: an Architectural Perspective 1291–1991* (Kilmallock, 1991), pp. 1, 39, 48.
22 Jennings, 'Brussels MS 3947', pp. 63–4; James Ware in BL, Add. MS 4821, fol. 107v.
23 BL, Add. MS. 4821, fol. 101r. The reference records the death of Maurice Fitzgerald, founder of the Youghal friary, in 1257.
24 BL, Add. MS. 4821, fol. 107v, 'Conventus de Athdara primus nobis impetratus et fundatus per D. Tho. Comitem Kildariae.'

and St Elizabeth, widow. Thomas, Earl of Kildare and his wife Johanna, daughter of James, Earl of Desmond, built the church and the fourth part of the cloister at their own expense. They also furnished the windows of the church with glass and presented the bell and two silver chalices. The convent was accepted, on behalf of the Order, at the provincial chapter held at Moyne, on the feast of the apostles Sts Peter and Paul in the same year, and the brethren of the family of the Observance entered into possession on the feast of All Saints following. The church was consecrated in honour of St Michael the Archangel, on his feast, in the year 1466. The following places outside the church were also consecrated that they might be used for burial of the dead: the whole circuit of the cloisters, inside and outside, both sacristies and the entire cemetery, except a portion at the south, which was set aside for those who might die without the right to Christian burial.

The other parts of the edifice were built by the following: the bell tower by Cornelius O'Sullivan, a pious and devout stranger who had settled amongst us (so the ancient book described him). He also presented us with an excellent chalice gilt with gold. Margaret Fitzgibbon, wife of Cunlaid O'Daly, the good poet, erected the great chapel. One of the small chapels was built by John, son of the Earl of Desmond; the other by Leogh de Tulcostyn, and Margaret, wife of Thomas Fitzmaurice. We owe another fourth part of the cloister to a Tertiary, Rory O'Dea, who also gave us a useful silver chalice. Another tertiary, Marianus O'Hickey, erected the refectory, and the wooden choir on the north side. He entered the Order later on and died in this convent, having spent a most holy life. Donald, the son of O'Dea and Sabina, his wife, finished another fourth of the cloister. Edmond Thomas, Knight of the Glen, and his wife, Honora Fitzgibbon, erected the infirmary. The latter died on the 13th May 1503. Johanna O'Loughlin, widow of Fitzgibbon, added ten feet to the sanctuary, under which she directed a burial place to be formed for herself. Conor O'Sullivan, who built the belfry, died on the 16th of January, 1492; Margaret Fitzgibbon, who built the Lady chapel, on the 23rd January, 1483; Donough O'Brien, son of Brian Duv who constructed the dormitory, on the vigil of St Francis, 1502; Thomas, Earl of Kildare, founder of the convent, on the 25th March, 1478; his wife Johanna, on the feast of St Anthony of Padua, 1486. The first to receive the habit in the convent was Theoderic Fitzmaurice, who died on the 18th June, 1484. There lived here also another laybrother named Quirke, who was held in great esteem for his sanctity. He died on the 13th December, 1532. John, Prior of Holy Cross, Limerick, who was the ordinary protector of the Fathers of Adare, died on the 2nd August, 1531.[25]

The survival of this passage gives a unique insight into the process of founding a friary, as well as providing important incidental information on the lives of the friars and their impact on contemporary society. It is clear that they enjoyed the support of both Anglo-Irish and Gaelic patrons and that the friary was completed in a relatively short time. It also shows that a number of benefactors were involved in the foundation and that the principal patron did not shoulder

[25] Jennings, 'Brussels MS 3947', pp. 63–4; translation from *The Franciscan Tertiary* (April 1895), pp. 354–7.

the entire cost of the enterprise. This is significant, because a similar process was probably repeated at other foundations where only the name of the main patron survives. The most striking feature of the account however is the extent to which the Fitzgeralds in all their ramifications were involved in establishing and supporting the house. In addition to the role played by the earl of Kildare as the foremost representative of the family, practically every other branch is represented as well: the families of the earl of Desmond, the Fitzmaurice lords of Kerry, the Knight of the Glen and the White Knight. It is possible that the benefactors were aware of the patronage of the Observants by magnates elsewhere in Europe and that their support represents their desire for religion a la mode. It is equally likely that they were keenly aware of their ancestral role as the first patrons of the Franciscans in Ireland and that their patronage represents a concerted effort to re-establish a dynastic association with the first foundation of a vibrant new reform of the Franciscan movement. The involvement of the secular tertiaries or Third Order members in establishing the foundation is significant as it provides important incidental evidence for their existence in late medieval Ireland and shows the Observants as promoters of this way of life. They were clearly established by the friars soon after their arrival and, apart from their spiritual purpose, were also an important source of material support to the community.

The friars took possession of the new friary on the feast of All Saints in 1464. Mooney refers to the dedication of the church to St Michael the Archangel on the feast of SS Pontian and Elizabeth, but this appears to have been a preliminary ceremony as the solemn consecration occurred on the feast of St Michael the Archangel in 1466. Three consecration crosses can still be seen on the internal wall of the western gable of the church. The church, bell tower, transept and transept chapels must have been complete at this stage. The sacristies and the cloister walks must also have been complete as they were consecrated for burials along with the cemetery, though it is possible that the cloister arcades initially consisted of temporary wooden structures. The south, east and north arcades of the cloister were completed at different stages between the foundation of the friary in 1464 and the death of the last named benefactor in 1503. Masons' marks indicate that some masons worked on all three sections of the arcade so the project may have been completed in a relatively short period of time. The simple design of the arcade arches is in keeping with the plain architecture of the rest of the building and may represent an expression of the Observants' desire for poverty and simplicity. After the initial flurry of patronage at the time of foundation the friars continued to attract the support of wealthy benefactors as the claustral complex was completed by the addition of a west range sometime after 1503. The cloister arcade in this section is more ornate than in the other three ranges and would have been more costly to endow. In addition a chamber, accessible only from the church through the crossing of the tower, was built above the south range of the cloister. This may have served as a private or gallery chapel in which distinguished visitors could attend services or listen to sermons. A number of free-standing buildings were also constructed adjacent to the friary. These may have been for food preparation, milling and the reception of guests but as their donors are not listed in the foundation account they may represent a later phase in the building campaign.[26]

The donation of items for liturgical or devotional use by the friars constituted another form of benefaction and was particularly popular because of the manner in which such artefacts associated the donor with the sacrifice of the mass and the liturgy of the hours. These donations included such inexpensive items as the bread, wine and wax used for the celebration of the liturgy donated to the Dominicans in Athenry, Co. Galway.[27] They also included costly high status gifts such as altar vessels, vestments, statues and stone sculpture, wall paintings, church furnishings and stained glass. The Adare community was the recipient of similar benefactions. In addition to the four chalices and the church bell donated at the foundation of the house, Mooney also records that as late as 1616 a ciborium, six or seven chalices and a processional cross still survived from the friary. The ciborium in particular attracted his attention for its craftsmanship. While none of these items is now known to survive, the Ballylongford cross, a silver gilt processional cross commissioned for the Observant Franciscans at Lislaughtin friary, about twenty miles from Adare, gives some idea of the standard of contemporary Irish church plate. This highly accomplished piece was presented to the friars in 1479 by Cornelius O'Connor, son of John O'Connor Kerry, the founder of the friary, and his wife, Juliana Fitzgerald.[28]

Mooney also expressed surprise at the number of liturgical vestments that had once belonged to the Adare friars. Such well-furnished vestries were not unusual however. In his account of his time as sacristan in the Observant friary in Donegal in 1600 Mooney records that the friars possessed forty suits of vestments including some made of cloth of gold or silver, the others made of silk. The Donegal community also possessed fourteen silver gilt chalices, two silver ones and two ciboria. He describes the surviving vestments from Enniscorthy friary as being ornamented with figures and designs.[29] No vestment is known to survive from an Irish Franciscan house but the late medieval set that survives from Waterford cathedral gives some idea of what the friars' holdings may have looked like. Though the Waterford vestments are a particularly fine imported set the friars' contacts with the upper echelons of Anglo-Irish and Gaelic society makes it quite likely that some of their vestments were of an equally high standard.[30] The English Observants were so disquieted by the magnificence of

---

[26] Ashling O'Donoghue, 'The Mendicant Cloisters of Munster: a Comparative Study of Six Franciscan Friary Cloisters' (unpublished BA thesis, Trinity College Dublin, 1995), pp. 11–16; Roger Stalley, 'Architecture and Patronage in Fifteenth-century Adare', *Irish Arts Review* 20:4 (2003), 110–15.

[27] Ambrose Coleman, ed., 'Regestum Monasterii Fratrum Praedicatorum de Athenry', *Archivium Hibernicum* 1 (1912), 201–21 (pp. 208, 210, 219).

[28] Colum Hourihane, 'Holye Crossys: a Catalogue of Processional, Altar, Pendant and Crucifix Figures for Late Medieval Ireland', *Proceedings of the Royal Irish Academy* 100 (2000), 1–85 (pp. 8–9).

[29] Jennings, 'Brussels MS 3947', pp. 40, 63–4, 84.

[30] Eamonn McEneaney, 'Politics and the Art of Devotion in Late Fifteenth-century Water-

the liturgical vessels and vestments that they had been given that they sought papal reassurance that these did not contravene the vow of poverty.[31]

In comparison with some of the unreformed Franciscan houses, particularly that at Ennis, Co. Clare, the Adare friary is conspicuous for the small amount of stone sculpture that survives.[32] Only one stone carving, an image of St Francis in the west cloister range, survives and none of the mural tombs are decorated with images of saints or intercessors such as those found on similar tombs in the Franciscan friary at Kilconnell, Co. Galway or in the Dominican houses at Strade, Co. Mayo and Sligo.[33] This reluctance to invest in stone sculpture seems to have been a feature of the early Franciscan Observant movement in Ireland as it is noticeable by its absence from the houses at Timoleague, Kilcrea and Sherkin in Co. Cork and Moyne and Rosserrilly in Co. Mayo. Four early modern wooden statues survive from Adare. These represent St Francis, St Louis of France, St Joseph and an image of the Madonna and child. While it is possible that the friars acquired them towards the end of the sixteenth century, it is more likely that they date to after the reoccupation of the friary in 1633. The presence of substantial brackets in the east walls of the chancel and transept indicate the location of statues in the pre-Dissolution period while three sockets beneath the east window of the chancel probably secured a retable over the high altar. Such altar pieces were relatively common features of late medieval Irish religious houses: a stone retable depicting the pieta survives at the Dominican house at Strade; the Dominicans in Athenry, Co. Galway possessed a Flemish altarpiece representing scenes from the life of the Virgin Mary and an alabaster retable was listed among the possessions of Holy Cross Priory in Limerick at the Dissolution of the monasteries. Extensive remains of wall paintings survived in Adare until the late nineteenth century and included figures of saints and geometric and floral motifs. All that survives today are the remains of a red-orange marigold in the arch of the piscina and fragments of a black letter inscription in a tomb niche, both in the south wall of the chancel.[34] From Mooney's description and from glazing grooves in the window frames it is clear that the windows of the church were glazed. Unfortunately nothing remains to show what this looked like. In general very little stained glass survives from medieval Ireland but archaeological excavations at two sites near the Adare

ford', in *Art and Devotion in Late Medieval Ireland*, ed. Rachel Moss, Colmán Ó Clabaigh and Salvador Ryan (Dublin, 2006), pp. 33–50 (pp. 40–46).

31   In the bull *Merentur vestrae*, *Annales Minorum* XV, pp. 663–4. This was a reiteration by Leo X of an earlier dispensation granted by Julius II to the friars at the instigation of Katherine of Aragon.

32   Rachel Moss, 'Permanent Expressions of Piety: the Secular and the Sacred in Later Medieval Stone Sculpture', in *Art and Devotion in Late Medieval Ireland*, ed. Moss, Ó Clabaigh and Ryan, pp. 72–97.

33   Colmán Ó Clabaigh, 'The Other Christ: the Cult of St Francis of Assisi in Late Medieval Ireland', in *Art and Devotion in Late Medieval Ireland*, ed. Moss, Ó Clabaigh and Ryan, pp. 142–62.

34   Karena Morton, 'Aspects of Image and Meaning in Irish Medieval Wall Paintings', in *Art and Devotion in Late Medieval Ireland*, ed. Moss, Ó Clabaigh and Ryan, pp. 51–71.

friary give some idea of how the friary windows may have appeared. The first excavation at the Fitzgerald castle adjacent to the friary produced rare evidence for the use of stained glass in a secular Irish context. The pieces discovered consisted of a rectangular quarry with a yellow stain wash and a fragment of red flashed glass with a curvilinear design dating to the fifteenth century.[35] The excavations at the Dominican friary in the nearby city of Limerick produced evidence for two phases of fenestration; the first, dating to the thirteenth and fourteenth centuries, relates to the foundation of the friary. The second phase, dating to the fifteenth century, corresponds with a period of patronage of the house by the Fitzgerald earls of Desmond. The glass from this second phase consists of large diamond quarries of white glass with minimal painted patterns highlighted with yellow stain. Similar quarries are found as a background to figure of the Archangel Gabriel in a window dated to c. 1440 in the south transept of York Minster.[36]

Sponsoring book production was another means by which benefactors endowed the friars. Bodleian Library, MS Rawlinson C 320 was produced for the Adare community in 1482 by Friar Donald O'Cahalyn and sponsored by Donough MacNamara and Margaret O'Brien.[37] The codex itself is significant as it contains the scripta ordinis or normative legislative texts of the Irish Observants.[38] These consisted of the 1223 rule of St Francis; his Testament (1226); the three definitive papal declarations on the Franciscan rule: Quo elongati (1230); Exiit qui seminat (1279) and Exivi de paradiso (1312). The bulk of the manuscript consists of a treatise on the training of novices by Friar Bernard of Bessa and the Abbreviatio statutorum, a compilation of Franciscan legislation adopted as normative for the Observant friars north of the Alps by the chapter of Barcelona in 1451.

The Adare Observants presumably were recipients of the type of casual small-scale almsgiving so characteristic of the mendicant economy elsewhere in Europe, though as is the case elsewhere in Ireland, little evidence survives for this. The most characteristic mendicant activity was the quest: the regular begging for alms for support of the friars from the local community.[39] Evidence for the practice comes from the instruction in the 1453 statutes of the synod of Cashel that the friars stay within the limits of the area in which they were licensed to beg.[40] While there is no reference to the Adare friars questing, their nearest Franciscan neighbours at Askeaton and Ennis certainly did. In 1491

[35] Josephine Moran, personal communication.

[36] Josephine Moran, 'The Shattered Image: Archaeological Evidence for Painted and Stained Glass in Medieval Ireland', in Art and Devotion in Late Medieval Ireland, ed. Moss, Ó Clabaigh and Ryan, pp. 121–41 (pp. 121, 125, 140–41).

[37] Richard Howlett, ed., Monumenta Franciscana, II, RS (London, 1882), p. xlviii.

[38] Two copies of an identical volume described as the scripta ordinis are listed in the Youghal library catalogue: Ó Clabaigh, Franciscans in Ireland, pp. 161, 174.

[39] For examples see Ó Clabaigh, Franciscans in Ireland, p. 119.

[40] J. Begley, The Diocese of Limerick: Ancient and Medieval (Dublin 1906), p. 433, nos 12 and 13.

the Askeaton friars secured a judgement from the minister general, Francis 'Samson' Nanni, against the Ennis community. The limits of their respective questing areas had traditionally been agreed to lie half-way between the two houses, but the Askeaton friars had been hindered in their begging by the Ennis friars. The minister general confirmed the rights of the Askeaton community and threatened the Ennis friars with excommunication if they did not accept the judgement. He also threatened the minister provincial and the other officials of the province with deprivation of office and excommunication if they did not uphold the decision.[41] The fact that the dispute had to be resolved at the highest level of the Order suggests that it may have been a long-running one.

Funeral offerings and (pro anima) testamentary bequests presumably formed a significant part of the Adare community's economy but little survives to illustrate this: in 1515 the guardian and community acknowledged a bequest of Renalda O'Brien remitted to them by Piers Butler, earl of Ormond.[42] The popular practice of seeking burial in a friar's habit or in a friary cemetery was another source of income for the friars and the disposition of the offerings made on these occasions were a constant source of friction between the mendicants and the secular clergy. From the mid-fourteenth century Ireland produced a number of significant contributors to the debate, most notably Richard Fitzralph, archbishop of Armagh.[43] While Fitzralph and his subsequent followers conducted the debate on the theoretical level, the disputes continued at the grassroots. Evidence suggests that tension between the friars of the various mendicant orders and the secular clergy over the issues of questing, bequests, funeral offerings and the 'canonical portion' was particularly pronounced in the ecclesiastical province of Cashel in the second half of the fifteenth century. In 1453 the Cashel provincial synod, meeting at Limerick, decreed that friars were not to quest for alms on the days on which it was customary for the secular clergy to receive their traditional offerings. Tertiaries were also warned to observe the appropriate legislation with regard to funeral offerings.

The presence of a copy of the (Apologia pauperum), or Defence of the Mendicants, by St Bonaventure in the library of the Franciscan Observants in Youghal further corroborates this. It was compiled c. 1269 and drew extensively on scripture, the Fathers and canon law to present a strong defence of the mendicant way of life, providing the intellectual basis for subsequent interpretations of the Franciscan rule. It was probably acquired by the Youghal community between St Bonaventure's canonisation in 1482 and the compilation of

---

41 G. Parisciani, *Regesta Ordinis Fratrum Minorum Conventualium 1484–1494* (Padua, 1989), p. 197, no. 1529.

42 National Library of Ireland, Deed 2014; calendared in E. Curtis, ed., *Calendar of Ormond Deeds*, IV, p. 27. For the situation in Dublin see Margaret Murphy, 'The High Cost of Dying: an Analysis of pro anima Bequests in Medieval Dublin', in *The Church and Wealth*, Studies in Church History, 24 (Oxford, 1987), pp. 111–22.

43 Katherine Walsh, *A Fourteenth-Century Scholar and Primate: Richard Fitzralph in Oxford, Avignon and Armagh* (Oxford, 1981), pp. 349–451.

the first section of the catalogue in 1491 and its acquisition is almost certainly connected to contemporary disputes with the secular clergy in Youghal and throughout the province of Cashel.[44] In 1493 the Cistercian abbot of Abbey-dorney was ordered to investigate the complaints of the archbishop of Cashel and his suffragans against the guardian and friars of Youghal and other named Franciscan houses in Munster over the friars' refusal to pay customary funeral offerings.[45] The dispute appears to have been ongoing as Francis O'Mahony gives the text of a 1514 judgement of Bishop John Fitz Edmund Fitzgerald of Cork in favour of the friars and against the warden of the secular college in Youghal. The friars also secured confirmation of this judgement from the archbishop of Cashel and the earl of Desmond.[46] Whereas the Adare friars are not specifically mentioned as being involved in this dispute, they were certainly aware of its implications as the section of the *Abbreviatio statutorum* in Bodleian Library, Rawlinson MS C. 320 dealing with the necessity of showing respect to the secular clergy and the obligation of paying the customary funeral offerings has been carefully erased.[47]

The experience of the Franciscan Observants at Adare provides an unusually comprehensive picture, in the Irish context, of a religious community embedded in the affections of their patrons and at odds with the ecclesiastical establishment. While this experience must have been replicated at numerous other foundations, the vagaries of Irish history have meant that little survives to illustrate this.[48]

---

[44] Ó Clabaigh, *Franciscans in Ireland*, p. 165.

[45] *CPL*, XVI, no. 116, pp. 79–80.

[46] Brendan Jennings, ed., *Wadding Papers* (Dublin, 1953), pp. 108–15.

[47] Howlett, *Monumenta Franciscana*, II, p. 91.

[48] Research for this article was undertaken under the auspices of the Mícheál Ó Cléirigh Institute, University College, Dublin, supported by a research fellowship from the Irish Research Council for the Humanities and Social Sciences.

6

The Augustinian Priory of Wombridge and its Benefactors in the Later Middle Ages

ANDREW ABRAM

The extent and richness of the late fifteenth-century cartulary of the Augustinian priory of St Leonard at Wombridge (BL, MS Egerton 3712) means that for a relatively 'unexceptional' community, in terms of the numbers of brethren and value of endowments, it is remarkably well documented.[1] The majority of donations to Wombridge occurred from the thirteenth century onwards, when the canons resolutely built up and maintained their properties and rights, chiefly within close proximity to the priory. Moreover, during the late medieval period the community not only attracted benefactions from its patrons, but also from a wide circle of knightly families holding local lordships and relatively small estates, who could be regarded, in the words of Una Rees, as the 'natural benefactors' of the priory.[2] The expansion of the community's estates and revenue, which accelerated from the mid thirteenth century onwards, was to a significant extent the result of a dynamic combination of a pro-active and accommodating religious community, and the continued donations of benefactors. At the heart of this, in essence, was the close and enduring relationship forged between the priory and its local lay supporters.

The community venerating St Leonard at Wombridge was the second Augustinian house established in Shropshire, after Haughmond Abbey which

---

[1] See G. R. C. Davies, *Medieval Cartularies of Great Britain* (London and New York, 1958), pp. 122–3. There also exist portions of a cartulary, probably a version of BL, MS Egerton 3712, and manuscript copies of four papal bulls, as well as episcopal and royal confirmation charters (Staffordshire Record Office, MS D593). Abstracts of BL, MS Egerton 3712, transcribed by George Morris in 1824, are printed in *Transactions of the Shropshire Archaeological and Natural History Soc.*, [afterwards *Trans. SANHS*] 1st series, IX (1886), 305–80; XI (1888), 325–48; 2nd series, I (1889), 294–310; IX (1897), 96–106; X (1898), 180–92; XI (1899), 331–46; XII (1900), 205–28. I would like to extend my gratitude to my doctoral supervisor, Professor Janet Burton of the Department of History at Lampeter, for her expertise, guidance and support, and to her and Dr Karen Stöber for providing me with the opportunity to give this paper.

[2] Una Rees, ed., *Cartulary of Haughmond Abbey* (Shropshire Archaeological and Historical Soc., 1985), p. 12.

was founded between 1125 and 1136.[3] Owing to the tenurial and socio-political influence, and religious aspirations, of the earls and constables of Chester, royal servants and their vassals and kin, the canons regular of St Augustine appeared in the north-west of the diocese of Coventry and Lichfield early in their movement's development. Beginning with the foundation of Runcorn by William the constable in 1115, a further six houses were established by the end of Henry I's reign. By c. 1204 twelve communities of canons and one of canonesses had been founded in the region.[4] Despite this not inconsiderable presence within the diocese, which can be paralleled in other areas of Britain, the Augustinian canons remain one of the least studied of the medieval religious orders. Since J. C. Dickinson's influential work and David Robinson's geographical survey, no major study has appeared, while there have been roughly a dozen papers relating to the Black Canons.[5] In terms of foundations, the Augustinians were the most commonplace religious group and thus no less important to ecclesiastical and lay society than the monastic orders that have been better served in historical scholarship. One approach to studying and contextualising the movement and in particular its relationship with founders, patrons and donors, is to consider in depth either a single community or a manageable number of houses in an ecclesiastical or geographical region.[6]

No foundation document for Wombridge Priory exists, but mid twelfth-

---

[3]   Shrewsbury Public Library [SPL], MS 6000 (late fifteenth-century Haughmond cartulary), fol. 165; *Cart. Haughmond*, no. 900.

[4]   The Augustinian foundations were at Runcorn (1115), Haughmond (1125 x 1136), Stone (c. 1125), Calwich (1125 x 1130), Norton (1134), Wombridge (c. 1130 x 1136), Ranton (after 1135), Lilleshall (c. 1143–4), Rocester (1141 x 1143), Trentham (1153), St Thomas near Stafford (c. 1174), Brewood (by 1189), Burscough (c. 1190) and Mobberley (c. 1204).

[5]   J. C. Dickinson, *The Origins of the Austin Canons and their Introduction into England* (London, 1950); 'Early Suppressions of English Houses of Austin Canons', in *Medieval Studies Presented to Rose Graham*, ed. V. Ruffer and A. J. Taylor (Oxford, 1950), pp. 54–77; 'English Regular Canons and the Continent in the Twelfth Century', *TRHS*, 5th series, 1 (1951), 71–89; David M. Robinson, *The Geography of Augustinian Settlement in Medieval England and Wales*, British Archaeological Reports, British Series, 80, 2 vols (Oxford, 1980). Some useful papers include C. W. Bynum, 'The Spirituality of Regular Canons in the Twelfth Century', in her *Jesus as Mother: Studies in the Spirituality of the High Middle Ages* (Berkeley, Los Angeles and London, 1982), pp. 22–58; and Ludo J. R. Milis, 'Hermits and Regular Canons in the Twelfth Century', in *Religion, Culture, and Mentalities in the Medieval Low Countries*, ed. M. Deploige, W. Simons and S. Vanderputten (Turnhout, 2005), pp. 181–246.

[6]   For example, see Janet Burton, *Kirkham Priory from Foundation to Dissolution*, Borthwick Paper, 86 (York, 1995); Allison Fizzard, 'Lay Benefactors of Plympton Priory in the Twelfth Century', *Reports and Transactions of the Devonshire Association for the Advancement of Science* 134 (2002), 33–56; Katrina Legg, *Bolton Priory: Its Patrons and Benefactors 1120–1293*, Borthwick Paper, 106 (York, 2004); Sarah Preston, 'The Canons Regular of Saint Augustine: the Twelfth Century Reform in Action', in *Augustinians at Christ Church*, ed. Stuart Kinsella (Dublin, 2000), pp. 23–40. My doctoral thesis (University of Wales, Lampeter, 2007), 'The Augustinian Canons in the Diocese of Lichfield and their Benefactors, 1115–1320', from which some of the material for this paper derives, considers thirteen Augustinian communities in the socio-political, tenurial and devo-

century evidence suggests that between c. 1130 and 1136 William, lord of Hadley, his wife Seburga and their eldest son Alan co-founded the community by granting for the salvation of their souls a small clearing in the royal forest of Hadley Wood with half a virgate of land in High Hatton. This initial endowment was confirmed by the Hadley's overlord, William I son of Alan, sheriff of Shropshire and founder of Haughmond, probably between 1155 and 1160.[7] Importantly, the charter describes the location of the monastery 'in Hadley Wood, bounded on one side by a rivulet, which divides the said wood from the King's forest; on another side, by a rivulet called Springwell Brook; on a third side, by Watlingstreet'.

In August 1181 Henry II confirmed the foundation,[8] and on 23 June 1187 Pope Urban III similarly confirmed the rights and possessions of the canons.[9] Wombridge's close proximity to other monasteries in Shropshire (twelve miles from Shrewsbury and five from Buildwas, for instance) had an important bearing on the pattern and nature of the properties available to its founders and benefactors.[10] The donations received by Wombridge during the first fifty years of its existence were modest, reflecting perhaps the relatively narrow tenurial and social orbit, and limited financial means of the founders and their close associates. Yet by the mid thirteenth century the priory had obtained a footing in the manors of Uppington, Harrington, High Ercall, Cherrington and Sutton Maddock, and had received the churches of Loppington and Sutton Maddock, and the chapel of Uppington, with their advowsons.[11] The canons attracted donations from a wide circle of benefactors, including the vassals and kin of the founders.

In accordance with common practice, the family of the founders of Wombridge acted as hereditary patrons of their community, and the advowson of the priory transferred in 1194 to Cecily, the daughter of Alan of Hadley and wife to Roger I

tional context of their supporters. See also Andrew Abram, *Norton Priory: an Augustinian Community and its Benefactors*, Trivium Occasional Papers, no. 2 (Lampeter, 2007).

7   R. W. Eyton, *The History of the Antiquities of Shropshire*, 12 vols (London, 1854–60), VII, 363. The confirmation was endorsed by kings Henry II in 1181 and Edward II in 1319, and by Pope Urban III in 1187 (BL, MS Egerton 3712, fols 79 (no. 1), 84v–85r; *CChR 1300–26*, pp. 404–6; *Monasticon*, VI, 388, no. i).

8   BL, MS Egerton 3712, fol. 79 (no. 1); BL, MS Harley 3868 (register of Lichfield Cathedral), fol. 5.

9   BL, MS Egerton 3712, fols 84v–85r (no. 4); Walther Holtzmann, ed., *Papsturkunden in England*, 3 vols, Abhandlungen der Gesellschaft der Wissenschaften zu Göttingen, phil.-hist. Klasse, neue Folge, 25 (1930–1); 3. Folge, 14–15 (1935–6); 33 (1952), III, no. 400; Morris, 'Abstracts' in *Trans. SANHS*, IX, 205–28 (pp. 205–7), no. 498. Urban III took the canons of St Leonard into the protection of St Peter, enjoined on them the Augustinian Rule, confirmed their possessions, both acquired and to be acquired (including those confirmed by Henry II), permitted them to celebrate divine services under certain restrictions, during the period of an Interdict, gave them the right of burial within their church, and also to hold free elections of the prior.

10   G. C. Baugh and D. C. Cox, *Monastic Shropshire* (Shrewsbury, 1982), pp. 12–24; Una Rees, 'The Leases of Haughmond Abbey, Shropshire', *Midland History* 8 (1983), 14–28.

11   BL, MS Egerton 3712, fols 79 (no. 1), 84v–85r (no. 4).

Corbet of Tasley.[12] Customarily, a monastic patron was the heir, direct or indirect, of the founder, and as such, he or she might expect certain benefits from the religious community in exchange for their protection and promotion.[13] An agreement of 1248 defined the privileges of the patron of Wombridge. Having sued the prior for presenting himself to the bishop before coming before him as patron, Roger II Corbet was permitted to take possession of the house during vacancies and to receive the canons' nomination of the prior-elect. However, he was denied custody of the priory's lands, whilst the canons were empowered to proceed to an election without waiting for his licence.[14] Yet despite such tensions the significance of a close, active, and continuous association between the canons of Wombridge and their patrons represented a vital element in the community's history, progress and existence. The gifts to Wombridge from its patrons were substantial. In the 1270s Thomas II Corbet gave a meadow in Eaton-upon-Tern, while in 1309 his son, Roger III, granted two burgages in Wellington to a vassal on condition that the annual rent was to be paid to the canons 'for the souls of the grantor and his wife Hawise'.[15] Later, in 1328, Roger granted rent from Hadley for the brethren to purchase wine 'for the celebration of masses in their church forever', and another rent from Hadley in exchange for the ninth part of that manor, granted originally by his ancestor, Alan of Hadley'.[16]

In 1354 Roger's grandson, Robert, leased his property in Uppington to Prior John for forty years, with its rent, and on 21 May 1377 he alienated a messuage, half a virgate, a mill and a croft in Hadley for ninety-nine years.[17] The later transaction meant more than a confirmation of his grandfather's earlier grant, with the addition of the mill and croft, for in return the prior was expected 'to provide a brother canon and a chaplain to celebrate services in the chapel, within the gates of Hadley manor house, for the salvation of the souls of the said Sir Robert, his wives, children, ancestors and heirs on Sundays, Wednesdays and Fridays weekly'. Adding to the continued interest of the patrons of Wombridge were donations from the family and kin-group of the founders. For instance, before 1278 John of Ercall, great-grandson of the co-founder, William of Hadley, gave lands and tenements in High Ercall.[18] John's son

12 Eyton, *Shropshire*, I, 86–101, VII, 355. In 1255 his grandson Roger II of Tasley held Hadley for half a knight's fee, Tasley for half a knight's fee, and High Hatton as one *muntator* of John III son of Alan (ibid., i, 92, vii, 356–7).

13 Susan Wood, *Monasteries and their Patrons in the Thirteenth Century* (London, 1955), p. 8; Janet Burton, *Monastic and Religious Orders in Britain, 1000–1300* (Cambridge, 1994), pp. 211, 215; Christopher Holdsworth, *The Piper and the Tune: Medieval Patrons and Monks*, The Stenton Lecture, 1990 (Reading, 1991), pp. 1–27 (p. 5).

14 Eyton, *Shropshire*, VII, 367; Wood, *Patrons*, p. 31.

15 BL, MS Egerton 3712, fols 2r (no. 2), 76v.

16 Ibid., fol. 77 (no. 2).

17 Ibid., fols 28v–29r (no. 176), 77r (no. 1).

18 *Monasticon*, VI, 391; Eyton, *Shropshire*, VII, 364.

and heir, William IV (d. 1304), permitted the canons to enclose wasteland at Shirlow.[19]

The benefactors of Wombridge expected and often received spiritual benefits from the community in return for their gifts. The most prominent motive was a religious one. It is likely that when a scribe wrote in charters phrases like 'for the salvation of his or her soul' or 'out of pious devotion', donors understood their well-determined meanings. Some writers have tended to regard those as merely formulaic expressions, yet more recent studies have recognised their religious significance.[20] Consequently, the most common reason given in charters granting or confirming property, was that it was done either *pro salute anime* ('for the salvation of the soul of') or *pro anima* ('for the soul of') the donor, and often members of their family, past, present and to come. For instance, when Robert of Montford, lord of Shifnal, donated c. 1274 a clearing in Wyke Wood, he did so for the salvation of his own soul and those of his wife Petronilla, and all his children and ancestors.[21]

Similarly, in 1248 Dionisia of Longnor granted to 'God and St Leonard of Wombridge' all her land in Wychley with her body, 'for the salvation of my soul and those of all my ancestors and successors';[22] Thomas Tuchet, lord of Leegomery, alienated to the brethren c. 1269 'free ingress and egress in my wood of Ketley, with their carriages, carts and workers, to hew and get stone in my quarry there, and to carry it away for their buildings and repairs, whenever necessary'.[23] Perhaps reflecting the extent and profitable nature of the grant, it was furnished 'on condition that the canons should yearly on the day of St Valentine the Martyr perform masses for the souls of my father Robert, Sir John Maunsell, and for the souls of myself and my wife Margery, whenever we shall depart this life, and for the souls of our children'. Furthermore, in June 1330 Fulk Lestrange, lord of Sutton Maddock, for the salvation of his own soul and those of his ancestors, released to the canons of Wombridge his rights in the land which they held in Brockton moor and Hadnall field.[24]

By some standards the majority of donations by lay benefactors were relatively modest; nevertheless, they enabled the community of Wombridge to build up a compact and economically viable estate located within close proximity of the priory, which itself served as an important centre for religious devotion,

---

[19] *Monasticon*, VI, 390.

[20] For example, Joel T. Rosenthal, *The Purchase of Paradise: Gift Giving and the Aristocracy, 1307–1485* (London, 1972), chap. 2. More recent works include Holdsworth, *Piper and the Tune*, pp. 1–27; Richard Mortimer, 'Religious and Secular Motives for Some English Monastic Foundations', *Religious Motivation: Biographical and Sociological Problems for the Church Historian*, ed. Derek Baker (Oxford, 1978), pp. 77–85.

[21] BL, MS Egerton 3712, fol. 43r (no. 50).

[22] Ibid., fol. 28r. The land amounted to a fifth part of a virgate, which she had been granted by her mother, Eleanor. Moreover members of the family, as heirs of Roger Mussun, were substantial benefactors of Wombridge, whilst both Dionisia's mother and Aunt Alina made donations *cum corpore meo* in the early 1240s (ibid., fols 19r–20v (nos 107–8)).

[23] Ibid., fol. 39v.

[24] Ibid., fol. 62 (no. 61).

family and identity for a tightly-knit group of men and women. A similar pattern emerges at other moderately sized Augustinian houses in Coventry and Lichfield diocese, such as Burscough, Mobberley and Ranton. At Wombridge the motivations of benefactors and the significance of their endowments should not be underestimated as these people were bound together by a combination of kinship, social class, land and lordship. As Arnould-Jan Bijsterveld suggests, 'landed property was the focus of a group's identity, prestige, power, and history'.[25] Moreover, the ceremonies at which their donations were made 'provided occasions for the establishment or reaffirmation of complex and enduring social relationships linking monastic communities to their neighbours'.[26] The numerous gifts to 'God and the church of St Leonard of Wombridge and the canons serving God there' illustrate the significance of patron saints to the devotional aspect of gift-exchange. This was vital, for religious communities represented that saint on behalf of the wider community, while saintly beneficiaries were to hold the 'tokens of esteem' of donors forever. Importantly too, gifts to saints were meant to be balanced by counter-gifts, which might range from burial in the monastery to items such as animals and money.

Some donors appealed for more specific services than the prayers and masses of the brethren. Before 1270 Henry of Woodhouse, a considerable donor, granted 'towards the lights of the church of the Blessed Mary and St Leonard of Wombridge', land and rent in Woodhouse.[27] Richard del Bury of Uppington made a similar gift of property in Uppington in September 1304 'for lights in the church of St Leonard at Wombridge and the chapel of St Nicholas at Uppington'.[28] The Wombridge cartulary contains a number of requests from benefactors during the later medieval period for entry into the *confraternitas* of the house. Confraternity is a rather imprecise term, but it meant generally that

---

[25] Arnould-Jan A. Bijsterveld, 'Gift Exchange, Landed Property and Eternity: the Foundation and Endowment of the Premonstratensian Priory of Postel (1128/1138–1179)', in *Land and Ancestors: Cultural Dynamics in the Urnfield Period and the Middle Ages in the Southern Netherlands*, ed. F. Theuws and N. Roymans, Amsterdam Archaeological Studies, 4 (Amsterdam, 1999), pp. 309–48 (p. 312).

[26] Stephen D. White, *Custom, Kinship and Gifts to Saints: the Laudatio Parentum in Western France, 1050–1150* (Chapel Hill and London, 1988), p. 20. This above all local perspective, emphasising the role of landed endowments in incorporating the *religiosi* and saints within a tightly knit, familiar network of benefactors and kin, is developed closely by Barbara Rosenwein's analysis of donations of property to Cluny in the tenth and eleventh centuries, and also Constance Bouchard's study of gifts to Cistercian houses in twelfth-century Burgundy (Barbara Rosenwein, *To be St Peter's Neighbor: the Meaning of Cluny's Property* (Ithaca, 1989), p. 202; Constance Bouchard, *Holy Entrepreneurs: Cistercians, Knights and Economic Exchange in Twelfth-century Burgundy* (Ithaca, 1991), pp. 170–84). On the subject of gift-exchange and social bonds with monasteries, see also Arnould-Jan A. Bijsterveld, 'The Medieval Gift as Agent of Social Bonding and Political Power: a Comparative Approach', in *Medieval Transformations, Texts, Power and Gifts in Context*, ed. S. K. Cohen and M. de Jong (Leiden, 2001), pp. 123–56 (pp. 130–1); Ilana F. Silber, 'Gift Giving in the Great Traditions: the Case of Donations to Monasteries in the Medieval West', *Archives Européennes de Sociologie* 36 (1995), 209–43 (pp. 220–1).

[27] BL, MS Egerton 3712, fol. 73; *Monasticon*, VI, 388.

[28] BL, MS Egerton 3712, fol. 3r (no. 1).

donors became participants in a religious community's prayers and good deeds. In 1264 Jane, widow of Hugh II of Beckbury, stressed the seemingly close bond with the canons of Wombridge forged previously by her husband's parents, by alienating half a virgate with its messuage in Harrington 'on condition that at my death my body should be buried at the priory, my name written in the martyrology of the house, the anniversary of my death to be duly kept, and special prayers offered up for my soul'.[29]

On 18 June 1245 William Dod, who seems to have been another 'very special' benefactor, conceded his land in Uppington and Wychley, given previously to the canons by his mother, in return for which he was allowed the benefit of the prayers of the convent.[30] Similarly, in 1270 Thomas of Brockton donated among other gifts a rent of 5s 6d in Priors Lee, stipulating that the brothers were to spend 2s on the priory's conventual buildings, 2s on lights in their church, and 1s 6d 'to keep the anniversary of the donor forever'.[31] In similar fashion John of Meeson granted land and rent that the canons 'should receive me into their confraternity and participation in all the benefits of their house forever'.[32]

The corrody accorded to William and Felicity Constantine is the only one mentioned by the Wombridge cartulary. Corrodies were a pension, in the form of lodging at a monastery or an allowance of food and clothing to a lay person. In 1253 Felicity donated land and 12d rent from her *maritagium*, her grant being later confirmed by William, who requested that the brethren should 'provide a certain maintenance and annuity for my wife Felicia and me for our lives'.[33] The full details remain unclear, but they were probably similar to one granted by the canons of Lilleshall in the 1270s to Hugh of Boningale. In exchange for the manor of Longdon-upon-Tern, he was permitted a room in the abbey beneath the great chamber, where he could reside for five or eight days with

[29] Ibid., fol. 51 (nos 3–4). During the 1220s and 1230s Alina and Hugh I of Beckbury made a series of small gifts to the canons of properties in the Uppington area. Moreover, as widow, she donated all her share of Winchley and the wood, waste, mill and fishpond of Uppington (ibid., fols 11v–12r (nos 69–72), 16v–17r (no. 107), 27r (nos 168–9)). Members of the family were also benefactors of the Augustinian abbeys of Haughmond and Lilleshall (SPL, MS 6000, fol. 213; *Cart. Haughmond*, no. 1198; BL, MS Add. 50121 (cartulary of Lilleshall), fols 65–6; Una Rees, ed., *The Cartulary of Lilleshall Abbey* (Shropshire Archaeological and Historical Soc., 1997), nos 118–19).

[30] Eyton, *Shropshire*, VIII, 185 (from an original 'in the possession of Mr George Morris of Shrewsbury'). William inherited 2¼ virgates in Uppington in 1244 as heir of Cecily Marshall, who before her death c. 1239 made a *cum corpore meo* gift to the priory with her husband William (BL, MS Egerton 3712, fol. 9 (nos 46–7)).

[31] Ibid., fol. 43v (no. 49).

[32] Ibid., fols 74v–75r (no. 7).

[33] Ibid., fol. 28r (no. 174). She was the sole heir of Henry of Burton in Uppington; her gift to the priory comprised all her portion of the demesne meadow in Uppington, and Holemaremeadow, plus a rent of 12d in Uppington. The witnesses, including John of Ercall (who succeeded his father William c. 1256), suggest a date of c. 1260 for her husband's confirmation charter.

two horses and two servants, who would be fed by the canons.[34] Also, Hugh and his wives Felicity and Sybil were received into the confraternity of the abbey and afforded the same benefits as the brethren. Similarly, Haughmond Abbey granted a generous corrody to Robert Lee of Uffington on 5 May 1415.[35] Among other things, Robert was required to serve the abbot as an esquire with a servant and two horses, and when Robert wished to reside in the house, he and his servant were to receive the same food, drink and clothes as the abbot's esquires and servants, and his horses to have the same fodder as theirs.

During the 1270s Hugh of Haughton rented a mill in Shifnal to the canons of Wombridge, but in March 1284 he granted it and its watercourse to them. His charter, which reflects what seems to have been a beneficial transaction for both parties, included a request from the donor for the rare privilege to present a canon. Hugh stipulated that in return for the mill

> the prior and all his successors shall, on the presentation of myself or heirs, always receive a fit person as a canon of their house, and on the death of one such nominee shall receive another so that forever they should have one in their house, doing services for the souls of myself and my wife Alice, of my ancestors and successors and of the chief lords of Shifnal, and all the faithful departed.[36]

Although Hugh's resources were necessarily modest, he was a prominent vassal of the Dunstanvilles, who were themselves important supporters of Wombridge. From the 1140s Hugh's ancestors had developed a lasting friendship with the canons, and it is possible that family members were buried amongst them.[37]

Burial within the priory of St Leonard seems to have been an honour much sought after and was accorded to either prestigious benefactors or those willing to purchase the privilege with a suitable donation. Interment represented a significant and potent gesture in which lay supporters could associate themselves in death with the *religiosi*. The choice of burial-place was equally crucial, both to the family of the deceased and the monastery. There is no indication that the founders, patrons and their relatives were buried at Wombridge, though it is distinctly possible. At Stone the patrons, the Staffords used the priory as their family mausoleum between the twelfth and sixteenth centuries,[38] while at Norton the Dutton family assumed the role of chief benefactors from the patrons, the constables of Chester, and provided endowments specifically intended for the construction of north-eastern chapels, which served as their burial place until 1536.[39]

---

[34] Shrewsbury, Shropshire Records and Research Centre, 1910/472.
[35] SPL, MS 6000, fol. 82; *Cart. Haughmond*, no. 449; *Monasticon*, VI, 110, no. 6.
[36] BL, MS Egerton 3712, fol. 41 (no. 29).
[37] For example, see ibid., fols 38r (nos 1–2), 41v–42r (nos 29, 44).
[38] Bodl., MS Dugdale 20, fol. 144v; *Monasticon*, VI, 230–1, no. ii.
[39] Archaeological excavation has revealed 140 burials of lay persons, most of which were located within the church and precinct. The choice of Norton as the burial place of the Duttons is confirmed by five surviving wills of family members produced between c. 1270 and 1527, two of which specify burial in the north-eastern lady chapel: Fraser Brown and Christine Howard-Davies, *Excavations at Norton Priory 1970–87* (Lancaster Imprints,

The late medieval period witnessed a widening of the privilege of interment in religious houses, and such burials were habitually facilitated by a donation in the form of *cum corpore meo* ('with my body'). However, the experience of Augustinian communities like Wombridge supports the view that up to the mid thirteenth century, and in some instances considerably later, burial in a monastery was a preferred choice of lay benefactors. David Postles has argued that it 'elicited the most effective intercession, as the resting place of the corpse amongst those of the monks or canons was a constant reminder and a direct invocation to the religious for their intervention'.[40] It was Urban III who granted burial rights to Wombridge in 1187. About 1240 Cecily and William Marshall gave the canons property in Uppington with their bodies, while in 1241 Eleanor, widow of Robert of Losford, granted her land in Uppington, including a share of the mill, in similar fashion.[41] Moreover, within twenty years, Eleanor's sister Alina and niece, Jane of Beckbury, donated properties *cum corpore meo*.[42] Also, before 1243 Jane's cousin, Reginald Corbrond, gave his rents in Uppington with his body.[43] Finally, in his will of c. 1308, Reginald's descendant, Richard del Bury, requested interment in the priory cemetery.[44]

Like other smaller Augustinian communities in the diocese of Coventry and Lichfield, such as Ranton and Calwich, Wombridge attracted the interest of a group of relatively local supporters. During the priory's lifetime at least thirty lords of Shropshire estates and members of their families chose to associate themselves with the canons through gift-giving, entry into confraternity, burial, and the witnessing of donations. The majority of these benefactors were vassals or kin of the founders, or their overlords. Although some families, such as the Dunstanvilles and Lestranges demonstrated their religious aspirations via a wider orbit of monasteries, most appear to have acted as benefactors solely of Wombridge. In many ways this emphasises the importance and vitality of the wider notion of 'community', of which the canons and their local donors were intertwined. The emerging picture is one of an adequate foundation endow-

---

2005), figs 18, 21, 27–30, 100–1, 104–7, 109, table 9; G. J. Jones, 'Quiet Witnesses: the Burials in the Lady Chapel, Norton Priory, Cheshire' (B.Sc. dissertation, Liverpool University, 1995); J. Patrick Greene, *Norton Priory: the Archaeology of a Medieval Religious House* (Cambridge, 1989), pp. 12 and fig. 10, 128–46 and fig. 56. See also Abram, *Norton Priory*.

40 David Postles, 'Monastic Burials of Non-Patronal Lay Benefactors', *JEH* 47 (1996), 620–37 (pp. 625, 629); Burton, *Monastic and Religious Orders*, p. 138. The subject of monastic burial has also been illuminated by Brian Golding, 'Burials and Benefactions: an Aspect of Monastic Patronage in Thirteenth-century England', in *England in the Thirteenth Century: Proceedings of the 1984 Harlaxton Symposium*, ed. W. M. Ormrod (Harlaxton, 1985), pp. 64–75, and 'Anglo-Norman Knightly Burials', in *The Ideals and Practice of Medieval Knighthood* I, ed. C. Harper-Bill and R. Harvey (Woodbridge, 1986), pp. 35–48.

41 BL, MS Egerton 3712, fol. 9 (nos 46–7, 52), 19r (no. 107). Cecily died c. 1239 and William in February 1244.

42 Ibid., fols 19r–20v (nos 108–18), 51 (nos 3–4).

43 Ibid., fols 18v–19r (no. 102).

44 Ibid., fol. 35 (no. 132). Richard was the great-grandson of Alice of Charlton, another sister of Jane of Beckbury.

ment, followed by a bout of gifts in the late twelfth century, then a rapid accumulation of possessions and rights in close proximity to the priory from the mid 1200s onwards. This included the extension of cultivation, especially in Uppington, Wychley and the lower slopes of the Wrekin, and the collection of small properties around the canons' granges at Cherrington, Shirlowe and Wychley. Additionally, the brothers exploited lucrative quarrying and coal mining resources at Grindle and Ketley, donated to them c. 1269 by Richard Grindle and Thomas Tuschet.[45] The grants of stone from quarries illustrate that building at Wombridge continued for several decades, which also allowed the completion of a Lady Chapel in 1328, probably funded by the patrons and benefactors of the house.[46] The myriad of grants are incorporated in an *inspeximus* of Edward II, issued in 1319,[47] which not only complements the cartulary evidence, but provides a valuable record of the priory's assets during the fourteenth century.

The decidedly enterprising canons of Wombridge depended on the generosity of their patrons and benefactors, and seem to have been especially accommodating in their relationship with them. To Richard Southern the stimulus of support for the Black Canons, in motivational terms, 'was provided by benefactors who saw in the communities of Augustinian canons a type of foundation within their means, and a religious ideal within their understanding'.[48] During the twelfth century at least, the Augustinian movement had been at the forefront of church reform, fashionable, and appealed to the practical nature of the royal family, *curiales* and the numerous lay founders and benefactors. This fits into a more general pattern in which the canons may have offered a relatively less expensive option to potential supporters, as well as a religious vocation associated with reform and practical religion. In return for their generosity, during the late medieval period the canons of Wombridge may have been especially willing to comply with the requests of donors for the special benefits of the community, as a way of securing donations in a region of Shropshire where competition for endowments from a number of religious communities was intense. Moreover, through such transactions of gift-exchange, St Leonard of Wombridge and the canons venerating him acted as an important focus for religious aspirations, family and identity for a close-knit group of men and women, bound together by a mixture of kinship, property and lordship.

The enduring relationship between the canons of Wombridge and their benefactors during the late medieval period supports the view that such houses were highly significant to local lay communities. It also challenges the notion

---

[45] BL, MS Egerton 3712, fols 39v (no. 12), 50r (no. 10).

[46] On 25 January 1328 Pope John XII granted an indulgence for the church and new chapel of St Mary and St Leonard for forty years to all visiting it (BL, MS Egerton 3712, fols 89r–90v); Morris, 'Abstracts' in *Trans. SANHS*, 2nd series, XII, 218–19.

[47] BL, MS Egerton 3712, fols 80r–84v; *CChR 1300–26*, pp. 404–6; *Monasticon*, VI, 388–9, no. i.

[48] R. W. Southern, *Western Society and the Church in the Middle Ages* (Harmondsworth, 1970), p. 245.

that the importance and value of moderately endowed religious communities were insignificant. This is particularly true when considering the relative scale of endowments from donors, themselves often lords or holders of modest fees, and possessing a limited tenurial and socio-political outlook. The association between with the canons and their supporters was both significant, and in many cases, long-lasting. Furthermore, the sheer extent and depth of the Wombridge cartulary demonstrates the inaccuracy of the view that small rural monastic houses tend to be poorly documented. Wombridge compares well with the Augustinian communities of Burscough, Ranton and Mobberley, each of whom possess valuable original and cartulary material, which provide considerable information about the development, endowments and donors of those communities.[49]

Visitation returns from the late fifteenth and early sixteenth centuries indicate that at least during the latter years of its existence, the community of Wombridge was relatively small, for instance numbering five brethren in May 1496.[50] Similarly, Ranton numbered six in 1377, seven in 1381, and six in 1496, 1518, 1521 and 1524 respectively.[51] However, at the priory of St Mary and St Margaret, Calwich, in 1385 the prior successfully petitioned for exemption from royal taxation on the grounds that there were only he and two canons in the priory, and alleged that this was the number required by the terms of the original foundation.[52] In contrast with Cistercian foundations, the nature of Augustinian foundations meant that few, if any, notions of 'ideal' numbers of brethren existed, and though the size of religious communities fluctuated, it would be imprudent to conclude that such modest numbers are symptomatic of unsuccessful management, lack of endowments and poverty. Wombridge Priory was dissolved with the smaller houses in 1536, showing a gross revenue of £72 15s 8d.[53] Yet the survey indicates that the canons met their obligations and that finance was sound, while a series of visitations between 1518 and 1524 reported good order and discipline.[54]

---

49 For Burscough see TNA (PRO), DL10, DLT25, DLT29 (original charters, 1199–1544), DL42/6 (cartulary, c. 1390 x 1400); for Ranton, BL, MS Cotton Vespasian C. XV (fourteenth-century cartulary); for Mobberley, Chester, Cheshire Record Office, DDX 553/1–7, 9–27 (thirteenth-century original charters). On the value of studying this type of community, see Linda Rasmussen, 'Why Small Monastic Houses should have a History', *Medieval History* 28 (2003), 1–27. See also the paper by Janet Burton in this collection, below, pp. 113–23.

50 London, Lambeth Palace Library, Register of Archbishop John Morton, i, fol. 149v.

51 Lichfield Record Office [LRO], B/A/1/5ii, fols 38–9; B/A/1/14i, fol. 19r; Lambeth Palace Library, Register of Archbishop John Morton, i, fol. 148.

52 LRO, B/A/1/5i, fol. 36. At the priory of St Thomas the Martyr, near Stafford, it appears that nine brethren represented the full establishment; in 1518 there were a prior, subprior, precentor and five canons, and according to the subprior this was one below the full complement (LRO, B/V/1/1, fol. 26).

53 VE, III, 194. The first ministers' account puts the value of Wombridge at £89 3s 8d (TNA (PRO), SC 6/Hen.VIII 3006, mm. 16–21).

54 LRO, B/V/1/1, fols 29, 39.

This paper has demonstrated that from the perspective of a well documented, if small and rural Augustinian house, it is possible to assert that, during the later Middle Ages in particular, the community of Wombridge developed substantially in economic terms and served as a focal point for religious devotion, family and identity, for both patrons and benefactors. These supporters were predominantly holders of local lordships, and their vassals and kin. In large part, the priory owed its success to the continued generosity and loyalty of its supporters, who alienated what were to them, substantial properties and rights. Equally, it is possible to argue that conventions of gift-exchange and particularly close links with benefactors meant that the brethren were frequently willing to accommodate their religious and social aspirations until the closure of the house in 1536. Evidently communities like Wombridge were both significant and successful.

7

The Rising Price of Piety in the Later Middle Ages

MICHAEL HICKS

It was a universal belief in late medieval England that religious benefits could be bought.[1] From well before the adoption of the official doctrine of purgatory in 1215 it was thought that the sufferings of the dead could be relieved by prayers and other good works, which could even be performed after death and financed on instalments from endowments. Witness the thousand or so religious houses, another thousand hospitals, numerous preceptories and colleges, and several thousand chantries that were endowed over nine centuries.[2] Many of these institutions endured until the Reformation, until the Dissolution of the Monasteries of 1536–40, or, if secular colleges, chantries, or hospitals, for a further decade. Together they expressed the religious aspirations, fashions, and generosity of almost a thousand years of Christian benefactors. Few generations apparently contented themselves with what they had inherited. The first twenty great Benedictine abbeys had been endowed principally by Anglo-Saxon royalty with swathes of territory. Such truly regal beneficence ceased to be feasible by the Norman Conquest, yet many new religious houses were founded. Some still were the work of kings and queens, but many more were created by earls and lesser aristocrats, generally on a smaller scale, almost all for dozens of inmates or fewer, often indeed endowed with wastelands and advowsons that were of little economic value to the donors. Even at the Dissolution a handful of religious houses still had founders amongst the country gentry, for example the Husseys of Harting in the case of the Premonstratensian Abbey of Durnford (Sussex), and in that of the Augustinian priory of Church Gresley, the Gresleys of Drakelow (Derbyshire).[3] Many more obscure people feature

---

1   See J. T. Rosenthal, *The Purchase of Paradise. Gift Giving and the Aristocracy* (London, 1972), especially pp. 12–13; D. Crouch, 'The Origin of Chantries. Some Further Anglo-Norman Evidence', *Journal of Medieval History* 27 (2001), 159–80, especially pp. 160–63. This paper benefits from the insights of my former and current research students Simon Phillips, Simon Roffey, Karen Stöber, and Cindy Wood.

2   *MRH*; R. M. Clay, *The Medieval Hospitals of England* (London, 1909); N. I. Orme and M. Webster, *The English Hospital 1070–1570* (New Haven and London, 1995), passim; A. Kreider, *English Chantries. The Road to Dissolution* (Cambridge, Mass., 1979), p. 73.

3   K. Stöber, *Late Medieval Monasteries and their Patrons. England and Wales c.1300–1540* (Woodbridge, 2007), appendix.

in the cartularies as contributors to the priories, preceptories, and cells that others had established. The thirteenth century witnessed the foundation of more modestly endowed chantries for single priests, both secular and monastic. Between 1310 and 1340 religiously competitive burghers of the provincial city of York founded forty chantries in their parish churches and the chapel on Ouse Bridge.[4] Two centuries later wills and churchwardens' accounts everywhere reveal mere parishioners commonly subscribing to the gilds, building projects and furnishings of their parishes, both in life and through bequests. Pre-Reformation Catholics continued to support such projects as long as they were permitted to do so: until the observances and their underlying doctrines, purgatory and the cult of saints, were suppressed and/or abolished.[5]

However the scale of endowments diminished. Very few new monasteries were established after 1300 and those that were, such as houses of Minoresses and Bonhommes, were modest in scale.[6] The peak of chantry foundations – and indeed of licensed alienations in mortmain over the whole period 1279–1547 – fell before 1350, after which licences dwindled almost to nothing.[7] Many factors contributed to this, with which historians are familiar: perhaps saturation point had been reached; certainly the Statute of Mortmain did prevent some new foundations and curtailed others; religious fashions were changing, as the public piety of the parish supplanted individual foundations; and pious giving often (and perhaps increasingly) took the form of cash and moveables. With an income of £400, Dean Worsley (d. 1497) certainly possessed the moveable wealth for a new foundation, yet, like so many church dignitaries, he chose not to make his own.[8] The chantry certificates reveal that much pre-Reformation endowment was funded by semi-permanent enfeoffments to use rather than from lands and rents properly alienated in mortmain. There is also a case, so this paper asserts, for explaining this decline in endowments in economic terms. Whilst this paper focuses on the later Middle Ages and on monasticism, its arguments may also be relevant to the central Middle Ages and to other expressions of late medieval piety.

4   R. B. Dobson, 'The Foundation of Perpetual Chantries by the Citizens of Medieval York', in his *Church and Society in the Medieval North of England* (London and Rio Grande, 1996), pp. 253–65 (pp. 257–8).

5   J. J. Scarisbrick, *The Reformation and the English People* (Cambridge, 1984); E. Duffy, *The Stripping of the Altars. Traditional Religion in England 1400–1580* (London, 1992), passim; but see the alternative view of R. Lutton, *Lollardy and Orthodox Religion in Pre-Reformation England: Reconstructing Piety* (Woodbridge, 2006), pp. 4, 37.

6   *MRH*, pp. 203, 286.

7   R. N. Swanson, *Church and Society in Late Medieval England* (Oxford, 1989), pp. 196–7; S. Raban, *Mortmain Legislation and the English Church 1279–1500* (Cambridge, 1982), pp. 156, 158; K. L. Wood-Legh, *Studies in Church Life under Edward III* (Cambridge, 1934), p. 125; A. D. Brown, *Popular Piety in Later Medieval England: the Diocese of Salisbury* (Oxford, 1995), p. 35; H. Colvin, 'The Origin of Chantries', *Journal of Medieval History* 26 (2000), 163–73 (p. 165).

8   H. Kleineke and S. R. Hovland, eds, *The Estate and Household Accounts of William Worsley, Dean of St Paul's Cathedral 1479–1497*, London Record Soc., 40 (2004), p. 31.

This paper contends that in the last two centuries of the Middle Ages – roughly from the Black Death to the early sixteenth century – the cost of pious benefactions increased greatly. Some donors were forced out of the market and could no longer afford to endow foundations of their own; many others had to curtail the scale of their generosity. Existing foundations became less prosperous and many failed. This is attributable to five interlocking factors, each of which is known to historians, but which have never been examined in combination. These five factors are: increases in clerical wages, in the capital value of land, and in building costs; a fall in landed income; and the costs of licences to alienate in mortmain. Each will be discussed in turn. The period 1300 to 1540 is deliberately treated as a whole. No allowance has been made for the sub-periods into which the era can undoubtedly be divided, and in particular none for the decades after 1500, when key trends in population and prices were reversed. The implied measure or template that underpins most of the paper is the cost of funding a single secular chantry priest; however, the more particular applications of this paper to English monasticism are also discussed.

Founding chantries was cheap around 1300. A single tenement yielding a rent charge of £1 sufficed as endowment for a London chantry in 1280. Dean William of Kilkenny (d. 1302) bequeathed only £50 to endow his chantry in Exeter Cathedral and William de Bosco in 1325 provided only 140 marks (£96 13s 4d) in 1325.[9] In Kermode's judgement £40 left in 1390, £30 in 1405, and £66 13s 4d in 1415, all at York, 'must have been insufficient to maintain a chantry priest in perpetuity'. Enormous capital sums were now required to found a perpetual chantry of a single priest: such as the £400 in 1396, £333 6s 8d in 1465, and £400 in 1509 left by merchants of York. Whereas founding a chantry was affordable for most of the early fourteenth-century York patriciate, a chantry for a term of years or an unendowed maisondieu was now a cheaper and much more realistic aspiration.[10]

A principal reason was the great increase in the wages of the chantry priests. The clerical proletariat were seriously underpaid around 1300, when many cantarists were paid less than five marks (£3 6s 8d), the sum that Rosalind Hill considered the minimum living wage. But their earning power was transformed by the Black Death. Though the number of clergy was sharply reduced, the number of posts was not. Demand exceeded supply and wages therefore rose. Naturally clerics migrated to the best paid jobs. Hence the disapproving perception of Chaucer, Langland, and the church authorities, that priests were deserting their arduous (but essential) duties as curers of souls in favour of

9   TNA C 146/376; D. Lepine, *A Brotherhood of Canons Serving God. English Secular Cathedrals in the Later Middle Ages* (Woodbridge, 1995), p. 149; see also D. Lepine and N. Orme, eds, *Death and Memory in Medieval Exeter*, Devon and Cornwall Record Soc., 46 (2003), pp. 130–8, 171–202.

10   J. I. Kermode, 'The Merchants of Three Northern English Towns', in *Profession, Vocation and Culture in Later Medieval England*, ed. C. H. Clough (Liverpool, 1982), pp. 25–6, 30–1.

easier and more lucrative appointments as chantry priests, especially at St Paul's. Archbishops sought to maintain the differentials in favour of curates and to restrict the earnings of cantarists – Islip in 1350 to five marks (£3 6s 8d), Zouche to £4, and Sudbury to 7 marks (£4 13s 4d). Even in the fifteenth century the statutory maxima were £6 for curates and £4 13s 4d for chaplains, at most only 4d a day. This was no more than the rate payable to other semi-skilled labourers. Chaplains in Lancashire were still receiving below these levels and York cantarists on average £4 13s 4d into the early sixteenth century, but this wage control generally failed. The normal wage of cantarists reached ten marks (£6 13s 4d) in late fourteenth-century London. £6, £8 or £10 was normal in the late fifteenth and sixteenth centuries.[11]

Two consequences followed. Chantries paying the old salaries failed and new ones had to provide far more generous emoluments. Kreider found that few early secular chantries were still in operation at the time of the chantry certificates.[12] The two chantries at All Hallows Barking, founded in the late thirteenth and early fourteenth centuries, offered perfectly respectable salaries of five and six marks apiece. In 1392, however, they were declared no longer viable, 'because of the scarcity of suitable chaplains and the dearth of victuals and other necessities', and had to be combined into a single chantry yielding eleven marks, £7 6s 8d. Several others worth as little as £2 were amongst the fifty-four at St Paul's that were amalgamated in 1391 by Bishop Braybrooke, who evidently regarded nine marks or £6 as the acceptable minimum. There were some chantries in every secular cathedral that were merged or even dissolved. In 1438, when Walter Lord Hungerford (d. 1449) obtained papal approval for the union of three chantries at Heytesbury and Upton Scudamore with the free chapel of Corston, all in Wiltshire, their combined incomes amounted to only £8 1s 4d and a house, a comfortable living for one cantarist. Escalating salaries greatly increased costs and help to explain why there were far fewer new chantries than were licensed before 1400. Thus the three chantries that Hungerford founded for himself paid salaries of £8 (twice) and a shared house, £10, and £10.[13] Evidently the tied house was valued at £2 a year.

Second, simultaneously the yield from endowments fell. From a peak before the Black Death rents fell sharply and consistently until the late fifteenth century. The worst period was apparently between 1420 and 1470. All great landowners were forced out of demesne farming. A 'second phenomenon – falling rents and farms – can be found throughout England ... There was a

[11] R. M. T. Hill, '"A Chaunterie for Soules": London Chantries in the Reign of Richard II', in *The Reign of Richard II*, ed. C. Barron and F. R. H. Du Boulay (London, 1971), pp. 242–55 (pp. 242–5, 249–50); T. Cooper, *The Last Generation of English Catholic Clergy. Parish Priests in the Diocese of Coventry and Lichfield in the Early Sixteenth Century* (Woodbridge, 1999), pp. 71, 113–14; Kermode, 'Merchants', p. 25.

[12] Kreider, *English Chantries*, pp. 73–8.

[13] Hill, 'Chaunterie', p. 244; Lepine, *Brotherhood of Canons Serving God*, p. 8; M. A. Hicks, 'Chantries, Obits and Almshouses. The Hungerford Foundations 1325–1478', in *The Church in Pre-Reformation Society*, ed. C. Barron and C. Harper-Bill (Woodbridge, 1985), pp. 123–42 (pp. 129–31).

reduction in the revenues received from most, if not all, manors in the years 1350–1500'.[14] Despite regional variations, estate accounts everywhere recorded long lists of decayed rents and arrears. Rents had to be reduced or were uncollectable, for numerous holdings lay vacant, especially in towns, where many houses collapsed into ruin. Rent-charges exceeded the rentable value and there was insufficient margin over salaries to meet the costs of maintenance attached to medieval urban property. 'The difficulty', so Raban observed, 'was due partly at least to houses standing empty.' It is not unreasonable to suggest that over two centuries rental values were halved. This had two effects on chantries. It meant, first of all, that endowments that were originally adequate now ceased to be so. Property that had brought in an adequate income when the chantry was established could only be let at reduced rents if at all. Hence 'many chantries, gilds and allied bodies withered to extinction. In Essex and Wiltshire more than three-quarters of those licensed in the first half of the fourteenth century had vanished by the dissolution.'[15] Obviously this decline in landed incomes meant, also, that more property was needed – perhaps double the amount – to achieve the necessary yield and to endow securely a chantry or any other type of foundation.

Third, over the same period the capital value or cost of land doubled. The capital value of property was calculated in multiples of the clear annual income. Ten years' purchase, which was the norm in the thirteenth century, meant that a purchaser had to pay ten times the annual revenues to purchase the property: thus £100 was required for a property yielding £10 a year. To express it another way, the purchaser could expect a yield of £10 a year on his outlay of £100 – a return of 10%. During and after the Middle Ages, however, capital values increased. K. B. McFarlane argued, and J. M. W. Bean has confirmed, that they roughly doubled, from the ten years' purchase of the thirteenth century to twenty years' purchase in the fifteenth. As early as 1376, Richard, earl of Arundel, expected to pay 13.33 years' purchase, twenty years' purchase was secured in some cases as early as 1388, and 'there is solid evidence that it was generally accepted by the middle of the fifteenth century'.[16] Sir John Fastolf paid on average 17.8 years' purchase, equating to a yield of 6%, but his costs approached twenty years when legal charges and litigation costs are taken into account.[17] Twenty years' purchase meant that £200 was now needed to secure an income of £10. In effect income, the return on capital, had fallen from 10% to 5%, en route to the thirty years' purchase of the eighteenth century and the

14 J. M. W Bean, 'Landlords', in *The Agrarian History of England and Wales*, III, *1348–1500*, ed. E. Miller (Cambridge, 1991), pp. 526–86 (pp. 583, 585).

15 Raban, *Mortmain*, pp. 136, 173; Kreider, *English Chantries*, p. 89.

16 K. B. McFarlane, *The Nobility of Later Medieval England* (Oxford, 1973), pp. 56–7; idem, *England in the Fifteenth Century* (London, 1981), pp. 191–2, 192n; Bean, 'Landlords' p. 567.

17 McFarlane, 'The Investment of Sir John Fastolf's Profits of War' in *England in the Fifteenth Century*, pp. 191–5.

derisory 2.5% of consols. No wonder that hard-pressed ecclesiastical corporations gave up purchasing land![18]

Individual churchmen and the laity nevertheless continued to endow religious institutions. Where did they find their endowments? Not from inherited land one might suppose, for inheritance was a fundamental right in medieval England and the current holders were expected to pass on what they had themselves inherited to their heirs. This obligation however was moral rather than legally enforceable and was not always observed. To alienate portions of the family inheritance was a cheap option in one sense, in that no cash had to be laid out to acquire the endowment, but it reduced the income of the donor, who often in consequence postponed the transfer, not infrequently failing to complete it before death. Heirs were often less sympathetic. Margaret, Lady Hungerford, for instance, allowed the hospital of her father William, Lord Botreaux (d. 1462), to dwindle and die.[19] The alternative was to purchase the endowment. The rising capital value of land is an indication that demand for it exceeded supply. Even though the land market seems to have grown and more land had become available, there were yet more purchasers of land – successful soldiers, merchants, and lawyers perhaps – with whom the makers of religious endowments had to compete. Whatever route was taken, the founder needed to convey a secure title, which involved buying out the residual rights of the heirs actual or potential – with inherited property, these were his own heirs and collateral relatives – who could otherwise wrest it back. There are examples where such acquisitions were recovered by such heirs. The generous endowment that Cardinal Beaufort made to his hospital of St Cross near Winchester, which he had purchased from the Crown after it escheated on the death of Sir Richard Montagu (d. 1429), was lost to Montagu's great-niece in 1461. Similarly the endowment of Middleham College with estates forfeited by John, earl of Oxford (d. 1513), was lost when the earl was restored in blood in 1485.[20]

Many important late medieval foundations were endowed neither from inheritances nor purchases but from lands already in the hands of the Church. When appropriating parish livings, bishops showed themselves sympathetic to the pleas of poverty of monasteries and to proposals to increase divine service (literally the number of masses). They habitually redeployed monastic wealth to fund their own foundations. Bishops particularly approved the new colleges at the universities of Oxford and Cambridge that sought to enhance the education of the clergy, and several of them founded such colleges themselves. Sadly university colleges did not appeal much to lay donors, who contributed relatively little to their scanty endowments, so that the founders – especially if bishops – had to recycle wherever possible whatever other resources the Church

[18] Raban, *Mortmain*, p. 176.
[19] Hicks, 'Chantries', p. 132.
[20] M. A. Hicks, 'The Neville Earldom of Salisbury 1429–71', *Wiltshire Archaeological Magazine* 72/73 (1980), 141–7 (pp. 144–5); idem, *Richard III as Duke of Gloucester: A Study in Character*, Borthwick Paper 70 (York, 1986), p. 21; see also idem, 'The Last Days of Elizabeth Countess of Oxford', *EHR* 103 (1988), 76–95 (p. 76).

possessed. First the properties of the dissolved Order of the Temple, then those of the dissolved alien priories, and finally those of failing hospitals and monasteries were diverted to this purpose.[21] In some cases, the failure of the previous holder was induced in order to release its resources for more beneficial purposes. Notoriously the unfortunate priory of Selborne (Hants) was suppressed by its founder and diocesan Bishop Waynflete – simultaneously plaintiff, judge, and beneficiary – in favour of his new Magdalen College at Oxford. Similarly Cardinal Wolsey's dissolution of some twenty religious houses as endowment for his own foundations overrode objections from patrons and viable houses alike.[22] Often substantial costs were involved. Bishop Wykeham paid the full market valuation to four continental houses for their cells.[23] It required royal approval – and hence often quid pro quos – to acquire resources lately belonging to the Templars and the alien priories. Even when bishops transferred livings in their gifts to their new foundations, this was to the permanent loss of their sees and required explicit confirmation by their cathedral chapters, who may have needed inducements to comply. Rather than alienating resources more readily useful to themselves, such as Crown lands or forfeitures, royalty also preferred to redistribute such earmarked ecclesiastical wealth to its own foundations such as Sheen Abbey, Eton and Windsor Colleges.[24] Also at the heart of many foundations of the aristocracy, such as chantry schools, chantry hospitals, and chantry colleges, was the appropriation of the rectory of the parish church within which they were sited: the colleges at Arundel (Sussex), Manchester (Lancs.), Middleham (Yorks.), North Cadbury (Som.) and Ewelme Hospital (Oxon.) are obvious examples. Appropriation itself was expensive, especially in relation to the more meagre revenues that remained available, as the most valuable livings had already been appropriated. They did not impact on the incomes of lay patrons, who undoubtedly valued the patronage of their new foundations over that of their ancient monasteries or parish livings.

The financial advantages of such recycling were all the greater as the costs rose of securing endowments on the open market. Permission to make alienations was now required from the Crown which, in practice, was far more willing to permit the recycling of the endowments of defunct religious houses, of which it took a share, than to permit large-scale alienation of secular land or indeed appropriated livings. The Crown had secured this right of veto as a result of the Statute of Mortmain of 1279, which forbade the acquisition of further land by the Church.[25] This was the fourth factor listed above. Property received in contravention of the statute was liable to confiscation by the Crown – a

---

21 S. D. Phillips, 'The Recycling of Monastic Wealth in Medieval Southern England, 1300–1500', *Southern History* 22 (2000), 45–71 (pp. 46–7, 67–8).

22 V. Davis, *William Waynflete, Bishop and Educationalist* (Woodbridge, 1993), pp. 147–8; P. Gwyn, *The King's Cardinal. The Rise and Fall of Thomas Wolsey* (London, 1990), pp. 464–70.

23 £1483 was paid to just two of them: Phillips, 'Recycling', pp. 61–2.

24 Phillips, 'Recycling', pp. 52–3, 55.

25 Raban, *Mortmain*, p. 1.

real penalty that can be demonstrated to have operated in practice. In 1391 an amnesty for illegal acquisitions resulted in no less than 378 retrospective licences that yielded fines exceeding £4,000.[26] Yet the statute was much less than absolute. Almost from the start kings granted exemptions from the act, licences for alienation in mortmain. Since these gave rise to inquisitions *ad quod dampnum*, which survive, and since licences were usually enrolled on the patent rolls, now calendared, it was possible for Dr Raban to calculate accurate numbers and trends in licences, the nature, quantity, and value of alienations from 1279 to 1500.[27] There is no such general measure for alienations before 1279, when many surviving chapels appear to have been constructed as chantries,[28] so it is not possible to measure how real a restriction to alienation the statute actually was. That many non-Londoners chose between 1300 and 1402 to found chantries in London, where mortmain did not apply, suggests that the statute was indeed limiting.[29] After 1279 there were very few licences for major donations worth £100 a year or more, but perhaps such large foundations had already almost ceased. Even if licences were granted relatively freely – and there were about 1150 such grants to monasteries under Edward III[30] – most fourteenth-century licences were for property worth less than £20 a year. From 1323, moreover, kings commonly set donations against the sum licensed at higher than their inquisition valuations, so that as little as a third of the value actually licensed might be secured.[31]

Endorsements on early inquisitions indicate that most applications for exemptions were approved. The Crown frequently remitted fines for the poor or deserving. However licences were granted more sparingly after 1400. There were virtually none in the last years of Henry V, when the king was abroad, during the youth of Henry VI, whose minority council felt unauthorised to alienate the king's rights, and during the reigns of Henry VII and Henry VIII,[32] when the technically illegal endowments by semi-permanent enfeoffments abounded. Licences might be altogether refused or delayed, so that intended endowments were never implemented.[33] Donors might have to bide their time, until they were better placed to induce favours from the king. Thus in 1469, as part of a much wider agreement with Margaret, Lady Hungerford (d. 1478), King Edward IV's brother Richard, duke of Gloucester, promised within sixteen months to obtain licences 'if he goodely can or may at the costes of the said

---

[26] Ibid., pp. 56 (graph 4), 63.

[27] Ibid., pp. 42–3, 45, 56, 57; see also Wood-Legh, *Church Life*, chapters 3–5, especially pp. 125–6; Kreider, *English Chantries*, pp. 74–6.

[28] S. Roffey, *The Medieval Chantry Chapel: An Archaeology* (Woodbridge, 2007); idem, 'Reconstructing the English Medieval Parish Church Chantries and Chapels: an Archaeological Approach', *Church Archaeology* 5–6 (2004), 62–8.

[29] Raban, *Mortmain*, p. 103.

[30] Wood-Legh, *Church Life*, p. 73.

[31] Raban, *Mortmain*, p. 65.

[32] Ibid., p. 43, as glossed by Hicks, 'Chantries', p. 139.

[33] Raban, *Mortmain*, pp. 20, 23.

Margaret'. The two licences for Heytesbury Hospital and a second Salisbury chantry that she obtained in 1472 fulfilled projects initiated thirty and thirteen years previously by Walter (d. 1449) and Robert (d. 1459), lords Hungerford respectively.[34] Thirty years passed from the death of Richard Beauchamp, earl of Warwick, in 1439, before the licences were granted for his mausoleum at Warwick.[35] Chantries were frequently financed from income long before they were permanently endowed. Thus Walter, Lord Hungerford, was funding the chantry at Farleigh Hungerford of his father Sir Thomas (d. 1398) years before it was licensed in 1426; he properly endowed it only in 1431, thirty-three years after his father's death. Masses were being celebrated at Salisbury Cathedral for Walter's son, Robert, in 1464–5, well ahead of the royal licence of 1472, and the chantry of Walter, Lord Ferrers of Chartley (d. 1485), at Windsor, although never licensed, was also operating before his death.[36]

The licensing system also involved expenses. Some were hidden, for example compensating the mesne lords and any costs in securing approval of the original petition, such as the intercession and lobbying by the powerful, which was always desirable. It is no accident that Walter, Lord Hungerford, royal councillor and then the Lord Treasurer, secured one of very few licences from Henry VI's minority government. There were obviously costs in initiating and stage-managing a successful inquisition *ad quod dampnum*. Even a supportive verdict did not guarantee approval by the king or, in the earlier period, parliament. There were also numerous standard if relatively small fees for each stage of approval, from the initial warrant to the writing and sealing of the patent of exemption and enrolment on the patent roll.[37] Altogether these may have added only a few pounds to the total, but the main expense was undoubtedly the fine that the king exacted for his licence. Only sporadic fines were recorded up to 1299, after which they became more systematic.[38] They could be substantial. Wood-Legh cited two examples, one for £10 to alienate £4 of rent in 1359 and in 1368 another of £20 for 8 marks rent,[39] respectively 2.5 and 4 years purchase. Restrictions were more absolute in the fifteenth century, when general licences were rarely granted – even more rarely without fines – and it became normal to exact fines for every implementation of general licences.[40]

Fines were levied at multiples of annual income, five years income being common in the period between 1391 and 1470, both higher and lower amounts being recorded.[41] 'Sir, hit ys to gret a good that ys axed of yow for youre lycens',

34 Hicks, 'Chantries', pp. 131–3.
35 M. A. Hicks, 'The Beauchamp Trust 1439–87', *BIHR* 54 (1981), 135–49 (pp. 139–41); *CPR 1467–77*, p. 153.
36 Hicks, 'Chantries', pp. 127–8, 132; C. Wood, 'The Chantry Chapels of St George's Chapel, Windsor' (MA dissertation, Southampton University, 2004), p. 45.
37 Raban, *Mortmain*, pp. 39–40, 65, 82, 180–1; Hicks, 'Chantries', pp. 127–8.
38 Raban, *Mortmain*, pp. 24–5, 38, 58–60.
39 Wood-Legh, *Church Life*, p. 64.
40 Raban, *Mortmain*, p. 67.
41 Ibid., pp. 69–70.

Sir John Fastolf was told in 1456, 'for they ax for every C. marc that ye wold amortyse D. marcz.'[42] That was five years' purchase or 25% of the total capital cost. Under Henry VIII fines of seven or ten times annual income were exacted. No wonder so many unlicensed enfeoffments appear in the chantry certificates. 'At worst their outlay reduced the value of what they had left to give', wrote Raban. 'Manifestly they could not continue to absorb the extra cost and buy as they had done before.'[43] But of course five years purchase – 25% – was in terms of fifteenth-century land values. Expressed in terms of fourteenth-century values, the fine was half (50%) – or under Henry VIII – three-quarters (75%) of the capital value of the land in 1300. Ironically, however, more sparing licensing and higher rates of fine were accompanied by less effective enforcement: indeed from 1457 religious houses received general pardons that covered evasion of the mortmain regulations.

The baseline for the viability of religious foundations increased very substantially in the two centuries after 1300. Endowments that had originally supported a secular cantarist – the standard measure applied here – no longer sufficed, both because much higher wages were required and because the underlying endowment no longer yielded the same income. Many such foundations vanished, presumably to be combined with or absorbed by others. What actually happened – whether former endowments were secularised – deserves further investigation. Many late medieval benefactors secured the prime benefits of existing chantries by merely supplementing their incomes. Aspirant founders had now to find much larger endowments if their foundations were to be viable. Not only had a much larger salary to be raised, but a substantially larger amount of land was required to fund it – land, moreover, at twice the capital cost. To all the usual legal expenses of acquisition and conveyance had now to be added those of the licensing system and normally a fine of up to a quarter of the gross capital value. Whilst this could be evaded – and perhaps was for smaller endowments of lights, obits, and even secular chantries – monasteries, colleges, chantry hospitals and chantry schools had to comply. Whilst each cost is individually significant – the Statute of Mortmain, for instance, may have diverted benefactions from land to furnishings – it is their operation in combination that is really significant. Together they were a powerful disincentive to new foundations and to endowments. Even before the mortmain legislation numerous smaller donors had replaced the great benefactors of the past. What few great givers there were in the fourteenth century were ever more discriminating – an indication in Raban's view of 'how tight the resources had become'.[44] Even such a plutocrat as Fastolf had cause to hesitate, delay, or to settle for more modest commemoration. Late fifteenth-century counterparts to the chantry-founding

---

[42] Ibid., p. 70.
[43] Ibid., p. 186; see also Brown, *Popular Piety*, p. 34.
[44] Ibid., p. 134.

early fourteenth-century York elite could not afford the increased costs. They and their inferiors had to trade down, to obits, to collaborative patronage of their parish or gild, or to cash donations.

Assessing the extent of this increase in costs is fraught with peril, yet it must nevertheless be attempted. The rise in salaries, fall in rentals, rise in capital costs, and exaction of fines did not represent continuous trends and varied, moreover, according to date, region, particular foundation and transaction. Sometimes no fine was charged or inflated ones were exacted. As a rough guide, however, the minimum salary acceptable to a cantarist doubled. More was sometimes paid, and indeed doubtless had to be paid, if men of good character or education or graduates were required. The capital value of the land itself expressed in years' purchase of the current income certainly doubled: hence the capital value of the endowment needed for double the salary actually quadrupled. And fines for exemption from the mortmain regulations imposed a further 25% cost on this inflated capital value (or 50% of the capital value at the rates of 1300). The price of such endowments therefore increased fivefold. Much more land was needed to raise the same income. A halving of income from land has been presumed: sometimes, perhaps, it was less, but often, in the Welsh marches and in towns, it was more. This did not affect the capital cost – it is important to avoid double-counting here – but it did mean that for a new foundation twice as much property, whether measured in manors, acres, or houses, was required to provide the same revenue. Twice as much land had to be purchased or twice as much allocated out of what donors had inherited.

A fivefold increase was what had to be borne by those who endowed wholly new chantries with land that they purchased on the open market and for which they paid the mortmain fines. Many donors did not pay all that. They alienated property they had inherited and thus did not suffer the costs directly. Often they evaded or were excused the fine. Even such fortunates experienced a doubling in the salaries to be financed. Those who endowed obits or alienated land for other purposes may have experienced inflation at different rates, but all did experience it, since the price of land, of manufactures such as vestments and plate, and of gild priests all doubled in this period.

That reminds us not to forget the cost of constructing and equipping a new foundation. Actually we know hardly anything of the altar furnishings, vestments, plate, service books, or household gear for most foundations, but can safely presume that the costs amounted to scores or hundreds of pounds. The cost of manufactures rose in the late Middle Ages as the wages of most craftsmen doubled. Moreover, all chantries required premises. Some chantries and most obits certainly operated from existing buildings, but many did not. Often new chapels were added or inserted, as at Salisbury Cathedral, where there are two cage chantries (Audley and Hungerford) and a further two freestanding Beauchamp and Hungerford chapels were erected to the north and south of the Lady Chapel. A few were constructed from scratch. Usually cantarists also required housing and sometimes quite extensive construction work was undertaken. Wotton-under-Edge (Gloucs.) required a schoolhouse, the chancel of North Cadbury church was reshaped as befitted a collegiate choir, and a quadrangle of conventual buildings was constructed at Cobham College.[45] At the top end of the market, the Beauchamp chapel at Warwick cost £3634 to build and the second Hungerford chantry at Salisbury cost £823 to build and equip.[46] Few conventual buildings survive, which may be indicative of less ambitious plans and elevations; even the ducal hospital at Ewelme (Oxon.), with collegiate church and cloister quadrangle, compares in dimensions to such a modest twelfth-century abbey as Titchfield (Hants). Late medieval projects were not comparable in size to most of the monasteries of the twelfth century. Perpendicular architecture and mouldings may have been simpler than what went before and thus inexpensive. Nevertheless the costs of building had increased and were indeed to rise sharply in the later Middle Ages. 'Building wages almost doubled between the Black Death and the end of the fifteenth century.'[47] Much inflated construction costs were a further burden for would-be founders.

The template applied throughout this paper has been the cost of a chantry priest – a secular priest – and does not therefore translate directly into monastic equivalents. Theoretically at least it should have been cheaper to establish a chantry within a religious house because the monastic officiant required no escalating salary from diminishing revenues. Similarly building costs only arose where new building was required. Partitioning off bits of churches, whether parochial or even monastic churches, or shared use of altars, were much more economical. However this perception is somewhat unreal. Monasteries as a whole were exposed to declining revenues, to rising expectations of living standards amongst inmates, and to increasing building costs, especially for the maintenance of extensive complexes of large and ancient buildings. Maintenance has generally been overlooked by modern historians. Revenues that had been just adequate ceased to be so. Instead of bankruptcy and closure, most monasteries were able to continue: they could draw on spare capital reserves which freestanding chantries lacked and they devised a variety of strategies to mitigate their adverse economic environment. Thus all orders, even including the Cistercians, abandoned direct farming. The quarters and churches of lay brothers were allowed to fall into ruin, and canons regular often stopped serving their appropriated churches. One compensatory device was to cut back on the scale – to support fewer monks. Another, commonplace among nunneries, was to rely on dowries for new inmates and subsidies from income. Some houses sold corrodies, raising short-term capital at the expense of future expenditure. Hence monasteries needed and welcomed new resources even to stand still, yet such additional endowments generally brought them extra commitments that exposed them further to the trends outlined above. There were already some

[45] N. Orme, *Education in the West of England 1066–1548* (Exeter, 1976), pp. 193, 198; N. Pevsner, *South and West Somerset* (Harmondsworth, 1958), p. 256; N. Saul, *Death, Art and Memory in Medieval England. The Cobham Family and their Monuments 1300–1500* (Oxford, 2001), p. 47.

[46] Hicks, 'Chantries', p. 133; 'The Beauchamp Trust', p. 140.

[47] D. L. Farmer, 'Prices and Wages, 1350–1500', in *Agrarian History*, ed. Miller, III, 492.

endowed chantries in monasteries in 1300, and yet others were to be founded there, often served by secular clerks. Religious houses also often became trustees of chantries founded elsewhere.

Raban's graphs of mortmain licences reveal clearly a great diminution in the legal acquisition of property by the Church, whether measured in numbers of licences or values. 'It must be concluded', wrote Wood-Legh, 'that the chantries had reached their greatest popularity well before the first appearance in England of the Black Death.'[48] Monasteries shared disproportionately in the decline. Before 1350, they represented half or more of recipients, afterwards significantly less of much diminished totals. Although Raban believes that illegal acquisitions by her Fenland abbeys were commonplace, each property was small and none of her examples postdate the fourteenth century.[49] Monasteries were also making considerable use of enfeoffments to hold their new acquisitions, but the statute of 1391 closed this loophole: 'evasion was mainly confined to chantry foundations and', wrote Raban, 'widespread abuse of mortmain by the religious was indeed a thing of the past'.[50] Henceforth there was little under-recording of new monastic endowments, which were as paltry as the licences suggest. Actually most monastic acquisitions in the fourteenth century were under general licences, usually for £20, that were gradually fulfilled – more slowly indeed than appears, since the Crown commonly inflated the annual values set against them. Even so, these permissions to acquire took time to fulfil. Thus the £20 licence awarded in 1312 to Spalding Priory was only exhausted in 1391, whilst Lesnes Abbey fulfilled its 1309 licence in 1500.[51] What were still accruing may have been donations by outsiders – a cost to donors. There were fewer benefactors prepared to meet the high cost even of reduced foundations in monasteries after 1400, when chantries were no longer cheap and might need as much, or half as much, endowment as a small nunnery. Internally financed purchases never absolutely ceased, but they became less common. The capital cost had become prohibitive. Too many years' revenue were needed to buy land that yielded enough. No wonder that even great founders of university colleges saved money by recycling monastic property.

Wood-Legh found that 750 grants to monasteries were unconditional, the donors being content with remembrance in their suffrages. That left 300 others that were earmarked – to particular obediences for vesture or better ale, for lamps, pittances, obits and chantries that entailed recurrent future expenditure. Initially the income covered the costs – indeed often more than covered them, accruing to the monastery what Wood-Legh saw as profit.[52] The celebrated royal chantries at Westminster Abbey were truly exceptional. As revenues were eroded, chantries often became loss-makers. Three Hungerford chantries, 'at Easton, Calne and Longleat, also represented exploitation, since the extra

48 Wood-Legh, *Church Life*, p. 125.
49 Raban, *Mortmain*, pp. 95–7.
50 Ibid., p. 129.
51 Ibid., p. 51.
52 Wood-Legh, *Church Life*, p. 73.

income was not commensurate with the additional burdens imposed'.[53] 'The most that many such founders could contribute from their own reserves was sufficient acumen to increase the existing wealth of the body', wrote Raban. 'All too often, therefore, there was a parasitic relationship between chantries and their hosts. Thus, even chantries which appeared to pay their way may in reality have absorbed wealth which would otherwise have accrued, unencumbered, to the house.'[54] Monks may have continued meeting obligations for which the original endowments no longer sufficed. It should be remembered that only direct costs were taken into account. The actual costs – the 46% overheads that we are familiar with today – covering administration, maintenance, clothing and such like, passed uncompensated. That monastic finances were exceptionally decentralised to obediences, where ongoing expenditure was not necessarily collated with falling receipts, may have been an aggravating factor.

One obvious example here is where chantries were manned by monks or canons. For founders, this was a cheap option as keep, not salary, was paid. For monasteries it merely involved designating which of the masses that each monk said daily was earmarked for this purpose. Ely Cathedral Priory was allowed to substitute two monks for two secular priests in 1398 because the endowment no longer covered the salaries.[55] Often allocated on a rota, such service may have been less than personal. Hence not infrequently the endowment went to fund an extra monk or canon at thirteenth-century valuations. Thus in 1328 Robert, earl of Oxford, granted land to Netley Abbey (Hants) to support two extra monks to be nominated by him and in 1342 an extra canon was funded at Christchurch Priory (Dorset).[56] In time such endowments were eroded and the newcomers ceased to be extra. At the Trinitarian friary of Easton (Wilts.), where Sir Robert Hungerford (d. 1352) had given only £1 0s 4d to endow an extra brother, the prior nominated himself in 1376. Some supplementary income at Calne Hospital obliged the warden additionally to celebrate masses for Sir Robert's soul.[57] Fulfilling such obligations became more expensive. Even finding a monk for the mass became more difficult as numbers of monks, and especially cloister monks, diminished. And of course if the foundation deed specified secular cantarists, potentially the monastery carried fixed costs against diminishing revenues. Consequently, Brown reports, monastic houses were reluctant to accept endowments or to honour their obligations: Milton Abbey 'had to be warned against the withdrawal of chaplains serving the chantries in the church'. Patrons may have been deterred by fear that their benefactions would simply be absorbed.[58]

[53] Hicks, 'Chantries', p. 140.
[54] Raban, *Mortmain*, p. 136.
[55] Wood-Legh, *Church Life*, p. 97.
[56] Ibid., p. 102.
[57] Hicks, 'Chantries', p. 126; Somerset Record Office, DD/SAS H348, fols 259v–60, 262.
[58] Brown, *Popular Piety*, p. 34.

*

If the price of endowing permanent institutions rose fivefold or merely twofold, it helps explain why new endowments and new buildings diminished so much. By the fifteenth century it cost twenty-five times as much to endow a cantarist as to pay him for a year. The cost of erecting him a freestanding chapel had become prohibitive. Even the secular colleges favoured by the great were primarily fourteenth-century phenomena. The circle of potential founders diminished. For most gentry and mercantile elites it was simply too expensive. Costs were cut by the recycling of ecclesiastical wealth by those plutocrats who could: kings and bishops. Unendowed hospitals were founded, and enfeoffments increasingly bypassed the mortmain regulations. Cantarists were worked harder – as schoolmasters, hospital wardens or both – for a single salary, and the prayers they offered were tailored to personal prescriptions. Lifetime giving counted for more and donors increasingly clubbed together in gilds. None of these devices favoured the monasteries.

FEMALE COMMUNITIES:
NUNS, ABBESSES AND PRIORESSES

8

Looking for Medieval Nuns

JANET BURTON

It has been rightly pointed out that just because a monastic house was, for whatever reason, small and poor, it does not follow that it is poorly documented.[1] Among the smallest and least well endowed houses in medieval England were priories of regular canons and of nuns. However, as Andrew Abram's paper in this collection demonstrates, the Augustinian priory of Wombridge may have numbered only a handful of canons and been classed as a lesser monastery at the Dissolution, but its cartulary bears witness to the significant role the canons had in the locality.[2] That other type of 'small and poor' religious house, the nunnery, has received increasing attention from historians in recent years, and it has been demonstrated that despite the lack of size and resources of many of them much can be known of their history. Yet for the nunneries of the north of England in the Middle Ages it remains the case that only one, that of Nunkeeling, has a surviving cartulary,[3] and only a handful have substantial numbers of surviving original charters[4] or other archives produced at the priory.[5] Casting the net more widely than the archives – in a strict sense – of houses of female religious provides opportunities to recover a little more of their history. This paper is concerned with the issue of how to approach the history of nunneries, and seeks to use a range of materials to explore what can be known not of the institutions themselves but of the women who lived in them.

For the monastic historian a staple source is the charter, containing as it does a record of the transfer of land and assets to or from a religious house. For my purposes, in terms of identifying individual religious, the charter has limited use. Charters issued by a nunnery are usually issued by an (often)

---

1 Linda Rasmussen, 'Why Small Monastic Houses Should Have a History', *Medieval History* 28 (2003), 1–27.
2 Andrew Abram, 'The Augustinian Priory of Wombridge and its Benefactors in the Later Middle Ages'; above, pp. 83–94.
3 BL, MS Cotton Otho C VIII, written between 1521 and 1536, and damaged in the Cottonian fire in 1731.
4 There are collections of original charters, for instance, from the priories of Marrick (Leeds University Library and Brynmor Jones Library, University of Hull) and Nun Monkton (Alnwick Castle).
5 On the account rolls of Marrick Priory, for example, see below, p. 122.

unnamed prioress and convent or nuns. Moreover, charters that I have examined in connection with the northern English nunneries suggest that nuns, unlike monks and canons, do not usually attest. Where we do find the names of nuns in charters they are likely to be the women whose entry into a nunnery accompanied a grant of land. I have discussed the evidence for the period up to the early thirteenth century extensively elsewhere.[6] I will give here three examples that had eluded me until recently. First, Amandus *pincerna* confirmed to God and St Mary the Virgin and St Helen and the prioress and convent of Nunkeeling the grant of land in Hatfield made by his wife Beatrice.[7] This land was of Beatrice's marriage portion (as grants to nunneries by women often were) and the grant was made *in sua legia potestate*. Amandus confirmed the land to Nunkeeling with one of their daughters, Avice, to maintain a lamp in the church before the body of our lord, and one in the dormitory *ante conventum*. Apart from the specific request for the use to which the donation should be put this is a fairly typical charter. Among the witnesses were Philip, master of Swine and Robert, priest of Keeling. The occurrence of the former allows us to date the charter to the latter part of the twelfth century or the early thirteenth[8] – Amandus himself died before 1218. Such evidence is valuable as providing not only the name of a nun, but her social background and geographical origin. Amandus was a member of the family of hereditary butlers who served the earls of Aumale, lords of Holderness.[9] He was associated with a number of religious houses, among them the nunnery of Swine and the Cistercian abbey of Meaux; when Amandus died his body was the subject of rather unseemly wrangling between the monks of Meaux and the nuns of Swine.[10] In the other two instances William de Gunneis donated land to Wilberfoss Priory with his daughter, Beatrice;[11] and Simon the cook of Butterwick granted rent from Butterick in the Isle of Axholme to his daughter, Gundreda, a nun of Yedingham for the term of her life.[12] There is a point that should be noted about such charter evidence. It exists for the late medieval period, but may not be as plentiful as it is for the twelfth century for two reasons. One is that what were effectively dowry grants could be seen as a form of simony, repeatedly legislated against by church councils. In the face of this and the frequent injunctions of the archbishops of York that nuns be received for love not money, such grants may

---

[6] Janet Burton, *Yorkshire Nunneries in the Twelfth and Thirteenth Centuries*, Borthwick Paper, 56 (York, 1979), and *The Monastic Order in Yorkshire 1069–1215* (Cambridge, 1999), pp. 125–52.

[7] Bodl., MS Top. Yorks. d 9, fol. 55r.

[8] For occurrences of Philip see Janet Burton, 'The Chariot of Aminadab and the Yorkshire Nunnery of Swine', in *Pragmatic Utopias: Ideals and Communities, 1200–1630*, ed. Rosemary Horrox and Sarah Rees Jones (Cambridge, 2001), pp. 26–42 (p. 28).

[9] B. English, *The Lords of Holderness 1086–1260: a Study in Feudal Society* (Oxford, 1979), pp. 92–3.

[10] Burton, 'Chariot of Aminadab', pp. 33–4.

[11] Bodl., MS Dodsworth 7, fol. 350v.

[12] Bodl., MS Dodsworth 95, fol. 33r.

have been concealed.[13] In addition, as grants to religious houses themselves dwindled, the likelihood of charter evidence decreases.

Avice, Beatrice, and Gundreda were just three nuns of three convents living at periods for which we may only be able to give an approximate estimate. Obtaining the names of an entire community is rather more difficult. However, there were occasions on which these names might be recorded and when we do get them, the evidence very often yields a precise date. One such occasion was the record of nuns electing a superior, which may appear in the registers of bishops and archbishops. On 3 August 1310 Margaret de Alta Ripa, or Dawtry, a 'woman of mature years' was elected as prioress of Wilberfoss in the chapter house (Margaret seems to have governed the house until sometime before 27 March 1319, when licence to elect a prioress was given to the nuns).[14] We are told that the 1310 election was a unanimous one. Those who voted for Margaret were Beatrice of Newton (subprioress), Matilda Gunneys, Alicia Uctred (sacrist), Margaret Chauncy (cellaress), Isolda Cayvill (precentrix), Elena Gra (the other sacrist), Lucy de Colburn (guest mistress), Margaret de Brampton (the second cellaress), and nuns Matilda Dive, Margaret of Preston, Hawise of Barton, Helewise of Langtoft (described as 'an old woman'), Agnes Darreins, Juliana Darreins, Agnes of Lutton, Joan of Portington, Isabella de Middleton, and Matilda de Wyktoft.[15] Thus we have evidence of a community of eighteen nuns, plus their prioress – a sizeable community – and of the eighteen, seven were office holders. On 20 August 1497 the nuns of Keldholme elected Elizabeth Davell, prioress of Basedale, as their prioress. We have the names of eight nuns who elected her: Katherine Anlaby (former prioress), Elizabeth Browne, Alice Norton, Agnes Wright, Christiana Redesdale, Joan Fleschewer, Elizabeth Semfold, and Margaret Talbot.[16] The community of Keldholme in 1497 thus numbered eight nuns plus the prioress. We can also name the eight nuns of Moxby who elected their prioress in 1424.[17]

---

[13] For further discussion of this point see Janet Burton, 'Yorkshire Nunneries in the Middle Ages: Recruitment and Resources', in *Government, Religion and Society in Northern England 1000–1700*, ed. John C. Appleby and Paul Dalton (Stroud, 1997), pp. 104–16.

[14] *HRH*, II, 619.

[15] William Brown and A. Hamilton Thompson, eds, *The Register of William Greenfield, Lord Archbishop of York 1306–1315*, 5 vols, Surtees Soc., 145, 149, 151–3 (1931–40), III, 177–8.

[16] Eric E. Barker, ed., *The Register of Thomas Rotherham, Archbishop of York 1480–1500*, I, Canterbury and York Soc., 69 (1976), p. 152.

[17] BI, SV Register 5A, fols 346v–347v (old fols 324v–325v), contains a report, dated 16 January 1423/4, of the resignation of a prioress of Moxby and the election of her successor. It states that the chapter of York, during a vacancy in the see, had received a letter declaring that Alice de Alta Ripa, prioress of Moxby, wished to resign on account of illness and old age, and asking the chapter to send someone to receive her resignation. These letters are said to have been dated 10 January 1423/4. The document further states that on 11 January the commissary went to the house, received Alice's resignation and that Joan was elected the following day, 12 January. I am grateful to Dr Philippa Hoskin for checking these details for me.

Lists of nuns might also appear in the records of a visitation, although it is more usual for those committing misdemeanours only to be named. However, there are some occasions on which the whole community might be identified. The six nuns of Arden in 1397 – Christina Darrel, Elizabeth Darrel, Elizabeth Sleyne, Alicia Barnard, Agnes of Middleton, and Elizabeth of Thornton – were loud in their criticism of Prioress Eleanor.[18] They accused her of mismanagement of the meagre priory resources, pawning the vessels of the church, and of selling wood without their consent. They reported that there were no candles in the choir and therefore insufficient light to say the offices, and that the buildings were in a state of disrepair. What emerges from their complaints is that this small community of seven women, living in the bleak environment of the North Yorkshire Moors, was suffering conditions of extreme poverty and hardship. It was life on the edge.

Let us just pause for a moment to ask what we can do with these names. First I would argue that the evidence of the names is sufficient to be able to build up a picture of recruitment in relation to geographical region. Several of the nuns of Arthington that I have been able to identify bear the names of local places, East Keswick (about four miles south-west of Wetherby), Batley, Tang, and Eccup. Those of Esholt Priory were also local: from Woodhall in Calverley, Calverley itself, and Hawksworth, about two miles to the west of the priory.[19] We might expect that such small institutions, closely tied to the local community, would attract local recruits. However, there were exceptions. Arthington, for which I have just cited evidence of local recruitment, also apparently accepted nuns from further afield, from Pontefract, Castleford, and Bawtry (Nottinghamshire), despite the existence of nunneries closer to those places.[20] A member of the Tocketts family, which was closely associated with the Augustinian priory of Guisborough, entered Moxby Priory, despite the fact that Guisborough enjoyed links with Basedale, and despite the greater proximity to the Tocketts lands of the priory of Handale.[21] So some nuns clearly did not enter their local house. Why not? Three factors seem to emerge from the evidence. One was personal contact and indeed pressure. In 1312 Hampole in the south of the county of Yorkshire accepted two nuns. One was called Mathilda of Driffield, whose name seems to place her in the East Riding of Yorkshire. However, she was the niece of the abbot of Roche, a Cistercian house fairly near to Hampole. At the same time the prioress received her niece into the house.[22] She may have come under pressure from a local churchman and her own family to accept these women, and she had to resign as a result,

18 Ibid., fols 228r–229r.
19 See, for example, *Reg. Greenfield*, II, 116, 124, 222; William Brown and A. Hamilton Thompson, eds, *The Register of Thomas Corbridge, Lord Archbishop of York 1300–1304*, 2 vols, Surtees Soc., 138, 141 (1925–8), II, 40, 92–3.
20 Ibid., I, 78.
21 R. M. T. Hill, D. Robinson, R. Brocklesby, and T. C. B. Timmins, eds, *The Register of William Melton, Archbishop of York, 1317–1340*, 5 vols, Canterbury and York Soc., 70, 71, 76, 85, 93 (1977–2002), II, 84, 126.
22 The case is discussed in Burton, 'Recruitment and Resources', p. 107.

because the archbishop had recently forbidden her to accept any more recruits. Another factor to affect recruitment was the location of priory estates. Thus as Tillotson has pointed out, Marrick Priory in Swaledale drew one of its prioresses from Hartlepool, where the priory held lands.[23] The third factor was the availability of places. We know that many of these nunneries were small institutions. We know that an archbishop sometimes tried to balance the size of the house with its resources.[24] It may be that the lack of available places at any given time forced postulants or their families on their behalf to seek entry into a nunnery further afield than their own local house.

Identifying the names of nuns can, as we see, help us discover their place of origin, and it can also help us to see links with local families. Alicia Uctred, who was sacrist of Wilberfoss in 1310, bears the name of a prominent Scarborough family.[25] Two nuns of Arden in 1397, Christina and Elizabeth, bear the name of Darel, and may well have been members of the Darel family of Sessay. Three prioresses of Nun Appleton were drawn from the local knightly family of Ryther.[26] Lists of nuns electing their superior and those who appear in visitation returns may also reveal the clustering of members of the same family in the same community, again not surprising if most recruitment was local. I have just cited two nuns of Arden who shared the same name, and there were two nuns of Wilberfoss with the name of Darreins in 1310.[27] There were two nuns of the same name, Elizabeth and Helewise Darreins, at Swine in 1290 and 1293 respectively, and Sir William Darreins, rector of Londesborough, is recorded as master of Swine in 1298.[28] Now this might all seem rather tentative, as sharing the same name does not necessarily mean a close family relationship. But closer investigation may throw further light on the degree of kinship. On occasions, however, the evidence is clear that members of the same family were present in the same nunnery. Archbishop Wickwane in 1268 found that three 'sisters of the flesh', Bella, Amia, and Sybil, created problems for their prioress at Swine by ganging up on her, and persuading at least three other nuns, Avice de Scruteville, Beatrice de St Quintin and Maud Constable, to join them.[29] Swine, therefore, in 1268 had three sisters of the same family, allied to three members of prominent knightly families of Holderness, the Scrutevilles, the St Quintins

23   John H. Tillotson, *Marrick Priory: a Nunnery in Late Medieval Yorkshire*, Borthwick Paper, 75 (York, 1989), pp. 5–8.

24   Burton, 'Recruitment and Resources'.

25   *Reg. Greenfield*, III, 178; David Crouch, 'Urban Government and Oligarchy in Medieval Scarborough', in *Medieval Scarborough: Studies in Trade and Civic Life*, ed. David Crouch and Trevor Pearson, Yorkshire Archaeological Society Occasional Paper no. 1 (Leeds, 2001), pp. 41–7 (pp. 43–5).

26   See my forthcoming paper, 'Documenting the Lives of Medieval Nuns', in the proceedings of the 2005 Harlaxton symposium.

27   *Reg. Greenfield*, III, 178.

28   W. Brown, ed., *The Register of John le Romeyn, Lord Archbishop of York, 1286–1296*, 2 vols, Surtees Soc., 123, 128 (1913–17), I, 177, 216, 225 and II, 222; *Reg. Corbridge*, I, 163.

29   W. Brown, ed., *The Register of Walter Giffard, Lord Archbishop of York, 1266–1279*, Surtees Soc., 109 (1904), p. 147.

and the Constables. In 1318 the archbishop forbad the priory of Nun Appleton to receive more than two or three nuns of the same family in the house to prevent discord. He may have had in mind the Normanvilles, whose women appear as prioress of Nun Appleton in 1303 (Joan), 1306, 1320 (Isabel) and 1322 (Sybil) – although the last two may be the same woman.[30] He might just as well have applied his remarks to Nun Monkton, where the name of Fairfax occurs with regularity. When we think that some convents numbered eight or ten nuns, then two or three from one family might seem two or three too many. A combination of sources enables us to see the persistent connection between, for instance, the family of Mohaut and the priory of Sinningthwaite, where the daughters of Simon I became nuns and so too did a granddaughter.[31]

So far the evidence I have been presenting suggests that it is possible to identify some nuns, and their geographical and social origins. But can we learn at what age they entered religion, how long they lived, and therefore how long they lived as nuns – what Marilyn Oliva has termed their 'nun years'?[32] Teasing out this information is more difficult. The evidence is often vague – girls are said to have been professed 'at a young age' or 'as a young girl', and that prioresses are said to have resigned from old age and sickness is a phrase that occurs so often as to sound formulaic – the same, perhaps, as politicians resigning to spend more time with their families. It is in the record of individual nuns that the evidence emerges. I am intrigued by the figure of Avice of Beverley, a nun of Nunburnholme. In 1280 it was reported to the archbishop that, having left the nunnery of Nunburnholme to lead a stricter life she had attempted to return but been refused entry. The nuns said that this was the third time she had left, and that the last time she had done so was fourteen years previously (that is, around 1266). They told the archbishop's commissioner, the prior of Warter, that they believed that during that time she had lived chastely, but that when she had lived with them she had been disobedient. They stated further that she had been a nun for thirty years before she last left, placing her entry into the religious life around 1236.[33] Let us place her birth around 1220. In 1280, when she sought re-entry into Nunburnholme, she would have been around sixty years old. This makes it unlikely that she was the Avice of Beverley, described as a nun of Nunkeeling, who was elected prioress of Nunburnholme in 1306 and died in 1310.[34] A case like this can highlight another difficulty, that of nuns sharing the same name, and Beverley is likely to have been a recruiting ground for both nunneries. A further likely nun to hail from the town was Agnes of

---

[30] *Reg. Corbridge*, I, 82; BI, Reg. 9A, fol. 173v; *CCR 1318–23*, p. 563; *HRH*, II, 592.

[31] See, for example, Bodl., MS Dodsworth 8, fols 140r–v, 142r–v.

[32] Marilyn Oliva, *The Convent and the Community in Late Medieval England* (Woodbridge, 1998).

[33] W. Brown, ed., *The Register of William Wickwane, Lord Archbishop of York, 1279–1285*. Surtees Soc. 114 (1907), p. 92.

[34] *Reg. Greenfield*, III, 121, 189.

Beverley. She was prioress of Nunkeeling in 1268 and although her election was originally quashed she seems to have ruled until 25 February 1304.[35]

Another occasion when nuns may make an appearance in archbishops' registers is when they were sent from one priory to another to do penance for a variety of misdemeanours, or when a nunnery was temporarily disbanded. In 1322 the five nuns of Rosedale were dispersed because of the damage done during a Scottish invasion. They are named as Alice de Ripplinghale, Avelina de Brus, Margaret of Langtoft, Joan Crouel, and Eleanor or Isabel Daiville.[36] There was no mention on this occasion of the daughter of John of Dalton, bailiff of Pickering, whom Archbishop Melton the previous year had enjoined Rosedale to receive as a nun. Yet Joan of Dalton – if she be the same women – was a nun of Rosedale in 1323 when the archbishop ordered the convent to receive her back following her expulsion.[37] Where she was in 1322 is not recorded but this emphasises the volatility of these communities at this time. The nuns of Moxby were dispersed at the same time as those of Rosedale.[38] Alice of Barton, prioress, was sent to Swine Priory. She had been prioress since her election in 1310. Sabina of Applegarth and Margaret of Neusom were sent to Nun Monkton. Of these two, we know a little more of Sabina. She was a former apostate nun who evidently held office of some kind, from which she was removed in 1318. Sabina went on to be prioress, but resigned by 26 March 1328.[39] Joan of Barton and Joan of Tocketts were dispatched to Nun Appleton. Joan of Barton subsequently became prioress but resigned in 1325 because of incontinence with a chaplain.[40] Joan of Tocketts was also later elected prioress, in 1328, and had died by 1331.[41] Agnes of Ampleforth and Agnes Jarkesmill went to Nunkeeling. Joan of Brotherton, on whom penance had been imposed in 1322 for twice being apostate, was sent to Hampole.[42] So of our eight nuns dispersed temporarily to other nunneries in 1322, four held the office of prioress within twenty years.

It would be easy to disparage this small and clearly unhappy community. But this was a desperate time for the nuns, who suffered poverty, and physical damage done to the priory buildings by the Scots. The enormity of what they went through is revealed in the actions of Archbishop Melton, who sent consecrated water to the rural dean of Bulmer and ordered him to cleanse the conventual buildings and the church of Moxby which had been polluted by the shedding of blood. He was to pay particular attention to the cleansing of the stalls of the nuns.[43] It is small wonder that the community was demoralised and lacking in leadership.

---

[35] *Reg. Giffard*, p. 50; *Reg. Corbridge*, I, 196; *HRH*, II, 594.
[36] *Reg. Melton*, II, 84.
[37] Ibid., pp. 88–9.
[38] Ibid., p. 84.
[39] Ibid., 14, 130
[40] Ibid., p. 105
[41] Ibid., p. 126.
[42] Ibid., pp. 75–6.
[43] Ibid., p. 86.

Let us stay with prioresses for a moment. I have already mentioned that archbishops' registers can contain lists of nuns who elected a prioress, so what of the
prioresses themselves, what can we know of them? We may have notice of their
election, and more detail on the seemingly frequent occasions on which they
resigned or where their appointment was accompanied by discord.[44] We may, if
we are fortunate, know the position they held when they were elected, if there
were special circumstances surrounding their election or appointment, if they
were chosen from within the convent or from outside. Cecily Conyers was the
illegitimate daughter of a married man and a single woman, and in 1474 she
received dispensation to hold the office of prioress of Ellerton in Swaledale. The
will of Christopher Conyers, of the family of Conyers of Hornby, made in 1483,
reveals Cecily to have been his sister.[45] The unnamed prioress of Hampole,
forced to resign in 1313 because she had disobeyed the order of the archbishop
concerning recruitment was one Constance de Cressy, who was daughter of
a local knight, Sir William de Cressy and sister of Sir Hugh. Mary de Ros,
prioress of Rosedale, was the daughter of Sir William Ros of Ingmanthorpe
– something we know because the archbishop gave her licence to visit him in
his sickness.[46]

The York registers reveal that the late thirteenth and the early fourteenth
centuries saw many disputed elections in the Yorkshire nunneries, and what
appears to be an increased inclination on the part of the archbishops of York
to intervene in nunnery affairs, intervention that was not always sought or
welcomed. I have discussed this evidence elsewhere, but I think it is useful to
recall it here as well, for the light it sheds in the composition of the community.[47] Keldholme had a particularly fraught few years beginning around the turn
of the century. Emma of Stapleton was elected prioress in 1294 and resigned in
1301. We hear of no prioress until 1309, when the archbishop appointed
Emma of York, a nun of the priory, after a vacancy. She resigned three months
later, a visitation having discovered the priory to be in a bad state. The archbishop then parachuted in Joan of Pickering, a nun of nearby Rosedale, but
this was far from being a safe seat. Six nuns refused to accept her appointment:
Isabella of Langtoft, Joan de Roseles, Amabilla of Lockton, Mary of Holme,
Orphania of Newton, and Beatrice of Roston. The troublemaking nuns were
dispersed to other houses: Handale, Swine, Wallingwells, and Nun Appleton, a
penance frequently used by the archbishop and sometimes resisted by the host
nunnery.[48]

The records of elections and their aftermath also reveal the close connections

[44] For some of these issues see Janet Burton, 'Cloistered Women and Male Authority: Power
and Authority in Yorkshire Nunneries in the Later Middle Ages', in *Thirteenth Century
England X*, ed. Michael Prestwich, Richard Britnell and Robin Frame (Woodbridge,
2005), pp. 155–65.

[45] *Test. Ebor.*, III, 287–93.

[46] *Reg. Greenfield*, III, 12–13; *HRH*, II, 601–2.

[47] Burton, 'Cloistered Women', pp. 160–2.

[48] *Reg. Greenfield*, III, 21.

between nunneries and their patrons. At Nunkeeling Avice de la More, subprioress, was elected prioress in 1304. She ruled until 1316, when she resigned, and she was given an allowance. She was to have a chamber to herself, a nun as a companion, and the portion of two nuns. Two years later (1318) she was warned about her 'conspiracies and disobedience'. Severe penance was laid on her, and a commission was set up to enquire into the state of the nunnery. Enter the figure of Isabella of St Quintin, doubtless a descendant of Alice of St Quintin, founder of the nunnery, whose family still held the patronage of the priory. In 1310 Isabella was suspected of incontinence and incest with two monks of Meaux; she was deprived of the office of cellaress, and the nuns were ordered to allow her to hold no further position of responsibility. Nevertheless the dean and chapter appointed her prioress on 20 August 1316, in succession to Avice de la More.[49] Could Isabella's elevation explain the 'conspiracies' and 'disobedience' of the former prioress? It is impossible to say, but there are parallels in other nunneries where the nuns (and sometimes former prioresses) resisted outside appointments, and where the close connection between a prioress and patron could be a cause for concern.

From the thirteenth century onwards the registers of the archbishops of York are perhaps the fullest source for identifying medieval nuns and prioresses. Another happy hunting ground is provided by wills. Wills can again give us some idea of from where recruits were drawn and their links with local families. In 1393 Sir John Fairfax, rector of Preston, bequeathed to his sister Margaret, prioress of Nun Monkton, several legacies of cups, mazers, spoons, a cloak trimmed with fur, and a basin.[50] His will reveals that Margaret's sister, Eleanor, was also a nun at Nun Monkton and that two other sisters were nuns of Sempringham: four sisters of one family had entered religion. The wills of several people from York demonstrate a connection with the priory of St Clement there. Roger de Moreton, a mercer, left four silver marks to his daughter, Isabella, a nun of St Clement's in order to buy black cloth, and one mark to his sister, Helen, who was also a nun of St Clements: aunt and niece were nuns in the same house. Not that the convent secured Roger's full devotion, for he also left legacies in the form of wax to Rosedale and Keldholme.[51]

Sometimes the evidence is ambiguous. Robert de Playce, rector of Brompton, left money for his niece to become a nun at Wykeham, Yedingham or Nun Monkton, so we do not know if she joined her aunt, Emota, a nun of Monkton, or was received into one of the other two convents.[52] And we would surely like to know if Joan and Katherine, the two daughters of Robert de Ros of Ingmanthorp, who made his will in 1392, and who are simply described as nuns, were indeed nuns of Rosedale as Mary de Ros was in 1310.[53] Agnes de Percehay, widow of Walter, who made her will in 1348, desired to be buried at the Gilber-

[49] Ibid., III, 187–8, V, 267–9.
[50] *Test. Ebor.*, I, 186–90.
[51] Ibid., pp. 133–4.
[52] Ibid., pp. 9–12.
[53] Ibid., pp. 178–80; see above, note 46.

tine priory of Malton next to her husband, and *inter alia* she left legacies to her daughter (unnamed) the prioress of Yedingham, and another daughter, Agnes, a nun of Watton.[54] In 1391 Agnes was also a beneficiary of the will of Agnes of Lockton, a member of the Percehay family.[55] In 1404 the will of Walter Skirlaw, bishop of Durham, left goods to his sister, Joan, who was prioress of Swine, and who was witness to his death bed codicil.[56]

This is not an exhaustive picture of the sources for study of Yorkshire nuns. Among others are the records of court cases, one of which, centring on claims to inheritance, has been studied extensively by Claire Cross.[57] Cause papers, that is, the working papers of court cases heard in the consistory court of York, have great potential. Nuns may appear as witnesses, and their depositions may give their ages and their 'nun years'. A prioress might also be a party to a case. One such was Ivetta, prioress of Handale who was mugged on her way to sort out a dispute over common pasture.[58] From the depositions we can build up a picture of some aspects of her career. Two nuns of the small nunnery of Thicket in 1441 appear as witnesses to the alleged demand, made in their priory church, by the prior and canons of Ellerton that the nuns pay tithes on the produce of certain lands. They were Alice Hadilsay, then aged over forty, and Margaret Broughton, aged forty-nine.[59] The archives of individual houses, scanty though they are, may help to construct a picture of the community. I am thinking here of the obedientiaries of Marrick who appear in the account rolls edited by John Tillotson. There we encounter in 1415–16 Agnes Gower, sacrist, Cecily de Blaykston, bursar, and Agnes of Wensley, granger. In 1435 we meet Agnes Wensley, Joan Colvell, and Joan Blaxton as beneficiaries in 1435 of the wills of Petronilla, wife of Richard Russell of York, and of her husband.[60]

To say that houses of female religious are poorly documented and 'had no history'[61] is clearly to overstate the case and this paper has demonstrated that the records have much to reveal. We have, as always, to remember the limita-

---

54   Ibid., pp. 53–4.
55   Ibid., pp. 165–6.
56   Ibid., pp. 306–25.
57   The case is that of Elizabeth Lutton, nun of Yedingham, which was heard in the Star Chamber between 1531 and 1533. See Claire Cross and Noreen Vickers, eds, *Monks, Friars and Nuns in Sixteenth-century Yorkshire*, YASRS, 150 (1995), pp. 550–1, and Claire Cross, *The End of Medieval Monasticism in the East Riding of Yorkshire* (East Yorkshire Local History Soc., 1993), pp. 15–17; F. Donald Logan, *Runaway Religious in Medieval England c. 1240–1540* (Cambridge, 1996), pp. 89–96.
58   BI, CP E.3, discussed in Janet Burton, 'The Convent and the Community: Cause Papers as a Source for Monastic History', in *The Foundations of Medieval English Ecclesiastical History: Studies presented to David Smith*, ed. Philippa Hoskin, Christopher Brooke and Barrie Dobson (Woodbridge, 2005), pp. 63–76 (pp. 71–2).
59   BI, CP F.221, discussed in Burton, 'Convent and Community', pp. 65–6, 69–70.
60   *Test. Ebor.*, I, 52–7.
61   This uses a phrase employed by Sally Thompson, 'Why English Nunneries had No History. A Study of the Problems of English Nunneries Founded after the Conquest', in *Distant Echoes: Medieval Religious Women*, I, ed. J. A. Nichols and L. T. Shank (Kalamazoo: Cistercian Publications, 1984), pp. 131–49.

tions of those sources. Elections are likely to be recorded when there was a dispute, and when communities appear as a result to be divided and divisive. Visitation returns note not the good but the bad and the ugly. We hear of pregnant nuns, apostate nuns, quarrelsome nuns, disobedient nuns, not those who lived out their careers in the quiet, devout and relentless round of prayer, reading and work. But something of the environment in which they lived – their buildings, their organisation, their books – does emerge from the records, and we have a glimpse of those institutions – and women – who held a lasting place in northern society for so long.

9

'Quhat say ye now, my lady priores? How have ye usit your office, can ye ges?'[1]

Politics, Power and Realities of the Office of a Prioress in her Community in Late Medieval Scotland

KIMM PERKINS-CURRAN

Historians have claimed that Scottish female religious houses and their inhabitants are not worthy of study. Traditionally the reasons they have given are the paucity of the sources about convents and nuns, the smallness of the houses themselves, the lack of importance that convents had in the locale, and the claim that female houses are simply 'too different' from male houses and therefore prove problematic in any study of medieval monasticism. Because of these assumptions, little work has been done on any aspect of female religious houses and nothing at all on female heads of houses. Indeed, Scottish historians have shied away from any discussion of medieval heads of houses, male or female: the publication *Heads of Religious Houses in Scotland* is concerned merely with the identification of abbots, priors and prioresses, with little further discussion.[2] In fact, very little has been done on heads of religious houses for the later medieval period in Britain or on the Continent.[3] Studies of female heads tend to focus on the early or central Middle Ages, when an abbess or prioress appears to have exercised a considerable degree of influence in her secular and religious community; these women were often of a particular rank, such as daughters of kings or members of the higher nobility, which allowed them to exercise authority and obtain a degree of independence.[4] When we move to the later Middle Ages,

---

[1] The quotation comes from Sir David Lindsay, *Ane Satyre of the Thrie Estaitis* (Edinburgh, 1989), p. 123, lines 3449–50.

[2] D. E. Watt and N. Shead, eds, *The Heads of Religious Houses in Scotland from the Twelfth to the Sixteenth Centuries*, Scottish Record Society (2001).

[3] However, see the paper by Martin Heale in this volume, above, pp. 51–68.

[4] See, for instance, Barbara Yorke, *Nunneries and the Anglo-Saxon Royal Houses* (London, 2003), p. 174; Sarah Foot, *Veiled Women, I: The Disappearance of Nuns from Anglo-Saxon England* (Aldershot, 2000), pp. 44–5.

however, what studies we do have of abbesses and prioresses tend to argue for a shift from their earlier positions of power, authority and influence. The confident picture of the influential role of female superiors begins to change, and we find female heads of houses being heavily criticised for their behaviour and their failures. The main focus of this paper is on the role of the prioress in a Scottish context, and on her active involvement in her communities, both secular and religious. This essay demonstrates that in the later Middle Ages Scottish prioresses were important because they played key roles within both their secular and religious communities. Often, it was the prioress who main-tained and forged valuable relationships with the outside world and balanced the needs of her nuns and convents with those of local communities.

Responsibilities and duties outside the cloister

A prioress had many duties to perform in order protect those in her care and her convent; these required her to be involved in the secular world. Female heads of religious houses could not sever their ties to the secular world, even if the Rule required them to do so and we find that these women were members of two separate but equally important 'familia': one religious and one secular. Patrons and founders were involved in monastic affairs, such as elections, and family interests may often have influenced many decisions that a superior had to make. The Rule does not specifically advise a superior on what role they were to have in the outside world or how to deal with family matters.[5] The superior had to make those decisions with the help from her obedientiaries and male officers. However, 'the success or failure of an individual house in filling its spiritual and temporal obligations depended on the leadership of the abbesses or prioress'.[6]

In her role as head of house, a prioress was an example to all those around her. Because she had 'lordship' over the lands of the convent she would have enjoyed the same prestige as any local lord or landowner in the area and been able to conduct her business with relatively little opposition from those in the secular world.[7] Often the prioress was well known already, as many heads of houses came from the local area or from influential local families. Local society would have accepted her because of her 'name' but also because of the 'authority' she had been given in her office. '[By] controlling the goods and powers of [her] community. ... [she] had considerable political power' locally and would have

---

5   RSB, chapter 54, addresses the question of letters or gifts to the monks from their family and how the superior had the authority and power to give the gifts or letters 'to whom he will'.

6   John Nichols, 'The Internal Organization of English Cistercian Nunneries', Cîteaux: Commentaria Cistercienses 30 (1979), 23–40 (p. 40).

7   As 'lord' over the land of their convents, prioresses swore fealty to Edward I in 1291 and 1296.

been a person of great importance and influence.[8] Whilst the abbess or prioress may have appeared to be acting in response to patron or family requests in some cases, it was often her governance and the network of connections to the outside world which allowed for the success of a convent – severing those ties would be detrimental to their survival, especially in difficult circumstances. Jo Ann McNamara states that 'abbesses were not simply slaves to family loyalties … [as] they played a power game with everyone else, relentlessly seeking the survival and enhancement of their communities'.[9]

Manager of monastic estates

In Scotland the leasing or granting in feu of church lands in the later Middle Ages was a common practice by many monastic houses and J. N. Hare has suggested, this 'management of [convent] estates reveals initiative and investment' on the part of the head of house and her convent.[10] As a local landowner the superior of a convent was in charge of collecting rents from lands as well as leasing lands in order to execute administrative tasks.[11] It was she who bore the burden of all the convent's costs and it was up to her to find revenue. There were many reasons for the leasing or granting of church lands but for the most part alienation was used for the financial gain of the convent. Many tacks or feu charters in Scotland indicate that land was granted to individuals because they helped provide money or goods for the maintenance and upkeep of monastic estates, to carry out repairs to ecclesiastical buildings or to pay taxes owed. But money from the rental and feu duty was also generated for general upkeep and to meet the food requirements of the convent.

As the Dissolution of the monasteries was taking place in England, King James V, rather than dissolve monasteries, began taxing the church. He requested a certain amount to be paid every year to go towards building his College of Justice and to also fund other rebuilding efforts such as the palaces at Linlithgow and Holyrood.[12] Evidence of the tax paid from Scottish convents can be found in the Accounts of the Master of the Works: the priory of Manuel paid £42 in 1541.[13] There was evidence that this particular tax created a burden on some female religious houses and some of them were unable to pay. In 1547

8   Jo Ann McNamara, *Sisters in Arms: Catholic Nuns through Two Millennia* (Harvard, 1996), p. 279.

9   Ibid., p. 226.

10   J. N. Hare, 'The Monks as Landlords: the Leasing of Monastic Demesne in Southern England', in *The Church in Pre-Reformation Society: Essays in Honour of F. R. H. Du Boulay*, ed. Caroline M. Barron and Christopher Harper-Bill (Woodbridge, 1985), pp. 82–94 (p. 94).

11   Nichols, 'Organization', p. 30.

12   W. Stanford Reid, 'Clerical Taxation: the Scottish Alternative to Dissolution of the Monasteries, 1530–1560', *Catholic Historical Review* 45 (1948), 129–53.

13   F. and W. Moncrieffe, eds, *Accounts of the Master of Works* (Edinburgh, 1929) [afterwards *MW*], p. 267.

the priory of Manuel was behind in its payment of the tax and was cautioned to pay £6 to the College of Justice.[14] In 1531, payments of taxes increased further when Pope Clement VII imposed a tax of three teinds: this became known as the 'Great Tax'.[15] In some feu charters, we have an indication that these taxes were difficult for female religious houses to pay: members of local society assisted them in making their payments and in return the prioress gave them land in feu. For example, John Carmichael and his wife Mariota Richardson were granted in feu-farm the land of Atherny by Isobella Hume, the prioress of North Berwick in 1536 for 'sums of money given' to the convent.[16] While the charter does not specifically state that the money was used to pay taxes it is not difficult to assume that these sums could have been used for this purpose.

With most of the money coming from goods in kind or from rents, many prioresses started feuing or granting land in tack to family, kin or members of local society in order to realize needed revenue or free the convent from the burdens of the labour of working the land. A prioress initiated the exchange for either a set number of years, in the case of a tack, or issued a feu charter that would grant land to a person on a heritable basis with consent of her convent and would usually call her sisters into council. In almost every feu charter or tack, the prioress was present with a notary, along with members of her convent and several witnesses. For example in 1552 Margaret Hume, prioress of North Berwick, granted in tack to Andrew Wood of Largo and his heirs the teindsheives of Largo, Balcormo and Stratherlie in the parish of Largo with rights to salmon fishing on the water of Leven for nineteen years and he was to pay the convent £48 for the teindsheives of the land and £13 for the salmon each year. The witnesses to the deed were George Hepburn, the son of the prioress's sister, John Whitehill, Alexander Gibson, Thomas Planamorche, Thomas Young, servant, John Whitehill, servant, Sir Alexander Romans, Sir Alexander Paterson, chaplains and Sir Robert Lauder, notary public. There was no evidence to suggest that her male support officers (bailie or servants) were instructing her to give particular lands to individuals or that her hand was forced, as the chaplains and servants of the priory were witnesses and not listed in the main body of the charter.[17] However, being a witness was not necessarily a passive act and these individuals may have been asked specifically by the

---

14 R. K. Hannay, ed., *The Acts of the Lords of Council in Public Affairs, 1501–1554* (Edinburgh, 1839), pp. 541, 563; see also National Archives of Scotland [NAS], Beveridge Papers, GD 215/1870, p. 2.

15 The tax of was to be paid each year for three years to help restore depleted revenues of the Crown: see R. K. Hannay, *The College of Justice: Essays by R.K. Hannay*, Stair Society (1990), pp. ix–x; MW, pp. xiii–xv.

16 J. M. Thomson et al., eds, *Registrum Magni Sigilli Regum Scottorum* (Edinburgh, 1882–1914) [afterwards RMS], IV, no. 2659.

17 National Register of Archives Scotland [NRAS] 3215, Writs of Largo, Bundle 3/2. In each consecutive confirmation of this particular lease there were different witnesses but the prioress was still acting on behalf of her convent. Convent seals were attached and members of the convent were present. No bailies were listed as witnesses. See NRAS 3215, Writs of Largo, Bundle 3/7, 8, 15; NRAS 3215, Writs of Largo, Bundle 5/5.

prioress to witness the deed. What should also be noted is that certain individuals, like chaplains or servants, may have had vested interests in conventual affairs and would be present to ensure the transaction was handled properly.

Another reason that a prioress would feu or lease land was to settle a debt. This might occur when members of her family or local families lent money or supplies to help in the rebuilding efforts of their local convents, especially after devastation. It was the responsibility of the prioress to make sure that accounts were in order; moreover, the heavy burden of having to pay off loans of money or supplies could eventually lead to further financial problems for the convent. For example, in 1540, Euphemia Leslie the prioress of Elcho, granted in feu to Alexander Dundas of Fingask and his wife Elizabeth Bruce the land of Cottis near Perth in return for his payment of 300 marks given for the reparation of the convent.[18] It is not clear from the feu charter what repairs the convent needed but we can assume that at the time it was in need of some repairs and that the prioress initiated rebuilding efforts. In 1559 for providing sums of money to help repair the convent after the destruction by the English army, the prioress of Abbey St Bathans feued to Robert Sleigh two acres of arable land near the village of Duns in return for an annual payment of 6s 8d to be paid by Robert or George Sleigh, his father.[19] In 1568, Alexander Carrick, burgess of North Berwick, received in feu from Margaret II, prioress of North Berwick, land on the north part of the Mains of North Berwick that Andrew Wood had once occupied and the land of Thomas Pantone on the west to show the convent's gratitude after he had given them a certain sum of money.[20] Alexander Carrick may be related to a burgess of North Berwick, Thomas Carrick, who once held lands of North Berwick Mains from the prioress.[21] The Carrick connection may also come from an earlier relationship that was established between the prioress, Elene Carrick, who may or may not be related to these burgesses.

Despite the favour being shown to particular family members or kin, feuing land could also be seen as management tactic by prioresses in order to keep monastic lands in the hands of laymen, rather than having the lands and rents revert to the Crown after the Reformation Parliament of 1560. Prioresses exercised good estate management and granting lands in feu must be looked at more carefully to determine whether or not such grants were really made with the consideration of family interests or in the interests of the convent.

Receiving feu duties or rents from newly leased lands provided the much-needed cash for paying taxes or for the general upkeep of the conventual household. In some cases the leases or feu charters stipulated that along with an annual feu duty, the grantee must also pay the convent with goods and kind, usually multures from mills. As a household manager, the prioress had to ensure that the goods in kind were delivered to supply food to her sisters, other members of the household and to the boarders of the convent. For example

---

[18] *RMS*, IV, no. 2746.
[19] *RMS*, IV, no. 1614.
[20] *RMS*, IV, no. 1612.
[21] NAS, Burgh of North Berwick, B56, fol. cccxxxi(v).

in 1547 the prioress of Manuel, Jonet Livingstone, granted in tack to 'our well-belovit' Henry Forrest and his wife Catherine Livingstone portions of the convent's corn mills and little mills: the payment annually was 30 bolls of oatmeal and 2 merks money.[22] In 1551 the prioress of Haddington granted in tack to John [Fl]oorhouse three acres of arable land in the Nungate for nineteen years for an annual payment of £4 yearly and a capon for each acre.[23] As seen above, Euphemia Leslie granted land to Alexander Dundas and his wife Elizabeth Bruce for their assistance; their feu duty was an annual rent of 20 marks, forty-eight chickens, thirty-six days' plough-service and thirty-six days' work for the harvest in autumn.[24]

The leasing of lands in tack or granting in feu by the prioresses to her family, kin or members of local society raises an interesting question regarding the management of monastic lands. From the examples above it appears that the prioress used both methods of lease and feu in order to provide for the needs of her convent. Members of local society, in particular, seem to be shown the most favour by the prioress and were granted lands in feu, especially when sums of money were provided for the repairs of the convent after devastation or to pay financial burdens, like taxes. This relationship between the convent and local society should not be taken for granted as they 'shared common geographical environments and influences ... estate administration was just [one] part of this relationship'.[25] The proficiency of estate management practised by the prioress in her use of both tacks and feus, indicates that there was a desire by the prioress to retain control over the assets of the convent and that she balanced the needs of the convent as well as see the needs of her family or kin.

Appointment of lay officers

Part of a prioress's role was to appoint officials, such as obedientiaries, servants or bailies for the convent, to ensure a smooth running of convent affairs. A bailie was not just any lay person, but one with sufficient power and prestige to exercise authority.[26] He was usually a local lord or a member of a prominent family in the area, often related to the head of house either directly or by marriage. Cowan has argued that these lay appointments may have furthered family interests and allowed for a particular family to acquire monastic assets.[27] On the other hand, Dilworth has suggested that when the bailie and head of house were from the same family or kin group the administration of the house

[22] NAS, Beveridge Papers, GD 215/1870, p. 17; the deed states 'feu-ferme letting' for nineteen years.

[23] NAS, Misc. Documents, GD 1/39/4/8. The carriage for the measuring of victuals which came from Fife was also listed as part of the payment.

[24] RMS, III, no. 2746.

[25] Hare, 'Monks as Landlords', p. 62.

[26] Mark Dilworth, Scottish Monasteries in the Late Middle Ages (Edinburgh, 1995), p. 47.

[27] Ian B. Cowan, The Scottish Reformation: Church and Society in Sixteenth-century Scotland (London, 1982), p. 29.

ran quite smoothly; if they were from different families or local rivals it was the cause of strife both for the head of house and for the convent.[28] What will become evident is that the prioress often chose her lay administrators carefully on the bases of who could provide the most protection, who had the most influence and who could best serve the needs of the convent. These may or may not have been members of her family.

Instances where such lay administrators were not from the same family as the head of house can be found at Coldstream and Eccles. In 1522 the prioress of Eccles had confirmed that the house's bailie was Alexander Home, father of George Home. His lands and titles, however, were forfeited to James V for treason and the king then presented George Home to the prioress so that he might receive and be given the office of heritable bailie of the convent.[29] In 1531 Eccles Priory had Robert Dickson of Hassington Mains as their bailie. The Dicksons were not as prominent as the Homes but they still were lesser lairds in the region and female members of this family can be found in the convent at the same time.[30] Despite this short break with the heritable office by the Homes in the 1530s, the Homes managed to gain back their position by 1569 when Alexander Home was listed as their bailie and supporter of his cousin Elizabeth Home for the office of prioress.[31]

In 1551, Jonet Hoppringle, prioress of Coldstream, with consent from her convent,

> undirstanding that it is verray necessar for the common weill and proffeit of the said abbey and convent, and of thair tennentis inhabitantis of all and sindrie the landis annexit to the said abbey, liand within [whatsoever] schirefdome, to have ane baillie that will accept the cuir and gyding of the saidis inhabitantis and ministration of justice upon thame baith in times of pece and weir; and becaus the saidis priores eftir the ripe advisement and lang deliberatioun fyndis na man mair abill, ganand nor convenient to exercise the office of bailliarie …[32]

granted the office to their well-beloved and trusted friend, Alexander, Lord Home. The Homes were considered to be one of the most prominent lords in the region and could be called upon for assistance in times of crisis or need.

Tom Graham has suggested that the Home family attaining of these offices was in reality an indication of how they could assert their power in the region

---

[28] Dilworth, *Scottish Monasteries*, p. 47.

[29] HMC, *12th Report*, appendix, p. 130.

[30] Maureen Meikle, *A British Frontier: Lairds and Gentlemen on the Eastern Borders, 1540–1603* (East Linton, 2004), p. 59; John Home was listed as their bailie prior to 1531: T. Maley et al., eds, *Selkirk Protocol Books, 1511–47*, Stair Society (1993), p. 80.

[31] HMC, *12th Report*, appendix, p. 137. Elcho elected Laurence Oliphant to the office of bailie in 1470 and this does not seem to have caused any problems for the convent. See J. Anderson, *The Oliphants in Scotland* (Edinburgh, 1879), no. 28.

[32] *RMS*, IV, no. 1709; see also NAS, Abbreviates of Feu Charters of Kirklands, E14/1, fol. 121v.

and gain control of monasteries.[33] Later a female Home did become head of house at Eccles – although contested – and at Abbey St Bathans. However, these appointments of bailies may indicate that prioresses and their convents were careful in their selection of these monastic officers and may have rewarded certain families for faithful services already rendered to a convent in time of need.[34] For example, at the convent of Elcho Sir John Wemyss their neighbouring laird came to their assistance after the 1547 invasion by the earl of Hertford that left the priory considerably damaged. After providing barley and money to help the needs of the convent and with repairs to their church and other buildings, he was appointed as their hereditary bailie and he continued to look after their affairs until 1572.[35] We cannot assume that there was always a direct relationship between a prioress and male officials as the prioress and convent may have chosen someone who would be able to assist them more fully – these were sensible political moves on their part. Contrary to Dilworth's assumption, there was no indication that there was any 'strife' caused by these appointments and we can assume that at the convent it was business as usual.

Protector of conventual assets

In times of crisis the convent and prioress might ask for assistance from their male officers in seeking reparation for damages done to monastic property, as it was her role to maintain the convent's assets. For example, Walter master of Coldstream (on the request of the prioress) wrote to Edward I in 1296 seeking reparation for damages done by the English army while they were encamped at Coldstream. The damage to the convent and monastic property was quite extensive and if reparation was not made the convent may not have survived the loss. The prioress was also in charge of making sure that not only were assets protected but also that the records of those assets were kept safe and in order and also, that the conventual seal was preserved. In 1434 John Lawrence, by apostolic authority, attested that Mariota Blackburn, 'a venerable and religious lady and prioress of Coldstream', gathered with her sisters in chapter and produced all of their charters, evidents, muniments, grants and confirmations. Partly because of the age of the documents but also in fear of English invasion, 'accidents like fire or flood, there was a danger that the truth of the original might parish' so she asked Lawrence to copy all the documents from the charter

33 T. W. Graham, 'Patronage, Provision and Reservation: Scotland and the Papacy during the Pontificate of Paul III' (unpublished Ph.D. thesis, University of Glasgow, 1992), p. 82.
34 Dickson served as a servant of Eccles in 1529 during the election of Christina Macdowell; Home was thanked for his service done to the convent, presumably after the devastation by the English army in 1547.
35 W. Fraser, Memorials of the Family of Wemyss of Wemmys, 3 vols (Edinburgh, 1888), II, nos 119, 120, 124; see also Perthshire Society of Natural Science, Pittmiddle Village and Elcho Nunnery: Research and Excavation on Tayside (Perth, 1988), p. 53.

chest.[36] In 1548, Margaret Hume of North Berwick detailed to the burgesses and notary public of North Berwick that an 'unknown person' had stolen the seal of the convent as well as many 'writings and discharges that were of great loss to the monastery'.[37] The convent eventually recovered its seal and documents with the help of the prioress's family after she lodged the complaint. The decision of Mariota, prioress of Coldstream, to save the documents of the priory should be emphasised. For Scotland there are no other surviving cartularies for Scottish female houses and the survival of the one at Coldstream, albeit incomplete, was down to the decisions made by the prioress. The conventual seal of North Berwick as well as many sixteenth-century documents of the convent also survived and it is to the credit of the prioress, Margaret and the influence of her family, that we have them today.[38]

Making sure that the assets of the convent such as commodities, lands, documents and chapter seals were protected inevitably meant that the prioress and convent would run into difficulties with the surrounding community. Many neighbours and even patrons encroached upon the rights of the convent in patronage of churches or even access to fishing or lands. Sometimes those who interfered with the rights or property of the convent were taken to court. Between 1518 and 1520 we find litigation between the convent of North Berwick, its prioress, Alison, and a certain William Ranton. She appeared in the episcopal court of St Andrews as the plaintiff against Ranton. We have no clear indication as to why she was in court since the case does not go into detail but we do know that the court ruled in her favour because of documentation she was able to provide.[39] In 1532 the prioress of Elcho, Euphemia Leslie, was in dispute with the burgesses of Perth regarding the fishing of certain parts of the River Tay.[40] In the same year, the prioress of Eccles was in dispute with William Brownfield regarding free passage over certain nunnery lands.[41] In April 1546 James Cockburn of Langton admitted that he had offended Dame Elizabeth, prioress of Haddington, and her convent by taking corn, cattle and goods from the land of Begbie and others; he was summoned to appear in court for his theft along with Elizabeth or her advocate.[42] And in 1551 there was a case between Janet Hoppringle against Andrew Ker of Hirsel, knight, and Walter Ker, his

[36] *Chartulary of the Cistercian Priory of Coldstream*, Grampian Club (1897), p. 74.

[37] NAS, Humes of Marchmount, GD 158/254; see also HMC, *14th Report*, iii, 72–3.

[38] Other conventual seals still survive from Eccles, Abbey St Bathans, Coldstream, Haddington, Sciennes and Manuel. See H. Laing, *Descriptive Catalogue of Impressions from Ancient Scottish Seals*, I, Bannatyne and Maitland Clubs (1850) and II (Edinburgh, 1866).

[39] T. Thomson, ed., *Liber Cartarum Prioratus Sancti Andree in Scotia*, Bannatyne Club (1841), no. 5.

[40] NAS, Court of Session Registers (Acts of the Lords of Council until 1535), CS6/1, fol. 54r. I am grateful to Elizabeth Ewan for pointing out the Court of Session Registers and the information they provide.

[41] NAS, Court of Session Registers, CS6/1, fols 27–28v.

[42] *The Acts of the Lords in Council in Public Affairs, 1501–1554*, ed. R. K. Hannay (Edinburgh, 1932) [afterwards *ADCP*], p. 545.

son, regarding the lands of Coldstream, Auldfinsall, Myrton and Teretoun and their troubling of the nuns and the prioress with their encroachment onto these lands.[43]

In most cases the prioresses appeared personally to plead their case for their convents but sometimes – as 'spiritual ladies' – they were not required. For instance, in 1532 the prioress of Eccles, Dame Christina Macdowell, notified the Lords of Council that she should not have been summoned before the sheriff in Stirling by a chaplain regarding a pension from the fruits of their parish church of Bothkennar as she was a 'spiritual woman' and letters were directed to a 'temporal judge' when she should have been called before a spiritual court.[44] Other times they would send someone in their place, such as their bailie or other official like a notary to plead their case in temporal courts. For instance, in 1549 Alexander Oliphant of Kelly 'invaded' the priory lands of Grange in Fife[45] belonging to North Berwick and 'besetting the way to the said prioress and her servants for their slaughter; and besieging them within the mansion house of the said lands'.[46] Alexander Hume of North Berwick and Alexander Wood, vicar of North Berwick, appeared for her in the court of the official at Edinburgh and pleaded the priory's case. In July 1501 we find David Balfour, procurator for the convent of Haddington in court for the prioress, Jonet, regarding the dispute between the convent and the Lord of Bass and the lands of Garvald that belonged to the nuns.[47] Later, John Hepburn, prior of St Andrews, was in court representing the prioress and claiming that 'this action between them and the Lord of Bass while it was a spiritual action ... should not hurt the church'.[48]

Diplomat or spy?

In order for the convent to survive difficult situations, a prioress might become involved in the worldly affairs of politics and support important figures, such as kings or queens. The prioresses of Coldstream, Abbey St Bathans and Eccles were involved in spying either for the English or the Scottish during the later part of the sixteenth century. Isabella Hoppringle, prioress of Coldstream, was noted as being a good spy for the English during the sixteenth century and 'congenial companion' to Margaret, James IV's queen and sister to Henry VIII of England. In 1515, the Regent Albany was pursuing Margaret (the Queen Mother) in the Borders and she sought refuge at the priory of Coldstream where she found the convent hospitable and the prioress, Isabella Hoppringle, to be

---

43 NAS, Misc. Eccl. Records, CH 8/11.

44 ADCP, p. 317.

45 This is possibly the grange of Elie that was held by the convent, see Derek Hall, *A Loop in the Forth is Worth an Earldom in the North: Monastic Granges of Scotland* (Perth, 2003), p. 18.

46 R. Pitcairn, ed., *Criminal Trials in Scotland from 1488 to 1627* (Edinburgh, 1833), I.i, 347.

47 ADCP, nos 203, 233, 243.

48 ADCP, no. 324.

an intelligent woman.[49] Margaret became the convent's patroness and protector and Isabella could rely on her to keep her priory safe from the English and Scottish armies.

We have letters detailing some of the prioress's spying activities in the 1520s, and in September 1523 an agent of Henry VIII, John Bulmer, received a letter from the prioress claiming that the 'lords are fallen from the queen and adhere to the governor'.[50] The prioress continued to write to the agent of Henry VIII, as a messenger of the queen and throughout the month of October she sent information regarding the intentions of the Scottish and French armies and the movements of the queen and Lords of Council.[51] Bulmer wrote to Surrey that the prioress had told him that the queen had been at Dumbarton, Glasgow and Stirling for eight days and seen the Lord Governor of Scotland's army and claimed that the queen 'never saw anything so great'. The prioress sent him a detailed list of the supplies of the French and where the army might muster and advised the English to 'put all things by the gate.'[52] The prioress of Eccles was also forthcoming with information regarding the Scottish and French army and had a 'friend' who promised to give warning to the English which direction the army would be heading.[53]

On 13 October, a kinsman of the prioress wrote to her stating that the Lords of Council had ordered Scots not to speak to any Englishman on the pain of death and that the Lords were 'evil contented at her' but he does not know why.[54] It is possible that the Lords of Council had discovered her spying activities and feared that she would continue to side with the English: 'They say in this town that the Prioress is an Englishwoman, as she was before.'[55] He begged the prioress to 'thresh out all the corn and put away the gear of the place' for fear of attack. Sometime later, however, possibly when the prioress found out that Albany was going to march south, she wavered in her attachment to the English and sided with Albany – for her own protection and the protection of her house.

Surrey met with the prioress on 4 November, and noted that she still gave good information but heard of her defection and threatened to burn her house.[56] In a desperate plea to save her friend's convent from destruction, the queen mother wrote to Surrey begging him not to burn the house because she was 'beholden to the prioress more than any other of her degree'.[57] She continued to write letters on the same day, desperate for an answer from Surrey regarding

49 Patricia Hill Buchanan, *Margaret Tudor, Queen of Scots* (Edinburgh, 1985), pp. 114–15.
50 *LP Hen. VIII*, III (2), nos 3304–5.
51 Ibid., no. 3404.
52 Ibid.
53 Ibid., no. 3303.
54 A note at the bottom of the reference states that the letter was to the prioress of C from her kinsmen, likely to be her nephew Robert or John of Tynnes who appeared in other letters to Henry VIII's agents in the 1520s.
55 *LP Hen. VIII*, III (2), no. 3426.
56 Ibid., no. 3508.
57 Ibid., no. 3553.

the convent, and asking Surrey to protect the prioress and convent 'so long as she was true' for she is the queen's 'only true messenger'. If Isabella was not 'true', however, then the queen did not hesitate to command Surrey to burn the place. Isabella proved her worth and the queen still continued to be warmly attached to the convent and her son, James V, granted to Coldstream lands held by his mother for their hospitality in receiving ambassadors of England in 1531. Isabella's successor at Coldstream, Janet Hoppringle, continued to help the English cause at least until 1539 but we do not have any more letters regarding her spying activities for the remainder of Henry's reign.[58]

Spying on the English and Scottish armies was not a difficult thing to imagine given the location of each of these convents along the Border. In 1509 James IV made it easier for this activity to occur. He granted a special licence to the priory allowing them to hold communication and buy or sell goods for the reparation of their place with the English and have as many as twelve persons from England on their premises.[59] In 1531, his son confirmed this licence 'as long as the prioress and convent or their tenants and servants do not attempt to own other things that may be prejudice or hurt to us, our realm or lieges'.[60]

As Maureen Meikle has remarked 'the everyday lives [of women of the sixteenth-century Borders] would not have been different to any other women's lot had it not been for the proximity of the international frontier ... which added complexity to the lives of women living on either side'.[61] The spying activities of the prioress of Coldstream were well documented but we also have indications that the prioresses of Eccles and Abbey St Bathans made some overtures to England during the 1520s and 1540s in order to save themselves and their convents. In June 1546 James V granted to Gavin Hume the priory of Abbey St Bathans because the prioress, Elizabeth Lamb, was convicted of 'treasonably favouring' England. Apparently she furnished them with 'weapons and other gear for their defence and invading of the realm [of Scotland]'.[62] Two months later, however, Elizabeth along with the priory's chaplain, Sir Thomas Hudson and William Lamb,[63] were pardoned for all their actions and crimes against the Scots.[64] However much these prioresses did for the English cause,

---

58 LP Hen. VIII, XIV (2), no. 723. The prioress 'hears that there was a man on the king's business that desired to speak to her brother, Robert, but that he was not present. She states that she does not wish herself or her family to appear in the matter for fear of displeasure from the king of Scots. If this were to happen it would be a great hindrance to obtaining further information.'

59 M. Livingstone et al., Registrum Secreti Sigilli Regum Scottorum (Edinburgh, 1908–) [afterwards RSS], I, no. 1865.

60 Ibid., II, no. 1194.

61 Maureen Meikle, 'Victims, Viragos and Vamps: Women of the Sixteenth Century Anglo-Scottish Frontier', in Government, Religion and Society in Northern England, 1100–1700, ed. John C. Appleby and Paul Dalton (Stroud, 1997), pp. 184, 173.

62 RSS, III, no. 1732.

63 In 1554 he was listed as the notary for Elizabeth: NAS Biel Muniments, GD6/81.

64 RSS, III, no. 1836.

it did not prevent their houses from being burned in 1545 alongside other monasteries during the invasion by the earl of Hertford.[65]

Patronage of the Arts and local tradesmen

A prioress could also show support for local tradesmen or artists by commissioning pieces of work. There are three surviving tomb effigies of Scottish prioresses and we have some evidence that one was commissioned by a prioress. The first effigy comes from the convent of Iona of Anna Maclean, daughter of Donald Maclean, who was prioress of Iona and died in c. 1543. Her tomb effigy is one of the best-known examples of West Highland sculpture as well as of prioress effigies in Britain. However, it has rarely been looked at as a significant piece of evidence showing how a prioress exercised her familial and conventual power by commissioning this important piece of work. It also shows a devotion to religious life and the realization that both the religious and secular were intricately entwined with her office.

Anna's effigy has been attributed to the Oronsay School of carvers and it has been remarked that she chose Oronsay because there were no other carvers on Iona for her to choose from and Oronsay was an Augustinian priory like her own.[66] The slab was originally divided in two panels with St Mary on the bottom half and the top half with the image of Anna (Fig. 9.1). She was carved wearing her habit, and in the background there are three turrets, with a looking-glass and comb on the panel. The looking-glass and comb were unusual symbols to be associated with a woman of religion, as they have been found more commonly on slabs of secular noble women. For example, C. Cessford states that on Pictish stones in Scotland mirrors and comb images are more likely to be 'a status qualifier' than anything else.[67] However, these images are present on three Pictish stones associated with women and it could be argued that these images are more symbolic of the feminine. It might also be suggested that the mirror may represent the image Anna had of herself: an image of the Virgin Mary as represented by the mirror image below Anna (Fig. 9.2). The Virgin has the sun and the moon on her panel representing symbols that were associated with her and were in the same placement of the mirror and comb found on Anna's panel. Anna's secular world was represented both by the presence of a comb and mirror but also by the two small dogs – showing

[65] Bodl., MS Top. Yorks. C. 45, fol. 68v. Elizabeth Lamb sided with the English again for the protection of herself, her tenants and servants in 1548. I am grateful to Maureen Meikle for this particular reference to Elizabeth Lamb.

[66] K. A. Steer and J. W. M. Bannerman, *Late Medieval Monumental Sculpture in the West Highlands* (Edinburgh, 1977), p. 70.

[67] C. Cessford, 'The Pictish Mirror Symbol and Archaeological Evidence for Mirrors in Scotland', *Oxford Journal of Archaeology* 16:1 (1997), 99–120. Mermaids were also depicted with mirrors and combs in medieval art and sculpture and these symbols usually were symbols of pride and luxury. I am grateful for the advice offered by Debra Strickland on the images of mirrors and combs in medieval art.

her fondness for her animals –which seems to be quite unusual for a prioress to have on her effigy. Much has been made of the presence of small animals at female convents and Eileen Power remarked that not only were dogs made into pets but also squirrels and small birds – which were an annoyance for other members of the convent.[68] Unfortunately, we cannot tell whether or not these particular symbols and representations of the secular world were common on other prioresses's slabs from the same period or geographic region as Anna's is the only to have survived.

Anna's patronage extended to the church of Soroby on the Island of Tiree, which was held by the convent, and she dedicated a large Celtic cross to the church. The shaft of the cross (Fig. 9.3) was dedicated to Archangel Michael by Anna, prioress of Iona, and depicts St Michael and the dragon with another image of a female ecclesiastic (nun) being led away by Death, who is wielding a spade.[69] St Michael was known as the collector of good souls at the moment of death and carried them into heaven. Anna may have chosen him as her protection on her journey to heaven – slaying all dragons and demons that may cross her path. The date of the cross is unknown but the symbolism may suggest that it was commissioned sometime before her death in 1543.

Madeline Caviness has suggested that having the names of donors inscribed next to their female images made their patronage public and indicated that their initiatives were respected. And by doing this, these women used their powerful offices (whether as queen or abbess) to emulate authority in their sphere of influence.[70] Both the tomb effigy and the cross reflect the piety of Anna and her choice for patronage in her locality as well as her authority and influence at the convent of Iona and in her surrounding communities.

The second tomb effigy comes from the convent of Abbey St Bathans and can be attributed to sometime between the late fifteenth and early sixteenth century (Fig. 9.4). Unfortunately we cannot ascribe the effigy to a particular prioress as we have a gap in the record: Margaret Kerr was prioress from c. 1412 to 1433, Agnes Sleigh (Sleych) was prioress in 1524 and the next prioress to appear in the record was Elizabeth Lamb in 1546.[71] To date there has been no follow-up work on this particular effigy and the only description we have of it comes from the Royal Commission inventory for the county of Berwick in 1915. The figure of the prioress measures six feet in length and the stonework shows her dressed in a habit, mantle and a veil covering her head. Her hands are folded in prayer and there are the remains of her crosier close to her head: the bottom point of the crosier rests on a small animal, which lies outstretched at her ankles. In the middle of the effigy there are angels on each side of her which show a 'girded alb, raised arms and outstretched wings, indicating that

---

68 E. Power, *Medieval English Nunneries c. 1275–1535* (Cambridge, 1922), pp. 662–3.

69 Steer and Bannerman, *West Highland Sculpture*, p. 71.

70 Madeline Caviness, 'Anchoress, Abbess and Queen: Donors and Patrons or Intercessors and Matrons?', *The Cultural Patronage of Medieval Women*, ed. J. H. McCash (Athens, 1996), pp. 105–54.

71 Watt and Shead, *Heads of Religious Houses Scotland*, p. 192.

Fig. 9.1. The Tomb Effigy of Prioress Anna Maclean of Iona showing the image of Anna. (Reproduced by courtesy of RCAHMS)

Fig. 9.2. The Tomb Effigy of Prioress Anna Maclean of Iona showing the mirrored images of Anna and the Virgin Mary. (Reproduced by courtesy of RCAHMS)

Fig. 9.3. Soroby, Tiree. The front of the shaft of a Celtic cross dedicated to the church of Soroby by Prioress Anna Maclean of Iona. (Reproduced by courtesy of RCAHMS)

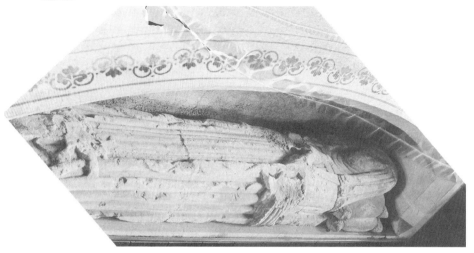

Fig. 9.4. Tomb Effigy of a prioress of Abbey St Bathans. (Reproduced by courtesy of RCAHMS)

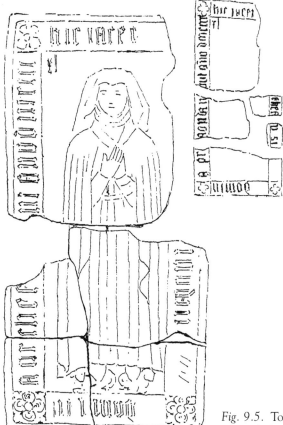

Fig. 9.5. Tomb Effigy of Prioress Blanche of Lincluden, c. 1390.

the angels were represented as rising up from beneath the effigy and supporting it with their backs, wings and arms'.[72]

This image of the prioress appears to be representative of other tomb effigies we have of prioresses in Scotland made during the later Middle Ages. The third effigy of a prioress is that of Blanche, the last prioress of Lincluden. This effigy (Fig. 9.5), like Anna's, shows some lettering, albeit incomplete, which indicates that this was the prioress of Lincluden. The effigy was found in the graveyard at the Cistercian abbey of Dundrennan as it became a refuge for Blanche after the suppression of her convent in 1394. She too is also depicted as wearing her habit with her hands folded in prayer. From the sketch of the remains of the broken slab it appears that small animals were laying at her feet, but what kind of animals is uncertain.

[72] RCAHMS, *Report and Inventory of Monuments and Constructions in the County of Berwick* (HMSO, 1915), p. 2.

We know very little of either of these last two effigies. For example we do not have any indication that these effigies were commissioned by the prioress or her family and the sculptors are also unknown. From the limited imagery on the effigies we can assume that these women held positions of power and authority in their localities and were seen as important individuals in their own right. They may also have had certain secular connections and developed networks between particular craftsmen. Because of the lack of analysis done on tomb effigies of late medieval prioresses in Britain it is difficult to determine whether or not these were representative of prioress effigies elsewhere. However, as we have seen, these effigies may help us in our understanding of how prioresses viewed themselves, and of how the secular world may have viewed these influential women.

Monastic rules do not clearly define the roles and responsibilities that a superior may have had in the secular world and we must piece together from existing evidence what these roles and responsibilities may have been. Scottish prioresses had varying duties to carry out in order to provide for the needs of their houses and the nuns under their care. We see prioresses granting church lands either in tack for a set number of years or feuing to family, kin and members of local society in order to pay off debts, maintain the monastic estate or rebuild after devastation. In some cases these grants were given as payment for money or goods given to the convent by her family, kin or other members of local society. The other duties of prioresses included appointing lay officers to support them in managing monastic estates. In many cases these men were appointed because of the influence and power they held in a locality and the convent could rely on these men for protection. Another aspect of her role as superior of her house would require a prioress not only to maintain conventual assets but also to protect them. The survival of the cartulary of Coldstream, conventual seals and other documents, attests to the quick thinking of Scottish prioresses. These women might also put themselves in a dangerous position by aligning themselves with important individuals to allow for the survival of their convent. We have evidence that prioresses on the Borders would spy on the English or Scottish armies in hopes that either side might spare them from destruction. Lastly, we know that prioresses showed support for local tradesmen by commissioning their tomb effigies, and the prioress of Iona also commissioned a cross for the church of Soroby. What these effigies indicate is that prioresses were important women within their convents and in their locality, a conclusion that is borne out by the documentary evidence considered in this paper.

MONASTERIES AND EDUCATION

10

Monasteries and Secular Education in Late Medieval England

JAMES G. CLARK

At the Dissolution of the Monasteries, as aspirational gentry and territorial nobility pestered Cromwell and his master for their portion of the spoil, an altogether more altruistic proposal emerged from the circle of humanist scholars and moderate reformers assembled around the king: the former abbeys and priories should be transformed into public schools not only for the social elite but also for the benefit of the whole commonweal.[1] The precedents for such a proposal were clear. Since the Black Death several ecclesiastical and secular patrons had recycled monastic resources for the purpose of scholastic foundations.[2] The most conspicuous contemporary case was perhaps also the least auspicious, since Wolsey's sequestered colleges at Ipswich and Oxford were incomplete, but it is possible the reformers were also aware of the greater progress of their continental counterparts, where schools and seminaries had already risen from the shells of surrendered monasteries.[3] There is no doubt their plan was also underpinned by a powerful commitment to the cause of humanism, which had been promoted so far only in a handful of high profile schools.[4] Their primary impulse, however, was surely the conviction, shared by many in early Tudor

---

[1] Thomas Starkey, *A Dialogue between Pole and Lupset*, ed. T. F. Mayer, Camden Soc., 4th Series, 37 (1989), pp. 124–5.

[2] For example, the twinned foundations of Henry VI at Cambridge and Eton that were raised on the resources of sequestered alien priories; Bishop William Waynflete's foundation at Oxford was endowed using the resources of the suppressed hospital of St John also at Oxford. See A. B. Cobban, 'Colleges and Halls, 1380–1500', in *A History of the University of Oxford, II: Late Medieval Oxford*, ed. J. I. Catto and T. A. R. Evans (Oxford, 1992), pp. 581–633 (pp. 610–16).

[3] See J. Newman, 'Cardinal Wolsey's Collegiate Foundations', in *Cardinal Wolsey: Church, State and Art*, ed. S. J. Gunn and P. G. Lindley (Cambridge, 1991), pp. 103–15. For schools founded from suppressed monasteries in Hesse and other Lutheran territories see O. Chadwick, *The Early Reformation on the Continent* (Oxford, 2001), pp. 151–8, 172; P. Schmitz, *Histoire de l'ordre de Saint Benoit*, 7 vols (Paris, 1948–56), IV, 271.

[4] N. Orme, *English Schools in the Middle Ages* (London, 1973), pp. 113–14, 213–14 and now idem, *Medieval Schools* (New Haven and London, 2006), pp. 119–21, 139–43. See also idem, *Education in Early Tudor England: Magdalen College and its School, 1480–1540* (Oxford, 1998).

England, that the monasteries had abandoned their traditional role as centres of education for the whole Christian community. The reformers fondly imagined a remote past when monasteries earned their endowments serving as beacons of education and enlightenment in an otherwise barren landscape.[5] But in their own time it was widely believed the monks had withdrawn behind their precinct walls to waste their resources upon themselves: 'they [i.e. the possessioners] are gloriously self satisfied', wrote Erasmus of Rotterdam, 'they believe it is the highest form of piety to be so uneducated they cannot even read'.[6]

The view of the monasteries as an obstacle to the spread of education – and of the Reformation as the first great stimulus to it – persisted for generations after these public and scholarly debates had subsided. The earliest modern historian of English education, A. F. Leach, shared many of the priorities and the prejudices of the sixteenth-century reformers and in his survey of medieval schools described the monasteries with the same degree of moral outrage, as the main obstacle to 'the advancement of science and learning': 'while monasticism prevailed', he wrote, 'that source of national energy [i.e. a cultured middle class] was cut off' and 'education made little impact on society at large'.[7] Even among his contemporaries, there were concerns over Leach's methods, and his partiality, but his general conclusions that the history of public education began at the Reformation, and that the notion of an ancient monastery teeming with schoolboys was nothing more than Romantic fantasy, were widely accepted.[8] Over the past thirty years, particularly in the pioneering work of Nicholas Orme, the authority of Leach has at last been undermined. Orme and others have acknowledged that the monasteries were more important (or at least less marginal) than earlier authorities allowed.[9] Yet there remains among these revisionists a strong conviction that the later Middle Ages were marked by progressive secularisation, not only of schools and schooling but also of the impulses that inspired the promotion and spread of popular education.[10]

The energy and enterprise of secular society in matters of education is expressed in a rich variety of sources, from a portfolio of property transactions that underpin a new school foundation, to a testamentary pledge that

---

[5]   The trope is evident in anticlerical commentaries of the late fourteenth and early fifteenth centuries. See, for example, *Piers Plowman* (B), Passus X, lines 305–8; also the critique of the Oxford theologians, Thomas Gascogine, *Loci e libro veritatum*, ed. J. E. Thorold Rogers (Oxford, 1881), pp. 72–3.

[6]   Erasmus, *Moriae encomium*, in *Opera omnia Desiderii Erasmi Roterodami recognita et adnotatione critica instructa notisque illustrate. Ordinis quarti, toma tertia*, ed. C. H. Miller (Amsterdam and Oxford, 1989), pp. 158–60.

[7]   A. F. Leach, *The Schools of Mediaeval England* (London, 1915), p. 331.

[8]   See W. E. Tate, *A. F. Leach as an Historian of Yorkshire Education with an index of the Yorkshire schools (c.730 to c.1770) referred to in his works*, St Anthony's Hall Publications (York, 1963).

[9]   Orme, *English Schools*, pp. 5–6, 224–51; idem, *Medieval Schools*, pp. 255–87, 300, 306, 342; J. H. Moran, *The Growth of English Schooling, 1340–1548: Learning, Literacy, and Laicization in Pre-Reformation York Diocese* (Princeton, 1985), pp. 12, 82 and note, 243.

[10] For example, Moran, *Schooling*, p. 226.

fatherless offspring be 'found to scole'.[11] It is the very number and variety of these documents, however, that has tended to obscure the enduring role of the religious orders. While seculars made conspicuous, even self-conscious, acts of educational patronage, the regulars' interest in and support for secular schooling, as an extension of their general charitable outlay, was seldom made explicit in accounts of their expenditure. The *Valor* commissioners of 1535 compounded this problem by returning incomplete, at times purely impressionistic, accounts of a convent's charity.[12] In respect of educational patronage it is possible their concealment was deliberate: Stephen Gardiner instructed the Winchester commissioners to deduct only alms for the poor from the monastery's gross income since 'the poor and wretched can live only by means of alms, while a school is not necessary for the children'.[13] The administrative records of the monasteries that remain will only ever yield a partial impression of their involvement in education but there are further insights to be recovered from other records, from domestic chronicles, *libri benefactorum* and even from the fragments of names and notes found in the margins of miscellaneous manuscripts. There are also some rare glimpses of the monasteries' involvement in secular education to be gleaned from the letters and papers of the laity themselves. It is true, as Nicholas Orme has observed, that medieval people did not discuss education as do their modern counterparts, but when the matter of school arose, it was not unknown, even in the shadow of the Dissolution, for them to acknowledge the debt they owed to the religious orders.[14]

The commentators of the 1530s were correct in sensing that the preceding two centuries had seen significant changes in the role of the monasteries as centres of education. The notion of the monastery which served as the sole focus of learning and literate culture in the surrounding community, an easy, open community – more akin to a minster than a post-Conquest *monasterium* – of men, women and children, which early Tudor readers continued to encounter in any number of popular printed histories and hagiographies, had no place in the realities of later medieval England. If there ever had been a kind of communality in early monastic precincts, as even anti-monastic commentators fondly imagined, it had been fractured before the beginning of the thirteenth century.[15] The practice of child oblation, never widespread in England, was almost extinct even in the last quarter of the twelfth century.[16] The cloister

---

[11] Orme, *English Schools*, pp. 197–8, 203–5; Moran, *Schooling*, p. 226; F. W. Weaver, ed., *Somerset Medieval Wills, 1383–1500*, Somerset Record Soc., XVI (1901), p. 166; *Test. Ebor.*, III, 205.

[12] The *Valor* returns frequently recorded the formula 'in elemosina ... diuersis pauperibus et lepros ab antiquo': see VE. For an early analysis of the *Valor* returns see A. Savine, 'English Monasteries on the Eve of the Dissolution', *Oxford Studies in Social and Legal History*, I, ed. P. Vingradoff (Oxford, 1909).

[13] Savine, 'English Monasteries', p. 11 and note.

[14] Orme, *Medieval Schools*, p. 160.

[15] For these early changes see especially Knowles, MO, pp. 489–92 (p. 491).

[16] Ibid., pp. 418–22, 635.

schools which since the tenth-century revival had served to educate secular clerks for a wide variety of careers – among them allegedly (at St Albans) Nicholas Breakspear, subsequently Pope Hadrian IV – were already diminishing in size and declining in number, eclipsed by the expanding number of secular schools.[17] At the same time, that other symbol of literate culture, the monastic *scriptoria*, had passed the peak of their activity. These changes, however, did not (as early Tudor commentators suspected) cause the monasteries to recline in an intellectual torpor that persisted to the Reformation. It is now generally acknowledged that the century after 1250 saw the resurgence of monastic learning in England.[18] From as early as 1247, responding to calls for reform first heard at Lateran IV, the provincial chapters of the Benedictine order, issued new injunctions for the formal instruction of monks in theology.[19] A code of statutes issued by the chapters in 1277 promulgated a programme of teaching, preaching, private study, and the study of selected monk scholars at the universities. In 1278 the first of three Benedictine *studia* was established at Oxford. Further reforms followed in 1336 and 1343 and were accompanied by comparable codes for the Cistercians and Regular Canons, both of which also eventually established *studia* at Oxford.[20] It would not be an exaggeration to suggest that by the mid-fourteenth century, the monk scholar had re-emerged as a public figure. There are signs at the same time of a return to in-house book production and the dissemination of original monastic scholarship in a diverse range of disciplines. These developments have been studied in some depth[21] but historians have largely overlooked the fact that at the same time the monks also re-emerged as educators in the non-monastic world.

The return of the monasteries to secular education has been interpreted as a purely practical response to the increasing liturgical burdens placed upon communities of even middling and smaller size.[22] Certainly as early as 1249,

---

[17] For Breakspear at St Albans see H. T. Riley, ed., *Gesta abbatum Monasterii sancti Albani*, 3 vols, RS (1867–9), I, 112.

[18] See J. Greatrex, 'Benedictine Monk Scholars as Teachers and Preachers in the Later Middle Ages: Evidence from Worcester Cathedral Priory', *Monastic Studies* 2 (1990), 213–25; idem, 'The English Cathedral Priories and the Pursuit of Learning in the Later Middle Ages', *JEH* 45 (1994), 396–411; A. Coates, *English Medieval Books: the Reading Abbey Book Collections from Foundation to Dispersal* (Oxford, 1999); J. G. Clark, *A Monastic Renaissance at St Albans: Thomas Walsingham and his Circle, c.1350–1440* (Oxford, 2004).

[19] See Knowles, *RO*, I, 9–27.

[20] See J. Catto, 'The Cistercians in Oxford, 1280–1539', in *Benedictines in Oxford*, ed. H. Wansbrough and A. Marett-Crosby (London, 1997), pp. 108–15; H. E. Salter, ed., *Chapters of the Augustinian Canons*, Canterbury and York Soc., 29; Oxford Historical Soc., 74 (1922).

[21] For example, J. P. Carley, *Glastonbury Abbey. The Holy House at the Head of the Moors Adventurous* (Woodbridge, 1988), pp. 138–44; Clark, *Monastic Renaissance*, pp. 79–123; R. B. Dobson, *Durham Priory, 1400–1450* (Cambridge, 1973), pp. 377–8; A. Gransden, 'Some Manuscripts in Cambridge from Bury St Edmunds Abbey: Exhibition Catalogue', in *Bury St Edmunds, Medieval Art, Architecture, Archaeology and Economy*, British Archaeological Association, Conference Transactions, 20 (London, 1998), pp. 228–85.

[22] For example, R. Bowers, 'The Almonry Schools of the English Monasteries, c.1265–1540',

the chapter of the Canterbury province of the Benedictines pinpointed growing pressures that might prevent a monk from private masses.[23] The concern was reiterated in the statutes issued by the chapter of the Canterbury province in 1277 although it was another thirty years (and then in the context of an epis-copal visitor's injunctions) before there was any explicit recommendation that the monasteries might recruit secular clerks to reduce the liturgical burden.[24] It is possible therefore that the provisions made by the leading Benedictine convents – notably the nine cathedral priories – may be connected directly to these capitular pronouncements, but they do not entirely explain the expansion of monastic provisions beyond the hierarchy of houses, or in houses of other orders.

The monks' renewed interest in secular education should be seen rather as the result of more fundamental changes in monastic attitudes to learning itself and its place and purpose in the religious life. The reform statutes of the later thirteenth and early fourteenth centuries not only transformed tradi-tional patterns of monastic education and formation but also stimulated a new receptiveness to the pedagogic practices of the secular clergy. That the monks should model themselves more closely on their secular counterparts was never explicitly stated, but it was the unequivocal message of the provincial and general chapters that they should recover their pre-eminence in the ranks of the priesthood, that they, rather than the parish clergy, were the true *magistri populi*.[25] The message was well received at least in some quarters of monastic England: at St Albans Abbey, a late fourteenth-century annalist (probably Thomas Walsingham) claimed that the monastery served as school for many who subsequently served in church and state.[26] While it would be an exag-geration to suggest that traditional monastic culture was now effaced, there is no doubt that English cloisters were now exposed to the textual traditions of popular, secular education, to the wide variety of grammar primers (not only for Latin but also for French and English), to manuals for the teaching of the *ars dictaminis* and even secular 'business skills'.[27] These texts conveyed to monastic

in *Monasteries and Society in Medieval Britain: Proceedings of the 1994 Harlaxton Symposium*, ed. B. J. Thompson, Harlaxton Medieval Studies, 6 (Stamford, 1999), pp. 177–222.

[23] W. A. Pantin, ed., *Documents Illustrating the Activities of the General and Provincial Chapters of the English Black Monks, 1215–1540*, 3 vols, Camden 3rd series, 45, 47, 54 (1931–7), I, 45; Bowers, 'Almonry Schools', p. 189.

[24] *Chapters*, ed. Pantin, I, 70–1, 96; Bowers, 'Almonry Schools', p. 190.

[25] *Chapters*, ed. Pantin, I, 64–92, especially 64, 75. For a more explicit statement see W. A. Pantin, 'A Sermon for a General Chapter', *Downside Review* 51 (1933), 291–308. A comparable note was sounded by the canons, *Summi magistri*, issued to the Benedictines by Benedict XII in 1336: *Concilia Magnae Britanniae et Hiberniae, a Synodo Verolamiensi, AD CCCCXLVI ad Londinensem AD MD CCXVII accedunt constitutiones et alia ad histo-riam Ecclesiæ Anglicanæ spectantia*, ed. D. Wilkins, 4 vols (London, 1737), II, 585–613.

[26] BL, Cotton MS Claudius E IV, fol. 333r.

[27] For the entry of these texts into monastic book collections after 1350 see D. Thomson, *A Descriptive Catalogue of Middle English Grammatical Texts* (London, 1979), pp. 114–31, 148–57, 182–4, 316–23. See also the variety of elementary dictionaries, glossaries and grammar treatises recorded in Benedictine book-lists between the fourteenth and the

readers the culture of the secular schoolroom even before they established such schoolrooms for themselves.

These attitudes were surely reinforced by a range of new, or newly sharpened, cultural influences which penetrated English convents in the course of thirteenth, fourteenth and fifteenth centuries. In the first place, the new practice of sending monks to study at university exposed a core group in each generation to the preoccupations and values of the secular clergy. The experience did not necessarily unsettle their monastic vocation but did mean that many of them returned to their convents bearing books, and sometimes a magisterial or scholarly agenda, absorbed from their secular colleagues.[28] Perhaps also traceable to the textual adventures of the graduate monks was the trickle of humanist texts that entered English monasteries from the last quarter of the fourteenth century. The earliest examples of humanist scholarship to attract a monastic readership were perhaps their new translations of Aristotle, but before the third quarter of the fifteenth century to these had been added a number of their manuals on Latin grammar and rhetoric.[29]

The changing outlook – and self-image even – of many later medieval monks, and especially monastic leaders, led them into a variety of new initiatives and involvements in secular education. The first and most conspicuous development was the foundation, from the turn of the thirteenth century forwards, of dedicated secular schools under the direct supervision of the monastery. The schools were conceived as an extension of the convent's charitable expenditure and as such were connected to the almonry, the formal frontier between the monastic community and the world beyond its walls. It is perhaps a further indication that the initiative was not purely the product of the Benedictines' preoccupations with their liturgical obligations that the earliest glimpse of such a school was at the Augustinian priory of Guisborough, in 1266. Nonetheless, the Black Monks soon made similar provisions. The earliest documentary evidence of the school at Norwich dates from 1272 x 1288/89; schools are also attested at Christ Church, Canterbury, Rochester, Ely, Westminster and Hyde between 1291 and c. 1325.[30] The first appearance of almonry schools at the Benedictine cathedral priories does confirm the primacy of practical concerns over liturgical

---

sixteenth centuries: *English Benedictine Libraries: The Shorter Catalogues*, ed. R. Sharpe, et al., CBMLC (1996), nos B24. 80; B30. 8, 10; B43. 77; B43. 82; B59. 22; B64. 9; B79. 212; B117. 24 (pp. 123, 139, 230–1, 306, 323, 522, 666); *Dover Priory*, ed. Stoneman, CBMLC (1999), BM1. 386b, 394c, 390c, 407, 410a, 411a, 412f, 433a, 441 (pp. 153, 155–6, 160–2, 167, 170); J. Willoughby and K. Friis-Jensen, ed., *Peterborough Abbey*, CBMLC (2001), BP21. 128a; BP21. 316 (pp. 103, 167).

28 For the evidence of this see Dobson, *Durham Priory*, pp. 375–6.

29 See R. Weiss, *Humanism in England during the Fifteenth Century*, 2nd edn (Oxford, 1957), pp. 30–38 (p. 36).

30 Bowers, 'Almonry Schools', pp. 182, 188–91. See also S. Evans, 'Ely Almonry Boys and Choristers in the Later Middle Ages', in *Studies presented to Hilary Jenkinson*, ed. J. C. Davies (Oxford, 1957), pp. 155–63; J. Greatrex, 'The Almonry School of Norwich Cathedral Priory in the Thirteenth and Fourteenth Centuries', *Studies in Church History* 31 (1994), pp. 169–81.

performance at least in the premier houses but there was no attempt to co-ordinate the creation of almonry schools across the congregation. In fact the adoption of the schools appears to be an unusual instance of unilateral action that nonetheless created common conditions throughout monastic England. The cathedral priories were the pioneers but before 1325 the phenomenon had spread to the independent abbeys.[31] Over the course of the next century schools also appeared at houses outside the hierarchy, and not only of those of the Benedictines but also others of the Cistercians and the Regular Canons. Roger Bowers has identified thirty schools whose existence can be documented in the period c.1270–c.1540, but even if the evidence is not always enshrined in a sequence of compotus rolls, there are grounds for suggesting there were many, many more.[32]

There was a significant difference in the constitution and the scale of the schools attached to the greater abbeys and priories and those attested at many smaller monasteries. At Canterbury Cathedral Priory, Durham, Ely, Norwich, and Worcester, and at Ramsey, Reading, St Albans and Westminster, the almonry schools must surely have closely resembled any secular school founda-tion, and since they appeared at the turn of the thirteenth century they could be seen to have anticipated the new generation of endowed schools founded in the century after the Black Death.[33] They were large institutions by any standard, with space for as many as forty schoolboys, supported by a profes-sional, stipendiary master, who was perhaps assisted by juniors as his counterpart would certainly have been at a secular school. The syllabus followed at these schools is not specified in the surviving documents – the extant ordinances offer only general statements on proficiency in grammar – but there are grounds for suggesting that the greatest of them provided their pupils with the oppor-tunity to progress as far as any endowed school of the period. According to the ordinance of 1339, the scholars of the St Albans almonry school were admitted for a maximum of five years, a period which would surely allow for progress beyond elementary grammar to the brink of university entrance. There was at least one occasion in the fourteenth century when the almonry boys and the boys of the town school at St Albans shared the same facilities, an arrangement that also supports the suggestion that they followed a common curriculum: the teaching of the town school was outlined in statutes of 1309; the *Priscianum magnum* was a principal textbook and senior scholars were prepared for a period of university study.[34]

In spite of its status as an adjunct of the almonry, it would appear the almonry school was never intended to provide purely for poor boys of proven ability, although the fiction that they were '*pauperes*' was frequently retained in the *compotus* rolls. At a number of the greater abbeys and priories the admission of

[31] Bowers, 'Almonry Schools', pp. 191–2.

[32] Ibid., pp. 180, 220–22.

[33] Bowers, 'Almonry Schools', pp. 188–94; Orme, *English Schools*, pp. 243–45; Dobson, *Durham Priory*, p. 60; Clark, *Monastic Renaissance*, pp. 72–8.

[34] H. T. Riley, ed., *Registrum abbatiae Johannis Whethamstede*, 2 vols, RS (1872–3), II, 305–15.

schoolboys was subject to the nomination of the convent, a process which of course gave disproportionate favour to the monks' own kinfolk. In a handful of cases, notably at a number of cathedral priories, nominations were negotiated between the convent and competing jurisdictions nearby (e.g. the diocesan).[35]

From an early stage, if not at their inception, the schools of the greater abbeys and priories were also opened to fee-paying pupils. There are no surviving figures that show the balance between the two constituencies but it seems likely that even the wealthiest houses willingly exploited the extra source of income. There were as many as forty schoolboys at Glastonbury in 1377 of whom half may have been paying pupils.[36] The entry of fee-paying alongside foundation pupils brought these schools closer still to the secular foundations of the fifteenth and early sixteenth centuries. To prospective pupils, and masters, and perhaps to the expanding number of lay patrons with an interest in education, these prestigious abbeys and priories must have appeared as partners, or indeed competitors, in a common enterprise.

As Roger Bowers has suggested, it may be helpful here to distinguish between the grammar schools established at these houses and the provisions they also made for the recruitment and training of singers. In the course of the fourteenth century the largest of the monastic cathedral priories began to train a cohort of singing boys alongside their almonry scholars.[37] Bowers rejects the formal appellation of 'song school' for these arrangements to avoid any confusion with not only the choral foundations of the secular cathedrals but also the professional, stipendiary choirs that a number of the greater abbeys and cathedral priories abbeys did form in the generation before the Dissolution.[38] Certainly, in several of the best documented cases, these singing boys were brought together for a specific duty, to assist in the services of the Lady Chapel. Nonetheless, in a number of instances their custody and training does appear to have been distinct from (or parallel to) that of the schoolboys of the almonry, with the appointment of a secular, stipendiary cantor-cum-organist to supervise their training. At Muchelney, Somerset, it was the responsibility of the secular cantor to recruit and train four singing boys to play the organ and perform the Lady Mass and other offices.[39] On the other hand there are early sixteenth-century examples where the singing boys were schooled alongside the almonry scholars under the supervision of a single master appointed to serve as cantor as well as schoolmaster, and sometimes also organist.[40]

---

35   Bowers, 'Almonry Schools', pp. 194–7.

36   Ibid., p. 203.

37   J. Fowler, ed., *Rites of Durham: being a description or brief declaration of all the ancient monuments, rites, & customs belonging or being within the monastical church of Durham before the suppression, written 1593*, Surtees Soc., 107 (1903), pp. 38, 54. See also Dobson, *Durham Priory*, pp. 71, 169–70; Bowers, 'Almonry Schools', pp. 208–12, 220–1; Orme, *English Schools*, pp. 243–6.

38   Bowers, 'Almonry Schools', pp. 208–12.

39   B. Schofield, ed., *Muchelney Memoranda edited from a breviary in the possession of J. Meade Falkner*, Somerset Record Soc., 42 (1927), p. 42.

40   For example, at Gloucester and Llanthony secunda: *VCH Gloucestershire*, II, 60; J. Rhodes,

The scale and structure of the greatest of these schools attracted secular masters of a stature not usually associated with the monasteries of the later Middle Ages. Evesham Abbey appears to have drawn to its free school a succession of well-qualified graduate masters.[41] In the early sixteenth century, if not in earlier periods, the monasteries secular schools were regarded by university graduates as preferment of great value. Leonard Cox abandoned a promising career in continental Europe for the position of schoolmaster at Reading, which he retained for more than a decade until the surrender of the monastery in September 1539.[42] There he published a textbook *The Arte or crafte of rhetorycke* (Richard Redman: London, c. 1535; STC 5947 / 5947. 5) based on Philip Melancthon's *Institutiones rhetoricae*, and he also translated Erasmus's *De pueris instituendis* and *Paraphrases* although neither work appeared in print. Cox's story serves as an exemplum of monastic educational patronage in this period. He was no monastic apologist and in fact at Reading associated with known religious radicals. Yet he does appear to have developed an intellectual affinity with Abbot Cook and, perhaps, other members of the monastic community, and used his association with them, as well perhaps as their library resources, to extend his own scholarly career. As an expression of their shared outlook in matters of scholarship, he even honoured Cook with the dedication of his *Arte*. The role of the monasteries, at least the 'great and solemn' monasteries, in the promotion of education, was acknowledged in early Tudor England even by those who favoured religious reform.

There was probably little common ground between the largest schools and those attached to monasteries of lesser status. The schools were almost certainly still attached to the almonry and under the administrative control of the almoner but they may have admitted only a handful of pupils, perhaps no more than a dozen even at their height. It is also unlikely that admissions were subject to the same controls as at the greater abbeys and cathedral priories. At Crowland Abbey even the episcopal visitor positively recommended the expedient of recruiting the convent's own kinfolk to ensure the available places were filled.[43] Here and in other similar houses the school may have amounted to no more than an *ad hoc* gathering of boys in the monastery precincts, notionally in the custody of almony staff. There may also have been some differences in the nature and organisation of the schoolboys' syllabus. At the greater abbeys and priories, a distinction was drawn between the schoolboys of the almonry and those boys, or young 'clerks' who were recruited and trained as singers.

ed., *A Calendar of the Registers of the Priory of Llanthony by Gloucester, 1457–66, 1501–25,* Bristol and Gloucestershire Archaeological Soc. Record Series, 15 (2002), pp. 195–7 (p. 196).

[41] N. Orme, 'Evesham Schools before the Reformation', *Research Papers, Vale of Evesham Historical Soc.* 6 (1977), 95–100.

[42] For Cox see Emden, *BRUO, 1501–40,* 145; S. F. Ryle, 'Cox, Leonard, b. c. 1495, d. in or after 1549', *ODNB,* 6525.

[43] A. H. Thompson, ed., *Visitations of Religious Houses in the diocese of Lincoln. Injunctions and other documents from the registers of Richard Flemyng and William Gray, AD 1420 to AD 1436,* Lincoln Record Society, 7 (1914), I, 37.

Following a visitation of Bradwell Priory in c. 1433 Bishop William Gray called for the recruitment of 'some teachable children to be ... instructed in reading, song and the other elementary branches of knowledge that they may serve the monks at the celebration of masses'.[44] It would be mistaken to assume, however, that the teaching in these smaller (and perhaps more informal) schools was at a lower level than in the larger monasteries. A notebook surviving from Barlinch Priory, dating from the turn of the fifteenth century, preserves extracts from contemporary preceptive treatises, which would suggest there was no obstacle to current trends penetrating West Somerset.[45]

It would be wrong to regard the almonry school, even as envisaged at the greater abbeys and priories, as simply a secular school in a monastic setting. It was commonplace, perhaps increasingly so in the pre-Reformation period, for the boys of the almonry and the novices of the monastery to share the same master. By the early sixteenth century, the requirement to teach on either side of the monastic enclosure seems to have become a standard feature of the schoolmaster's contract. The 1502 indenture that bound Thomas Browning to Llanthony Priory to serve as schoolmaster required him to offer teaching to both the canons and 'the boys of the house' ('scolam grammaticalem tenebit et stupabit et omnes et singulos canonicos et pueros in eodem existentes prioratus illius ad scolam illam venientes libenter et diligenter').[46] The arrangements were the same at Gloucester where the novice school joined thirteen almonry boys in 1515.[47] There are also one or two accounts that suggest a professed monk served as master to the boys as well as to the novice monks. The only surviving witness to the presence of schoolboys at Kirkham Priory suggests the master was a canon of the community itself.[48]

It has been suggested the sole purpose of the almonry school was to provide personnel for the monastic community, first a cohort of competent boys to assist in the choir, and subsequently candidates suitable for profession as monks. There is no doubt the daily rhythm of the almonry school did echo that of the monastic community and the periods of teaching were punctuated by regular periods of observance. The regime of the 'children of the aumerie', as reported in the post-Reformation memoir of Durham Priory, not only required the school-boys' presence in the choir but also their completion of other ceremonial duties, including the chanting of the complete psalter during the vigil for deceased brethren.[49] However, the burden of observance varied between one house and another. The sheer scale of the performances seen at the greater abbeys and cathedral priories required the assistance of professional singers and as early as

[44] Ibid., p. 23. For comparable injunctions issued elsewhere see I, 89, 106.

[45] N. Orme, 'A School Notebook from Barlinch Priory', in idem, *Education and Society in Medieval and Renaissance England* (London and Ronceverte, 1989), pp. 113–21.

[46] Rhodes, ed., *Registers of Llanthony*, pp. 59–61.

[47] *VCH Gloucestershire*, II, 60. For the same arrangement at Winchester see J. Greatrex, *BRECP*, p. 657 and note.

[48] J. Burton, 'Priory and Parish: Kirkham and its Parishioners, 1496–7', in *Monastery and Society*, ed. Thompson, pp. 329–44 (p. 338).

[49] *Rites of Durham*, ed. Raine, pp. 15, 44.

the end of the fourteenth century there were already stipendiary singers permanently employed at Westminster.[50] In these institutions the almonry boys made a token appearance and were never the mainstay.[51]

It may be similarly unsafe to assume the almonry school served as the sole source of recruitment to the monastic community. The number of schoolboys whose names and biographical details are documented remains very small and there is only a handful of these that can be shown with some certainty to have progressed to profession as a member of monastic community.[52] Although monastic recruitment in the later Middle Ages is still under-researched it is already clear that men continued to enter the cloister from a variety of routes. There were a significant number, even in the fifteenth and early sixteenth centuries, recruited from the ranks of the secular clergy, in some cases directly from the Oxford and Cambridge schools.[53] The most prestigious abbeys and priories proved as selective as they always had been and if not a schoolman they still preferred those offering the very best educational credentials. Social origin may also have been a factor at the greater abbeys and priories: it may be more than coincidence that several ex-almonry scholars entered the staff of the monastery rather than making their profession.[54] It should also be recognised that monasteries, even the prestige abbeys and priories, also recruited men possessing only rudimentary education, perhaps especially in the earlier part of this period. The appearance of elementary primers in the cloister cupboards of some convents, and the marginal annotation in a number of extant manuscripts are surely testimony to the presence of monks whose literacy fell below the standard of an almonry alumnus.[55] It should also be remembered the period saw a marked shift in the rate of monastic recruitment. There may have been occasions, at least once in a generation, when there was no place in the monastery for the aspirant almonry boy.

Like their secular counterparts, in fact, the monastic almonry schools appear also to have prepared boys for a variety of careers beyond the convent walls. An almonry school education could prepare a boy for university, and the names of those who progressed from the monastery to the schools are occasionally

---

[50] See also R. Bowers, 'An Early Tudor Monastic Enterprise: Choral Polyphony for the Liturgical Service', in *The Culture of English Monasticism*, ed. J. G. Clark (Woodbridge, 2007), pp. 21–54.

[51] See, for example, arrangements at Abingdon, Newnham, Thornton and Ramsey: R. E. G. Kirk, ed., *Accounts of the Obedientiars of Abingdon Abbey*, Camden Soc., ns, 51 (1892), p. 90; *Visitations of Religious Houses*, ed. Thompson, I, 89, 106, 121.

[52] For example, Bowers, 'Almonry Schools', p. 206. Bowers records the names of two almonry boys subsequently professed at respectively Christ Church, Canterbury, and St Osyth. See also Moran, *Schooling*, p. 115 and note. In her biographical register of the cathedral priories, Joan Greatrex recognises the difficulty of handling references that are 'resistant to unambiguous interpretation'. Whilst it would seem reasonable to surmise that the route into the monastic life of many of the men she records was indeed the almonry school it is rarely proven. See *BRECP*, p. 656.

[53] For example, Clark, *Monastic Renaissance*, p. 15; Dobson, *Durham Priory*, p. 61.

[54] For example, Bowers, 'Almonry Schools', p. 206.

[55] See note 27 above.

recorded: Thomas Grey entered Oxford before 1538 after three years passed in the 'fermery' of Newburgh Priory.[56] Their fee-paying scholars, of course, were never destined for the monastery but returned to a pre-ordained place in gentry, noble or even courtly society. If the courtier-bishops John Barnet and Thomas Hatfield were indeed *alumni* of the St Albans almonry, as the author of the *Gesta abbatum* claimed, then this was certainly their progression.[57] It was surely the same story for Christopher Urswick, scion of a substantial Cumbrian family, who is said to have attended the school at Furness Abbey.[58] Whether or not their attendance at the almonry school had been free or funded, there were a number of merchants and tradesmen of St Albans who identified themselves as alumni of the monastery. Thomas Fayrman (d. 1440) conducted much of his career at the Calais Staple but was returned to the abbey church for burial, when the convent remembered him as an *alumnus*.[59] A fuller of the town, John Bayley (d. 1429) may also have been a former almonry boy, since he bequeathed 12d to the *magister scolarum*.[60] At St Albans at least there were also *alumni* whose association with the abbey school was best forgotten. The ringleader of the 1381 rebellion was the abbey's own *alumnus*, William Grindecobbe.[61]

The ordinances and other early documents attesting to the almonry schools encourage an impression of permanence which in the case of many is probably unwarranted. For all their codification in conventual registers and *libri memorandum*, the early fourteenth-century foundations faced natural and unavoidable disruption, in some cases from the urban uprisings of 1327 and 1381, and in many cases from the Black Death. There may have been many schools of middling size which faced leaner years after 1400 than they had done before. The sporadic references to 'poor scholars' in the Abingdon accounts underline the uneven fortunes of an almonry school even at a well endowed and independent abbey: regular payments to the scholars are recorded in the final quarter of the fourteenth century but are absent from subsequent records.[62] The canons of Thornton told their visitor in 1422–3 that it had been the old custom to have fourteen boys in the almonry; such times were slow to return since only two schoolboys were recorded in 1440.[63] Even at the cathedral priories numbers appear to have contracted at the turn of the fifteenth century although this may be connected with a shift in priorities and a new concentration on the recruitment and training of singing boys for the monks' choir.[64] In an expanding market place, it was not only schoolboys that monasteries strug-

---

[56] Moran, *Schooling*, p. 264.

[57] BL, Cotton MS Claudius E IV, fol. 333r.

[58] J. B. Trapp, 'Urswick, Christopher, 1448?–1522', *ODNB*, 28024.

[59] BL, Cotton MS Nero D VII, fol. 138r. See also Royal Commission on Historical Monuments, *Inventory of Historical Monuments of Hertfordshire* (1910), p. 184.

[60] Hertfordshire Record Office, ASA, AR1, fol. 14v.

[61] *Gesta abbatum*, ed. Riley, III, 300.

[62] *Obedientiars of Abingdon Abbey*, ed. Kirk, pp. 25, 44, 50.

[63] *Visitations of Religious Houses*, ed. Thompson, I, 121; III, 371.

[64] See, for example, Norwich Cathedral Priory: A. Jessopp, ed., *Visitations of the Diocese of Norwich, AD 1492–1532*, Camden Soc., ns, 43 (London, 1888), p. 192.

gled to recruit but also suitably qualified masters. There may have been many other convents confounded as were the monks of Christ Church, Canterbury, when the master of their school was poached by the corporation of Kingston-upon-Thames.[65] The prior and convent refused to send on his baggage but it was small revenge.

Like many features of monastic life – liturgy, learning, even estate management – the provision of teaching in the almonry fluctuated from one generation to another dependent, more than any other factor, upon the commitment of the abbot and convent itself. Clearly there were convents where commitment had evaporated by the beginning of the sixteenth century. At a visitation of Bromhill in 1514 Bishop Nix of Norwich found the 'scholehouse chaumbre' had fallen into ruin.[66] There were monasteries, however, and not only the more prestigious, premier institutions, which maintained these provisions down to the Dissolution. Some may have benefited in terms of recruitment, as Bowers has suggested, from the decline of episcopal schools in the early sixteenth century.[67] The commissioners confronted schoolboys not only in the 'monastic' north, but also in the midlands, south and west during their circuits of 1535 and 1536. The school at Cerne, Dorset, continued as the suppressions spread southwards: elderly witnesses in an estate enquiry of 1575 recalled their early careers as scholars of the abbey during the 1510s and 1520s.[68]

For the most part, these school facilities were established only at the parent monastery rather than a dependency but in the case of Canterbury Cathedral Priory they were also replicated at their Oxford *studia*. The support of secular schoolboys on the foundation of Canterbury College was prescribed by Archbishop Courtenay's revised statutes of 1384 but it may be wrong to interpret it as an innovation since the surviving rolls record *ad hoc* arrangements for schoolboys as much as a decade before.[69] Courtenay called for five *pueri collegii* to be funded from the same source of revenue as the student monks, an appropriated parish church. They were to be selected by nomination, of the prior and convent of Christ Church, and the archbishop, *ex officio*.[70] The position of the *pueri collegii* matched that of their counterparts in the monastery; in academic and domestic matters they were supervised by a secular master but they were to wait upon the warden and fellows at mealtimes and to serve them in the *Opus Dei*.[71] The *compotus* rolls are well preserved for the century before 1540 but the *pueri* appear only rarely and it is possible that places were filled only irregularly.

[65] J. B. Sheppard, ed., *Literae Cantuarienses. The Letter Books of the Monastery of Christ Church, Canterbury*, 3 vols, RS (1887–9), II, 465–6.

[66] *Visitations*, ed. Jessopp, p. 86.

[67] Bowers, 'Almonry Schools', p. 217.

[68] K. Barker, ed., *Cerne Abbey Millennium Lectures* (Cerne Abbas, 1988), p. 50.

[69] W. A. Pantin, *Canterbury College, Oxford*, 4 vols, Oxford Historical Society, ns, 6–8, 30 (1947–85), IV, 85.

[70] Ibid., III, 179.

[71] Ibid., III, 179; IV, 87–8.

Provisions for secular scholars were also made at Durham College, the *studium* of the prior and convent of Durham Priory. In his 1381 statutes Bishop Thomas Hatfield directed that eight secular scholars were to be supported on the foundation. Four were to be recruited from Durham (city and/or diocese) and two respectively from Allertonshire and Howdenshire, an arrangement that reflected the priory's supervision of secular schools. This connection with the convent's grammar schools indicates that the eight were intended to be undergraduates and not *pueri* on a par with almonry boys.[72]

It is remotely possible that provisions of this kind were also made at Gloucester College, the third of the Benedictine *studia* at Oxford. In spite of its status as the *studium* for Benedictines of the southern province, the college lacked the communal buildings of its counterparts and until the mid-fifteenth century comprised little more than a cluster of cottages. A number of the greater abbeys and priories appear to have rented their cottages on the open market and this may have made the college accessible to secular sojourners: Walter Baynon, a secular who submitted to the *prior studentium* in July 1461 after an act of indiscipline, appears to have been resident at the college.[73] There may be stronger grounds for supposing that secular sojourners were supported on the endowment of Oxford's other monastic *studia*, the Cisterican St Bernard's College (founded 1437) and the regular canons' St Mary's College (established by 1448). Like Gloucester College, St Bernard's lacked the full complement of communal buildings but since monk students themselves were sparse, there may well have been recourse to secular sojourners to fill the space and supplement the income. St Mary's College was better equipped and is known to have opened its gate to fee-paying seculars.[74]

The almonry school may have been the most striking development in the monasteries' provision for lay education, since it established a permanent, or at least semi-permanent, presence within the precinct, but it should not obscure the other forms of educational patronage that many monasteries initiated or revived in this period. The larger abbeys continued to exercise their jurisdiction over the schools within their own liberty, foundations, for the most part, which pre-dated the advent of the almonry boys. In the traditional monastic boroughs the monasteries' right over these schools was never seriously threatened and the period saw only cosmetic changes in the manner of their supervision. The prior and convent of Durham retained their role in the schools at Allerton and Howden as well as Durham itself.[75] The monks of Bury maintained right of appointment of master of town grammar school in fifteenth century and also

72 Dobson, *Durham Priory*, pp. 170–71.
73 For Gloucester College see J. Campbell, 'Gloucester College', in *Benedictines in Oxford*, ed. Wansborough and Marett-Crosby, pp. 37–47. For Baynon see Emden, *BRUO*, I, 135.
74 The east range of the quadrangle at St Bernard's College was never completed. See also W. C. Costin, *The History of St. John's College, Oxford, 1598–1860*, Oxford Historical Soc., ns, 12 (1958) and H. M. Colvin, 'The Building of St. Bernard's College', *Oxoniensia* 24 (1960), 37–48.
75 See above, note 72.

provided his stipend.[76] There were cases where the monasteries' claims over the school, and schooling within the liberty in general, were strongly contested. A dispute at Walden, Essex, in 1423 led to the summary departure of all secular schoolmasters from the town.[77] However there were perhaps as many where the monastery sought the extension of its jurisdiction over the operation of schools and schoolmasters even on the very border of the liberty. The abbot and convent of Bury laid claim to the supervision of the school at Beccles, nearly fifty miles from the monastery and far beyond the limit of its ordinary jurisdiction.[78] These interventions undoubtedly were part-and-parcel of the general reassertion of spiritual and temporal rights in which many monasteries were engaged perpetually, but they might also be regarded as the application of the claims made by contemporary monastic leaders, that they were indeed the *magistri* of the people. Even where it was not a matter of their rights, monastic superiors might show an interest in the affairs of secular schools: the prior of Worcester intervened on behalf of a Coventry master challenged by the city authorities.[79]

There was something of this renewed determination to supervise the instruction of their secular subjects also to be seen in the monasteries' management of their churches, chapels, and some of the other secular institutions under their jurisdiction. The conversion of the church of Hemingbrough into a collegiate foundation by Prior Washington of Durham in 1426–27 may have been driven forward by his concern to provide material comfort for his 'benefice-hungry clerks' but as Dobson has suggested after some early struggles he succeeded in creating a corporate body with a distinct, and apparently scholarly, *esprit de corps*.[80] Prior Washington was not untypical in the patronage he showed to the secular clerks in his service and, whether or not the motive was material, there are many comparable examples of exceptionally well qualified clerks, even doctoral graduates, clustered together in the livings the local monastery. There may have been others in the mould of William Trebilville, an Oxford scholar and former protégé of Abbot Wheathampstead of St Albans who was presented to the vicarage of St Mary's, Wallingford. Trebilville was the consummate pastor and left a pastoral manual of his own compilation.[81]

The greater abbeys and priories may have made formal provision for teaching at their hospital foundations. The largest of the secular hospitals supported teaching: the endowment of St Leonard's, York, was enough to provide for two schoolmasters as well as a substantial library.[82] The only monastic hospital known to have maintained a schoolmaster was the hospital of St Mark at

76 T. Arnold, ed., *Memorials of St Edmund's Abbey*, 3 vols, RS (1896), III, 249.
77 *VCH Essex*, II, 518–19.
78 *Memorials of St Edmund's Abbey*, ed. Arnold, III, 182–3.
79 J. M. Wilson, ed., *The Liber Albus of the Priory of Worcester*, Worcester Historical Soc., 33 (1919), p. 65.
80 Dobson, *Durham Priory*, pp. 156–62 (p. 162).
81 Clark, *Monastic Renaissance*, pp. 17, 95.
82 *VCH Yorkshire*, III, 336–43 (pp. 337, 343).

Bristol, a special case since it adopted the Benedictine rule only in the four-teenth century.[83] There is circumstantial evidence to suggest similar provisions were made elsewhere. The master of the almonry school at Durham Priory was obliged to celebrate mass at St Mary Magdalen hospital: perhaps he performed other services there.[84]

The almonry boys may have been the only properly constituted school in the monastic precincts – excepting the presence of a cohort of singing boys – but they represented only one of several groups of youths present there for academic and practical instruction. Monastic superiors still admitted the sons of founders or other leading benefactors into their own households for the benefit of both clerical and domestic training, as many had done since earliest times. It has been suggested the practice declined sharply after 1200 but evidence from that later period is equal to that from the monastic 'golden age'.[85] The monasteries could no longer claim their old monopoly on the ecclesiastical patronage of the magnates in this period but many families of both high and middle rank continued to turn to them for the education, training and protection of their children. These secular sojourners are glimpsed only rarely in surviving monastic sources. A fuller picture of their place in the monasteries of this period is often provided by the papers of the patrons themselves. It is not uncommon for the claustral custody of children to be found among testamentary bequests. In 1500 John Lepyngton willed that his son be boarded with the prior of Bridlington, East Riding, for four years.[86]

There were occasions in the later period when a poor boy was supported in this way through the personal charity of the superior. The distinguished scholar monk, Richard of Wallingford (c.1290–1334), a son of the smithy, received his early education at Wallingford Priory through the philanthropy of Prior William de Kirkeby.[87] Perhaps it was the poverty of the unnamed undergraduate Bodenham that persuaded Abbot Walter de Monington of Glastonbury to support him at Oxford in 1365.[88] Probably there were many more cases where the charity of the monastic community began even closer to home. The case of John Mason (b. 1503) of Abingdon combined charity both to home and heartland: Mason was the son of an Abingdon cowherd but also the nephew

---

[83] J. H. Bettey, *Suppression of the Religious Houses in Bristol* (Bristol, 1990), pp. 2, 20; *VCH Gloucestershire*, II. 117–18. There were both children and choristers present at the surrender on 9 December 1539.

[84] *VCH Durham*, II. 119–20; *Rites of Durham*, p. 78.

[85] Elizabeth Gardner sees secular sojourners as primarily a pre- and post-Conquest phenomenon: E. J. Gardner, 'The English Nobility and Monastic Education, c.1100–1500', in *The Cloister and World: Essays on Medieval History in Honour of Barbara Harvey*, ed. J. Blair and B. Golding (Oxford, 1996), pp. 80–94 (p. 92).

[86] See also C. Cross, 'Monasticism and Society in the Diocese of York, 1520–40', *TRHS*, 5th series, 38 (1988), 131–45 (p. 137).

[87] Richard's early life is recalled in *Gesta abbatum*, ed. Riley, II, 181–3. See also J. D. North, *God's Clockmaker: Richard of Wallingford and the Invention of Time* (London, 2005), pp. 18–25.

[88] Emden, *BRUO*, I, 208.

of an Abingdon monk. He received his education at the expense, if not the direct hand, of his uncle, and later prospered at Oxford and in the service of the king.[89]

The admission of a boy into the abbot (or prior's) *familia* was a favour to a 'friend' of the monastery but it was also a formal transaction sealed on payment of a fee and the exchange of indentures. The executors of Ralph Snaith were instructed to agree with the prior an appropriate sum for the 'burds and lernyng' of his two sons.[90] The register of Prior Edmund Forest of Llanthony Secunda preserves an indenture of 1513 recording the admission of one William Peryeman of Westbury-on-Severn into his household 'to be the servaunt of the said Edmunde and to dwell with him during the terme of 3 yeris ... and all the precepts and commaundements lawfull of the said Edmunde the said William shall well and truly and diligently observe'.[91] While there may have been families which placed their boys in a monastic household purely to experience the workings of a great establishment, in this case a curriculum of study was clearly prescribed: 'the said Edmunde shall cause the said William to be taught and informed in playing at organs by the space of oone yere of the said 3 yeres and in gramer the othr 2 yeres'.[92] There was probably greater scope here than in the almonry school for personal variations in the programme of study. When Lord Lisle placed his stepson, James Basset, into the custody of Abbot Hugh Cook of Reading in 1534 he specified that he should be 'plythe hym to his learning bothe Latin and Frenche', the latter unlikely to be taught in the almonry at this date as a matter of course.[93]

There is no sign of a sudden decline in the practice prior to the Dissolution. The rhetoric of Robert Aske regarding the care of the religious houses for the children of the gentry may not be persuasive in itself, but the presence of well born youths is well documented in the Dissolution decade and not only in the northern counties.[94] Writing to Cromwell in 1535, Abbot John Sheppey of Faversham (1499–1538) bore witness to 'suche feithfull approved servauntes whome I have brought upp in mye poure house frome their tendre yeres'.[95]

The support of individual scholars was probably not the sole preserve of monastic superiors but was a form of patronage practised by other officers of the monastery. At the greater abbeys and priories the senior obedientiaries gathered their own cohort of *familiares* – indeed some even convened their own coun-

---

89 Emden, *BRUO, 1501–1540*, pp. 386–88 (p. 386).
90 *Test. Ebor.*, III, 204–5.
91 Rhodes, ed., *Registers of Llanthony*, pp. 114–15.
92 Ibid.
93 *VCH Berkshire*, II, 68–9.
94 In his apologia Aske claimed, 'their young sons there succoured and in nunneries their daughters brought up in virtue'. See R. W. Hoyle, *The Pilgrimage of Grace and the Politics of the 1530s* (Oxford, 2001), p. 47. For such youths at Boxgrove and Woburn see *VCH Bedfordshire*, I, 367; *VCH Sussex*, II, 59.
95 T. Wright, ed., *Three Chapters of Letters relating to the Suppression of Monasteries*, Camden Soc., os, 26 (1843), pp. 103–7 (p. 104).

cils – and there may have been young men among them who, in some way or another, were considered to be under instruction.

The greater abbeys and priories also appear to have played host to young men seeking various forms of vocational training. It was perhaps only to be expected that the chancery of pre-eminent monastic prelates such as the abbot of St Albans and the prior of Durham should attract legal professionals at the beginning of their career. At St Albans there appears to have been a small group of apprentices-at-law present in the precincts at least for much of the first half of the fifteenth century. The mere fact of their presence at the abbey does not prove their close interaction with the monastic community as a whole but it is worth noting that the name of one notary is preserved on the flyleaf of manuscript from the library and, according to a fifteenth-century inventory of burials, three unfortunate apprentices were accorded the singular privilege of burial in the cloister.[96] The letters and fragments of letters preserved in a fourteenth-century Durham manuscript attest to a similar presence at the priory as much as a century earlier. It is not unlikely that a number of civil lawyers and notaries launched their careers in a monastic context.[97]

These forms of patronage were focused on the monastery and its own resources but this period also saw a surprising number of monasteries extend their support to scholars and scholarship beyond the convent walls. Most commonly, as compotus rolls, registers and other documents record, they made regular *ad hoc* payments to particular scholars to support periods both at grammar school and university. The Bolton Priory compotus records a payment in 1395 of 2s for 'cuidam pauperi scolari eunti ad scolas'.[98] In a number of cases the financial assistance of the abbot and convent was accompanied by their letters of recommendation dispatched to masters or other officials outside the liberty, documents that are occasionally preserved in conventual registers.[99] Pre-Reformation records show that several convents contributed to regular exhibitions for students of the city or diocese. At the Dissolution, Gloucester Abbey funded no fewer than thirteen students at the town's grammar school.[100] The sixteenth-century accounts of Tewkesbury Abbey record an annual contribution of £3 11s 8d to clothe sixteen of the town's schoolboys.[101] At York, the abbot and

---

[96]   H. T. Riley, ed., *Annales Monasterii S. Albani, a Johanne Amundesham Monacho, ut videtur, conscripti (A.D. 1421–1440)*, 2 vols, RS (1870–71), I, 439, 441–2.

[97]   C. R. Cheney, 'Law and Letters in Fourteenth-century Durham: a Study of Corpus Christi College, Cambridge, MS 450', *Bulletin of the John Rylands University Library of Manchester* 55 (1972), 60–85. See also Dobson, *Durham Priory*, pp. 131–42. For a parallel community of professional lawyers at Christ Church, Canterbury, see R. A. L. Smith, *Canterbury Cathedral Priory. A Study in Monastic Administration* (Cambridge, 1969), p. 70.

[98]   I. Kershaw and D. M. Smith, eds, *The Bolton Priory Compotus, 1268–1325, together with a priory account roll for 1377–1378*, YASRS, 154 (2000), p. 560.

[99]   Clark, *Monastic Renaissance*, pp. 72–8 at 74.

[100] Savine, 'English Monasteries', p. 231.

[101] Ibid., p. 232.

convent of St Mary's contributed, together with other regular and secular institutions, to the city's support of poor scholars.[102]

It is worth noting that the continuing interest of the monasteries in lay education was matched in many nunneries. There was no formal school foundation in the precincts of the female monastery, even for prospective novices, but anecdotal and documentary evidence suggests many provided schooling *ad hoc*. The pioneering Eileen Power found forty-nine female houses, dispersed across twenty-one counties, which harboured children between 1282 and 1537.[103] In some case this *schooling* may have been simply an extension of provision the nuns already made for the care and custody of infants: there are examples – e.g. St Katherine's Priory, Lincoln – of orphanages in the precincts of a nunnery.[104] The larger houses, however, appear to have admitted children into their custody apparently more-or-less on the same basis as the men. In her survey of the pre-Reformation records of Yorkshire, Jo-Ann Moran found references to 'schools', no doubt of varying degrees of formality and size, at a dozen different nunneries.[105] There were no fewer than twenty-six 'chyldren of lordys, knyghttes and gentylmen' seen at St Mary's Abbey (Nunnaminster) Winchester, when the Cromwellian commissioners arrived in 1535.[106] The appearance, at Winchester, of boys in the custody of the women religious does not appear to have been exceptional despite the disapproval it drew from their (male) monastic or episcopal governors. The placement of a girl in the custody of women religious, of course, was frequently invested with different impulses from the entry of a young gentleman into the household of an abbot or prior. Any educational benefit accrued may have been secondary to the political or social purpose of securing her temporary withdrawal from the world although recent studies of the books of the pre-Reformation nunneries suggest the greatest houses were certainly capable of offering a modicum of 'book learning'.[107]

The continuing profile of the greater abbeys and priories as patrons of schools and schooling now persuaded a growing number of lay patrons to engage them, as they might a secular prelate, in their own educational schemes. Several school founders of the fifteenth century placed their foundations in the trust of

---

102 *VCH County of York*, I, 421.
103 E. Power, *Medieval English Nunneries* (Cambridge, 1922), pp. 237–84 (pp. 261–77, especially 262, 264). Power's findings have been repeated by Elizabeth Gardener, 'English Nobility and Monastic Education', pp. 80–94.
104 J. J. Scarisbrick, *The Reformation and the English People* (Oxford, 1984), p. 6.
105 Moran, *Schooling*, pp. 100 and note, 115–16, 238, 263, 268, 271, 278.
106 *VCH Hampshire*, II, 125.
107 Power doubted that the teaching of nunnery children amounted to more than the alphabet, the *Credo*, *Ave* and *Pater noster*: *Medieval English Nunneries*, pp. 276–77. Gardener followed her, 'so far as book learning was concerned [the education they received] was extremely limited': 'English Nobility and Monastic Education', p. 94. However, for recent studies see D. Bell, *What Nuns Read* (Kalamazoo, 1995); P. Lee, *Nunneries, Learning and Spirituality in Late Medieval English Society* (Woodbridge, 2001); M. C. Erler, *Women, Reading and Piety in Late Medieval England* (Cambridge, 2002). See also evidence of the books at pre-Reformation Barking: *English Benedictine Libraries*, ed. Sharpe et al., B7. 6 (p. 15).

their neighbouring monastery. Under the terms of her will Joan Huddleston of Winchcombe entrusted the endowment of a school for poor boys to the town's Benedictine monastery.[108] The prior and convent of Lenton, Nottinghamshire, were named as supervisors of the endowment bequeathed for the foundation of a school at Lenton that was to be directly administered by the town's governors.[109] A Lewes testator left £20 to the prior and convent of the Cluniac priory to appoint a schoolmaster for the Sussex village of Southover.[110] The abbot and convent of Sherborne were bound to provide three exhibitions (at a total value of 78s) for scholars of the town school at Sherborne under the terms of one of their own benefactor's wills.[111]

There are also a surprising number of examples when either the abbot, or the abbot and convent as a corporate whole, collaborated with the secular patron as co-founder of a secular school. Bruton School (1519) was the co-foundation of Richard Fitzjames, former warden of Merton College, Oxford, and (from 1506) bishop of London, and Abbot William Gilbert of the Augustinian abbey. The school was positioned directly opposite the abbey gatehouse.[112] In the same way, the new school founded at Milton, Dorset, in 1521 was the co-creation of magnates Sir Thomas Arundel and Sir Giles Strangeways, who shared the stewardship of the monastery, and Abbot William Middleton.[113] Of course, it could be objected that the common ground between these clerical and lay patrons was in large part circumstantial. Bishop Fitzjames was bound to Bruton and its environs by family ties and before the school foundation had made a major benefaction to the parish church.[114] In the same way, Strangeways derived much of his income and influence from his supervision of the Milton estates; his co-foundation of the school might be said to have simply added another dimension.[115] However, at least some of these school patrons also shared a common cultural and perhaps scholarly background. Abbots Gilbert and Lichfield were graduate monks, educated and formed in the same environment as the scholar-bishops Alcock and Fitzjames and quite possibly (although none of their books or personal papers survive) sharing the same early humanist enthusiasm as their episcopal colleagues.[116]

It is perhaps as an expression of the common – and quasi-humanist – conception of education that had emerged among some secular and regular clergy, and some lay patrons, in early Tudor England, that we can explain the first form of Brasenose and Corpus Christi Colleges founded at Oxford between 1512 and 1517. From the beginning Brasenose was conceived as a secular college,

---

[108] VCH *Gloucestershire*, II, 420–21; Savine, 'English Monasteries', p. 231.
[109] VCH *Nottinghamshire*, II, 98–9.
[110] VCH *Sussex*, II, 412–13.
[111] VE, I, 284.
[112] VCH *Somerset*, II, 136–7.
[113] VCH *Dorset*, II, 61. See also J. P. Traskey, *Milton Abbey: a Dorset Monastery in the Middle Ages* (Tisbury, 1978).
[114] VCH *Somerset*, II, 136. For Fitzjames see also Emden, *BRUO*, II, 691–2.
[115] VCH *Dorset*, II, 61.
[116] Emden, *BRUO*, II, 691–2 (Fitzjames); 768 (Gilbert); 1183 (Lychefeld).

but the pattern of religious observance proposed by its co-founder Sir Richard Sutton (a common lawyer, and also steward of Syon Abbey) was unquestionably monastic.[117] Corpus Christi College was first offered to the university in 1513 by Bishop Richard Fox as a monastic foundation, an Oxford *studium* for the monks of St Swithun's Priory, Winchester. It was only after the building work had begun – and, apparently, a number of student monks had already taken up residence – that Fox's anti-monastic colleagues persuaded him to secularise the scheme.[118]

There is no doubt the monasteries' involvement in secular education on the eve of the Dissolution was more extensive than it had been in earlier centuries. The provision of a school for poor boys and other fee-payers was no longer the preserve of a handful of prestige abbeys of the Benedictines. In fact between the fourteenth and the sixteenth centuries there were schools to be found at houses of all orders, even at those in remote, rural locations, where the schoolboys surely outnumbered the convent's own *schola* of novices. Moreover, many monasteries now reclaimed their early role as guardians of popular education, through their patronage of parish churches, and of the range of clerical communities that remained under their jurisdiction. They also sponsored individuals as well as institutions: in the half century before the Henrician Reformation there may have been a significant minority sustained at school and university by a monastic patron. Their prominence in this field even persuaded a handful of secular clerical and lay benefactors to entrust them with their own endowments. Barely twenty years before the Dissolution there emerged the prospect of further fruitful collaboration between the monastic order and leading figures in the clerical and educational establishment, for example, Bishop Fitzjames of London and Bishop Fox of Winchester.

These developments were driven at least in part by the different demands of monastic life in the later Middle Ages. The inexorable expansion of their liturgical obligations made the monasteries increasingly dependent upon the assistance of secular clerks, and the almonry school was promoted (by the monks and by their episcopal supervisors) as the principal means of their recruitment and training. Their return to secular education was surely also stimulated by a shift in their corporate outlook, their determination, as expressed, from the turn of the thirteenth century onwards, in the preamble to capitular statutes, in capitular sermons, and other official texts, to recover – from the mendicants, the secular clergy, from secular lordships even – the spiritual as well as the seigniorial supervision of their lay subjects. At this level there was no altruism in the almonry school and their other scholastic provisions: they represented another territory in which the war over jurisdiction might be prosecuted. Yet it would be wrong to interpret the involvement of the monasteries in secular schooling

---

[117] I. S. Leadam, 'The Early Years of the College', in *Brasenose College Quatercentenary Monographs, II. Special Records*, ed. A. J. Butler et al. (Oxford, 1909), pp. 13–51 (pp. 23, 33–4). For Sutton see J. G. Clark, 'Sutton, Sir Richard, c. 1460–1524', *ODNB*, 26802.
[118] For the foundation of Corpus Christi see *VCH Oxfordshire*, II, 219–28 (pp. 219–20).

purely in practical or political terms. These changes can also be connected to the cultural influences that entered English convents in the centuries before the Dissolution. The thirteenth-century reform of monastic studies exposed monastic communities more thoroughly than ever before to the culture of the secular clergy. Over time it was not only the textbooks and teaching methods of the seculars that entered the cloister, but also a taste of their prejudices and preoccupations. Monastic preachers now opined to their brethren on the problems of the parish, the priesthood and the spectre of popular heresy, and for many of their listeners it seemed the vocation of *monachus* had become overlaid with the obligations both of *magister* and *pastor*. It was perhaps only to be expected in this climate that convents (and individual monks) should seek to secure a stronger purchase on the educational provisions in their own locality. These concerns coloured their patronage towards the secular schools, parish churches and possibly also the hospitals under their jurisdiction. It appears they also served to soften something of the old animosity between a monastery and the secular clergy, in some instances leading to their collaboration in schemes to increase opportunities for schooling in the liberty, or even the diocese. In the second half of the fifteenth century, as humanist values spread among the graduate clergy, both regular and secular, this common outlook on matters of learning was only strengthened.

There is no indication that their commitment to these issues diminished in the countdown to the Dissolution. The little that is known of the reading patterns of pre-Reformation monks suggests there was considerable interest in modish textbooks and pedagogical tracts.[119] At an institutional level, the monastic patronage of schoolmasters continued under the eyes of the *Valor* commissioners, even, in the case of Leonard Cox, when the master in question consorted with known heretics.[120] Indeed it may be that their hybrid identity – *monachus, magister* – their interest in education *per se*, eased the passage of some of these monks into post-Dissolution society. Certainly it is worth noting the number of ex-monks known to have served as schoolmasters, not infrequently in the same locality as their former community. Several also sought to establish schools of their own. The former prior of Guisborough, Robert Pursglove, served for a time as provost of Rotherham College and himself endowed a grammar school at his home village of Tideswell.[121] Richard Boreman alias Stevenage, former abbot of St Albans, secured a grant of the former Lady Chapel to serve as a schoolhouse, and surely a deliberate substitute for the former almonry school suppressed a decade before.[122] It has often been remarked how rapidly at the Dissolution the ex-religious seemed to assume the role (and stipends) of the

---

119   *English Benedictine Libraries*, ed. Sharpe et al., B55. 71, 85, 138, B117. 55 (pp. 277, 279, 287, 670).
120   S. F. Ryle, 'Cox, Leonard, b. c. 1495, d. in or after 1549', *ODNB*, 6525.
121   Emden, *BRUO, 1501–1540*, pp. 467–8, 735. See also M. F. H. Hulbert, *Bishop Pursglove of Tideswell, 1504–80* (Tideswell, 1994).
122   J. G. Clark, 'Reformation and Reaction at St Albans Abbey, c. 1530–58', *EHR* 115 (2000), 297–328.

secular clergy, as if it was a reflection of how alienated from the monastic vocation many of them had already become.[123] The examples of ex-monks pursuing
pedagogic careers could be seen, on the contrary, as an indication of the conti-
nuities in their pre- and post-Dissolution self-image. In this way it might also
be argued that a new generation of schools (and schoolmasters) was indeed
raised from the resources of the monasteries, although hardly in the way the
Henrician reformers had intended.

---

[123] For example, G. Baskerville, *English Monks and the Suppression of the Monasteries* (London,
1937), pp. 246–70 (pp. 254–8).

11

'Make straight in the desert a highway for our God': The Carthusians and Community in Late Medieval England

GLYN COPPACK

The Carthusians were exceptional among medieval religious in that they were, in theory at least, in business for the salvation of their own souls. Guiges de Saint-Romain, fifth prior of the Grande Chartreuse, who wrote the order's customs before 1133, said that 'it was not for the temporal cure of other folk's bodies but for the eternal welfare of our own souls that we took refuge in the retirement of this desert'.[1] While that was the reason for discouraging guests and hospitality, a central tenet of Benedictine monasticism, it underlined the separation and exclusiveness that were the Carthusians' contract with God, symbolised by their withdrawal to desert places.[2] Yet in the later Middle Ages we find that the Carthusians were clearly respected by broad elements of society, supported by princes, and building their monasteries not in the wilderness, but in well-watered deer parks, on the edges of major towns, or alongside major roads.[3] The order proudly proclaimed that it was *nunquam reformata quia nunquam deformata*, yet it had changed substantially by the late fourteenth century and was still developing in the early sixteenth century. Henry VIII expected, and desperately needed, the Carthusians to endorse the 1534 Acts of Succession and Supremacy. Their opinion counted with society at large, despite their small numbers – there were only nine Carthusian monasteries out of approximately 836 monastic houses in England and Wales. The priors of London, Axholme

[1]   E. M. Thompson, *The Carthusian Order in England* (London, 1930), p. 25, from her partial translation of Guigonis I. *Carthusie Majoris Prior V. Consuetudines*, in J.-P. Migne, ed., Patrologiae Cursus Completus, Series Latina, 153, cols 635ff.

[2]   On the theme of the Cistercians and hospitality see the paper by Julie Kerr, above, pp. 25–39.

[3]   While the first English foundation of Witham in Somerset was established on a remote site in the royal forest of Selwood in 1178/9, subsequent foundations at Hinton (1227) and Beauvale (1343) were established in the deer parks of their founders. London (1371), Coventry (1381), and Hull (1377) were all immediately suburban; Axholme (1397/8) and Mount Grace (1398) were rural but not remote; and Sheen (1414) was adjacent to the royal palace of Sheen/Richmond.

Fig. 11.1. The small Carthusian church at Mount Grace. (Glyn Coppack)

and Beauvale died not because they refused to swear the oaths attached to these acts, but because they said it was none of their business to get involved with affairs of state. There is no evidence in 1534 that any Carthusian monk in England opposed the early stages of the Reformation. It was their failure to promote it that destroyed many of them.[4] So how did the Carthusians become so important and influential in the later Middle Ages? By looking at the charterhouses of London and Mount Grace, and particularly the latter, it is possible to reconstruct their relationship with society.

First and foremost was the wish for many people to be buried in a charterhouse, or if that was not possible to be remembered in the monks' prayers, something which translated specifically into the purchase of obits by the 1480s and confraternity somewhat earlier. A typical compromise would be for a man or woman to will his or her body to the friars, but at the same time to seek prayers and obits from the Carthusians. At London and Mount Grace this manifested

---

[4]   For the government attack on the Carthusians see Knowles, RO, III, 222–32.

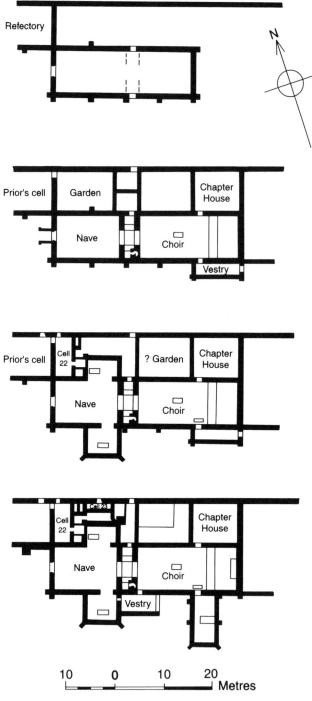

Fig. 11.2. The four phases of development of the Mount Grace church. (Glyn Coppack)

itself in a rapidly growing church, with the addition of burial chapels and the extension of altar space. Carthusian churches were by their very nature small and plain. At Mount Grace (Figs 11.1 and 11.2), the four-bay church of about 1400, one of the first buildings to be erected, was substantially modified, yet it was used by the community only for vespers and the night offices. Its growth can be directly related to the demand for burial.[5] In 1417 the General Chapter granted Thomas Beaufort the right of sepulture in the priory church,[6] and the extension of the presbytery and the erection of a bell tower are associated with his burial in 1427 at the centre of the choir. Effectively Beaufort had installed himself as a second founder. Before this date, the only burial recorded was that of Thomas de Holand in 1411, and wills provide evidence of only two bequests to Mount Grace, one specifically for the building of a cell. Between 1420 and 1440 there were four further bequests, three of them associated with burial. In 1432 William de Authorp, rector of Kirk Deighton and a kinsman of John de Ingleby, with Thomas de Holand co-founder of the house, desired to be buried in the church at Mount Grace, and he left to the prior and convent a silver cup, 12 silver spoons, and a book called *Pupilla occuli*.[7] In 1436 Thomas Lokwood of Estharlesey Graunge, a tenant of Rievaulx Abbey, willed 20s and requested that his body be buried in the church at Mount Grace,[8] and in July 1438, Eleanor de Roos was buried there and left to the convent a silver vessel with a cover, and a noble apiece to the other eight English charterhouses.[9]

By the 1460s, the church was already too small and it was extended, first by the addition of a transept chapel on the south side of the nave, and then by a second on the north side, though in this period only one burial was specifically willed to the site (Fig. 11.3). Joan Ingleby, widow of Sir William Ingleby, died in October 1478, and although she made no pecuniary bequest to the convent, she bequeathed her body for burial there, suggesting that she or her husband had supported the community during their lifetimes.[10] It must be admitted that the evidence from wills is only partial, for both chapels contain clear evidence of several burials. From 1480 to the suppression in 1538 there was a steady series of bequests purchasing obits, though less than half required the burial of the donor. Burial was still common, however, with a third chapel added to the south side of the presbytery in the 1520s (Fig. 11.3), associated with the Strangwayes family of East Harlsey who had been patrons of the house from as early as 1456 and whose first recorded burial there was in 1476. On 2 September 1532 Sir Thomas Stangwayes of Harlsey Castle desired:

to be beriede at Mountgrace where as the Prior of the same house thynkes best. Also I gif to my corseprisaunce my best horse. Also I give to the Mountgrace, if it please God that I be beriede there, on other horse. Also I gif to the saide house

5 On patrons and burials see the essay by Karen Stöber, above, pp. 11–24.
6 Thompson, *Carthusian Order in England*, pp. 231–2.
7 *Test. Ebor.*, III, 351.
8 Ibid., III, 483.
9 Ibid., II, 65.
10 Ibid., III, 243.

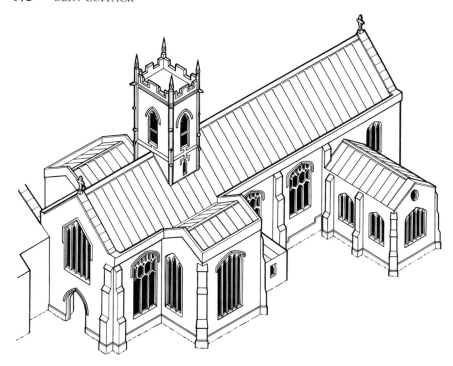

Fig. 11.3. Reconstruction of the Mount Grace church as it appeared in the early sixteenth century. (Simon Hayfield/English Heritage)

> of Mountgrace, and the brether of the same, for to pray for my saull, lxs. ... also I will that the Prior of the Mountgrace have, to pray for my saull and Cristen saulles that God wold have praid for xxs.

He also provided £4 for three years to support the priest 'that synges at our Lady chapell of Mountegrace'.[11]

The picture at London was almost identical, but there we know that individuals actually provided the chapels, or at least the altars, associated with their burials. That the church should be heavily modified not for the benefit of the community but for the advantage of the laity might seem surprising in an order that wished to cut itself off from the world. It was not just the building that reflected this ideology; the aspirations of the Carthusians also extended to the furniture within the church. When the chapel of St Jerome and St Bernard was built at the expense of Sir John Popham who was buried there in 1453 it was fitted up with:

> an alter table wythe a Crucyfyx of Marye and John, ij Imagys at ether ende of the sayd alter, the one of Irone the other of saint Barnard, the sayd Chappell being partelye scelyd wyth wayn skotte.

11   Ibid., V, 115–16.

Within there were 'ij seates and a lyttell Coffer', and to these can be added rich altar cloths and vestments, Turkey carpets and cushions, all out of keeping with the rule.[12]

While the strictness of Carthusian life obviously added to the effects and desirability of the community's prayers and led lay people to want to be associated with the Carthusians, the Carthusians were also happy to accommodate them in a manner that was far from their own ideals. This compromise indicates a close association in life, underlined by the fact that well connected lay men, for instance Sir Thomas More in London, might live for a time within the charterhouse. Lay people might sponsor cells or even individual monks, just as Dame Jane Strangways left sums of 10s to Dan Richard Methley and Dan Thurstan of the Mountgrace in 1500.[13] That Carthusian monks should be in receipt of money at all was a serious infraction of the customs, but at both London and Mount Grace it appears to have been the norm. As we will see, it was not only bequests that came into the hands of the religious.

It was to the prior of Mount Grace, Nicholas Love, to whom Thomas Arundel turned in 1410, commissioning him to make an English translation of Bonaventure's *Meditationes vitae Christi* 'to the confusion of all fals Lollardes and heretikes'.[14] Love's *Mirrour of the Blessed Lyfe of Jesu* was to circulate widely outside Carthusian circles, providing an extensive English commentary on the Gospels, and finally appearing in print towards the end of the fifteenth century. So detailed was the commentary that Love had virtually produced an unofficial English translation of the Gospels, surely some thing of which Archbishop Arundel could hardly have approved, though he did accept the confraternity of Mount Grace. Love was not the only monk of Mount Grace writing for the outside world. An unknown monk of the house wrote to an equally anonymous monk of London:

> in this last yere I sent to a devoute preeste of my knowlegge a copy of the Reuelacion ... Which ye sende me. And the same preste sent dyuers copies to certeyn of hys Frendes, of whom ther was a good husbond man harde of the grete vartu and grace of the forsaid prayers he vsed it dayly as deuoutly as he coulde.[15]

Effectively, Carthusian teaching, which made great use of the vernacular as opposed to Latin, could be spread outside the monastery without monks leaving the enclosure of the great cloister. Mount Grace produced two other authors of distinction, John Norton, prior to 1521, and Richard Methley who entered religion in 1485 and who was still alive in 1507/8. Both wrote primarily for their

12 W. H. St J. Hope, *The History of the London Charterhouse from its Foundation until the Suppression of the Monastery* (London, 1925), p. 185.
13 *Test. Ebor.*, IV, 189.
14 Thompson, *Carthusian Order in England*, p. 339, n. 3, quoting a note on Bodl., MS 634 in *Catalogue of Western MSS in the Bodleian Library*, No. 27689, and n. 4, Arundel's Register, fol. 121d.
15 F. Wormald, ed., 'The Revelation of the Hundred Paternosters: a Fifteenth-century Meditation', *Laudate* (1936), 165–82.

Fig. 11.4. The excavations of the eastern cells of the great cloister at Mount Grace. (Laurence Keen)

own communities but Methley also wrote for laymen outside the monastery. His letter 'to Hew Heremyte' was clearly a reply to a request for spiritual guidance.[16] While the documentary evidence is intriguing, it is more than confirmed by the archaeology of the great cloister and its enclosed cells.

The Carthusian cell was essentially a private monastery, and provided everything an individual monk required. At Mount Grace, eight cells have been excavated since 1968, providing exceptional evidence for what happened inside them (Fig. 11.4). The cell is a two-storey house, with an entry passage, living room, study, and bedroom and oratory on the ground floor with a work room above, set typically in the corner of a garden about 15m square and surrounded by walls 3m or more high. The garden was the receptacle of choice for any rubbish produced in the cell, and it is unlikely to have migrated. Thus the gardens themselves tell us quite a lot about individual members of the community. The latest garden of Cell 8 was nothing exceptional, a vegetable garden dug in rows with rather unimpressive paths of gravel. The rubbish spread around it was, however, quite exceptional. The last monk in this cell had been a book-binder and the garden was littered with the detritus of his trade: bindings, strap ends, and clasps from books. We even have his pliers. This would have not

---

[16] J. Hogg, ed., 'Richard Methley: To Hew Heremyte, a pystyl of solytary lyfe nowadayes', *Analecta Cartusiana* 31 (1977), 91–119 (p. 101).

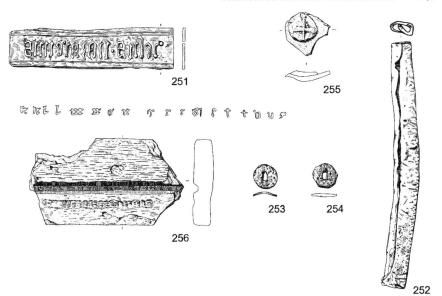

Fig. 11.5. Finds from Cell 11 at Mount Grace, including a retrograde *Iesus Nazarenus* strip (251) and the mould for casting type (256). (English Heritage)

been so significant if it were not for finds from several other cells in this part of the cloister that indicated without a doubt that the Mount Grace community had been producing books on an industrial scale. Cells 10 and 11 produced copper alloy pen nibs and Cell 10 lead dry points, Cells 12 and 13 had oyster shells containing coloured pigment, and Cell 12 also produced a stone 'rubber' for grinding pigment or polishing parchment. One can almost imagine the lay brother on his rounds around the great cloister taking copied folios from the hatches of Cells 10 and 11, placing them in the hatches of Cells 12 and 13 to have colour added, and finally taking the finished work to Cell 8 where it was bound. The scale of this work was too great simply to be mere evidence copying of books for the house's own library or even circulation within the order. The monk in Cell 11 seems to have tried his hand at printing. Within the cell was found a stone mould (Fig. 11.5, 256) with a groove approximately 6–7mm wide at the bottom, 11mm at the top, and 5–6mm deep with incised gothic lower-case letters from k to x. There is a fragment of a letter before the first k; both k's are divided, rather like 1c; there is insufficient space for the tails of the p and q; and x is broken. A groove of this nature and size could only be used to cast in metal a strip of letters to be cut up and rearranged as required. What seems clear is that the letter-forms are based on contemporary handwriting and compare well with the typefaces in printed books with which the monks would have been familiar. But to what purpose might the type have been put? It seems unlikely that the monks would have even contemplated full-scale book printing, though this object implies more than a passing understanding of the process. One is surely looking at a much smaller and less exacting enterprise.

As it is clear that the charterhouse was giving out letters of confraternity (two examples are known – one for 1515, the other for 1520), and such letters were being printed for other monasteries and gilds, the possibility emerges, therefore, that the monks might have attempted to print their letters of confraternity. The proof, however, must await the discovery of a printed Mount Grace example.

Mount Grace Priory is exceptional for the provision of its guest accommodation. For a Carthusian house to encourage guests was contrary to the twelfth-century customs. Mount Grace, however, lay on the pilgrimage route between York and Durham, a day's journey north of York, which probably explains why there are two guest houses, and by the 1520s a hostel called *le Inne* sponsored by Sir John Rawson, master of the Irish Hospitalry of Kilmainham before the siege of Rhodes.[17] The northern guest house contained four small apartments, one large apartment, and the guest hall, and the southern guest house a further four small apartments and a common dormitory on two floors. Clearly Mount Grace took its obligations to travellers seriously and at some considerable expense. The whole of the western side of the inner court was given over to visitors.

Just what the monks made of their visitors becomes very clear when the contents of the excavated cells are further examined. The most common non-monastic objects to be found were cast lead strips with the legend *iehus nazarenus* in retrograde (Fig. 11.5, 251). No fewer than four of these were excavated, but what purpose did they serve? They are not furniture fittings, for they have no fixings. The current thought is that they are the moulds for clay plaques, the religious equivalent of seaside ashtrays inscribed 'a Present from Whitby', or they could have been used for producing a clay mould which would then have been used to print images on paper. Clearly, if pilgrims travelling between the shrines of St William and St Cuthbert were going to stay at Mount Grace they might as well be exploited before they left! More seriously, the community had found a way of serving society, and it would be strange if the souvenirs were not seen as a form of indulgence. One further object may have been the result of this trade in religious items, a stone plaque with the demi-figure of Christ and an indulgence inscription from Cell 10. This object (Fig. 11.6) is not in itself a devotional item, but it could have been used for producing a clay mould which would then have been used to print images on paper. The result would not have been entirely successful, and this object was carefully buried in the latrine pentice of the cell to prevent it falling into the wrong hands.

Money was clearly involved in the transaction evidenced by these objects, because the second commonest category of small finds were coin balances and weights, from Cells 10, 11, and 14 and the great cloister alley. The presence of balances and weights indicate that money must have been present in some quantity. Individual members of the community were receiving money from outside the monastery; so much is clear from wills. At London, such bequests

---

[17] 'Wee have a proper lodging at our place wich a marchand of London did buld and he is now departed from hus and made knight at the roddes', for which see BL, MS Add. 48965, fol. 6, a letter from Prior John Wilson written to Henry, Lord Clifford, on 13 December 1522.

Fig. 11.6. The pardon panel from Cell 10 at Mount Grace. (James Barfoot)

were vested in the prior and used for the purchase of books, repairs to the fabric, and other 'approved' uses, even though this was specifically forbidden by the statutes and was regularly complained about by the visitors up to the 1520s. Thus there was no lessening of this rule, though it appears to have been more honoured in the breach up to the suppression, yet members of the Mount Grace community appear to have been handling coin as individuals.

Finally, we have to consider the members of the community themselves. Most seem to have come to the Carthusians later in life, and had previously been in contact with society. We have a waiting list written in 1527 which was used to explain to a generous patron, Henry, lord Clifford, why the convent could not accept his chaplain.

Morouer my lord wee haue but too celles voide and for thone wee haue promysed to receyve shortlie affter th'fest of th'epiphanie a worshipfull man S(ir) Willm Malev(er)er and he is brether childer a(nd) also he is both Comissarie and officialle to the bushop of Rochester a(nd) may spend better than xlli benefesse. His habbett is made redye for hym. And th'oder celle is not p(er)fetlie finished. Ther was a monke in it a yere a(nd) more and because I thought it nedefull to be mended putt hym in another celle. Albeit I had promised it to Mr Willm Stapilton who I here say is departed from this wretched liffe whos soule Ihs p(ar)done and affter hym wee graunted the supp(ri)or of Burton Abbaye, and then the p(ar)son of sanct Saueyour in York, and then a yong prest wich was shaven w^t huss v yere sence … and yesterday I receyuyd a l(ett)re from a graduett of Cambrige wich saithe he has a graunte in my predecessours tyme with diuersse other that makith grete instance.[18]

These were men with connections and men of status, much more so than the average choir monk. From the late fifteenth century there was also a growing number of university educated monks.

Their style of living, solitary though it might have been, was substantial. The cost of building a cell at London was £20, enabling endowment by individuals. At Mount Grace Thomas Beaufort 'built and endowed five cells in the same [place]'. Endowment and building need not have been contemporary events. Cell 1 bears the arms of Archbishop Richard Scrope of York who died in 1405, at least a decade before the cell was built. Cells 4 and 5, although the evidence is no longer clear, had label-stop shields with the arms of Gascoigne. Thus the likely founder was Sir William Gascoigne, chief justice of King's Bench and a friend of Scrope, who died in 1419. The arms of Redman quartering Aldburgh found on the label-stops of the door to the first prior's cell in the south-west cloister range are those of Sir Richard Redman, MP for Yorkshire between 1405 and 1421. At London, the founders of cells ranged from Bishops Hatfield of Durham and Buckingham of Lincoln, through the aristocracy represented by the countess of Pembroke and the earl of Suffolk, to substantial lay women like Felicia Aubrey and Margaret Tilney (wife of the butler of Boston). It was not just the buildings that were sponsored, but some of their contents. When Thomas Golwynne transferred from London to Mount Grace, he brought with him 'a wyde sloppe furryd to put ouer all my gere of the gyfte of my lady Conuay … a newe pylche of the gyft of Mr Saxby … a newe mantell by the gyfte of syr John Rawson Knyght of the Roods, [and] a new chafyng dysshe of laten gevyn to us and ij new tyne botylls gevyn by a kinsman of owres'.[19] Clearly there was a close relationship between individual monks who were so sponsored and their patrons. There is every indication that individual monks corresponded with their patrons – Richard Methley wrote at least twice to Henry, lord Clifford, both on the business of the house and on spiritual matters.[20]

---

[18] Ibid., fol. 7, in a letter from Wilson to Clifford dated 4 January 1523.
[19] TNA, State Papers Domestic Henry VIII, ix, fol. 170.
[20] BL, MS Add. 48965, fols 1–4.

The cell itself is highly indicative of the Carthusians' connections. The late medieval Carthusian cell takes its inspiration from contemporary provision in colleges and monastic halls in the universities. Thus the outside world was providing the framework for Carthusian life, perhaps not surprising when monks were drawn from the outside world, often towards middle age. The provision of a house that mirrored the life of a scholar or a secular priest is very apparent in the excavated Cell 10 at Mount Grace. With timber floors, a heated living room, timber partitions and plastered or panelled walls, this was hardly the home of a hermit. It was a form of accommodation that was to spread outside the Carthusian order. The Cistercians at Fountains, Byland, and Kirkstall were all to adopt two-roomed apartments within their infirmaries. They did not have the gardens that the Carthusians enjoyed but they did have everything else.

The gardens at Mount Grace could be vegetable gardens like the late garden of Cell 8. More usually, however, they were formal gardens of delight, employing designs that were normally the prerogative of the lordly classes. The early garden of Cell 8, of the last quarter of the fifteenth century, comprised regular raised beds and paved paths. In Cell 9, the garden had square knots and grass paths, and the garden of Cell 10 had raised paths around its garden beds and planting pits for shrubs. Quite clearly, the choir monks in these cells were very much aware of developments in gardening outside the monastery.

The picture which emerges in late medieval Carthusian monasteries is one of strong contrasts. The religious were maintaining an eremitic life within their cells, but were in close contact with society. Their church was given over to lay burial, to the extent that it was severely modified, and altar space was provided for the numerous obits the monks were contracted to say. Members of the community were writing for secular clergy and even laymen, and moreover they were writing in English. Guests were no longer actively discouraged, and at Mount Grace were openly exploited for the income they would provide, and the cloister was attracting men of substance and high status. Individuals were corresponding with their own patrons and they were handling coin. They were also very aware of developments outside the cloister, be it printing or gardening. Yet the Carthusians were highly regarded and their life considered hard and unremitting. Their prayers and advice were regularly sought right up to the suppression, and even the king believed he needed their support at the start of the Reformation. Perhaps most significantly, the order considered that it had not changed from its early simplicity.

MONASTERIES AND URBAN SPACE

12

Early Franciscan Legislation and Lay Society

JENS RÖHRKASTEN

The members of religious communities organised their lives according to the guidelines usually set by charismatic founder figures and eventually formulated into written norms. Apart from the rule which offered the foundation for all activity within and by the community, there could be customs (*consuetudines*), summarising past practices, and constitutions or statutes. Such legislative texts performed a number of functions. They were to ensure uniformity in liturgical practice, dress, food, work and discipline in a single monastery or in groups of convents geographically remote from each other, thus defining a religious order as a distinctive and separate legal body. In this sense they were points of reference for the internal government and administration which could be located in different geographical areas. They were also to guarantee the observance of principles which in their totality constituted the perfect life to be led by all members of the community. The texts preserved these principles for future generations, thus ensuring continuity.[1]

Given these main purposes, the normative texts in question were intended for the religious, that is, those who were immediately affected and not for a wider public. Although even the older religious orders had dealings with lay society, being involved in local economies and sometimes even in political ventures, this was hardly reflected in their normative texts. Exceptions were rare; one could think of the references to novices and to *pauperes*, recipients of alms, in the Benedictine rule.[2] Although the Franciscans remained influenced by earlier eremitical traditions, the order at large embraced a radically new

---

[1] G. Melville, 'Regeln – Consuetudines – Texte – Statuten. Positionen für eine Typologie des normativen Schrifttums religiöser Gemeinschaften im Mittelalter', in *Regulae – Consuetudines – Statuta. Studi sulle fonti normative degli ordini religiosi nei secoli centrali del Medioevo*, ed. C. Andenna and G. Melville, Atti del I e del II Seminario internazionale di studio del Centro italo-tedesco di storia comparata degli ordini religiosi, Bari/Noci/Lecce, 26–27 ottobre 2002; Castiglione delle Stiviere, 23–24 maggio 2003, Vita regularis, 25 (Münster, 2005), pp. 5–38.

[2] R. Hanslik, ed., *Benedicti Regula*, Corpus Scriptorum Ecclesiasticorum Latinorum, 75 (Vienna, 1960), XXXI, 9 (p. 88), LXVI, 3 (p. 156). Another reference to the outside world is made in LVIIII (pp. 138–41) and in LXVII (pp. 157–8): 'De fratribus in viam directis'.

way of interacting with lay society. Franciscans acted as preachers, confessors and spiritual advisers; they were involved in arbitration and conflict settlement; they acted as missionaries; they could be found at royal courts and were entrusted with political tasks by the papacy. They were visible and in permanent contact with the laity, not least because their convents were invariably located in or close to urban centres, where lay fraternities held their regular meetings in their churches.[3]

The aim of this paper is to identify the order's legislative responses to the consequences and problems arising out of the public nature of their life and work. The observations made here will be based on normative texts, mostly decisions made by general chapters up to the early fourteenth century. They can only be preliminary because medieval Franciscan legislation is still an enigmatic phenomenon, a statement perhaps best proved by the fact that the order's early general statutes have only very recently been published in a critical edition.[4]

At first sight the Franciscan *Regula bullata* of 1223 only appears to be dealing with internal matters. In its twelve chapters it addresses the conditions for joining the order, sets regulations for the conduct of divine service, deals with questions of discipline, fasting and work, defines the poverty ideal and regulates the election of superiors and the holding of chapters.[5] The legislation produced

---

[3] P. Adam, *La vie paroissale en France au XIVe siècle*, Histoire et Sociologie de l'Église, 3 (Paris, 1964), p. 68; J. Chiffoleau, *Les confréries, la mort et la religion en comtat venaissin à la fin du moyen âge*, Mélanges de l'École Française de Rome, 91 (1979), pp. 785–815 (pp. 792, 806). On the new forms of spirituality as a response to social change cf. B. H. Rosenwein and L. K. Little, 'Social Meaning in the Monastic and Mendicant Spiritualities', *Past and Present* 63 (1974), 4–32. M. B. Becker, 'Aspects of Lay Piety in Early Renaissance Florence', in *The Pursuit of Holiness in Late Medieval and Renaissance Religion*, ed. C. Trinkaus and H. A. Oberman, Studies in Medieval and Reformation Thought, 10 (Leiden, 1974), pp. 177–99 (pp. 183–4); S. da Campagnola, 'Gli ordini religiosi e la civiltà comunale in Umbria', in *Atti del VI Convegno di Studi Umbri Gubbio 1968*, 2 vols (Perugia, 1971), II, 469–532 (pp. 488–503); A. Cazenave, 'Les Ordres mendiants dans l'Aude et l'Ariège', in *Les Mendiants en pays d'Oc au XIIIe siècle*, Cahiers de Fanjeaux, 8 (Toulouse, 1973), pp. 143–76; D. Dedieu, 'Quelques traces de religion populaire autour des frères mineurs de la province d'Aquitaine', *La religion populaire en Languedoc*, Cahiers de Fanjeaux, 11 (Toulouse, 1976), pp. 227–49; E. W. McDonnell, *The Beguines and Beghards in Medieval Culture* (New York, 1969), pp. 213, 219, 318; D. S. Bachrach, 'The Friars go to War: Mendicant Military Chaplains, 1216–c.1300', *Catholic Historical Review* 90 (2004), 617–33.

[4] M. a Neukirchen, *De Capitulo Generali in Primo Ordine Seraphico* (Rome, 1952) traces the composition of the early general chapters. E. Wagner, *Historia Constitutionum Generalium ordinis Fratrum Minorum* (Rome, 1954), pp. 41–3; R. B. Brooke, *Early Franciscan Government. Elias to Bonaventure* (Cambridge, 1959), pp. 210ff; J. Röhrkasten, 'Franciscan Legislation from Bonaventure to the End of the Thirteenth Century', in: *Regulae – Consuetudines – Statuta*, ed. Andenna and Melville, pp. 483–500; *Constitutiones generales Ordinis Fratrum Minorum*, I (Saeculum XIII) eds. C. Cenci and G. Mailleux (Grottaferrata, 2007).

[5] *Expositio Quatuor Magistrorum super Regulam Fratrum Minorum (1241–1242)*, ed. L. Oliger (Rome, 1950), pp. xii–xiii. On the complexities of the early sources: K. Esser, *Anfänge und ursprüngliche Zielsetzung des Ordens der Minderbrüder*, Studia et Documenta Franciscana, 4 (Leiden, 1966), chap. 1; M. D. Lambert, *Franciscan Poverty. The Doctrine of the Absolute*

by the order prior to 1260, discovered and published as the 'Praenarbonenses' by Cesare Cenci, quite naturally also focuses on internal affairs, the authority of custodians and provincial ministers, the conduct of visitations, the conditions for the reception of novices or disciplinary matters.[6] It is designed for the internal regulation of the order and this focus on the preservation of the friars' distinctive poverty ideal and matters of internal administration can unsurprisingly also be found in the new phase of the order's legislative history which begins with the constitutions of Narbonne of 1260. Here again one finds norms relating to the interpretation of the order's ideal of absolute poverty, the friars' dress, fasting practices, the conduct of visitations, the election of ministers or the principles according to which discipline was to be maintained in the community. These internal matters were confidential. The legislation itself, the possibly controversial discussions at the general and provincial chapters, the 'secretum capituli' and anything 'unde Ordo noster possit turbari vel infamari' were not to be revealed to outsiders.[7] At the general chapter of Padua in 1310 virtually all internal affairs, disagreements between officials and diffinitors or even simple friars, were defined as 'secreta ordinis'.[8] The concern here was the disrepute into which the order could be brought through the public knowledge of its internal problems. There also appears to have been a strong desire to limit outside influence on the order's internal affairs and structure. This is indicated by additions to the general constitutions made during the general chapters of Assisi and Paris in 1279 and 1292, where a new danger was identified. It was defined as a serious disciplinary offence for any friar to approach either prelates or lay princes or other members of the laity in an effort to make any alteration affecting the order, for example to divide a province or merge two provinces or to move friars from one place to another. An addition to this section outlawed the use of lay influence to bring about alterations to the decisions taken by general chapters.[9] A related problem was secular interference in the order's personnel policies. The constitutions of 1279 state that no friar shall be either retained in or removed from office because of outside pressure, a demand

---

Poverty of Christ and the Apostles in the Franciscan Order 1210–1323 (London, 1961), pp. 9–31; A. Quaglia, Origine e sviluppo della regola francescana (Naples, 1948), pp. 102–36; B. Vollot, Hugues de Digne et la règle de 1216, Collectanea Franciscana, 66 (1996), pp. 381–429. Neukirchen, De Capitulo Generali in Primo Ordine Seraphico, p. 7, points out that a Pentecostal chapter but no general chapter is mentioned in the rules of 1221 and 1223.

[6]   C. Cenci, De Fratrum Minorum Constitutionibus Praenarbonensibus, Archivum Franciscanum Historicum, 83 (1990), pp. 50–95.

[7]   Statuta Generalia Ordinis edita in Capitulis Generalibus celebratis Narbonae, an. 1260, Asisii, an. 1279, atque Parisiis, an. 1292, ed. M. Bihl, Archivum Franciscanum Historicum, 34 (1941), pp. 13–94, 284–319 (pp. 84, 12).

[8]   C. Cenci, Le Costituzioni Padovane del 1310, Archivum Franciscanum Historicum, 76 (1983), pp. 505–88 (p. 544).

[9]   Statuta Generalia Ordinis, ed. Bihl, p. 90 (12a, b); p. 94 (6).

repeated at the general chapter of 1310.[10] Equally outlawed was the practice of procuring secular sponsors for friars going to university.[11]

Although the rule and the general constitutions were only meant to deal with the order's internal affairs, a closer reading of the legislative material reveals a constant concern for issues connected with the friars' relations with the laity. Unlike earlier orders the Franciscans and their fellow mendicants actively sought contact with the secular population in town and countryside and they largely depended on its support for their material survival. In order to be effective they had to maintain their spiritual ideals, they had to be seen to pursue the evangelical life as set out in the *Regula bullata* and they had to be careful not to give offence. Already in the rule of 1223 friars were admonished not to become 'compatres virorum vel mulierum' to avoid 'scandalum' either 'inter fratres' or 'de fratribus'.[12] The sentence forms part of the short chapter XI, which restricted the friars' contacts with female religious houses, intended to avoid the 'suspecta consortia' with women. The basic guidelines for the friars' appearance and behaviour in public were given in chapters III to VI of the Rule, where they are forbidden to quarrel and argue, to be judgmental on outsiders, where they are admonished to be meek, peaceful, modest, and humble, to be respectful in their speech and to avoid travel on horseback. Under no circumstances are they allowed to receive coins, not even for their work, and the Franciscan poverty ideal is clearly defined: the friars have no house, no place nor anything and of course they must not covet the property that their novices are obliged to give away in order to reach the state of evangelical poverty. The friars' behaviour is to be matched by their appearance: 'fratres omnes vestimentis vilibus induantur'; they have to be seen to be poor; worn out clothing is to be repaired with sackcloth and rags. These indirect references do not reveal the full scope of Franciscan interaction with the laity. A further clause was dedicated to the order's preachers, who had to be licensed by their superiors, who were to obey the local diocesan bishop and who were to address the 'populus' briefly, edifying and benefiting the laity, explaining virtues and vices, punishments and rewards.[13]

The *Regula bullata* set the themes for the order's subsequent legislation. Centred on the Gospel, its purpose was to provide a concise set of regulations addressing mainly spiritual concerns and the practical issues arising out of them. It was designed as an improvement on the order's less organised earlier

---

10 Ibid., p. 91 (12d). In 1310 it was clarified: 'propter principum vel aliorum petitiones': Cenci, *Costituzioni Padovane del 1310*, p. 546.
11 *Statuta Generalia Ordinis*, ed. Bihl, p. 72.
12 *Regula bullata*, c. XI.
13 On techniques and contents of Dominican and Franciscan preaching: D. d'Avray, *The Preaching of the Friars. Sermons Diffused from Paris before 1300* (Oxford, 1985); idem, 'Sermons to the Upper Bourgeoisie by a Thirteenth-century Franciscan', in *The Church in Town and Countryside*, ed. D. Baker, Studies in Church History, 16 (Oxford, 1979), pp. 187–99.

rule.[14] Members of the laity only feature as novices, as postulants who have to divest themselves of their property. The way in which the order is perceived by the laity does not appear to be a major concern at this early date. The rule is dealing with the friars' spiritual welfare. A good example is the admonition not to despise others for their coloured and more comfortable clothing, for the high quality of their food and drink. Although it is left open whether other members of the clergy or the laity are meant, the purpose of the clause is to protect the friars: outsiders only feature indirectly.

References to relations with the laity feature more prominently in the order's early constitutions and they can be grouped into distinctive themes. The first focus is on novices. Like other regular religious groups the Franciscans investigated the background of those who wanted to join their community, setting conditions and a minimum age. The rule of 1223 places emphasis on the orthodoxy of their faith and their marital status but this was modified in subsequent legislation, which probably reflected the experience of the first decades. The 'Praenarbonenses' already reflect the order's development into a community dominated by clerics, demanding that they shall only be accepted as novices if they are educated, either in grammar, philosophy, medicine, law or theology. Members of the laity were only of interest if they were no burden and the order benefited from their presence: 'laicus, de cuius ingressu esset valde famosa et celebris edificatio in populo et in clero', in itself a significant statement as to how the Franciscans defined their task in society at large.[15] This distinction between clerics and laymen, the latter being excluded from participation in the general chapters, was maintained in the constitutions of 1260.[16] The status of lay friars was reduced by the revised constitutions of 1316 which require a licence of admission by the general minister. The 'Lugdunensis compilatio', dated 1325, offers the exception: 'nisi esset persona multum nobilis et multum insignis de cuius receptione esset magna edificatio in populo et in clero'.[17]

Of importance was also the setting of a minimum age of eighteen years for novices which in exceptional circumstances could be reduced to fifteen.[18] Novices as well as the order itself could be confronted with a hostile reaction from relatives and friends if the decision to join had been taken without their approval. The relatives of Brother John, one of those who joined the as yet young community in Assisi, were desperate when they heard of his step which also endangered their economic survival.[19] Later in the century Salimbene di Adam almost took pride in the disappointment and anger caused by his deci-

---

[14] On the rule of 1221: J. R. H. Moorman, *A History of the Franciscan Order* (Oxford, 1968), pp. 51–2.

[15] Cenci, *De Fratrum Minorum Constitutionibus Praenarbonensibus*, pp. 75, 76 (nos 30, 31).

[16] NARB I, 3, *Statuta Generalia Ordinis*, ed. Bihl, p. 39; Neukirchen, *De Capitulo Generali in Primo Ordine Seraphico*, pp. 77–8.

[17] A. Carlini, *Constitutiones generales Ordinis Fratrum Minorum anno 1316 Assisii conditae*, Archivum Franciscanum Historicum 4 (1911) pp. 269–302, 508–36 (pp. 277, 527).

[18] NARB I, 2, *Statuta Generalia Ordinis*, ed. Bihl, p. 39.

[19] 'Videntes autem parentes eius et fratres qui adhuc erant parui quod uolebat dimittere eos, ceperunt ipsi et omnes de domo tam fortiter lacrimari et plangere alta uoce ...': R. B.

sion to join the Franciscans. As his father's heir, his family had had other plans for him and they also disapproved of his choice of a new and still dubious religious affiliation.[20] Sometimes even supporters of the friars could turn against them when a son unexpectedly joined the community. Well known is Thomas of Eccleston's story of Richard Gobiun, who had provided the first accommodation for the Minorites in Northampton but ordered them to leave when he learned that his son John had become a Franciscan.[21] 'Maledicta sit hora qua te unquam vidi', answered the sister of Friar Solomon, one of the first novices in the English province, when her brother, who had joined this order of beggars, came to her door to beg alms.[22] Another wealthy father, who had sent his young son to Oxford, where he had promptly joined the order, allegedly drew his sword and told his servants to send him away when he, perhaps provocatively, came to his father's house.[23]

The second theme was central to the order's poverty ideal: the handling, receiving and storing of 'pecunia', a term extending beyond the meaning of coinage or money. Franciscans were not to receive, touch or carry money and alms could not be accepted in the form of coins.[24] It was equally forbidden to store money or other valuables in a convent, a regulation which not only outlawed certain forms of economic management by the friars themselves but equally ruled out the use of a priory as a safe storage place by outsiders, most likely members of elites and potential or past benefactors. This principle of the order's early legislation was integrated into the constitutions of Narbonne in 1260 which added the exception that such deposits were allowed if they could not be avoided without 'gravi scandalo', a notion reiterated at the revision of the constitutions in 1316.[25] Since it was not uncommon to use religious houses

Brooke, ed. and transl., *Scripta Leonis, Rufini et Angeli Sociorum S. Francisci* (Oxford, 1970), p. 120.

20 '... toto tempore vite sue doluit pater meus de meo ingressu in Ordinem fratrum Minorum nec consolationem accepit, eo quod filium non habebat qui ei in hereditate succederet': Salimbene de Adam, *Cronica*, 2 vols, ed. G. Scalia, Scrittori d'Italia, 232 (Bari, 1966), I, 54. Still in the 1250s, more than a decade after his joining the order, a Parmese compatriot showed his anger: 'Vade miser, vade! Multi mercenarii in domo patris tui panibus abundant et carnibus, et tu vadis hostiatim mendicando panem ab his qui non habent, cum posses tu multis pauperibus abundanter tribuere. Deberes modo cum dextrario per Parmam discurrere et cum hastiludio tristes leto efficere, ut esses dominabus spectaculum et ystrionibus consolatio. Nam et pater tuus dolore consumitur, et mater tua amore tui, quem videre non potest, quasi de Deo desperat.' *Ibid.*, I, 61–2. Another friend of the family, bishop Gratia of Parma, who had shown appreciation of Salimbene's brother Guido, withdrew his patronage when Guido joined the order: '... sed, postquem Ordinem fratrum Minorum intravit, non curavit de ipso': ibid., I, 97.

21 A. G. Little, ed., *Fratris Thomae vulgo dicti de Eccleston Tractatus de adventu fratrum minorum in Angliam* (Manchester, 1951), p. 23.

22 *Ibid.*, p. 12.

23 Gray's Inn Library, MS 7 fol. 62r; cf. J. Röhrkasten, 'Mendicants in the Metropolis: the Londoners and the development of the London friaries', *Thirteenth Century England* VI, ed. M. Prestwich, R. H. Britnell and R. Frame (Woodbridge, 1997), pp. 61–75 (p. 73).

24 *Regula bullata*, c. IV, V; NARB III, 6, *Statuta Generalia Ordinis*, ed. Bihl, p. 46.

25 Cenci, *De Fratrum Minorum Constitutionibus Praenarbonensibus*, pp. 87–8, 90 (nos 62,

as safe deposits for treasure or documents, it is no surprise to find that Franciscans were also confronted with such requests. In 1303 two thousand marks sterling from the estate of Queen Blanche, widow of Edward I's brother, were found in the priory of the London Grey Friars.[26] She and her husband were the founders of the city's Franciscan nunnery and it would have been difficult for the friars not to agree to a request for assistance.

The third theme concerns the friars' legal relations with the outside world. Franciscans were to avoid litigation and any involvement in arbitration.[27] When the subject of avoiding recourse to legal procedure re-emerged in the constitutions of 1260 it was introduced as a measure to protect the ideal of poverty: the friars were to preserve the purity of absolute poverty and neither they nor an intermediary on their behalf could sue for material possessions or an 'iniuria temporali'.[28] However, it seems that it was not just the friars' identity as mendicants which is at stake here but also the outside perception of the order.

A related aspect was the friars' involvement in the execution of wills. This was forbidden in the legislation before 1260 and it is known that this law was enforced by Bonaventure in his time as general minister.[29] However, when the clause was incorporated in the revised constitutions of 1279, it was modified. Friars were not to take on the task of executor if it seemed likely that their role would involve them in litigation.[30] A similar subtle change can be detected in the Franciscans' attitude to bequests. It was not unexpected that Minorites were consulted in the drafting of wills and that they acted as advisors to laypeople. Clearly neither the friars nor their relatives were to derive any material advantage out of this, a clause formulated in 1260. The revision of 1279 modified this regulation, stating that the bequests made by the relatives or friends of such a Franciscan advisor could be received.[31] The order's ambivalent attitude to bequests clearly emerged in the legislation of the late thirteenth century. The general chapter of 1279 pronounced that friars involved in the drafting of wills had to make sure that no member of the order was named as heir. When the constitutions were revised next in 1292 this clause remained unchanged,

---

63, 70); NARB III, 8, *Statuta Generalia Ordinis*, ed. Bihl, p. 46; Carlini, *Constitutiones generales Ordinis Fratrum Minorum anno 1316 Assisii conditae*, p. 280.

[26] J. Röhrkasten, *The Mendicant Houses of Medieval London 1221–1539*, Vita Regularis 21 (Münster, 2004), p. 169.

[27] Cenci, *De Fratrum Minorum Constitutionibus Praenarbonensibus*, pp. 88–9 (nos 65, 67).

[28] NARB III, 24, *Statuta Generalia Ordinis*, ed. Bihl, p. 49. Confronted with a legal action the London Franciscans simply denied any claim to the property in question in the 1280s: Röhrkasten, *Mendicant Houses of Medieval London*, pp. 292–3.

[29] Cenci, *De Fratrum Minorum Constitutionibus Praenarbonensibus*, p. 88 (no. 66); Bonaventura, *Opera Omnia*, VIII, p. 469b; disputes about wills between Minorites and the parish clergy have been noted in France: Adam, *La vie paroissiale en France*, p. 93. In medieval Constance the Franciscans received clearly more bequests than the other mendicant convents: P. Baur, *Testament und Bürgerschaft. Alltagsleben und Sachkultur im spätmittelalterlichen Konstanz*, Konstanzer Geschichts- und Rechtsquellen, 31 (Sigmaringen, 1989), p. 136.

[30] ASS, PAR VI, 6a, *Statuta Generalia Ordinis*, ed. Bihl, p. 75.

[31] NARB III, 7, *ibid.*, pp. 46, 49.

however, friars were now told to recommend the convent of Paris to testators for support, perhaps a reaction to the economic pressures on the students caused by the monetary changes in France. The order, which still refused to accept bequests of rents and regular incomes, was now quite happy to have bequests, as long as the phrases in the will were suitable, that is, in those cases where an inheritance was not given to the friars but was said to be made available for their needs, in line with Nicholas III's bull 'Exiit qui seminat' of 1279: 'pro fratrum necessitatibus expendendam'.[32]

The fourth theme addressed in the legislation concerned the friars' appearance and behaviour outside the convent. A wide range of issues was involved, some of which had already been raised in the *Regula bullata*.[33] It is difficult to decide whether these clauses were motivated by a concern for observance within the order or a worry about the way in which the members of the young community were viewed from the outside. It has to be kept in mind that the Franciscans served as a model for smaller mendicant communities, for example the Fratres de Poenitentia Jesu Christi or Segarelli's Apostles in Italy, who had a tendency to copy the Franciscan habit.[34] In any case, further detailed legislation followed: friars were not to carry a purse on their journeys, they were not allowed to carry money, not to have a servant let alone a servant who carried their money; they were to be accompanied by their 'socius', they were to stay in the convents of their order and not to eat and drink in public if it could be avoided, they were not to carry anything 'in verbis vel scriptis' which could cause a 'scandalum' and bawdy songs were strictly outlawed by the general chapter of Padua, meeting in 1310.[35]

Clear guidelines were set on begging, which was not allowed in streets and public places, perhaps to distinguish the mendicants from the involuntary destitute.[36] Alms boxes and altars converted for the purpose of begging were also outlawed, presumably because such items were associated with collecting coin.

32 ASS, PAR III, 7b; PAR III, 7a; PAR III, 7c, 7e, *ibid.*, p. 50. *Corpus Iuris Canonici*, 2 vols, ed. E. Friedberg (Leipzig, 1881), II, col. 1117. The Franciscans of Liège held property already in the thirteenth century: P. Bertrand, *Commerce avec dame Pauvreté. Structures et fonctions des couvents mendiants à Liège (xiiie – xive s.)*, Bibliothèque de la Faculté de Philosophie et Lettres de l'Université de Liège, 285 (Geneva, 2004), pp. 213, 216.

33 *Regula bullata*, c. III.

34 R. Orioli, *Apostoliker*, in *Lexikon des Mittelalters*, vol. I (Munich, 1980), cols 792–3; P.-A. Armagier, 'Les frères de la Penitence de Jesus-Christ ou du Sac', *Provence Historique* 15 (1965), 158–67; H. F. Chettle, 'The Friars of the Sack in England', *Downside Review* 63 (1945) 239–51; G.M. Giacomozzi, *L'Ordine della penitenza di Gesù Cristo*, Scrinium Historiale, 2 (Rome, 1962).

35 Cenci, *De Fratrum Minorum Constitutionibus Praenarbonensibus*, pp. 84–5, 91 (nos 55, 57, 73); NARB IV, 8; V, 6, 7, 12, 18, *Statuta Generalia Ordinis*, ed. Bihl, pp. 56, 63–5. G. Abate, *Memoriali, statuti ed atti di capitoli generali dei frati minori dei secoli XIII e XIV*, Miscellanea Francescana 33 (1933), pp. 15–45, 320–36; 34 (1934) pp, 248–53; 35 (1935) pp. 101–6, 232–9 (pp.31–2): 'quod cantus fractos et dissolutos, vel a nota Ordinis discrepantes, studiose de Provinciis suis exterminent, graviter puniendo fratres, quod de cetero cantus huiusmodi intra vel extra didicerint, docuerint, vel cantaverint'.

36 Cenci, *De Fratrum Minorum Constitutionibus Praenarbonensibus*, p. 88 (no. 64).

The same regulations allowed begging for food – specifically mentioned are bread and wine – from within the convents and 'humiliter'.[37] Similarly important was the friars' clothing which identified them and their vocation. Restrictions on quality and quantity can already be found in the *Regula bullata*. In the constitutions of 1260 a separate chapter was devoted to this topic.[38] Later, in 1310 and 1313, there were calls for these regulations to be observed more strictly and for the habits to be uniform.[39]

The fifth topic identified in the legislation, the hearing of confessions made by members of the laity, was one of the major points of friction between the mendicants and the secular clergy. The problem emerged gradually over the course of the thirteenth century as Franciscans increasingly encroached on parochial rights. The general chapter of 1282 gave instructions to exhort the laity in 'secreto' to confess to their parish clergy once a year, in line with the privileges contained in the bull 'Ad fructus uberes' of December 1281.[40] The order's constitutions of 1292 also contained a clause reflecting the tension which had arisen between the parish clergy and the friars, who were neither to hear deathbed confessions nor to act in the confessional at Easter.[41] Seen in conjunction with other legislation on the subject this clause perhaps reveals important information on the Franciscan practice of hearing confession, a matter which had generated hostile criticism and resistance from early on.[42] Already the pre-1260 legislation ruled that neither the confessor nor the convent were to derive any material gain in the process.[43] The constitutions of 1260 were slightly more precise, prohibiting any demand by the confessor for anything from the penitent as penance. An additional clause in 1292 warned confessors not to give absolution to usurers unless they had made restitution first.[44]

There was an aspect of hearing confession that caused even more concern in the order. This leads to the sixth theme: the friars' relations with women. As mentioned above, the rule of 1223 instructed Franciscans not to be 'compatres' of men or women and to avoid 'scandalum'. But the friars were very popular confessors in the period under investigation and much as they may have wanted

---

[37] NARB III, 5, 6; *Statuta Generalia Ordinis*, ed. Bihl, p. 46. In some Franciscan provinces it seems to have been common to combine begging with the hearing of confessions and to focus on the harvest season, cf. Adam, *La vie paroissale en France*, pp. 229–32.

[38] *Ibid.*, pp. 42–4.

[39] Abate, *Memoriali, statuti ed atti di capitoli generali dei frati minori dei secoli XIII e XIV*, pp. 30–1 (no. 4), 32–4 (no. 8).

[40] G. Fussenegger, 'Definitiones capituli generalis, Strassburg 1282', *Archivum Franciscanum Historicum* 26 (1933) 127–40 (p. 135); Moorman, *History of the Franciscan Order*, p. 182.

[41] PAR VI, 6b, *Statuta Generalia Ordinis*, ed. Bihl, p. 75.

[42] Adam, *La vie paroissale en France*, p. 230; J. L. Copeland, 'The Relations Between the Mendicant Friars and the Secular Clergy in England during the Century after the Issue of the Bull Super Cathedram (1300)', unpublished M.A. thesis (London, 1937), pp. 148–82; Y. Dossat, 'Opposition des anciens ordres à l'installation des mendiants', *in Les mendiants en pays d'Oc*, Cahiers de Fanjeaux, 8 (Toulouse, 1973), pp. 263–306.

[43] Cenci, *De Fratrum Minorum Constitutionibus Praenarbonensibus*, p. 89 (no. 68).

[44] NARB III, 7; PAR VI, 4a, *Statuta Generalia Ordinis*, ed. Bihl, pp. 47, 74–5.

to, they could not exclude women. Hearing confession was particularly problematic because the confessor had to be physically close to the penitent. The
legislation of 1260 prohibited the confessor to sit or stand close to the female
penitent unless he could see his 'socius' and this companion would be able to
see him.[45] Students were deemed to be specifically exposed and the legislation
of 1313 and 1316 forbade them to hear the confessions of women unless they
happened to be the only friars in the convent who spoke the required vernacular.[46] Damaging suspicion and gossip were seen as threats to the order's integrity
and efforts were made to maintain a distance: friars were not to receive a vow
from a woman, those who were notorious for 'colloquiis suspectis et consortiis
mulierum' were warned and in 1279 it was decided that women should not be
allowed to eat in a convent.[47]

Various religious duties and services which brought the Franciscans into
contact with the laity are grouped into the seventh theme, which includes
problems relating to burials, memorial masses, preaching and friars in their roles
as missionaries and inquisitors.[48] While some of these aspects, preaching, memorial masses, mission and inquisition, hardly feature beyond general guidelines to
choose men well suited for the task and not to offend the secular clergy when
preaching to the laity,[49] the issue of burials, another contentious issue between
the friars on the one hand and the secular clergy and even other regular religious on the other, is given more prominence. Already the legislation prior to
1260 warned friars not to conduct burials and baptisms outside their convents
and to act in accordance with papal privileges, a reference to the bulls 'Nimis
iniqua' of 1231 and 'Cum a nobis petitur' of 1250.[50] The general constitutions
of 1260 added that laypeople should not be buried in a Franciscan friary unless
it could not be avoided without 'scandalum' and the revised version of 1279
warned not to enter into disputes in order to obtain bodies for burial. At the
same time it was decided not to advertise the option of burial with the 'fratres
minores', not to induce anyone to choose a burial site different from the one
where the ancestors had been buried.[51]

Conflicts about the burial of laypeople did occur and they were often
conducted in full view of the public, as happened, for example, in late thir-

---

45   NARB VI, 5, ibid., p. 70.
46   Abate, Memoriali, statuti ed atti di capitoli generali dei frati minori dei secoli XIII e XIV, pp.
      32–4 (no. 3); Carlini, Constitutiones generales Ordinis Fratrum Minorum anno 1316 Assisii
      conditae, p. 292.
47   NARB VI, 6, VII, 8; ASS PAR IV, 8a; Statuta Generalia Ordinis, ed. Bihl, pp. 60, 70–1,
      84.
48   From 1246 the minister general had the right to choose the inquisitors: M. d'Alatri,
      L'inquisizione francescana nell'Italia centrale nel secolo XIII (Rome, 1954), p. 14.
49   Cenci, De Fratrum Minorum Constitutionibus Praenarbonensibus, p. 80 (no. 45); NARB VI,
      10; PAR VI, 11e, Statuta Generalia Ordinis, ed. Bihl, pp. 71, 77.
50   Cenci, De Fratrum Minorum Constitutionibus Praenarbonensibus, pp. 89, 94 (nos 69, 86);
      NARB III, 20, Statuta Generalia Ordinis, ed. Bihl, p. 48; Moorman, History of the Fran-
      ciscan Order, pp. 94, 122.
51   NARB III, 22; ASS III, 22b; ASS PAR 22, Statuta Generalia Ordinis, ed. Bihl, pp. 48,
      53.

teenth-century Worcester. A confrontation between the cathedral priory and the town's Grey Friars in 1289 led to unpleasant scenes and an exhumation in 1290.[52] After a successful appeal to the – Franciscan – archbishop of Canterbury the friars continued these practices, even burying William, earl of Warwick, in their convent, rather than in the cathedral – the place where his ancestors were buried – and carrying his corpse in a procession through the town like the spoils of war, as the annalist of Worcester sourly remarks.[53]

Legislation concerning relations with princes and prelates forms the eighth theme. The order's attempts to avoid outside pressures were mentioned earlier; in return friars were admonished not to procure for themselves secular 'negotia' from princes, prelates or towns and certainly not to initiate any involvement in secular affairs.[54] It is hardly necessary to stress in this context that royal and official support was crucial for the Franciscans, probably more so than for other religious orders. Franciscans did act as royal ambassadors; they received royal support for their general chapters and in England also for their provincial chapters.[55] From 1306 onwards the convents of Oxford and Cambridge received regular annual payments of 50 and 25 marks sterling respectively, strictly speaking a contravention of the order's principle not to accept regular incomes.[56]

The ninth theme, restrictions on architectural display, reflects both concern for observance and the way in which the order presented itself in local communities. Franciscan architecture was to represent the poverty ideal, avoiding large dimensions and unnecessary 'curiositas' in ornaments, decoration, windows and similar stylistic features. The construction of church towers was prohibited and vaulted roofs were equally frowned upon. This legislation of 1260 remained

---

[52] *Annales de Wigornia*, in *Annales Monastici*, 5 vols, ed. H.R. Luard, RS (London, 1864–9), IV, 499–501.

[53] *Ibid.*, p. 537. It has been alleged that French Franciscans were even prepared to bury those under sentence of excommunication: Adam, *La vie paroissale en France*, pp. 201, 236–40. Franciscan convents were the most coveted burial places for members of the laity in parts of France: J. Chiffoleau, *La compabilité de l'au-delà. Les hommes, la mort et la religion dans la région d'Avignon à la fin du moyen âge (c. 1320–c. 1480)*, Collection de l'École Française de Rome, 47 (Rome, 1980), pp. 166, 259–60.

[54] NARB VI, 7; PAR VI, 7, *ibid.*, pp. 71, 76. Cf. a forthcoming article by Dr Michael Robson (St Edmund's College, Cambridge) on Queen Isabella and the Franciscans, and A. Crawford, 'The Piety of Late-Medieval English Queens', *The Church in Pre-Reformation Society*, ed. C. Barron and C. Harper-Bill (Woodbridge, 1985), pp. 48–57 (pp. 51, 54). On the political importance of the Franciscans in Germany, see B. Degler-Spengler, *Das Klarissenkloster Gnadental in Basel (1289–1529)*, Quellen und Forschungen zur Basler Geschichte, 3 (Basle, 1969), p. 19; J. B. Freed, *The Friars in German Society in the Thirteenth Century*, The Mediaeval Academy of America, 86 (Cambridge, Mass., 1977), pp. 17, 133, 138, 160; L. K. Little, 'Saint Louis' Involvement with the Friars', *Church History* 33 (1964), 125–48.

[55] Examples are: TNA E403/90 m 3, a payment for the Franciscan general chapter of Assisi in 1295, and E403/106 m 4, a payment for the provincial chapter held at Stamford in 1300.

[56] TNA E403/134 m 2.

almost unchanged in 1279 and 1292.[57] The subject was still on the agenda in 1310, when it was demanded that architectural excesses be rectified, and in 1316 when friars were encouraged to be content with humble buildings. Already in 1310 the general chapter acknowledged outside pressure directed against the removal of decorations and ornaments – it is easy to imagine lay donors who were not keen to see their additions to a Franciscan convent removed. In such a case disciplinary measures were threatened against the local house.[58]

This survey shows how the Franciscans tried to regulate their relations with the laity, how they used legislation to set standards for themselves and to avoid outside influences and pressures, most of all 'scandalum'. Since the order – despite is rapid and extensive development – sometimes received a muted or even hostile reception, its relations with the laity were an important concern. On occasion the Franciscans were even confronted with stinging criticism, a potential problem for a religious community which at least in theory rejected all property and thus relied on continuous support from the outside.[59] There was an awareness of the danger of losing esteem, especially among the elite, directly addressed at the general chapter of 1274 where it was impressed on all officials to observe the constitutions: 'pro eo quod apud graves personas Ordo in magnum dignoscitur venire contemptum'.[60] Such problems were addressed by successive general chapters and the legislation was developed cautiously, even though internal criticism of malpractices could be sharp, for instance when Bonaventure addressed the problem of relations with the laity writing that many people feared to encounter Franciscans on their journeys as much as they feared to meet robbers.[61]

In their attempt to ensure cohesion of the order as a whole the general ministers could have recourse to the papacy. Popes favouring the order were quite prepared to respond to requests for privileges or even a new interpretation of the Rule like the bull 'Exiit qui seminat' (1279);[62] however, papal legislation was not simply a tool which could be used at will. Popes like the lawyers Boniface VIII or famously John XXII were not under the spell of the Francis-

---

[57] NARB III, 15–17, ASS III, 15–18, PAR 18–18b, *ibid.*, pp. 48, 51–2. On the enforcement of these regulations in the English province, see A. G. Little, *Studies in English Franciscan History* (Manchester, 1917), pp. 62–3; *Tractatus de adventu fratrum minorum in Angliam*, ed. Little, pp. 23, 45.

[58] Abate, *Memoriali, statuti ed atti di capitoli generali dei frati minori dei secoli XIII e XIV*, pp. 31–2 (nos 7, 8); Carlini, *Constitutiones generales Ordinis Fratrum Minorum anno 1316 Assisii conditae*, p. 281.

[59] Adam, *La vie paroissale en France*, p. 235; J. Batany, 'L'image des Franciscains dans les «revues d'états» du XIIIᵉ au XVIᵉ siècle', in *Mouvements Franciscains et Société Française*, ed. A Vauchez, Beauchesne Religions, 14 (Paris, 1984), pp. 61–74.

[60] *Memoriali, Statuti ed Atti di Capitoli Generali dei Frati Minori dei Secoli XIII e XIV*, ed. Abate, p. 18.

[61] 'Occurrit importuna petitio, propter quam omnes transeuntes per terras adeo abhorrent Fratrum occursum, ut eis timeant quasi praedonibus obviare': *Sancti Bonaventurae Opera Omnia*, vol. VIII (Quaracchi, 1898), p. 469.

[62] A. Maggiani, *De relatione scriptorum quorumdam S. Bonaventurae ad bullam 'Exiit' Nicolai III (1279)*, Archivum Franciscanum Historicum 5 (1912), 3–21.

cans and neither the minister general nor the general chapter had the right to disregard papal bulls as a matter of principle.[63] Their only critical reaction could be a decision not to make use of a privilege, as happened for instance at the general chapter of 1282, when it was decided not to make use of the privileges of preaching and hearing confession recently specified in 'Ad fructus uberes', unless a written agreement by the local bishop could be obtained.[64]

Relations between Franciscans and the laity extended beyond the themes covered so far in this paper. From the late 1220s groups of penitents in Italian towns wanted to be associated with the Franciscans, eventually forming the third order, which was given its own statutes in 1289.[65] This lay branch of the Franciscans extended into many parts of Europe and added another element of diversity as well as a new dimension of interaction between the mendicants and the laity.[66] The statutes of the lay friars of Brescia show that there were regular meetings in the Franciscan convent, involving the mendicants in the commemoration of the dead as a matter of course and giving them important tasks in visitation, religious instruction and in the electoral processes of the lay community which appears to have had access to many areas of the convent.[67] Brescia was not an exception and the locations as well as the legal status of Franciscan houses made it difficult to exclude the laity.[68] Parts of Franciscan

---

63 On the legislation of these two popes see Copeland, 'The Relations Between the Mendicant Friars and the Secular Clergy in England', pp. 29, 34; T. S. R. Boase, *Boniface VIII* (London, 1933), pp. 189–99; L. Hödl, 'Der Kommentar des Kardinals Johannes Monachus zur Dekretale *Super Cathedram* des Papstes Bonifatius VIII (18. Februar 1300)', *Revue Mabillon* 77 (2005), 133–78; P. Nold, *Pope John XXII and his Franciscan Cardinal. Bertrand de la Tour and the Apostolic Poverty Controversy* (Oxford, 2003), p. 140ff. Generally see B. Gratien, *Histoire de la fondation et de l'évolution des Frères Mineurs au XIIIe siècle* (Paris, 1928), pp. 111ff, 354ff; Lambert, *Franciscan Poverty*, pp. 170, 213–6; Wagner, *Historia Constitutionum Generalium ordinis Fratrum Minorum*, pp. 1–5, 18–20; I. J. Lipinski, *Rapporti fondamentali tra la regola di San Francesco e la legislazione dei Frati Minori nel secolo XIII*, Orizzonti Francescani 14 (Rome, 1975), p. 27.

64 Fussenegger, *Definitiones capituli generalis, Strassburg 1282*, p. 135.

65 H. Golubovich, *Acta et statuta generalis capituli tertii ordinis Poenitentium D. Francisci Bononiae celebrati an. 1289*, Archivum Franciscanum Historicum 2 (1909) pp. 63–71; S. W. Whitfield, *The Third Order of St Francis in Medieval England*, Franciscan Studies 13 (1953) pp. 50–9.

66 G. G. Meersseman, *Ordo Fraternitatis. Confraternitate e pietà dei laici nel medioevo*, 3 vols, Italia Sacra, 24, 25, 26 (Rome, 1977), I, 34, 362–4, 371; the statutes of a lay fraternity by a Franciscan are printed in idem, 'Dossier de l'Ordre de la Pénitence au XIIIe siècle', *Spicilegium Friburgense* 7 (1961), 295–307. M. Ronzani, 'Penitenti e ordini mendicanti a Pisa sino all'inizio del Trecento', *Mélanges de l'École Française de Rome* 89 (1977), 733–41; A. Vauchez, *Les laïcs au Moyen Âge* (Paris, 1987), pp. 93–107.

67 P. Guerrini, 'Gli statuti di un'antica congregazione francescana di Brescia', *Archivum Franciscanum Historicum* 1 (1908) 544–68.

68 On the location of mendicant convents see M. d'Alatri, 'I più antichi insediamenti dei mendicanti nella provincia civile di Campagna', *Mélanges de l'École française de Rome* 89 (1977), 575–85 (p. 576); T. Berger, 'Die Ausbreitung der Minoriten in der Erzdiözese Mainz und in den Diözesen Speyer und Worms im 13. Jahrhundert', in *Könige, Landesherren und Bettelorden*, ed. D. Berg, Saxonia Franciscana, 10 (Werl, 1998), pp. 37–59 (pp. 44–5); L. Butler, 'The Houses of the Mendicant Orders in Britain: recent

convents and churches were used as public spaces by the laity, sometimes by an urban or even royal administration.

This paper has surveyed the connections between the Minorites and the laity only on the basis of the order's normative sources which refer to an abstract laity. However, the friars were confronted with very diverse realities in different parts of Europe. Even though it is a commonplace, it needs to be emphasised that legal and political realities, economic and social structures and ecclesiastical organisation in European towns differed widely and that these factors determined the conditions under which a mendicant convent existed. If they wanted to engage with the laity the friars had to adapt to differing contexts. This was a continuous process because the contextual setting was constantly changing. It is possible to detect attempts by the order's leadership to adapt to such changes but the problem of Franciscan legislation is more complex. Not all underlying causes for changes to the norms can be identified. While it is quite possible that the changes to the building regulations reflected outside pressures, legislative processes during the general chapter meetings may well have developed a dynamism of their own.

These observations could help to define the direction of future research. The legal material mentioned here will only come to life if it is embedded in the realities of Franciscan existence as they can be reconstructed from sources produced in the different provinces, custodies and convents and also produced by the laity. Despite the attempts to create a coherent legal structure, the practices and customs followed in the order's provinces could be different, a state of affairs generally accepted: 'diversae provinciae diversis consuetudinibus varientur'.[69] An analysis of the contrasts between norm and ideal on the one hand and reality on the other may be valuable. It may reveal the process of change which affected the order in this period, identifying the nature of the outside pressures and the responses. It may show how the Franciscans, who clearly defined their role in society in their normative texts and other writings, tried to fulfil these ideals in different circumstances. It may also turn the emphasis away from the order held together by a common rule, a hierarchy and shared constitutional processes to reveal a more complex religious community characterised by strong local identities.

---

archaeological work', in *Archaeological Papers from York Presented to M. W. Barley*, ed. P. V. Addyman and V. E. Black (York, 1984), pp. 123–36 (p. 123); Freed, *The Friars in German Society*, p. 50; E. Guidoni, 'Città e ordini mendicanti. Il ruolo dei conventi nella crescita e nella progettazione urbana del XIII e XIV secolo', *Quaderni medievali* 4 (1977), 69–106 (p. 75); H. Martin, *Les Ordres mendiants en Bretagne (1230–1530). Pauvreté volontaire et prédication à la fin du moyen âge* (Rennes, 1975), p. 14 (Guingamp). B. Stüdeli, *Minoritenniederlassungen und mittelalterliche Stadt*, Franziskanische Forschungen, 21(Werl, 1969), pp. 22, 87ff. On the legal status of Franciscan property see S. W. De Vine, 'The Franciscan Friars and the Feoffment to Uses and Canonical Theories of Property Enjoyment before 1535', *Journal of Legal History* 10 (1989), 1–22.

[69] Cenci, *Costituzioni Padovane del 1310*, p. 574.

13

The Austin Friars in Late Medieval Canterbury: Negotiating Spaces

SHEILA SWEETINBURGH

Boundaries were closely defended in late medieval towns and urban records are full of territorial disputes among individuals and institutions, who sought to guard against possible encroachments into their space. Much was at stake because control brought financial and judicial rights and privileges, issues that were of special importance to town governors and to others, including the friars, who at times resisted the demands of those in authority. Even though conflict was not inevitable, many studies of the role of urban monastic houses have highlighted the ways leading citizens attempted to wrest lordship from their powerful ecclesiastical neighbours.[1] Other studies have considered this question of control over the spatial dynamics of the urban landscape by looking at the relationship between sacred and profane space, and the differing ways churches and other ecclesiastical buildings have been used by individuals, groups and institutions. To date some work has been done on the role of friaries in the English urban landscape, though in terms of detailed case studies the place of the London friaries has received more attention than those in provincial towns. In particular, Jens Röhrkasten's work on the London mendicants has highlighted the different experiences of the various orders both within and between towns, leading him to conclude that 'the Orders, [though] large international structures, were highly sensitive to local influences'.[2] This essay seeks to explore such ideas using the Austin friars of Canterbury whose history over a two hundred year period may shed further light on the place of the mendicants in provincial English society.

As Röhrkasten notes, friaries were often established in the suburbs, or close to gates or town walls and frequently adjoining a major thoroughfare, often

---

[1] Though Fleming explores a particular aspect of conflict at Bristol, such issues for other towns have been much discussed in the academic press; P. Fleming, 'Conflict and Urban Government in Later Medieval England: St Augustine's Abbey and Bristol', *Urban History* 27 (2000), 321–43.

[2] J. Röhrkasten, 'Secular Uses of the Mendicant Priories in Medieval London', in *The Use and Abuse of Sacred Places in Late Medieval Towns*, ed. P. Trio and M. De Smet (Leuven, 2006), pp. 135–51 (p. 151).

resulting in their proximity to market places, harbours or rivers.[3] Among the Italian friaries he sees evidence of a long-term strategy regarding their location, though how far this was replicated in England remains open to discussion, and in some cases their late arrival onto the urban scene left them few alternatives other than marginal sites.[4] Yet aristocratic or similar patronage might provide a more central location which could result in an increasingly complex urban landscape, requiring them to negotiate their place within urban society.[5]

The Austin friars of Canterbury were apparently particularly sensitive to such spatial concerns, and, from the time of their arrival in the early fourteenth century until the dissolution of their house in 1538, the friars were engaged in numerous negotiations over space, both physical and metaphysical, with different sectors of society: individuals, groups and institutions. As a consequence they developed a wide range of relationships with those outside their walls, based on such measures as gift exchange, but also through the use of litigation. Their friary occupied a contested space within Canterbury's urban landscape, which meant that at times competition and conflict were as important as co-operation and mutual assistance for the friars, who seem to have seen themselves – and were seen by others – as offering a wide variety of benefits: hospitality, commemoration and burial – services they were prepared to defend even if this proved confrontational.

Late medieval Canterbury

Canterbury was small compared to the great provincial centres of York, Norwich and Coventry. Nevertheless, it had a disproportionately large number of parish churches, there being twelve within the walls. In addition, there were the great churches of Christ Church Priory and St Augustine's Abbey, the former the cathedral church within the walls, the latter outside; both houses having considerable property portfolios in Canterbury and its suburbs, including the advowson of several city parishes.[6] St Gregory's Priory and St Sepulchre's nunnery were also close by; there were several hospitals locally and the archbishop held two neighbouring manors. Arriving in the early thirteenth century, the first friars settled close to the river away from the city centre, while a third order, the friars of the Sack, had a very modest house in the north-west ward of Westgate.[7] Thus ecclesiastical jurisdiction in Canterbury and its suburbs was extremely complex, the various parties jealously guarding their particular rights

---

3   J. Röhrkasten, 'The Origin and Early Development of the London Mendicant Houses', in *The Church in the Medieval Town*, ed. T. R. Slater and G. Rosser (Aldershot, 1998), pp. 76–99 (p. 82).

4   Ibid., p. 83.

5   London, being far larger, was better able to accommodate the relocation of certain friaries: ibid., p. 90.

6   T. Tatton-Brown, 'Medieval Parishes and Parish Churches in Canterbury', in Slater and Rosser, eds, *Church in the Medieval Town*, pp. 236–71 (pp. 236–8).

7   The Franciscans arrived in 1224, while the Dominicans settled before 1237; they were

and privileges. The corporation, too, was greatly concerned about jurisdiction, the members of several prominent, long-established families seeing themselves as patrons and guardians of their city. In some cases this involved defending the city's property and its rituals, as well as asserting its privileged status, which, with regard to the crown, culminated in Edward IV's grant that made Canterbury 'independent of Kent forever'.

Yet, even though matters of jurisdiction were important, there were points of cross-over between the corporation and Christ Church, both having a considerable vested interest in the pilgrims visiting Becket's shrine in the cathedral. Apart from their offerings and their need for accommodation, pilgrims brought many other benefits. Nevertheless, the level of their contribution to the city's economy during the later Middle Ages is unclear, but the allegedly large numbers of pilgrims attending the various jubilees would seem to indicate their continuing value.[8]

Some migrants and townsmen were able to capitalise on the opportunities presented in late-fourteenth-century Canterbury but often their ambitions were thwarted by escalating royal taxation and the rapacious activities of certain local landlords.[9] The resulting political instability continued into the fifteenth century, the city also witnessing increasingly dilapidated dwellings and falling rent rolls, a major concern for institutional landlords such as Christ Church Priory.[10] The period also saw the disappearance of several of the prosperous, long-established families, some returning to the neighbouring countryside where they acted as agents for monastic houses whose interests crossed the boundary between town and country. Nonetheless, throughout this period there were still wealthy citizens residing in and around the city; yet most having made their fortune were apparently unable to pass it on to the succeeding generation. This inability was not confined to the city's elite, and poverty, like disease, had serious implications for family survival and commemoration.[11]

Even though the Austin friars arrived in Canterbury before the calamities of the mid fourteenth century, they did enter a city where the Church was a major institution, both physically in terms of territory and in the minds of the local populace (see Fig. 13.1). This may have been a mixed blessing because the friars needed to establish a house in what was a highly competitive environment that would allow them successfully to undertake their work in the city. Initially, the

joined by the Austin friars in 1318: MRH, pp. 214–15, 222, 224, 240–1; W. Page, ed., VCH Kent, II (London, 1926), pp. 177–8, 190–4.

8   C. Woodruff, 'Financial Aspects of the Cult of St Thomas of Canterbury, Archaeologia Cantiana 44 (1932), 13–32. J. Zeiger, 'The Survival of the Cult of St Thomas of Canterbury in the Later Middle Ages' (MA dissertation, University of Kent, 1997).

9   A. F. Butcher, 'English Urban Society and the Revolt of 1381', in The English Rising of 1381, ed. R. Hilton and T. Aston (Cambridge, 1984), pp. 84–111.

10   A. F. Butcher, 'Rent and the Urban Economy: Oxford and Canterbury in the Later Middle Ages', Southern History 1 (1979), 11–43 (pp. 39–42).

11   S. Sweetinburgh, 'The Archangel Gabriel's Stone and Other Relics: William Haute's Search for Salvation in Fifteenth-century Kent', Archaeologia Cantiana 126 (2006), 311–30.

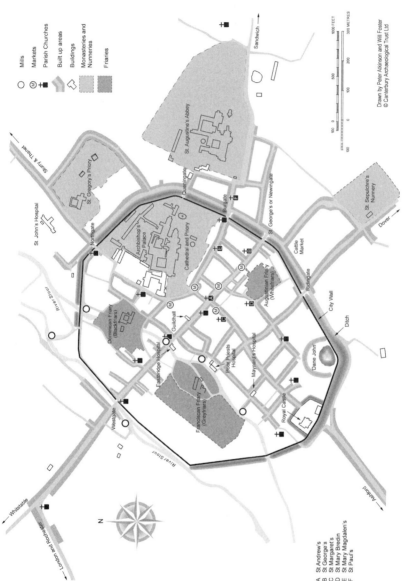

Mills ○

Markets ㉟

Parish Churches +■

Built up areas

Buildings ◇

Monasteries and Nunneries

Friaries

Drawn by Peter Atkinson and Will Foster
© Canterbury Archaeological Trust Ltd

A St Andrew's
B St George's
C St Margaret's
D St Mary Bredin
E St Mary Magdalen's
F St Paul's

Fig. 13.1. Canterbury c. 1500. (Map organised by Andrew Savage, Canterbury Archaeological Trust, and drawn by Peter Atkinson and Will Foster, Canterbury Archaeological Trust)

Austin friars in England had adopted an eremitical lifestyle, but in obedience to a papal directive of 1256 they started to serve in urban communities, and by 1300 the order had established friaries in many English cities.[12]

Canterbury's first Austin friary was in the suburbs, but in the early 1320s the friars relocated to a new site in St George's parish within the walls.[13] Constructed in stages, the new house was needed to accommodate the growing band of friars that had increased from eight in 1319 to eighteen in 1336.[14] This second friary probably followed the conventional plan of a church, and a chapter house, cloister, guest house, dormitory, infirmary and refectory, with gardens surrounded by a wall.[15] Access by the laity, especially women, was severely restricted, so keeping a physical distance between the friars and others, though in death such barriers were less rigorously enforced, even allowing a few women to gain a special burial space in the friary church itself.

Relations with the Church

At their second site, the Austin friars were encroaching on the territory of the prior of Christ Church and the incumbent at St George's, who held his living from Christ Church. This prosperous parish was in the south-eastern sector of the city, St George's Street being the southern section of the city's primary thoroughfare.[16] As a serious rival in the parish the Austin friars were not welcome, the prior showing great reluctance when asked to give permission for them to move into a house there.[17] He may have expected that any questions about the legitimacy of the friars' arrival in St George's would be decided in the church courts, but their next move presumably angered him still further. Apparently without waiting for the initial dispute to be resolved, the friars constructed an oratory where they celebrated divine service, an even greater infringement of parochial rights, especially as they had not sought archiepiscopal approval first. The archbishop convened an inquiry but the commissioners did not proceed according to canon law, providing the friars with an opportunity to seek a compromise with their opponents.[18] In 1326 an agreement was reached between Prior William Berneye of the Austin friars, and Christ Church Priory

---

12 F. Roth, *The English Austin Friars 1249–1538*, 2 vols (New York, 1961–6), I, 231.
13 The friars' first house was a gift of Archbishop Reynolds who had received royal approval to alienate two acres of land in Westgate to the north-west of the city in 1318: Roth, *Austin Friars*, II, 260 citing the Letters Patent for 4 July 1318.
14 Page, *VCH Kent*, II, 199; *MRH*, p. 241.
15 Roth, *Austin Friars*, I, 232–40.
16 W. Urry, *Canterbury under the Angevin Kings* (London, 1967), p. 267.
17 J. B. Sheppard, ed., *Literae Cantuarienses: the Letter Books of the Monastery of Christ Church, Canterbury*, I (London, 1887), pp. 100–1.
18 Canterbury Cathedral Archives and Library [afterwards CCAL], MS DCc/Register A, fol. 426v; E. Hasted, *A History and Topographical Survey of the County of Kent*, 12 vols (1778–1801; repr. Canterbury, 1972), XI, 110. Roth, *Austin Friars*, I, 254; Sheppard, *Literae* I, 160.

and the rector, Sir John of Nakington, whereby the priory and incumbent were to be compensated for the loss of revenue and tithes from the messuage held by the friars, the friars paying 10s 8d each year (the rector receiving 9s, the priory 20d).[19] This agreement strengthened the friars' position, encouraging both the friars and their supporters to consolidate their presence in the parish; and using a vacant plot they had been given that abutted St George's Street at the cloth market, they built their outer gatehouse, agreeing in 1356 to pay 2s 4d annually to Christ Church.[20]

During their first decade in St George's parish the friars were extremely active, their financial position aided in 1328 when the king gave permission for them to sell their former site in Canterbury.[21] This may have allowed them to start building a grand church on their new holding, a structure that dwarfed St George's church which was on the opposite side of the main street.[22] In addition to its impressive size, the friary church had images of Our Lady of Pity and St Katherine, the chapel of St Didier, and probably altars dedicated to the Assumption of Our Lady and to SS Crispin and Crispinianus.[23] However, probably the most significant altar was that dedicated to Scala Coeli, a new devotion that had first arrived in England in 1500.[24] At the Austin friars the altar was in place by 1519, the only church in Canterbury to secure this new and popular focus of devotion, an illustration, perhaps, of their privileged position, and one which was advantageous financially and in terms of their status.[25]

The relationship between the Church and the Austin friars was to a large extent predicated on the spiritual economy which, like any economy, was complex, changeable and subject to external as well as internal factors.[26] When the friars first arrived the enthusiasm displayed by certain members of the laity was not shared by those whose space the friars were invading. Consequently, the friars needed to negotiate successfully with the priory through a series of gift exchanges which would allow them to establish their position in the community. Even though the parties became involved in litigation, suggesting in some senses a breakdown of the negotiation process, the court may be viewed as a means of formalising the use of arbitration. The prior at Christ Church needed

[19] CCAL, MS DCc/Register A, fols 426–8.
[20] Ibid., fol. 426.
[21] Roth, *Austin Friars*, I, 254; *CPR 1327–1330*, p. 233.
[22] Recent archaeological excavations by Canterbury Archaeological Trust (unpublished). The boundary of the lane at the west end: 'soil of five buttresses fixed to the gable of the Austin Friars church'; CCAL, MS CC/FA2, fol. 295; CC/Supp. MS11, p. 105.
[23] The choice of St Desiderius (or Didier) of Vienne is particularly interesting and may relate to the link between Bishop Desiderius and St Augustine when the saint travelled to Canterbury (and England); H. Thurston and N. Lesson, eds, *Butler's Lives of the Saints*, 5 (London, 1936), pp. 281–2.
[24] E. Duffy, *The Stripping of the Altars: Traditional Religion in England, c.1400–c.1580* (New Haven and London, 1992), p. 375.
[25] The first known reference is the will of John Hebbyng: Centre for Kentish Studies [afterwards CKS], MS PRC 17/14, fol. 17.
[26] R. N. Swanson, *Church and Society in Late Medieval England* (Oxford, 1989), pp. 209–28.

to balance the demands of his house and the wider community, especially the parishioners of St George's who were indirectly his responsibility. Furthermore, the convent's requirements were complex because in addition to financial concerns, the prior had to consider the status and reputation of his monastery, and its relationships with those outside its gate. To be seen to be opposing the establishment of his fellow religious whose express mission included aiding those for whom he had a duty of care was presumably unacceptable, necessitating his active participation in the process of negotiation. Even though the incumbent at St George's church was directly involved, as the prior's spiritual and social inferior he was expected to follow the prior's lead, probably seeing himself as having to balance his own and his congregation's needs. Thus the agreement whereby the friars gave to the prior and rector regular monetary gifts forever and in exchange received permission to reside and to work in the parish was a public demonstration of their inter-dependency. The prior of the Austin friars presumably took his offering to a room known as the 'Cheker' at the priory which was reserved for the receiving of payments from Christ Church's tenants.[27] By entering this room he was signalling his house's subservient position in the ecclesiastical hierarchy, but he was equally notifying all concerned that the friars had a place and a role in the city's spiritual life which they could legitimately claim, possibly at a time when Christ Church was viewed as oppressing rather than sustaining Canterbury's less prosperous citizens and their rural neighbours.[28]

Unfortunately the surviving evidence provides little indication concerning the relationship between the priory and the friars during the later fifteenth and early sixteenth centuries, but for the same period something can be said about the attitudes of certain local clerics.[29] Even though the numbers involved are small, of the Canterbury clergy known to have made a will 50% included the Austin friars among their beneficiaries. Most gave money, some indicating the spiritual services they expected as counter gifts, though a few sought a more personal relationship with their chosen house. Among the latter was Dom. William Walpole (1482), chaplain at the Arundel chantry in the cathedral, who wished to be buried in the friary church.[30] Walpole was particularly concerned to strengthen his links with the Austins: the four friars who carried him to his grave were each to be given 20d, and each friar at his death and at his month's mind was to receive 12d to celebrate for his soul. Interestingly, he wanted a graduate in theology from among the friars to celebrate for his soul during the following year; a reflection of his own level of learning?[31] Of the

---

27 B. Dobson, 'The Monks of Canterbury in the Later Middle Ages, 1220–1540', A History of Canterbury Cathedral, ed. P. Collinson, N. Ramsey and M. Sparks (Oxford, 1995), pp. 69–153 (p. 93).

28 Butcher, 'English Urban Society', pp. 99–106.

29 Though possibly an isolated incident, a century earlier the parson at the neighbouring parish of St Andrew had given a messuage worth 12d annually to the friars; CPR 1354–1358, p. 50.

30 CKS, MS PRC 32/2, fol. 578.

31 Walpole was neither an alumnus of Oxford nor of Cambridge.

four local parish priests whose wills survive, three made at least one bequest to the Austin friars. Sir John Williamson (1521) and Sir Henry Ramsey (1501) each left 6s 8d, but Sir Didier Bargier (1503) was extremely generous, intending that a featherbed, two blankets, two pairs of sheets, a coverlet and two pillows should be given to the infirmary, and his little 'brevett' mass book covered in red leather should be used at St Didier's altar.[32] As a result, his book would act as a constant reminder, reinforcing the bond of the shared name which he may have hoped would allow him to become part of their community, receiving their prayers for the benefit of his soul. Sir John and Sir Henry might also have been expected to look to Christ Church for their spiritual well-being. Yet only Sir John left anything in his will to the monks, and even he apparently wished to develop stronger ties with the heads of other monastic houses in Canterbury and Faversham. Thus, even though the evidence is extremely limited, it may indicate a more harmonious relationship between the Church and the Austin friars on the eve of the Reformation compared to the situation two hundred years earlier, a shift in the place of the friars and monks in the lives of the secular clergy whether as patrons, benefactors or beneficiaries.

Relations with the corporation

The extra-parochial status of the Austin friars was important with regard to the Church, but the boundary also marked a physical reality. Though able to construct their outer gatehouse on St George's Street in the mid 1350s, the friars were seemingly unable to enclose their precincts within a wall until the early fifteenth century. They were still acquiring land in the area during this period, and in order to gain seclusion for their community they needed to control two lanes that ran through their premises. As part of the process of consolidation, Prior John of Sturry leased from the city chamberlains at 4s per annum a crooked lane which ran from the north or outer gatehouse of the friary, next to the cemetery and church, towards another lane.[33] Two years later, in 1431, and at a combined cost of 5s, the friars leased a second lane from the chamberlains which ran from opposite St Mary Bredin's church via their postern (west) gate in the new stone wall towards the friary gardens in the east.[34] To strengthen their claim to these lanes, and thus to their perimeter wall, the friars petitioned the king and in 1431 Henry VI granted the two lanes to them on the grounds that they 'are lonely and little used but in which there is so much stench and filth that many infirmities daily befall those dwelling there'. He also agreed that 'by alms and great labour the friars have their house partially built but the building cannot be properly finished unless it is much larger' and so in addition

---

[32] Williamson (St George's parish): CKS, MS PRC 17/15, fol. 101; Ramsey (St George's parish): CKS, MS PRC 17/8, fol. 100; Bargier (St Andrew's parish): CKS, MS PRC 17/9, fol. 191.

[33] CCAL, MS CC/FA1, fol. 188; CC/PA2, p. 69.

[34] CCAL, MS CC/FA1, fol. 209.

to the lanes he permitted them to receive a messuage and a garden for which they would pay 5s annually to the fee farm of the city.[35] Nevertheless, the friars seem to have encountered some opposition to their actions, and the prior was summoned to appear before the king's court to substantiate the friary's rights to the area. He was successful, his attorney securing judgement in favour of the Austin friars in 1438.[36] A few years later they were apparently building again, and their second great gate may have replaced an earlier wooden structure.[37]

Such points of contact between the friars and the civic authorities were important, it being understood that the friars should open their gates every morning and close them at night.[38] Nonetheless, as a mark of their autonomy, the friars were apparently prepared to defend their walled enclosure and to offer sanctuary to those who sought their protection. In 1525 the prior, William Mallom, and four friars drove off the coroner with sticks and knives when he tried to arrest for felony a woman who had sought sanctuary at the friary.[39] However, they were unable or unwilling to defend Alice the prostitute in 1499, who was fined 12d at the assize court for Newingate ward when she was convicted of having gone to the friary at night to meet certain Austin friars, something she was said to have done on many occasions.[40] Yet when it was friars who were the transgressors, it was the provincial in England who was expected to restore order. In 1527 William Wetherall was ordered by his superior to investigate several charges against the prior and two named friars at Canterbury who were said to have eaten and slept in local inns.[41] There they and other friars had played dice, cards and ball games, activities that the civic authorities were similarly seeking to curtail in an attempt to halt what they saw as moral and spiritual decay.

Nonetheless, for most of this period the friars and the corporation were on good terms, and in 1476 the city came to an arrangement with the friars whereby the corporation's guests were accommodated at the friary. The mayor and aldermen had quarrelled with St Augustine's Abbey over certain property rights and two senior crown appointees conducted the hearing in Canterbury. These men stayed at the friary for a week in March and again in August, and on both occasions the corporation lavishly entertained their guests.[42] How far such activities were also a drain on the friars' own resources is impossible to ascertain because their wealth may primarily have been in the form of bricks and mortar. Yet their activities on the city's behalf seem to have provided them with a sympathetic hearing when the corporation wanted them to pave the street outside their gate. The members of the burghmote accepted their plea

---

35 Roth, *Austin Friars*, II, 313, citing the Letters Patent 18 Nov. 1431.

36 Page, *VCH Kent*, II, p. 200.

37 Richard Pargate bequeathed 40s towards the new gateway in 1457; CKS, MS PRC 17/1, fol. 20; CCAL, MS CC/FA1, fol. 272v; CC/FA14, fol. 16.

38 CCAL, MS CC/Supp MS11, p. 23.

39 Ibid., p. 100.

40 CCAL, MS CC/J/B/298, fol. 96.

41 Knowles, *RO*, III, 60.

42 CCAL, MS CC/FA2, fols 180–80v.

of poverty, agreeing to give 26s 8d to them against the cost of pavage.[43] These incidents suggest that the Austin friars were seen as suitable exchange partners by the corporation, their elegant and well-constructed house mirroring their wealth and status, which in turn reflected well on the corporation in its bid to impress senior crown officials. Consequently the gift of hospitality was a highly significant bond between the friars and the corporation, the friary guest house providing the right level of accommodation in which the mayor and aldermen could entertain their guests, thereby honouring all the parties concerned. For the corporation, the provision of entertainment was a vital part of its work on the city's behalf in the pursuit of good lordship, patronage and favour, its guests ranging from the king to the civic representatives of neighbouring east Kent towns, and it was important that each should be suitably provided for as befitted their status. Thus at a time when the provincial chapter of the Austin friars regularly met in Canterbury, this prestigious friary seems to have become a valued partner in the corporation's strategy of civic manoeuvring for survival, or better still favour and advancement. Why the friary was seemingly not used in the same way during the early sixteenth century is unclear, especially as senior members of the order apparently sought to strengthen the relationship between the friars and the civic authorities.[44]

Relations with the laity

The first lay patron of the Canterbury Austin friars was the extremely powerful Hugh Despenser, earl of Warwick, and it was to him the friars turned when they initially entered St George's parish.[45] Having secured a substantial stone house on Brewers Lane from Thomas of Bonnington, the friars subsequently received the adjoining tenement on the other side.[46] This first gift from Thomas, a member of one of the leading local families in the fourteenth century, brought them into conflict with Christ Church Priory, but as noted above the dispute only temporarily halted the Austin friars. They acquired the old jail in 1329, a messuage from Henry son of Robert atte Gayole; and in the next decade they received three further messuages, a garden and a vacant plot of land from several benefactors, including Richard Fraunceys and John Chich, member of a prominent Canterbury family.[47] More gifts followed, but a messuage and garden from John Chertesey in 1394 may mark the end of the friars' property acquisitions from local benefactors.[48] The expansion of the friary was presum-

[43] CCAL, MS CC/Supp MS6, p. 90.
[44] In 1500 the provincial of the Austin friars in England issued a letter of confraternity to the mayor of Canterbury and to his successors; CCAL, MS CC/Supp MS6, p. 91.
[45] Sheppard, *Literae*, I, 100–1.
[46] CCAL, MS DCc/Register A, fols 431, 433.
[47] CPR 1327–1330, pp. 456, 457; CPR 1334–1338, p. 60; CPR 1343–1345, p. 195; W. Somner, *The Antiquities of Canterbury* (1703, repr. Wakefield, 1997), p. 68; Hasted, *Kent*, XI, 110.
[48] CPR 1391–1396, p. 404.

ably accompanied by a policy of creating a suitable range of buildings: Michael Denne bequeathed five thousand tiles to the friary church in 1394 and eleven years later Amelia Gobion left ten marks towards the new work there.[49] All these activities may have led the friars to overstretch themselves because they were seeking royal assistance in 1408. In that year Henry VI allowed the friars to become landlords by giving them permission to rebuild houses and other buildings on their own land which was adjacent to St George's Street.[50] The friars rented out these houses and another messuage and garden, which apparently allowed them to continue building and to pay their dues. However, like their monastic neighbours, the returns were seemingly insufficient to cover their expenses, leading the friars to seek additional royal aid in order to enclose their premises.

Nevertheless, the imposing friary church and the friars' activities in the neighbourhood presumably drew alms from local citizens and visitors to Canterbury, but the level of such giving is impossible to quantify. Consequently any analysis of the support enjoyed by the Austin friars in Canterbury must rest on the level and type of bequests recorded in wills. Of the eleven hundred known Canterbury testators between 1380 and 1538, 20% made at least one bequest to the Austin friars, and of the fifty-eight parishioners in St George's parish making wills during the same period, 35% included the Austin friars among their beneficiaries. Comparing the level of testamentary support enjoyed by the friars and the monastic houses as a way of placing the Austins among the city's religious institutions, each of the three friaries received more bequests than any of the monasteries. The Austin friars were slightly less favoured compared to their Franciscan and Dominican brothers, though the difference is not significant. There was some variation in the level of support each of the friaries received on a parish basis and in five of the sixteen parishes in Canterbury and its suburbs the Austin friars were the most frequent beneficiaries. Support was particularly strong among testators from St George's parish (see above), they were also the leading recipients in the abutting parishes of St Andrew, St Mary Magdalene and St Paul, the latter outside the city walls. Thus proximity to the friary was seemingly a determining factor, even in a city as small as Canterbury.

For these Canterbury benefactors, the Austin friars were valuable members of the spiritual economy. Among the counter gifts they sought were burial, the provision of pall bearers, the provision of masses at the three funeral services, at obits and the establishment of temporary or permanent chantries. The small size of the friary cemetery, it was squashed into a space between the church, the tenements abutting St George's Street and the crooked lane, may have limited the number of people seeking burial there, but the friary church itself was chosen by at least twenty-eight local people. The value of the friary as a family mausoleum was recognised by several married couples, including the

49 Denne: CKS, MS PRC 32/1, fol. 7; Gobion: CKS, MS PRC 32/1, fol. 15.
50 *CPR 1405–1408*, p. 433.

Courtmans (1501, 1511); while William Catbury (1479) wanted to be near to his friend Christopher Hamer.[51] Although some testators indicated their choice of burial site in terms of the church as a whole, such as in the south side, others selected particular altars or images and of these the image of Our Lady of Pity in the nave was especially favoured. Only William Haute and his wives are known to have chosen burial before the image of St Katherine, his gift to the friars of a piece of her hair shirt a perpetual reminder of his devotion to this virgin martyr.[52] The request for burial at the friary was rarely linked to a specific post-mortem gift, though Richard Dyne did give the considerable sum of 20s.[53]

Instead, many sought other spiritual gifts in addition to burial or left specific instructions concerning their desires. Several citizens wanted the Austin friars to act as pall bearers regardless of whether they would be carrying the deceased to the friary church for burial. George Haslet (1532) left seven vessels of single beer to the friars to take him to his grave at St Augustine's Abbey; while John Cornwall (1489) gave 10s on condition the friars carried him to his burial at his parish church of Holy Cross and sang a dirge and requiem mass.[54] That it was the friars rather than the friary church that was the main attraction for some is interesting, the friars expected to celebrate masses and other services at the testator's home parish church. To have the friars at one's grave side may have been seen as advantageous for several reasons. Like the poor they were seen as worthy recipients of charity, they were seen as chosen by God for their humility and poverty and, as professional prayers, they would be particularly efficacious for the benefit of the benefactor's soul.

Others adopted a different approach, seeking commemoration for far longer periods, and the idea of an obit at the friary was an attractive addition or alternative for a number of benefactors. The longest obit was fifty-two years, William Bonnyngton (1463) also specifying the type of masses he wished should be celebrated on his behalf in the choir of the friary church.[55] The funding of a temporary or perpetual chantry was beyond the means of many of the friary's benefactors, but Sir John Fyneux intended that his gift exchange with the friars would provide a chaplain to say mass daily at the altar of the Visitation of Our Lady for his soul, for that of his wife and for the souls whom he named.[56]

This understanding of the worthiness of the Austin friars as advocates for the dead might be enhanced through the celebration of requiem masses and other services at particular altars. The testamentary evidence suggests that the most important was the Scala Coeli altar, which was especially favoured in the 1520s, though whether this was in response to its general popularity or its promotion

---

[51]   John Courtman: CKS, MS PRC 17/8, fol. 167; Johanna Courtman: CKS, MS PRC 17/12, fol. 26; Catbury: CKS, MS PRC 17/3, fol. 287.

[52]   CKS, MS PRC 32/2, fol. 79; Sweetinburgh, 'Gabriel's Stone', 315, 321–2.

[53]   CKS, MS PRC 17/4, fol. 26.

[54]   Haslet: CKS, MS PRC 17/19, fol. 245; Cornwall: CKS, MS PRC 17/5, fol. 350.

[55]   CKS, MS PRC 32/2, fol. 132.

[56]   Somner, Canterbury, appendix 18.

by certain friars is unknown.[57] The selection of the altar of Our Lady of Pity was longer lasting, a response, perhaps, to the widespread and enduring popularity of her cult; and at the friary church Isabel Walker (1515) not only wanted to be buried there but intended that a taper should burn before the image of Our Lady at the time of mass and compline for as long as the taper lasted.[58]

As well as their services for the dead, the friars were seen as valuable exchange partners for the living. Even though the evidence is limited, there may have been at least two fraternities at the friary. One dedicated to St Erasmus was presumably open to local laymen, like William Furnour (1524) of St Margaret's parish, who gave two half-pound tapers to the fraternity.[59] The second may have met in St Katherine's hall at the friary, and seems to have had strong links with the neighbouring parish of St Andrew: in 1505 the churchwardens paid for the hall to be cleaned and for rushes for the floor.[60] Moreover, the friars were prepared to store timber on behalf of the churchwardens when they were constructing substantial alterations to the rood loft, receiving gifts in return of a hundred herring, and 4s 10d worth of figs and raisins.[61]

In addition, from the same period (and maybe earlier) the guild of shoe-makers, curriers and cobblers held their patronal services at the friary church.[62] On both days each guild member provided a penny offering at the mass, the guild wardens giving lights to the appropriate altars on behalf of the brethren. After the procession, which presumably accompanied the high mass, the members retired to their guild house to dine and to execute guild business. Even though this was outside the friary precincts, the relationship between the fraternity and the friars, articulated through the public performance of these fraternal rituals, would have been viewed as mutually beneficial. For the guild, the friary offered a suitable space in a richly-decorated prestigious church for its spiritual activities. And for the friars, the presence and gifts of this craft frater-nity were valuable signs of a relationship that had the potential to continue forever, a link that they might seek to extend to individual guild members as special beneficiaries.

The value of personal connections between individual friars and members of the laity can also be seen from the testamentary evidence. Although very few named friars were the recipients of such largesse at any of the Canter-bury friaries, these bequests may denote strong connections, especially where the friar was called upon to perform special actions: Sir Thomas Fogge (1407) wanted Austin friar John Clerke to be his executor; while Walter Grene was to celebrate a trental of masses at St Paul's church for the soul of Thomas

57 These included a testator from Alkham, near Dover: CKS, MS PRC 17/17, fol. 335.
58 CKS, MS PRC 17/12, fol. 525.
59 CKS, MS PRC 17/16, fol. 29. For fraternities at Austin friaries more generally: F. Andrews, *The Other Friars. The Carmelite, Augustinian, Sack and Pied Friars in the Middle Ages* (Woodbridge, 2006), pp. 145–7.
60 CCAL, MS U3/5/4/1, fols 27, 27v.
61 CCAL, MS U3/5/4/1, fols 25, 25v.
62 CCAL, MS CC/Woodruff Bundle 54/2.

Marre (1528).[63] Friar Grene was the chosen beneficiary of two other St Paul's parishioners, receiving from Eleanor Lyncoln (1530) a platter, dish, saucer and candlestick, personal items that might denote Eleanor's gratitude to the friar, as marks of regard and/or as mnemonic aids in her search for commemoration and salvation.[64]

Yet the friars' relations with the local townspeople may not always have been harmonious and there may have been some difficulties with regard to the renting of their five tenements from the late fifteenth century, a problem experienced by other ecclesiastical landlords in Canterbury. Unfortunately relatively few Canterbury wills survive pre-1460 which means that it is impossible to ascertain any trends in the level of support the friars received over time. Consequently it is not clear whether there was any significant local opposition by the late 1530s to the Austin friars, though they were said to be poverty-stricken which might indicate indifference to the state of their house.

In conclusion, this case study of the Austin friars' place in late medieval English society has revealed the importance of the relationships the friars established with their fellow religious, the civic authorities and the laity. Being mendicants they remained heavily dependent on the community outside their gate, and benefaction and patronage were significant issues, allowing them to develop social solidarity through processes of gift giving and reciprocity. Moreover, the Austin friars recognised the value of arbitration in their dealings with others, yet they were not afraid to become involved in litigation when negotiation had seemingly faltered. This apparently flexible strategy necessitated a detailed understanding of the wants and aspirations of other groups and individuals in Canterbury, which seems to endorse Röhrkasten's conclusion regarding the friars' high sensitivity to local conditions. Like the London mendicants, the Austin friars of Canterbury were successful, finding themselves a niche by negotiating spaces. As a result the house and order prospered, its prestige in the fifteenth century mirrored in its dealings with others in Canterbury and beyond. The sixteenth century brought different challenges. Even though the introduction of new cults was apparently successful in strengthening the friary's ties with the locality, making them respected participants in the spiritual economy in the early decades of the century, local knowledge did not save them in 1538 and, though extreme, Friar Stone's death presumably generated a diverse response from Canterbury's townspeople.[65]

---

[63] Fogge: CKS, MS PRC 32/1, fol. 16; Marre: CKS, MS PRC 17/13, fol. 367.
[64] CKS, MS PRC 17/19, fol. 25.
[65] Page, *VCH Kent*, II, 201. CCAL, MS CC/FA13, fols 69v–70.

RELIGIOUS HOUSES IN THE REGIONS

14

Monasteries in Medieval Cornwall: Mediocrity or Merit?

NICHOLAS ORME

It is said that the Devil, having travelled through Devon, reached the edge of Cornwall and decided to go no further. 'Over there everywhere's called Saint this and Saint that, and anything strange that moves they put into a pasty.' Medieval monks were more adventurous, but for them too Cornwall was unrewarding territory. Although it acquired twelve monasteries after 1100, most of these were small foundations dependent on religious houses elsewhere. As a result few Cornishmen became monks, since the opportunities to live the monastic life were limited even for those who wished to do so.[1]

Cornwall had no monasteries in 1066. They had existed in about the seventh and eighth centuries, but by the late Saxon period there were only minsters of canons, priests, or clerks.[2] Then, in the twelfth century, the great tide of monastic foundations in England caused ripples in Cornwall. The first monastery to be founded was the priory of St Nicholas on the Isles of Scilly, in about 1114. This was a daughter house of Tavistock Abbey (Devon), which had been given half of the islands by Henry I.[3] The priory of Scilly, as it was known, would have been staffed by only two or three monks and a couple of servants, was wholly dependent on Tavistock, and sent its surplus revenues to its mother house. The abbots of Tavistock were apparently fond of the exotic foods that the islands produced, and reserved a supply of dried and salted puffins and seal meat when they leased the islands in 1501.[4] Six other monasteries, all fairly small and offshoots of larger institutions, made their appear-

---

1   This article is based on the research for *VCH, Cornwall*, II: *Religious History to 1559*, by Nicholas Orme (forthcoming: Woodbridge, 2008).
2   On monasteries in Cornwall before the Norman Conquest, see L. Olson, *Early Monasteries in Cornwall* (Woodbridge, 1989).
3   G. Oliver, *Monasticon Dioecesis Exoniensis* (Exeter and London, 1846), p. 73; H. W. C. Davis et al., eds, *Regesta Regum Anglo-Normannorum*, 4 vols (Oxford, 1913–59), III, 119.
4   Devon Record Office (hereafter DRO), W1258 M/E37.

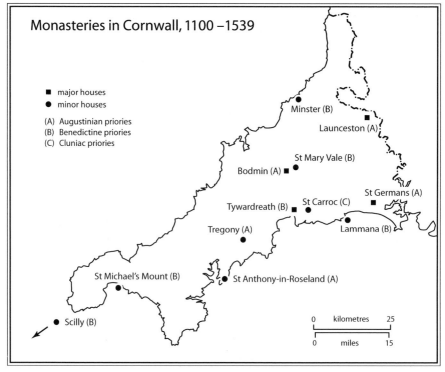

Fig. 14.1. Monasteries in Cornwall, 1100–1539.

ance during the twelfth and thirteenth centuries. These, with their mother houses in brackets, were the Cluniac priory of St Carroc (Montacute) and the Benedictine priories of Lammana (Glastonbury), St Mary Vale (Tywardreath), St Michael's Mount (Mont St Michel), and Minster and Tywardreath (both St Serge, Angers). Tywardreath was the biggest and wealthiest with seven monks, while St Michael's Mount probably had six, and the others only two or three each. These six monasteries, even at the height of their prosperity in about 1250, contained only about twenty-two monks, nearly all of whom were Frenchmen supplied from Angers and Mont St Michel. The English residue came mostly from Somerset.

Monks in the narrow sense did not account for the whole of monasticism in medieval Cornwall, however. There were three larger houses of regular canons whose origins lay in the minsters that survived the Norman Conquest. During the 1120s the bishop of Exeter, William Warelwast, turned the two richest of these, Bodmin and Launceston, into bodies of Augustinian canons, and another bishop of Exeter, Bartholomew, did the same at St Germans in about 1180. The Augustinian rule seems to have suited Cornwall better, or else the relatively wealthy endowments of the three Augustinian houses supported larger and more viable communities. All three houses were independent and all contained more inmates: about eighteen at both Bodmin and Launceston up to the Black

Death, and a dozen or so at St Germans. When we reach the fourteenth century and begin to have records of their canons' surnames, many and probably nearly all came from Cornwall, or more precisely from the more anglicised eastern half of the county. To these houses we can add two other small Augustinian priories: St Anthony-in-Roseland, a cell of Plympton Priory (Devon), and Tregony, a dependency first of St Marie du Val (Normandy) and later of Merton (Surrey). Neither is likely to have contained more than two or three canons: from Devon in the first case and from France, later Surrey, in the second.

There were, then, twelve Cornish monasteries – seven fairly small and poor, one of middling wealth (St Michael's Mount), and the big three with Tywardreath coming close behind them. Middling and big means only by Cornish standards. This relatively modest monastic presence partly reflected the lack of large landowners in the county. There was only one great nobleman – the earl of Cornwall, to whom Launceston was indebted for some of its property, but the earldom was vacant for much of the twelfth century. The bishops of Exeter who reorganised the three Augustinian houses gave them virtually no property, and Bodmin and St Germans had to make do with their ancient minster endowments. The second richest Anglo-Norman family, the Cardinans, founded Tywardreath – the wealthiest of the small houses – but the remaining founders were lower in status and their foundations were correspondingly smaller. Some Cornish landowners who wished to give lands or churches to monasteries gave them to houses out of the county, including Beaulieu, Glastonbury, Rewley, and Tewkesbury. The result was that the monastic houses of Cornwall never contained more than about eighty to ninety monks and canons, even at their acme in the 1200s, compared with perhaps four hundred parish clergy. No Cistercian monastery was founded, nor Premonstratensian, nor Carthusian. Nor was there ever a nunnery, although a few Cornish women are mentioned joining religious houses elsewhere.[5]

As time went on even the small group of monasteries started to dwindle. Two little ones went in the thirteenth century because their mother houses found them too expensive to run: Tregony between 1282 and 1286, and Lammana in 1285. St Mary Vale probably faded out within the next fifty years or so, and another two disappeared as a consequence of the Hundred Years War and the interference by the crown with the property of French abbeys in England. These were Minster, converted to a parish church in 1408, and St Michael's Mount, given by Henry V as an endowment to Syon Abbey between 1417 and 1420 and thereafter a chapel staffed by three secular priests. Scilly seems to have vanished in the second half of the fifteenth century. As early as about 1300 the mother house, Tavistock Abbey, tried to persuade the king to give it new endowments in exchange for the Isles of Scilly,[6] and during the mid fourteenth century the

5   E.g. F. C. Hingeston-Randolph, ed., *The Register of Edmund Stafford* (London and Exeter, 1886), pp. 210, 406.
6   TNA, SC 8/75/3720; H. P. R. Finberg, *Tavistock Abbey*, 2nd edn (Newton Abbot, 1969), p. 15.

abbey withdrew its monks from the islands, pleading their dangerous situation.[7] The priory was subsequently restored but the last reference to a prior occurs in 1452, and by 1492 Tavistock was keeping a single monk on the islands to deal with its business there.[8] By 1500 the number of houses had fallen by half to include the three bigger Augustinian foundations, Tywardreath, and the two small cells of St Anthony-in-Roseland and St Carroc.

Sites and buildings

Small and short-lived though some of these houses were, they are not without interest. Let us begin with their locations: where were they founded and why were such places chosen? The bigger three houses replaced older minsters, but even the little twelfth- and thirteenth-century foundations adopted locations where there had been a previous religious presence such as a shrine or chapel. St Carroc and Minster each claimed to have a local saint buried in them.[9] The foundation charter of Scilly talks of earlier monks or hermits, and St Anthony, Lammana, and St Michael's Mount all seem to have occupied older holy sites. Only Tregony and Tywardreath appear to have stood on virgin soil, the first beside a new town and castle and the second at the centre of a group of churches given for its endowment.

More foundations were made in the eastern half of Cornwall than in the western, perhaps reflecting the greater remoteness, poverty, or difference, of the west where Cornish was spoken. Two houses, Bodmin and Launceston, were situated close to towns on the main road from England through Cornwall. They had the most urban settings, although strictly speaking suburban ones, and the greatest advantages from passing traffic. A third house, Tywardreath, was not far from the town and seaport of Fowey. In contrast five of the smaller priories occupied romantic and other-worldly locations. Three of them – Lammana, the Mount, and Scilly – were on small islands, renewing the tradition of such sites in Britain so typical of pre-Viking times and paralleled elsewhere in England after the Norman Conquest.[10] Lammana, dedicated to St Michael, looks like an attempt to imitate the Mount, and we are told that pilgrims came to it by boat.[11] Two other houses were in rocky wooded places – St Mary Vale and Minster, adjacent to settlements but secluded from them. Clearly some twelfth-century monastery founders were captivated by remote surroundings.

[7] Oliver, Monasticon, p. 74; CPR 1343–5, p. 480.

[8] C. Harper-Bill, ed., The Register of John Morton, Archbishop of Canterbury 1486–1500, 3 vols, Canterbury and York Soc., 75, 77, 89 (1987–2000), II, 81.

[9] See below, note 48.

[10] E.g. Farne (Northumberland), Steep Holme (Somerset), and West Mersea (Essex) on islands, and several monasteries (especially Cistercian houses) in wild places.

[11] W. M. M. Picken, 'Light on Lammana', Devon and Cornwall Notes and Queries 35 part 8 (1985), 281–6.

The Cornish monasteries have left us little in terms of standing buildings or even ruins: about two thirds each of the churches of St Germans, St Michael's Mount, and St Anthony-in-Roseland; some vestiges of Minster in the parish church there; and a few remains of Scilly. Launceston was excavated in the late nineteenth century, and something of Bodmin's layout can be imagined from William Worcester's description of it in 1478. There is no space here to attempt the reconstruction of these buildings, and all that can be offered are simple summaries. The smaller monastic foundations had churches correspondingly smaller in size. St Carroc is referred to in documents and on Tudor maps as a chapel.[12] St Michael's Mount, Minster, and Scilly each consisted of a modest nave, choir, and little else. St Anthony had additional transepts. These last three, and probably also Tregony, were parish churches as well as religious houses. The only one of them to undergo architectural development was the Mount, which added a Lady chapel during the late fourteenth or early fifteenth centuries.[13]

The three bigger monasteries had appropriately larger churches. St Germans, the best preserved today, was about 50 metres (165 feet) long. It was entered by a grand west door, flanked by two towers, and possessed aisles alongside the nave, the nave being the local parish church. These aisles did not apparently continue past the choir. A Lady chapel was added later, probably in the south transept built in the fourteenth century, which was itself extended to be a south aisle for the nave in the fifteenth.[14] Bodmin, a wealthier house than St Germans, had a correspondingly longer church, about 58 metres (192 feet) in length. This seems to have had aisles alongside nave and choir as well as a retrochoir behind the high altar, containing the shrine of Bodmin's saint, Petroc. The shrine faced a Lady chapel which extended a further 9 metres (30 feet), and a bell tower stood at the north-west corner of the nave.[15] Launceston had the largest church, reflecting its greater wealth than Bodmin. This was about 84 metres (275 feet) long. In its original twelfth-century form it consisted of a narrow nave and choir. A north aisle was later added to the nave and north and south aisles to the chancel, a south nave aisle being precluded by the presence of the adjoining cloister. Here too a Lady chapel was eventually constructed east of the choir and the high altar.[16]

[12] E.g. *John Norden's Manuscript Maps of Cornwall and its Nine Hundreds*, ed. W. L. D. Ravenhill (Exeter, 1972), facsimiles 2, 5, 10.

[13] On the buildings of the Mount, see P. A. S. Pool, 'The Ancient and Present State of St Michael's Mount, 1762', *Cornish Studies* 3 (1976), 29–47.

[14] On the buildings of St Germans, see L. Olson and A. Preston-Jones, 'An Ancient Cathedral of Cornwall? Excavated Remains East of St Germans Church', *Cornish Archaeology* 37–8 (1998–9), 153–69.

[15] W. Worcester, *Itineraries*, ed. J. H. Harvey (Oxford, 1969), pp. 86–7, 90–1.

[16] O. B. Peter, 'Launceston Priory: the Substance of a Lecture' (Launceston, 1889); idem, 'Excavations on the Site of Launceston Priory', *Journal of the Royal Institution of Cornwall* 11 (1891–3), 1–6; J. Gossip, *St Thomas' Priory, Launceston, Cornwall*, Cornwall Archaeological Unit (Truro, 2002).

Launceston is the only monastery where traces remain of the domestic buildings. South of the nave there was a cloister, as usual with a grassy plot in its centre. On the west side of this lay the prior's lodgings, and on the south and east sides the refectory for meals, the frater or common room, and the dormitory. Further out were kitchens, stables, and accommodation for servants who probably numbered about twice the canons. A guest hall is mentioned where it seems that guests were fed and servants ate. In the fifteenth century four tables stood in this hall for the use of grooms, clerks, workmen, and gentlemen, and inscriptions were written on the walls enjoining the observance of good manners as well as the giving of charity to scholars and the poor.[17]

Lands, wealth, and self-importance

Cornish monastic income came partly from lands and rents, partly from commercial sources (markets, fairs, and tolls), and partly from tithes of churches. All the houses had lands, Launceston's being the most extensive and spreading for several miles north, west, and south of the priory. Three monasteries held lordship over towns. Launceston owned Newport, the northern suburb of the borough of Launceston, but had no rights over the borough itself. Bodmin owned the borough of Bodmin, and Tywardreath owned Fowey. These monasteries handled law and order in their towns, supervised fairs and markets, and took the profits – powers resented in Bodmin, the biggest of these places, which was denied the self-government of its sister Launceston until the 1530s when the end of the priory's power was in sight. A further irritant at Bodmin was the monastery's possession of the surrounding woodlands and a major fishing river, the Allen, from which local people wished to take wood and fish. This led to Bodmin becoming a remote outlier of the Peasants' Revolt in 1381. According to a local inquisition, held in July of that year, three Cornishmen including a chaplain, having heard of the revolt in London, gathered a large band of men and usurped the royal power in Cornwall. On Saturday 15 June, the day that the revolt collapsed in London, they came to the priory's river, broke down a weir, and destroyed a building.[18]

Figures for the total incomes of the Cornish monasteries in 1291 are provided by the papal taxation of that year and of those that still existed or had successors in 1535 by the valuation of the Church made by the government of Henry VIII.[19] No figures survive for Lammana, St Mary Vale, Scilly, or Tregony. The

---

[17] Bodl., MS Bodley 315, fol. 268r, printed by F. Rose-Troup, 'Verses in the Hall at Launceston', *Devon and Cornwall Notes and Queries* 19 (1936–7), 154–6, and (with full discussion) by R. H. Robbins, 'Wall Verses at Launceston Priory', *Archiv für neuere Sprachen und Literaturen* 200 (1964), 338–43.

[18] *Calendar of Inquisitions Miscellaneous*, IV, 102.

[19] F. C. Hingeston-Randolph, ed., *The Registers of Walter Bronescombe and Peter Quivil, Bishops of Exeter* (London and Exeter, 1889), pp. 466–72, 479–80; VE, I, 196, 426; II, 376–8, 396, 400–3, 405.

records of 1291 excluded some revenues and were generally undervalued, so that the 1535 figures give a better idea of values, although even these fell somewhat short of the truth:

Table 1. Incomes of Cornish monasteries

House	1291	1535
St Anthony	£9 11s 2d	£28 10s 0d[20]
Bodmin	£50 0s 8d	£289 11s 11d
St Carroc	£10 6s 8d	£11 1s 0d
St Germans	£27 9s 6d	£243 8s 0d
Launceston	£88 11s 0d	£392 11s 2¼d
St Michael's Mount	£28 6s 4d	£33 6s 8d
Minster	£6 0s 0d	£22 17s 0½d
Tywardreath	£73 9s 4d	£151 16s 1d

These figures show that Launceston was the richest house, followed by Bodmin and then by St Germans, Tywardreath, and St Michael's Mount. The smaller cells had very low incomes.

Monastic functions in Cornwall must have embraced the usual triplet of prayer, administration, and hospitality. Bodmin and Launceston both lay on the main road through Cornwall, and important travellers like bishops, judges, noblemen and gentlemen expected to be entertained to meals or housed over-night. The heads of the three big houses had little weight nationally, but they served their turn as conveners of the Augustinians' national councils and as visitors of other west-country monasteries on the order's behalf. Since Cornwall had few rich resident parish clergy, the heads of the three big houses prob-ably had a good deal of status and influence. The prior of Bodmin possessed a country house at St Margaret east of Bodmin and another at Rialton near Newquay. All three larger monasteries were inclined to give themselves airs. St Germans claimed incorrectly that it was the oldest Augustinian monastery in England, founded by Bishop Leofric in about 1050.[21] Bodmin boasted that it had been founded by St Petroc in the fifth or sixth centuries.[22] In 1498–9 the prior of St Germans elicited a papal grant of the mitre, staff, and insignia of a bishop,[23] and in 1509 the prior of Launceston got permission from the bishop of Exeter to wear a fur almuce or cape – a privilege of the canons of Exeter Cathedral.[24] In 1517 the prior of Bodmin, Thomas Vivian, capped both his rivals by being made a suffragan bishop. He marked his importance by acquiring

[20] This figure includes a further element to cover revenue from land.
[21] Oliver, *Monasticon*, p. 4; *CPR 1381–5*, p. 316; J. Leland, *Collectanea*, ed. T. Hearne, 2nd edn, 6 vols (London, 1774), I, 75.
[22] P. Grosjean, 'Vie et miracles de. S. Petroc', *Analecta Bollandiana* 74 (1956), 163–4.
[23] *Calendar of Papal Registers*, XVII part 1, 643.
[24] DRO, Chanter XIII (The Register of Hugh Oldham), fols 182v–183r.

a coat of arms from the king's heralds (a showy piece in four colours, featuring three lions' heads),[25] and was eventually buried in a magnificent tomb beneath an effigy, now in Bodmin church.

Mediocrity

Each house had a patron: the bishop of Exeter in the case of the big three, and the earldom or duchy of Cornwall or the crown in the case of Tywardreath and eventually St Michael's Mount. In the fourteenth century the crown and the duchy of Cornwall made several attempts to challenge the bishop's patronage, but these failed, although the crown succeeded in claiming the minster of St Buryan as a royal chapel and withdrawing it from the diocese. Patronage sat uneasily with the tradition that monks and canons should elect their own leaders. Bishops intervened to quash elections that were disputed or allegedly irregular, but on one notable occasion the bishop failed in this respect.[26] In 1430 the fourteen canons of Launceston met to choose a new prior. They met three times and failed. On the fourth occasion they decided to cast votes. One candidate got four votes, the other eight. The bishop refused to confirm the election, but the eight canons declared their candidate the victor and he took control of the priory. Then he appealed to powerful figures – Humphrey, duke of Gloucester, and Cardinal Beaufort – who put pressure on the bishop. The bishop was forced to give way, but in 1443, when Henry IV had attained adult-hood and Humphrey and Beaufort were less strong, he had his revenge by forcing the prior and his main adjutant to make a public apology for slandering him and resisting his authority.[27]

Episcopal visitations of monasteries in Cornwall, like those elsewhere, contain plenty of complaints about misdeeds and shortcomings. The most formidable bishop of Exeter, John Grandisson (1327–69), battled for nearly twenty years, between 1327 and 1346, with the prior of Launceston, Adam of Knolle.[28] Grandisson found much wrong with Adam's regime. The prior was spending time outside the monastery with secular persons, some of them women. He was keeping too many servants, and impoverishing the monastery. He had stopped giving alms to the poor. The canons were drinking immoderately in their refec-tory and in private. They were keeping dogs and hawks, presumably for hunting. Eventually, in 1344, Grandisson removed Adam from control of affairs in the monastery and commissioned two canons to take charge instead. The canons

[25] London, College of Arms, MS L 10, fol. 71r; MS M 3, fol. 79v.

[26] On what follows, see, for the bishop's record of the election, F. C. Hingeston-Randolph, ed., The Register of Edmund Lacy, Bishop of Exeter, vol. I (London and Exeter, 1901), pp. 132–43, and for the priory's, Bodl., MS Tanner 196, fols 8r–54r (pp. 15–107).

[27] G. R. Dunstan, ed., The Register of Edmund Lacy, Bishop of Exeter: Registrum Commune, 5 vols, Devon and Cornwall Record Soc., ns 7, 10, 13, 16, 18 (1963–72), II, 300–2.

[28] On what follows, see F. C. Hingeston-Randolph, ed., The Register of John de Grandisson, Bishop of Exeter, 3 vols (London and Exeter, 1894–9), I, 564–5; II, 837, 955–6, 989–92, 1003–4.

began to carry out reforms, but the prior resisted. He appointed other people to do administrative jobs, abstracted money, and continued to spend time with a married lady friend. The angry bishop denounced the prior as 'a son of damnation', a man 'who has for many years led a life detestable to God and man, scorning and undermining our commands, punishments, and sentences with damnable audacity'. Adam managed to hold out for a couple more years, but in the end the bishop was too strong for him. On 19 June 1346 he was forced to agree to resign and sent the bishop a letter certifying that he had done so. In the following year the bishop turned his attention to Bodmin. Its affairs were no better. The canons were wearing secular clothes such as buttoned and hooded tunics, thigh boots, and pointed shoes. They were playing dice, backgammon, and chess, and talking to women. Some of them were living in private rooms, dogs were being kept, and the monastery was badly in debt.[29]

Thomas Colyns, who ruled at Tywardreath from 1506 to 1535, has become Cornwall's most notorious prior. This may be unfair to Colyns, but his character was certainly larger than life. He came to Tywardreath from Devon, apparently as an adult, and is recorded in the priory in 1506 when he persuaded the old prior to resign and recommend him, Colyns, to be his successor. In return Colyns promised to pay the old prior a pension of £40 a year, 20% of the monastery's income. Colyns got the job and benefited again when the bishop cut down the pension to £20.[30] The new prior then began an expansive career. He gained papal permission to hold one of the priory's parish churches in tandem with being prior, eventually becoming vicar of Fowey. He badgered the pope for other privileges, claiming that Tywardreath had suffered attacks from pirates.[31] He recruited a musician to improve the priory's services, a musician who had to be versatile because he was expected to act as the prior's barber.[32] He bought himself a beautiful seal – a copy of an antique Roman one, reflecting Renaissance tastes.[33] And, when Prior Vivian of Bodmin got his own coat of arms, Prior Colyns decided that he must have one equally ostentatious, displaying a griffin and three Cornish choughs.[34]

By the 1520s matters were not going well at Tywardreath. The bishop found that the monks were not performing the services properly. They were going out of the precincts on their own, through the windows as well as the doors. Women were coming in by similar routes.[35] By the end of the decade quantities of bottles were seen being carried into the prior's lodging. Colyns was often drunk, or so it was said.[36] Word spread, and the most powerful man in the South

---

29 Ibid., II, 1011–13.
30 Truro, Cornwall Record Office (hereafter CRO), ART 4/5–6.
31 CRO, ART 4/10–11.
32 N. Orme, 'Music and Teaching at Tywardreath Priory, 1522–1536', *Devon and Cornwall Notes and Queries* 36 part 8 (1990), 277–80.
33 C. W. King, 'Seal Set with an Intaglio of Laocoon', *Archaeological Journal* 24 (1867), 45–54.
34 College of Arms, MS M 3, fol. 79v.
35 DRO, Chanter XV (The Register of John Veysey, vol. ii), fols 7v–8r.
36 TNA, E 134/31Eliz/Hil24, m. 2; A. L. Rowse, *Tudor Cornwall* (London, 1941), p. 162.

West, Henry VIII's cousin, the marquess of Exeter, decided to get Colyns out. Cardinal Wolsey was enlisted to help. Wolsey wrote to Colyns, advising him to resign and promising him a good pension. Colyns refused. The marquess sent two of his gentlemen to order Colyns to go – or else he would be dismissed. Colyns again refused.[37] In 1529 nobody knew quite what to do with an obstinate prior, and Colyns was left alone for the next five years. Then things changed. Henry VIII became head of the Church and Thomas Cromwell became its effective leader. Cromwell did not waste time on obstructive monks. A letter was sent by Cromwell to Colyns in 1534–5 requiring him to give up the priory's jurisdiction over Fowey. The king, said Cromwell, 'thinketh that you be very unworthy to have rule of any town that cannot well rule yourself'. He warned Colyns that he would report whatever Colyns replied to Henry VIII.[38] It is likely that such pressure soon forced Colyns out altogether. He went towards the end of 1535 or early in 1536. The priory was closed soon afterwards. He died in 1539, and his tombstone can still be seen in Tywardreath parish church.

Merit

This is the kind of material that has dominated the writing of so much monastic history from the Reformation to the late Dom David Knowles. Cornish monasteries have seemed like Cornish pasties: attractive outside with little of substance within. The Cornish historian Charles Henderson applied the following words to Tywardreath in less than a page of writing: extravagance, mismanagement, deplorable, wretched, dissolute, and grave scandals. He concluded 'Records make it difficult to believe that the priory ever justified its existence, and no house can have been more ripe for dissolution.'[39] This, I believe, is unjust. The story is more complex at Tywardreath and all the monasteries.

Take the case of St Michael's Mount. Ostensibly its history after 1350 is one of decline. In 1350 it was still a viable priory of the Benedictine order, dependent on Mont St Michel, with a French prior and French monks. By 1374 there were only a prior and two monks, and after French monks were ordered to leave England in 1378 there is no evidence of any monks at the Mount from that date except for the prior. By 1383 the last French prior had been replaced by an Englishman who was not even a Benedictine but an Augustinian canon, although he was succeeded by an English Benedictine and then by one who may have been French but came from another French dependent house in England. After 1383 the priory had no formal links with Mont St Michel, and was virtually independent. The fact that by the 1420s the Mount was staffed by chaplains makes it very likely that chaplains had been introduced in the

[37] CRO, ART 4/14–19, printed in Oliver, *Monasticon*, pp. 45–7 (nos XXV–XXX).

[38] J. Polsue, *A Complete Parochial History of the County of Cornwall*, 4 vols (Truro and London, 1867–72), II, 23.

[39] C. Henderson, *The Cornish Church Guide and Parochial History of Cornwall* (Truro, 1925, repr. 1964), p. 196.

late 1370s as the only way that the priory could maintain its religious duties. In about 1415 the last prior disappeared, and the Mount was given by Henry V to Syon Abbey.

Yet the severing of connections with Mont St Michel led to at least two developments. One was the production of a cartulary listing all the Mount's property – essential for an independent monastery.[40] The other was the adoption by the Mount of a legend that had hitherto belonged to its mother house.[41] Since the tenth century Mont St Michel had claimed that the Archangel Michael had instructed and helped its founder, Aubert, to build the monastery at a place called 'Mount Tomb' (*Mons Tumba*). Up to the late fourteenth century references in England to *Mons Tumba* relate to Mont St Michel, the Mount being called simply *Mons Sancti Michaelis*. In 1402, however, a royal writ provides an early example of the application of the term St Michael of *Mons Tumba* to the Mount, rather than to its mother house. At about the same time John Mirk, canon of Lilleshall Abbey (Shropshire), described in his *Festial* the occasions on which the Archangel had manifested himself, and stated that the appearance hitherto associated with Aubert was 'to another byschop at a place that ys called now Mychaell yn the mownt in Corneweyle'. The details that follow were entirely taken from the legendary of Mont St Michel, and show that the Mount had appropriated the foundation story of its mother house. By the fifteenth century it was well understood in England that St Michael had made one of his four historic appearances at the Mount, ignoring the claims of Mont St Michel, and visitors were shown the archangel's seat at the top of the island. Arguably the Mount did well to survive as a priory for a generation after the expulsion of the French monks. If Henry V had not wanted it for Syon it might have continued yet further.

The story of Tywardreath is one of greater success. In the middle of the fourteenth century it too had a prior and monks who were French. It too must have been affected by the expulsion of French monks in 1378, and by 1381 the house was staffed by the French prior and three English chaplains, presumably employed for lack of monks.[42] Like the Mount Tywardreath continued with a succession solely of priors, although in its case they were all French and they lasted longer than they did at the Mount, the last one resigning only in 1433. These lonely Frenchmen managed to defend Tywardreath from a grant of much of its revenues by Henry V to a layman, and fought a successful claim in the king's courts that their priory was 'conventual' or a community, despite the lack of evidence for monks. In 1433 the crown appointed an English monk as prior (although he came from a French abbey), and this man, John Brentyngham, began to gather English recruits, one of whom, Walter Barnecote, succeeded him and brought in others. Under Barnecote Tywardreath regained its ancient

[40] P. L. Hull, ed., *The Cartulary of St Michael's Mount*, Devon and Cornwall Record Soc., ns 5 (1962).

[41] On what follows, see N. Orme, 'St Michael and his Mount', *Journal of the Royal Institution of Cornwall* ns 10 part 1 (1986–7), 32–43.

[42] TNA, E 179/25/5.

strength of seven monks, instituted lawsuits to recover lost property, and regained some moveable goods. By the end of the fifteenth century the priory was in a healthy state, to the extent that a local boy named John Porth from St Blazey, who was brought up in the priory during his youth (perhaps as a page or boarder), went on to become a servant of Henry VIII in London and a man of some wealth.[43] These are facts that need to be weighed alongside the career of Prior Colyns.[44]

For all their usefulness, most of the surviving records of monasteries skew our perceptions about them. We know something about property, government, and the occasions when bishops dealt with matters of discipline. Most other areas of monastic life are scarcely recorded. Worship went on day by day, but little is extant about it. It is clear, however, that lay people went into the Cornish monasteries to pray or to watch the worship. Bodmin had the shrine of St Petroc behind the high altar, and aisles along which visitors could go to see it. In 1274 we are told that people visiting the town on days of county court business entered the priory to listen to the services.[45] They also made offerings to an image and light of the Virgin Mary in the Lady Chapel.[46] St Germans acquired a relic of its patron saint in 1361, miracles were claimed, and the bishop and the pope granted indulgences to those who came to the church to honour the saint.[47] People gave offerings to the saint of St Carroc, and miracles took place at the shrine of the saint of Minster.[48] St Michael's Mount was the biggest pilgrimage centre in medieval Cornwall, and this was probably the case during its monastic period up to 1415 although most of the evidence comes from after that date. The Mount attracted pilgrims by a generous indulgence of one third of all penance, either in this life or the life to come, the same entitlement as at Compostella. People travelled to the Mount from as far as Somerset, Herefordshire, Dorset, Hertfordshire, and Norfolk, and the Cornish regularly remembered the Mount in their wills. We are lucky to possess a manuscript of Tywardreath which names the members of its confraternity: lay people in Cornwall and elsewhere who supported the priory with money and received prayers in return. The names include not only those of local gentry but, from around 1500, Henry VII's councillor Sir Reginald Bray, Sir John Percival, lord mayor

[43] N. Orme, ed., *Cornish Wills 1342–1540*, Devon and Cornwall Record Soc., ns 50 (2007), p. 171.

[44] Hingeston-Randolph, ed., *Reg. Lacy*, I, 158, 364.

[45] Hingeston-Randolph, ed., *Reg. Bronescombe*, p. 31; O. F. Robinson, ed., *The Register of Walter Bronescombe, Bishop of Exeter 1258–1280*, 3 vols, Canterbury and York Soc., 82, 87, 94 (1995–2003), II, 66–7.

[46] Hingeston-Randolph, ed., *Reg. Grandisson*, II, 982; Harper-Bill, ed., *Reg. Morton*, II, 79.

[47] Hingeston-Randolph, ed., *Reg. Grandisson*, III, 1226; M. H. Laurent et al., eds, *Lettres communes des papes du XIVe siècle: Urbain V, letters communes*, 12 vols (Paris, 1954–85), III, 542.

[48] F. C. Hingeston-Randolph, ed., *The Register of Thomas de Brantyngham, Bishop of Exeter*, 2 vols (London and Exeter, 1901–6), II, 582; Worcester, *Itineraries*, ed. Harvey, 28–31, pp. 106–7.

of London, and his Cornish wife Thomasine.[49] There must have been similar networks of supporters at Bodmin, St Germans, and Launceston.

Another difficult area to investigate is the role of monasteries as places of study and learning. Bodmin certainly supported learning in the twelfth century. One or more people there wrote works in Latin: two lives of St Petroc (one in verse) and a list of the saint's miracles, while a canon named Robert of Tawton compiled an account of the theft of the saint's relics which took place in 1171.[50] After 1200 it is harder to say what was going on. We know of only a handful of surviving books that belonged to the Cornish houses, and these are mostly books used for worship like the famous Bodmin Gospels. In about 1300, however, when the Franciscan friars of Oxford decided to produce a union catalogue of theological works and the places in England where you could find them, they asked their colleagues in the Franciscan friary at Bodmin to investigate the book collections at Bodmin Priory and Launceston Priory. The friars reported 41 titles of works held by Launceston and 52 by Bodmin: titles rather than volumes, some volumes perhaps including more than one title. There were works by Augustine, Jerome, John Chrysostom, and Bede, yet were it not for the friars we would not even know that Bodmin and Launceston had such books.[51]

A few Cornish monks went to university. We hear of two from Bodmin and one each from Launceston and Tywardreath, but such men were not common, as they were not in English monasteries generally. Most monks probably had more practical or popular interests in literature. A manuscript in the British Library contains some pages of a commonplace book made by a late fifteenth-century canon of Bodmin called John Bowyer. The texts he copied, in English, included a prayer or meditation directed to Jesus, a poem about the childhood of Christ called 'The Infancy of the Saviour', and a poem called 'How the Wise Man Taught his Son', containing sensible practical advice for a young man.[52] In 1478 the historian William Worcester passed through Bodmin on his way to St Michael's Mount. He met and talked to two canons, William John (later prior) and John Stevyns, who were interested in 'physic' (natural science, especially medicine). John showed him 'several ancient books' on the subject.[53]

[49] CRO, RS/60.

[50] Grosjean, 'Vie et miracles de. S. Petroc', pp. 131–88, 470–96.

[51] R. H. and M. A. Rouse, eds, *Registrum Anglie de Libris Doctorum et Auctorum Veterum*, Corpus of British Medieval Library Catalogues, 2 (London, 1991), pp. 281–2.

[52] BL, MS Harley 2399, fols 47r–64v; C. Brown and R. H. Robbins, *The Index of Middle English Verse* (New York, 1943), nos 250 (printed in C. Horstmann, *Sammlung altenglisches Legenden* (Heilbronn, 1878), pp. 101–10), 1985 (printed in R. Fischer, ed., *How the Wyse Man Taught hys Sone* (Erlangen and Leipzig, 1889), pp. 42–9), and 4232 (printed in T. Wright and J. O. Halliwell, eds, *Reliquiae Antiquae*, 2 vols (London, 1841–3), II, 173–4); R. H. Robbins and J. L. Cutler, *Supplement to The Index of Middle English Verse* (Lexington, 1965), 711.5.

[53] Worcester, *Itineraries*, ed. Harvey, pp. 88–91.

The Reformation

There was no formal resistance to the dissolution of the Cornish monasteries. Tywardreath closed first in the spring of 1536. The last prior, Colyns's successor, was given a pension and became vicar of the nearby church of St Winnow. The big three houses surrendered in February 1539, and the two other cells faded out unobtrusively at about the same time. The last prior of St Germans, Robert Swymmer, was awarded a handsome pension of £66 but his colleagues received only the usual small ones of £6 or less. Prior Shere of Launceston had been having trouble with his canons, and was apparently only too willing to arrange a surrender. He gained a pension of £100, the largest in Cornwall.

Prior Wandsworth of Bodmin was a man of conservative views. He later got into trouble for trying to smuggle out of England the arm of the Carthusian martyr John Houghton, and was condemned to be executed although he was released after suffering imprisonment.[54] He saw the coming end of monasticism more clearly and earlier than most people. In the summer of 1537 he summoned all the canons into the chapter house and said to them 'The king is going to take his pleasure on our house, and we must do good to those who have been good to our house, so they will be good to us hereafter.'[55] Wandsworth's Bible studies had evidently included the parable of the unjust steward![56] An orgy of giving ensued. Wandsworth leased as much property that he could to the local gentry. The Prideaux got Padstow, the Kendalls Withiel, the Lyteltons Lanhydrock, and Sir John Chamond Bodiniel. Wandsworth's own relatives, the Mundys, gained possession of the rich manor of Rialton with the lovely manor house that Prior Vivian had rebuilt, and Wandsworth arranged marriages for three of them with the Prideaux and Kendall families. By the time that the crown realised that such transactions were taking place in England and a statute was enacted forbidding them, Wandsworth's arrangements were too long established to be reversed. He showed defiance of a kind, one to which historians have given less attention than they have to those fewer, more dramatic acts of resistance that led to imprisonment and death.

Conclusion

Cornish history is often seen, particularly by those who live in the county, as having a special 'Celtic' character. More accurately this should be termed a 'Brittonic' character, relating to the language and culture of Brittany and Wales, in some of which Cornwall shared. There is little sign that monasti-

---

[54] C. Wriothesley, *A Chronicle of England*, ed. W. D. Hamilton, vol. I, Camden Society ns 11 (1875), pp. 184–5.

[55] J. Maclean, *Parochial and Family History of the Deanery of Trigg Minor*, 3 vols (London and Bodmin, 1873–9), I, 135.

[56] Luke, xvi. 1–9.

cism changed its nature when it crossed into Cornwall, however, or that it was coloured by much that was Brittonic. Our twelve monasteries certainly partook of Cornishness in matters such as building materials, the recruitment of local men as monks and servants, the food on their tables, and the dialect of English that they spoke. Only three or four of the twelve, however, honoured a Brittonic saint. Bodmin venerated St Petroc, St Carroc the saint of the same name, and Minster St Mertherian, while St Anthony's saint was originally a Cornish Entenin, although it is likely that after 1100 he was chiefly identified with a Roman St Anthony.[57] Bodmin and Launceston kept the feasts of some of the Brittonic saints of the Cornish parish churches that they owned, but taking the monasteries as a whole the cults of the Brittonic saints were far outweighed by those of international saints to whom most of the priories were dedicated and who received veneration even at the houses with Brittonic patron saints. Monks who spoke the Brittonic language of Cornwall must have been rare, since the majority of the houses were in the English speaking eastern half, and those that were not were largely staffed by French or English speakers. The Cornish monasteries were distinguished not so much by Cornishness but, as we have observed, by their modest resources – the result of their relative remoteness and lack of wealthy and powerful patrons.

If Cornwall had little discernible effect on its monasteries, the monasteries certainly had effects on the county. They acquired property, owned churches, and appropriated tithes. The monastic buildings of Bodmin and Launceston were the largest structures in those towns, and even the smaller and remoter houses stood out in terms of their appearance and importance. When Leland visited St Germans after the Dissolution, he rated the place 'a poor fisher town' and added, 'The glory of it stood with the priory.'[58] Whether the effects of the monasteries were positive or negative is harder to say. Rents and tithes were taken from lands and churches and often left Cornwall altogether. Yet this was true of landlordship in general. The appropriation of tithes reduced the stipends of some parochial vicars to low levels, and Tywardreath was particularly exacting in this respect. Equally this meant that those benefices had resident vicars rather than wealthy non-resident clergy who appointed curates to do their work. Appropriation did not affect the duty of parishioners to maintain and furnish the naves of parish churches, and much money and devotion was forthcoming in Cornwall for that purpose, as it was elsewhere in England. The monasteries provided careers for some local boys as monks or servants, some charity to the poor, and some money for rebuilding the chancels of appropriated churches. None of this can be quantified, however.

Mediocrity or merit? No absolute judgment can be made on either side. It is difficult to claim much for the Cornish monasteries in the context of English and Welsh monastic history, whether in terms of buildings, possessions, books, shrines, or art. Even the largest were in the second or third division of the

[57] On these saints, see N. Orme, *The Saints of Cornwall* (Oxford, 2000), pp. 65–6, 85–6, 115–16, 189–90, 214–19.
[58] Leland, *Itinerary*, ed. L. Toulmin Smith, 5 vols (London, 1907–10), I, 210.

monastic league – the traditional fate of teams from the South West of England. All that can be pleaded in their favour is that, whatever their faults, they were not without some learning, spirituality, or popular support. When many Cornishmen rose in protest against the Reformation, in 1549, the demands that they and their colleagues from Devon sent to the king included a call for two foundations to be made 'where two of the chief abbeys was within every county … and there to be established a place for devout persons which shall pray for the king and the commonwealth'.[59] It is a reminder that something good about the monastic past was remembered by some people.

[59] F. Rose-Troup, *The Western Rebellion of 1549* (London, 1913), p. 221.

15

Monasteries and Society in Sixteenth-Century Yorkshire: The Last Years of Roche Abbey

CLAIRE CROSS

Between 1536 and 1540 the government of Henry VIII destroyed seventy-nine religious houses in Yorkshire containing well over a thousand monks, friars and nuns. At first sight there would seem to be little cause for singling out the apparently unremarkable Cistercian abbey of Roche, but the fortuitous survival of three manuscripts, a near contemporary account of its suppression, an ordination certificate of 1555 alluding to the apparent revival of the monastery, and, most intriguingly of all, topographical notes on neighbouring churches attributed to one of its members, provides more detailed information on the process and consequences of the Dissolution both for the monks and the local inhabitants than exists for almost anywhere else in the county. After briefly exploring the relationship between the abbey and lay society in the earlier part of the sixteenth century, this paper will use this evidence to examine reactions to the surrender of Roche in the summer of 1538, assess the significance of the events in the Marian period, and follow the fortunes of the last generation of monks.[1]

Founded about 1147 by two local landowners in a valley in the parish of Maltby some five miles from the small town of Tickhill in the extreme south of the West Riding, Roche enjoyed a clear annual revenue of around £222 in 1535. This placed it way below Fountains, by far the richest Yorkshire Cistercian abbey valued at over £1000 a year, and the considerably less wealthy Kirkstall, Meaux, and Rievaulx, at about the same level as Byland and Jervaulx, and substantially above Sawley, the only Cistercian monastery in the county with an annual income below £200. In other words it possessed a reasonable competency, which allowed it to maintain a convent of around eighteen monks, but could in no sense be regarded as a major religious house.[2]

Although it had acquired a few dispersed properties over the years, its chief

---

[1] C. Cross and N. Vickers, eds, *Monks, Friars and Nuns in Sixteenth Century Yorkshire*, YASRS, 150 (1995), pp. 4–5; the spelling of all quotations has been modernised.

[2] Janet Burton, *The Monastic Order in Yorkshire, 1069–1215* (Cambridge, 1999), p. xix; W. Page, ed., *VCH, Yorkshire*, III (1913), pp. 131–58; *LP Hen. VIII*, X, no. 364 (p. 142); XIII pt. II app. 25 (2).

estates lay in a relatively confined area in the vicinity of the abbey in south Yorkshire, north Nottinghamshire and north Lincolnshire, which constituted its main sphere of influence at the end of the Middle Ages. On entering religion Cistercians usually changed their surname to that of their place of origin. The pensions list for Rievaulx quite exceptionally supplies both the monastic and family names of most of the monks, and while no such material exists for Roche, it would seem likely that the abbey observed the same custom, and consequently that an analysis of the surnames of its monks would yield some information on the geographical origins of the community. Virtually half of the forty-two religious ordained from the abbey between 1480 and 1538 had identifiable toponymics. Seven seem to have lived within a fifteen mile radius of the house in Conisbrough, Doncaster, Hampole, Houghton in Darfield, Hoyland in Wath, Norton in Campsall and Dodworth. A further five had apparently come from Temple Hirst, South Milford, Drax, Burn in Brompton and Middleton in Rothwell, villages some fifteen to thirty miles from the abbey, with the remaining eight drawn from Cundall, which furnished two novices, Helaugh, Guiseley, York, Haxby, Gargrave and Jervaulx between thirty and sixty miles away. Without exception all these settlements were in Yorkshire, the great majority in the West Riding. Since the abbey only owned property in Campsall, Conisbrough, Doncaster and York, landholding does not seem to have greatly affected recruitment. The admittedly scant evidence from wills seems to confirm the essentially local nature of its intake. In a rare allusion to a family relationship, in 1534 John Colson, husbandman, of Armthorpe just north of Doncaster, bequeathed 40d 'to my brother of Roche abbey and the convent'.[3]

At their visitation in February 1536 Layton and Lee reported on a miraculous image of Christ crucified at Roche, but while pilgrims may still have been frequenting the abbey, very few aspired to be buried within its confines. Wills made in the last two decades before the Dissolution reveal that almost without exception the laity wished to be interred in their parish church or churchyard. Only one testator, Thomas Storres of the Folds in Tickhill, opted for burial in the monastic church before Our Lady and St Katherine, paying to the abbey 3s 4d for the privilege and a further 3s 4d to the convent.[4]

Lay people showed rather more interest in the abbey as source of intercession. In 1521 William Johnson of Braithwell left the abbot 12d to have a mass said for his soul 'afore the crucifix'. A year later Nicholas Hall of Stainton paid the abbot and convent 40d to celebrate a mass of requiem, while Robert Sikes of Stainton offered 12d for the same intent in 1529. In 1532 Thomas Nicholson of Conisbrough bequeathed the abbey 3s 4d, and in the following year John Howland of Thurnscoe gave 2s to the abbot and 12d to each of his monks in return for prayers. Formal absolution cost considerably more, with Richard Oldfeld of East Retford in north Nottinghamshire and Agnes

---

3   Cross and Vickers, *Monks, Friars and Nuns*, pp. 170–1, 186–8; BI, Prob. Reg. 11 pt. I, fol. 74r (Colson).
4   *LP Hen. VIII*, X, no. 364 (p. 138); BI, Prob. Reg. 9, fol. 427v (Storres).

Frankishe of Stainton in 1522, and William Whiteheid of Maltby in 1538 all granting the abbot and convent 6s 8d 'to be assoiled.' The only benefaction of any size received by the abbey in these years came in the will of the Doncaster lawyer, Thomas Strey, who conferred 20s upon each of four south Yorkshire monasteries of Nostell, Monk Bretton, Pontefract and Roche.[5]

Northerners still occasionally turned to religious houses to oversee the execution of their wills and protect their children's inheritance. John Hugh of Armthorpe, perhaps a tenant of Roche, named the abbot as supervisor of his will in 1526, rewarding him with an ambling stag for his pains. In his will of 23 July 1530 Edmund Kaye, gentleman, of Linthwaite in Almondby in the north of the West Riding, assigned the lease of Barnby Grange, which he held of the abbot and convent of Roche, to William Saville on condition that within two years he married his daughter, Anne, and discharged the testator's bond to the abbey.[6]

The monastery also played a role in the social life of the region. Just as Butley Priory in Suffolk was providing *fêtes champêtres* for the delectation of the local aristocracy, the abbot of Roche, like any great secular lord, was hosting more traditional hunting and hawking parties on his outlying manors on the eve of the Dissolution. After four centuries the abbey seemed a permanent fixture on the local ecclesiastical, political and economic scene, and the sudden change in national policy in 1529 seems to have taken the monks, their tenants and the laity in general completely by surprise.[7]

In the same way as the Cistercians of Jervaulx enjoyed a special relationship with the Carthusians of Mount Grace, by the early sixteenth century the Roche monks had developed spiritual ties with Axholme charterhouse in north Lincolnshire, a few miles across the county border. Members of both these elite communities now tried vainly to oppose the break with Rome. Alongside the priors of the London and Beauvale Charterhouses, Augustine Webster, the prior of Axholme, paid with his life for his adherence to the papacy in May 1535, and his stand may well have inspired some resistance at Roche. At their visitation of the abbey at the beginning of the following year government officials reported on the imprisonment in York castle of one of the monks, John Robinson, for speaking against the king's headship of the Church, though Robinson, unlike George Lazenby of Jervaulx executed for treason in August 1535, eventually thought better of his protest and returned to his house unscathed.[8]

5   BI, Prob. Reg. 9, fols 173v (Johnson), 454r (Sikes), 245r (Hall); Prob. Reg. 11 pt I, fols 19r (Nicholson), 52r (Howland); Prob. Reg. 9, fols 243v (Oldfeld), 265r (Frankishe); Prob. Reg. 11 pt I, fol. 288r (Whiteheid); Prob. Reg. 10, fols 15r–16r (Strey).

6   BI, Prob. Reg. 9, fol. 350v (Hugh); Prob. Reg. 11 pt I, fols 13v–14r (Kaye).

7   A. G. Dickens, ed., *The Register or Chronicle of Butley Priory, Suffolk, 1510–1535* (Winchester, 1951), p. 23; G. W. O. Woodward, *Dissolution of the Monasteries* (1966), p. 144; J. W. Clay, *Yorkshire Monasteries. Suppression Papers*, YASRS, 48 (1912), p. 16.

8   *LP Hen. VIII*, V, no. 226; W. Page, ed., *VCH, Lincoln*, II (1906), pp. 159–60; *MRH*, pp. 133, 134; A. G. Dickens, *Lollards and Protestants in the Diocese of York, 1509–1558* (1959), pp. 79–82; Clay, *Suppression Papers*, p. 16.

With an income below £200 a year the Cistercian abbey of Rufford in Nottinghamshire came within the remit of the act for the dissolution of the lesser monasteries, and on its confiscation in the summer of 1536 at least one of the monks, the subprior, Thomas Welles, chose to transfer to Roche rather than seek a career in the secular Church. By the autumn the crown had seized six more religious houses within twenty-five miles of the abbey, Blyth in Nottinghamshire, Torksey, Thornholme, and Gokewell in Lincolnshire, and Drax and North Ferriby in Yorkshire.[9]

Because of its location, the abbey must very soon have had word of the rising of the commons at Louth on 2 October 1536. On 5 October at Sawcliffe the Lincolnshire rebels captured Robert Aske on his way to London from his home at Aughton in the East Riding, and forced him to swear their oath. Five days later he assumed the leadership of the Yorkshire revolt, styling himself 'chief captain of the Marshland, the Isle and Howdenshire'. Having first gone north to take possession of York, he moved south to secure Pontefract on 20 October. Throughout November the duke of Norfolk at the head of the king's much smaller forces encamped just south of Doncaster attempted to negotiate a compromise with the rebels, and at last on the promise of a free pardon persuaded the commons to disband on 4 December. Despite all this unrest on their doorstep, and in marked contrast with their less circumspect sister house of Jervaulx, declared forfeited to the crown on account of the abbot's treason in May 1537, Roche managed to avoid any direct involvement in the Pilgrimage of Grace and in Sir Francis Bigod's abortive attempt to rekindle the rebellion in the succeeding January.[10]

The rising, nevertheless, had the effect of bringing all the remaining monasteries under suspicion, and it soon became clear that the government would not allow them to continue for much longer. Under a new system of inducements all the members of a community, and not just the head, as in the past, stood to receive compensation on the voluntary surrender of their house. Clearly having lost the will to fight, Roche was the first of the major Yorkshire Cistercian abbeys to capitulate under these terms on 23 June 1538. The abbot, Henry Cundall, secured a substantial annuity of £33 6s 8d, the subprior, Thomas Twell, and the bursar, John Dodsworth, £6 13s 4d and £6 a year respectively, the eleven other monks pensions of £5 and the four novices 66s 8d a year. At his departure the officials in charge of the proceedings allowed the abbot his books, a fourth part of the plate, the cattle, and the household stuff, a convenient portion of corn, a chalice, a vestment and £30 in money, and gave every one of his brethren his half year's pension in advance and an extra 20s towards his apparel by way of reward.[11]

9   BI, Abp Reg. 23, fols 461v, 462r; Reg. 25. fol. 119v; W. Page, ed., VCH Nottingham, II (1919), pp. 83–8, 101–4; VCH Lincoln, II, pp. 156, 166, 170; VCH Yorks., III (1913), pp. 205–8, 241–2.

10   R. W. Hoyle, 'Aske, Robert (c. 1500–1537)', ODNB, II, 707–8; Cross and Vickers, Monks, Friars and Nuns, pp. 132–3.

11   LP Hen. VIII, XIII, pt II, app. 25.

Most unusually a local man recorded the reactions of some of the monks and the laity to the loss of their abbey. Early in Elizabeth's reign Michael Sherbrook, a native of south Yorkshire appointed rector of Wickersley in 1567, began writing a treatise on 'The Fall of Religious Houses', in which he included a number of reminiscences concerning the destruction of Roche. Materialism seems to have been the order of the day with lay people out for all they could get, and not even the monks were immune to a little private enterprise. Sherbrook remembered hearing as a child how

> every one of the convent had given to him his cell, wherein he lied: wherein was not anything of price, but his bed and apparel, which was but simple and of small price. Which monk willed my uncle to buy something of him, who said, 'I see nothing that is worth money to my use.' 'No', said he, 'Give me iid. for my cell door, which was never made with vs.' 'No', said my uncle, 'I know not what to do with it.' (For he was a young man unmarried, and then neither stood need of houses nor doors.)[12]

Sherbrook pondered long and hard over the problem of why the villagers had not made any effort to defend their monastery, deploring the fact that immediately after its surrender

> every person bent himself to filch and spoil what he could; yea, even such persons were content to spoil them that seemed not two days before to allow their religion, and do great worship and reverence at their matins, masses and other service, and all other their doings: which is a strange thing to weigh; that they that could this day think it to be the house of God, and the next day the house of the Devil ...[13]

Greed alone, he concluded, could explain 'the inconstancy of the rude people'.

> For the better proof of this my saying, I demanded of my father, thirty years after the suppression, which had bought part of the timber of the church, and all the timber of the steeple, with the bell frame, with other his partners therein (in the which steeple hung viii, yea ix bells, whereof the least but one could not be bought at this day for £xx, which bells I did see hang there myself more than a year after the suppression) whether he thought well of the religious persons and of the religion then used? And he told me, 'Yea'. 'For', said he, 'I did see no cause to the contrary.' 'Well', said I, 'Then how came it to pass you was so ready to destroy and spoil the thing that you thought well of?' 'What should I do?' said he, 'Might I not as well as others have some profit of the spoil of the abbey? For I did see all would away: and therefore I did as others did.'[14]

---

[12] M. Sherbrook, 'The Fall of Religious Houses', in *Tudor Treatises*, ed. A. G. Dickens, YASRS, 125 (1959), pp. 89–142 (p. 123).

[13] Ibid., pp. 124–5.

[14] Ibid., p. 125.

Sherbrook failed to mention any individual monks, apart from the one who unsuccessfully tried to dispose of his cell door, though in fact many stayed on in the area and six were still drawing their pensions when he began writing his treatise. Immediately after the Dissolution the abbot, Henry Cundall, retired to the adjacent town of Tickhill, where he lived in some style in a well furnished house in the company of at least one servant. He may have occasionally officiated in the parish church, and was certainly on friendly terms with the vicar, Robert Stanley, and the stipendiary clergy, John Knagges, John Emerie, John Yaitts and William Marshe. He accumulated a number of godchildren in both Tickhill and the north Lincolnshire village of Crowle, most probably his birthplace, where he owned a mill with all its appurtenances and sufficient beehives to produce some 20 gallons of honey a year. At his death in the spring of 1555 the greater part of his estate went to his relatives, Thomas Willee and Katherine Moore.[15]

Without the substantial compensation which enabled Henry Cundall to maintain his status in society, the rest of the Roche monks needed to supplement their pensions with paid employment as secular clergy to achieve financial independence. The majority at first seem have taken free lance posts in the neighbouring parish churches, though the more fortunate soon obtained permanent benefices in the form of perpetual chantries. Within five months of leaving the abbey Nicholas Collys had secured the chantry of the Holy Trinity in Tickhill parish church, perhaps through the intervention of his former abbot, to whom he left a furred gown at his death. Taking his pension into account, this effectually doubled his earnings. The acquisition of the chantry of the Blessed Virgin Mary in Kirk Bramwith church some time in December 1540 brought up the income of the former bursar, John Dodsworth, to £8 10s a year. Two of the monks moved south into Lincolnshire, Thomas Wells procuring the Stretton Wolfe chantry in Lincoln cathedral with an annual stipend of a little over £3 10s, Henry Wilson that of St Mary and St Nicholas with a similar stipend in the affluent church of Heckington in the Fens. Thomas Harrison may also perhaps be identified with the cleric of the same name who held the Southill chantry in Wakefield parish church in 1548, and Thomas Middleton with one of three priests serving the chantry of Our Lady in Bedale church in the North Riding.[16]

Richard Drax had died before Michaelmas 1540, John Happa before Michaelmas 1543, and Christopher Herster or Hirst and the novice Thomas Smith may also not have survived for long after the Dissolution, but as many

15 TNA (formerly PRO), LR6/122/8, m. 23; BI, Prob. Reg. 14, fols 78v–79r.
16 BI, Prob. Reg. 14, fols 78v–79r; Cav. BK 1, fol. 28r; W. Page, ed., *The Certificates of the Commissioners appointed to survey the Chantries, Guilds, Hospitals etc. in the County of York. Part I*, Surtees Soc., 91 (1894), pp. 115, 183, 194; *Part II*, Surtees Soc., 92 (1895), p. 307; A. Kreider, *English Chantries: the Road to Dissolution* (Cambridge, Mass., and London, 1979), p. 225, n. 71; G. A. J. Hodgett, ed., *The State of the Ex-Religious and Former Chantry Priests in the Diocese of Lincoln, 1547–1574*, Lincoln Record Soc., 53 (1959), pp. 19, 119.

as fourteen out of the eighteen monks who signed the surrender deed lived to see Mary's reinstatement of Catholicism. In addition to the former abbot, Collys, Dodsworth, Wells, Wilson, Harrison and Middleton a further seven, Thomas Twell, Thomas Cundall, Richard Fishburn, William Carter, Richard Morresley, John Robinson and William Hellay appear to have remained in the vicinity of Roche, presumably augmenting their pensions by working as curates or stipendiary priests.[17]

In his contemporary chronicle Robert Parkyn, curate of Adwick le Street near Doncaster, asserted that within weeks of the queen's accession 'in many places of Yorkshire priests unmarried was very glad to celebrate and say mass in Latin with matins and evensong thereto, according for very fervent zeal and love that they had unto God and his laws', and in the circles in which he moved there does indeed seem to have been a whole-hearted welcome for the return of catholic services and the reconciliation of the nation to Rome. While the laity may have held back, these conservative clergy did not hesitate to invest in the old religion, and Parkyn himself and his clerical friend William Watson, of Melton on the Hill, expended a considerable amount of effort and money at this time arranging for intercessionary prayers to be offered for their souls and the souls of their ancestors and benefactors after their deaths.[18]

Parkyn counted some of the dispossessed Yorkshire religious among his acquaintances, making the prioress of Hampole a beneficiary of his trental and subsequently bequeathing a book to Robert Scolay, the vicar of Brodsworth and a former member of Monk Bretton, and rejoiced in 1555 that 'all such as had been cloisterers before time, yea as well women as men, was commanded to take their habit or vestures unto them again'. The re-creation of monasteries where these monks and nuns could resume the religious life seemed the logical next step, and Mary herself lead by example, refounding six houses in and around London at Westminster, Sheen, Syon, Dartford, St Barthlomew's, Smithfield, and Greenwich. No fewer than six Mount Grace Carthusians together with two from Hull joined the Sheen charterhouse, known after its migration to the continent in the following reign as Sheen Anglorum.[19]

Other Yorkshire religious were clearly anticipating the restitution of monasticism in the north of England. As early as November 1554 a former canon of Bolton left his chalice and two vestments 'to the monastery of Bolton whensoever it shall please God that it shall be restored'. Some four years later a onetime Kirkstall monk made arrangements for all the books in his custody to 'be redelivered by my said executors to Christall abbey if it go up in their times'.

17 TNA, LR6/121/1, m. 50; LR6/121/3; E164/31, fol. 53; D. S. Chambers, *Faculty Office Registers, 1534–1549* (Oxford, 1966), p. 144; BI, 1555 1/13.

18 'Robert Parkyn's Narrative of the Reformation', in *Reformation Studies*, ed. A. G. Dickens (London, 1983), p. 309; A. G. Dickens, 'South Yorkshire Letters 1555', *Transactions of the Hunter Archaeological Soc.* 6 (1950), 282–4.

19 Dickens, *Reformation Studies*, pp. 291, 312; Dickens, 'South Yorkshire Letters', p. 283; C. B. Rowntree, 'Studies in Carthusian History in Later Medieval England' (D. Phil. thesis, University of York, 1981), pp. 491, 506, 510, 521, 529, 532, 533, 536, 537, 544.

Even nearer to Roche, four former Benedictines from Monk Bretton, who had been systematically buying back their monastic library at their own expense, together with five other of their brethren beneficed in the area were holding themselves in readiness to reoccupy of their house.[20]

This apparently fairly widespread expectation of the return of monasticism in the region goes some way to explain the wording of an extraordinary document of 1555. In an attempt to improve the academic and pastoral standard of the parochial clergy the Marian authorities introduced a scheme which required all candidates for ordination to provide a certificate attesting their suitability for the priesthood. A small cache of these letters testimonial preserved at the Borthwick Institute includes one character reference for Richard Moresley, then of Kellington near Pontefract but previously a novice at Roche, subscribed by fourteen clerics and four laymen. Three of the local clerical signatories, John Geffrason, the chaplain of Kellington, the vicar of Campsall, John Lommas, and the vicar of Rolleston, John Thomson, appear never to have been other than seculars, but all the rest like Moresley himself were former Cistercians of either Roche or Rufford. Quite remarkably they wrote as if both their monasteries had already been re-established, styling themselves

> We Roland Blyton, the abbot of Rufford, with our successors, Sir Thomas Doncaster, the abbot after him, and the convent of the same abbey, with our subprior of the same, Sir Thomas Welles, remaining at St Clement's in Lincoln, Sir Thomas Arthure, Sir Thomas Steyentone, Sir Edward Knaysburghte; also the abbot of Roche, Sir Thomas Condall, Sir Thomas Medyllton, Sir Thomas Twelles, Sir Richard Fyestburne, with others ...[21]

Apparent discrepancies in this listing on further examination turn out not to be discrepancies at all. In a highly contentious election Thomas Cromwell had imposed Roland Blyton upon Rievaulx in 1533, and Thomas Doncaster had then succeeded to his office, and this accounts for two religious being designated as abbot of Rufford in 1555. Thomas Wells, a member of Roche in 1538, who had only transferred there on the dissolution of Rufford two years earlier, had now understandably reverted to his original allegiance. No more evidence has so far come to light on these monks' attempt to reclaim their houses, but at the very least the document reveals the existence of two virtual Cistercian communities ready and waiting to revive their former abbeys in south Yorkshire and north Nottinghamshire in the Marian period .[22]

Some of these clerics did not live to see their hopes confounded. Mindful

---

[20] BI, Prob. Reg. 14, fols 118r–119r (Richmond); Prob. Reg. 15 pt III, fol. 59v (Hepton-stall); J. W. Walker, ed., *Abstracts of the Chartularies of the Priory of Monk Bretton*, YASRS, 66 (1924), pp. 5–9; Claire Cross, 'A Yorkshire Religious House and its Hinterland: Monk Bretton Priory in the Sixteenth Century', in *Christianity and Community in the West: Essays for John Bossy*, ed. S. Ditchfield (Aldershot, 2001), pp. 82–3.

[21] BI, Ord. 1555 1/13; the document is printed in full in C. Cross, 'The Reconstitution of Northern Monastic Communities in the Reign of Mary Tudor', *Northern History* 29 (1993), 200–4.

[22] Cross and Vickers, *Monks, Friars and Nuns*, pp. 171, 188.

of 'the manifold changes and perils of this foul world and also the diseases wherewith I am and oft times have been grieved with, and most of all calling to remembrance the uncertainty of this mortal life', the last abbot of Roche, Henry Cundall, had made his will at Tickhill in October 1554, and died before the beginning of May in the following year. In addition to endowing a perpetual obit for himself and his parents at Blyth, where he had been serving as a stipendiary priest, Thomas Twell, his subprior, in his will of 1558 bequeathed sacred vessels and vestments to Sheffield parish church on condition that the vicar or his deputy said 'the collect secret and post communion *per sacerdote* so oft as they shall mass with the said chalice'.[23]

Within months of Elizabeth's accession, parliament passed the acts of supremacy and uniformity, and the remnant of this band of former Roche monks had finally to accept that their house would never be brought back. Richard Fishburn, who had become vicar of North Muskham in Nottinghamshire in 1557, died in 1563. John Dodsworth, Henry Wilson, William Carter, John Robinson and William Wike all appeared on the pensions list of 1564. Still in receipt of his two pensions to which he was entitled as both a former monk and a former chantry priest, Henry Wilson died at Brauncewell in Lincolnshire in April 1573. William Carter, assessed on his pension for the parliamentary subsidy in the same year, can perhaps be identified with the curate officiating in St Martin's chapel in Swine in 1575. Neither John Robinson, nor William Wike, also still alive in 1573, seems ever to have obtained promotion in the Church.[24]

John Dodsworth, the bursar, fared much better. Presented some time after 1548 to the rectory of Armthorpe, formerly appropriated to the house, he gave evidence in a tithe case in 1569, when he said that he was seventy years old and had been 'a white monk of Roche abbey twenty years together and more next and immediately before the dissolution'. Early in the sixteenth century the monastery had acquired a lease of the rectory of Tickhill from Nostell Priory, and as its steward or surveyor for the next nineteen or twenty years he 'did weekly twice in one week resort to the town of Tickhill to see the tithes gathered both in harvest time and other times'. Dodsworth subscribed the Thirty-Nine Articles of Religion in 1571 and paid the subsidy on his pension two years later. In his will of May 1574, apparently by this date an orthodox protestant, he consigned his soul 'unto God Almighty my creator and redeemer', trusting 'to be saved by the merits of Christ's passion'. Having asked to be buried beside his sister in Armthorpe churchyard, and made small legacies to the poor man's box, to his servant, Dorothy Vicars, to his god children and other children in

23 BI, Prob. Reg. 14, fols 78v–79r (Cundall); Prob. Reg. 15 pt III, fol. 18v (Twelves); J. Hunter, *Hallamshire: the History and Topography of the Parish of Sheffield in the County of York* (1819), p. 140; Cross, 'Reconstitution of Northern Monastic Communities', pp. 200–4.

24 TNA, LR6/122/8, m. 23; BI, Inst. AB 2 pt II, fol. 21v; Hodgett, *The State of the Ex-Religious*, p. 149; T. M. Fallow, 'Names of Yorkshire Ex-Religious, 1573: Their Pensions and Subsidies to the Queen thereon', *YAJ* 19 (1907), 100–4; J. S. Purvis, *Tudor Parish Documents in the Diocese of York* (Cambridge, 1948), p. 117.

the parish, he went on to bestow the bulk of his household goods, livestock and the residue of his estate upon relatives John and Robert Jepson.[25]

The story does not quite end with the death of the last known member of the Roche community. In 1696, three years after graduating from Cambridge and then spending some months as a curate at Broughton near Brigg in Lincolnshire, Abraham de la Pryme returned to Hatfield to throw himself into writing the history of his birthplace. Two years into the task he noted in his diary that he had sent the much older Yorkshire antiquary, Dr Nathaniel Johnston, transcripts of epitaphs in Doncaster and Snaith churches that he had copied 'out of an old manuscript formerly belonging to Dunscroft cell', which also contained material on the churches of Fishlake, Hatfield, Thorne, and Howden in south Yorkshire, and Crowle, Haxey, Epworth and Belton just over the county border in Lincolnshire. He had come across the document, much worn and scarcely legible, among the papers of a local landowner, Edward Canby of Thorne, 'bound up with many records relating to his estate, so that he will not part with the same out of his presence'. When Joseph Hunter attempted to track it down a little over a century later, it had disappeared without trace.[26]

De la Pryme depended heavily upon this manuscript for his description of the interior of Hatfield church in the late Middle Ages:

Over against the organs a little on the west side of the reading desk stood all the singing boys, some on one side of the church, and some on the other, with their books on their stands before them, who made most sweet and pleasant music the times of their devotions ...

The chancel was all beautiful and glorious likewise within. Hung about with many curious pictures of saints and religious men. The altar was all of alabaster, curiously wrought, upon which stood a crucifix with our saviour thereon above a foot and a half high of mazy silver with several less images of the saints on the right hand and on the left.

In the window was excellently painted in the glass the Virgin Mary in her full bigness sitting with our saviour in her lap, encompassed about with beams of glory and all the heavenly host about her doing her worship and honour.[27]

---

[25] BI, CP G 1384; Ins. AB 2 pt III, fol. 139r; Abp Reg. 30, fol. 182r (Doddesworth); Fallow, 'Names of Yorkshire Ex-Religious', 100–4.

[26] C. Jackson, ed., *Diary of Abraham de la Pryme*, Surtees Soc., 54 (1870), pp. 175–6: J. Hunter, *South Yorkshire*, I (1828), preface; I am most grateful to Dr P. S. Barnwell, Dr Sarah Brown, Dr J. Binns, Dr P. Cullum, Professor R. B. Dobson, Dr D. Dymond, Dr P. J. P. Goldberg, Professor R. Marks, Dr C. Norton, Mrs A. Rycraft and Mr P. Rycraft for sharing with me their opinions for and against the authenticity of the manuscript.

[27] BL, MS Lansdowne 897, fol. 152r; this is printed in a slightly modernised form in Hunter, *South Yorkshire*, I, 188–9; B. Sprakes, *The Medieval Stained Glass of South Yorkshire* (Oxford, 2003) pp. 123–5, reproduces the two pages from Hunter in an appendix without comment. The medieval wills which survive for the parish contain references to the image of St Mary of Hatfield, to St John the Baptist's altar, to lights before the Rood, St Mary, St Crux, St Katherine, St Peter, St John the Baptist, St Nicholas and St George, and to gilding the Rood loft in 1531: BI, Prob. Reg 2, fols 2v (Snytall), 140v (Stanford), 280r (Snytall); Prob. Reg. 9, fol. 95r (Pawger); Prob. Reg. 11, fols 18v (Coward), 420v (Ranalde), 565r (Staynton), 615v (Grave).

The church possessed numerous paintings in addition to the glass. 'On the wall on the north side of the window on the north end of the altar hung a curious picture representing the whole passion of Christ, with the picture of a man looking upon him ...' 'Upon the south wall on the south side of the great window was another table representing the picture of the blessed Trinity, by the effigies of an old man, our saviour and a dove set in a triangle ...' Beneath this by a holy water stoop stood an image of St Peter with his cock. Almost all these carried Latin inscriptions, usually in verse, explaining their theological significance.[28]

If authentic, and de la Pryme would seem to have been too reputable a historian to have manufactured his evidence, a major question hangs over the manuscript's authorship and dating. In 1828 Joseph Hunter attributed the document to 'a monk of Roche'. Later in the nineteenth century James Aveling referred even more confidently to one of the Roche monks who 'shortly before the dissolution went about making notes of the churches in Yorkshire'. The epitaph to Jane Rastal of May 1530 provides a date before which it could not have been written. While it would seem to be somewhat unlikely that a religious would have devoted himself to antiquarian pursuits as his monastery was about to be suppressed, it might perhaps be a little more plausible to imagine the document being produced in the Elizabethan period when Michael Sherbrook was compiling 'The Fall of Religious Houses', Roger Martin setting down his recollections of the glories of Long Melford, and an anonymous writer expatiating upon the medieval 'Rites of Durham'.[29]

If the lost Yorkshire manuscript can very tentatively be assigned to a member or past member of the Roche community, and in addition to de la Pryme's statement that it derived from Dunscroft, a grange of Roche, internal evidence suggests that it was put together by a man conversant with south Yorkshire and north Lincolnshire, then the author may just possibly have been John Dodsworth, who by his own admission had frequently travelled around the area on the abbey's business in the early sixteenth century. He would have been in a position to have made notes on local churches in his very last years as bursar of Roche or, more probably, to have recorded his memories of pre-Reformation church life when rector of Armthorpe in the first part of Elizabeth's reign. To take conjecture one step further, since Hatfield had constituted the abbey's most valuable appropriation, some of the monks may even have had a hand in the design of the decidedly Marian and Christological subject matter of the windows and wall paintings in the parish church.[30]

This is little more than speculation, though there can be no doubt that early

---

28 BL, MS Lansdowne 897, fol. 152r–v.

29 BL, MS Lansdowne 897, fol. 153v; Hunter, *South Yorkshire*, I, 188; J. H. Aveling, *Roche Abbey* (1870); Dickens, *Tudor Treatises*, pp. 89–142; D. Dymond and C. Paine, *The Spoil of Melford Church: the Reformation in a Suffolk Parish* (Ipswich, 1992); D. Dymond, 'Martin, Roger (1526/7–1615)', *ODNB*, XXXVI, 975–6; J. T. Fowler, ed., *Rites of Durham*, Surtees Soc., 107 (1903).

30 BI, CP G 1384.

in Elizabeth's reign some conservatives were already beginning to romanticise the medieval Church. Sherbrook's 'Fall of Religious Houses', however biassed, the more dispassionate testimonial of eleven surviving members of Rufford and Roche of 1555, and the ecclesiastical reminiscences of a south Yorkshire antiquarian all point in the same direction. Accustomed for almost four hundred years to look upon Roche as a source of spiritual power, as an influential landlord and employer, perhaps even as a patron of the arts, when left to their own devices neither the monks nor the local laity would have voluntarily relinquished their abbey in the third decade of the sixteenth century.[31]

---

[31] Dickens, ed., *Tudor Treatises*, pp. 27–32; BI, Ord. 1555 1/13.

Index of Religious Houses mentioned in the text

Index

Other Volumes in
Studies in the History of Medieval Religion